NEWNES'
PICTORIAL KNOWLEDGE

VOLUME SEVEN

NEWNES'
PICTORIAL KNOWLEDGE

General Editors
R. H. POOLE
PETER FINCH, M.A.
WALTER SHEPHERD

Art Editor
A. H. J. HUMPHREYS

VOLUME 7 ·

GEORGE NEWNES LIMITED
CARLTON HOUSE, GREAT QUEEN STREET,
LONDON, W.C.2

PRINTED IN GREAT BRITAIN
BY THE WHITEFRIARS PRESS LTD., LONDON AND TONBRIDGE, AND
BOUND BY HAZELL, WATSON & VINEY LTD., AYLESBURY AND LONDON
N.P.K. 7055.   W.P. 5316

CONTENTS OF VOLUME SEVEN

Colour Plates

Special Colour Supplement

Photo=tone Supplements

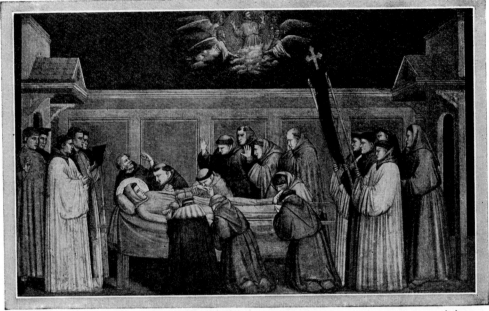

Anderson.

THE BEWAILING OF ST. FRANCIS

The picture above is reproduced from a fresco (*i.e.*, painting on a wall) at the Church of Santa Croce in Florence. It was the work of Giotto, an artist who was born in 1266 and lived until 1337. St. Francis, seen on his death-bed, was the great apostle of humanity; and Giotto one of the very early Italian painters who brought back humanity to art after the stiffness that followed the fall of the Roman Empire.

IN THE BEGINNING

APELLES, greatest of Greek painters, was famous for his pictures of " Venus Rising from the Sea " and " The Three Graces." Another picture of his, " Alexander Wielding a Thunderbolt," was known all over the ancient world.

Apelles was an intimate friend of Alexander the Great, and the historian Pliny tells a story of how one day Alexander visited the painter's studio and began to talk about pictures, but knew so little of art and blundered so badly that Apelles whispered to him he had better be silent because even the boys who were mixing the colours were laughing at him.

Advice to a Cobbler

The most famous story of Apelles concerns him and a cobbler. At an exhibition of the great artist's work, Apelles himself stood behind one of his pictures, listening to what the people said about them. A cobbler, looking at a picture, found fault with a shoe, or rather sandal, depicted in it, and Apelles at once set to work to alter it and put it right. The cobbler was immensely pleased and got rather a swelled head—so much so that next day he came back and began to criticise the legs in the picture. Out came Apelles in a fine rage and told the cobbler to stick to his last, advice which has been famous all through the twenty-three centuries which have passed since Apelles painted.

What a sad thing it is that not one of the paintings of this great Greek master remains for us to admire and study! There is not even a copy of one. All the pictures painted by the many great artists of Ancient Greece have long ago turned to dust and ashes. We still have some of their wonderful sculptures, and from these we know what marvellous artists lived in those days, but not a single painting.

We believe we are right in saying that the only examples of the paintings of classical times which still exist are frescoes or wall paintings found in long-buried cities such as Pompeii, in this case preserved by the ashes flung out by the volcano Vesuvius. Of one of these, a picture of the Greek hero Ulysses with his wife Penelope, enough remains to show how wonderfully the artists of those long-past days were able to paint.

When Art was Discouraged

For centuries after Rome was destroyed by the flood of Northern barbarians the art of painting almost vanished from the Western world. It is true that the monks in their monasteries illuminated their missals with lovely colours, but there were no great painters of pictures, or if there were they have been utterly forgotten. As Sir William Orpen has written: " In the early days of the Church the

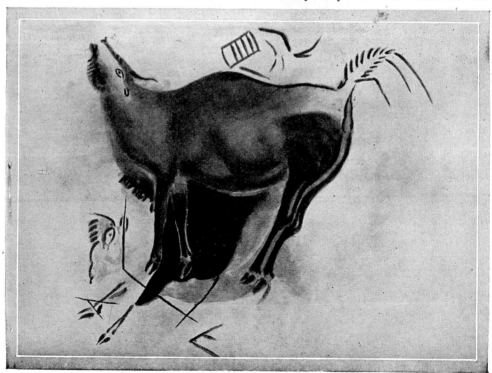

PAINTED BY CAVE-DWELLERS   *Giraudon.*

In a large cave near Santander, in Northern Spain, wall-pictures were discovered about half a century ago, and one of them is reproduced above. When we consider that it belongs to the prehistoric period and that it was the work of a person (or persons) who lived the life of a cave semi-savage, we must appreciate the high quality of the draughtsmanship. The drawing is attributed to a late period of the Stone Age.

Giraudon.

A PREHISTORIC WORK OF ART

Here is another painting from the cave in Northern Spain which was once the habitation of people of the Stone Age. The animal in the background is plainly a bison, such as once roamed the prairies of North America. Many of the paintings in the Altamira cave were carried out on the roof. Deer, elk, bison, wolves and bears figured among the subjects chosen. No one can say whether the work was that of one man or of several people.

Fathers gave little encouragement to Art, and 'cursed be all that paint pictures' is a sentiment frequently found in their writings." They were like the strict Mahommedans who to this day hate the taking of photographs.

Giotto's Sample

And so we skip sixteen centuries from Apelles and come to the Italian Giotto di Bondone. There is a story about Giotto which illustrates not only his skill, but his character. The Pope of the period sent a messenger to him, to ask for a specimen of his work, with a view to commissioning him to paint a picture for the Vatican. Giotto took a sheet of paper and a brush dipped in red paint, then, resting his elbow against his side so as to form a sort of compass, with one turn of his hand drew a perfect circle and handed this to the messenger as proof of his skill.

Giotto, greatest of early Italian painters, was born at a village near the town of Florence about the year 1266. He knew nothing of painting, he had no education, yet from his earliest childhood he did his best to represent the things he saw around him by lines drawn in the dust. One day when the lad was ten years old he was out in the field looking after his father's sheep, and, as usual, was drawing. His canvas was a flat stone, his pencil a bit of burnt stick and his model a lamb.

Suddenly a shadow fell across him and, looking up, he saw a tall bearded man with a kindly face watching him. This was Giovanni Cimabue, first of

Anderson.

FIVE HUNDRED YEARS AGO

This beautiful angel was painted about five hundred years ago by Giovanni da Fiesole, better known as Fra (*i.e.*, "Brother") Angelico, for he became a monk. His works were all of a religious character. Angelico was born in 1387 and died in 1455.

the restorers of painting in Italy, and painter of two remarkable pictures of the Madonna which, after 700 years, are still in existence. The master, greatly impressed by the work of the little shepherd lad, took him to Florence and had him taught. Before he died he had the happiness of seeing Giotto paint a series of magnificent frescoes in Florence. In one of these, the "Paradise," Giotto introduced portraits of a number of his friends, including the great poet Dante. These splendid pictures were afterwards covered with a coat of whitewash, but this has now been removed, and the frescoes can be seen in the Museo Nazionale at Florence.

In 1334 Giotto was made Master of Works of the Cathedral and City of Florence and he decorated the cathedral with fine statues. He was an architect as well as a painter, and the west front of Florence Cathedral was designed by him, as well as the Campanile or Bell Tower.

A Painter of Angels

Although to us Giotto's paintings seem stiff and conventional, yet they were life itself compared with the dull Byzantine art of earlier times. If the Byzantine artist painted a human figure the background was left blank or filled in with gilding. Giotto was the first to paint backgrounds with buildings and trees, and we can judge of the effect of his work on the people of the time by what the novelist Boccaccio said of him:

"Giotto was such a genius that there was nothing in Nature that he could not have represented in such a manner that it not only resembled, but seemed to be, the thing itself."

The name Giovanni da Fiesole means little to most of us, but when we speak of Fra Angelico we mention a name familiar to all lovers of art. Fra Angelico was born in 1387 and became a monk. He was a gentle, kindly person, a little brother of the poor, who rarely

The above picture is reproduced from a painting by Giotto, the first of the great Florentine painters. He produced many frescoes depicting the Life of St. Francis, known as the Saint of Assisi. Not only was Giotto a painter, but he was also an architect, and was made Master of the Works of the Cathedral at Florence. Its campanile, or detached bell-tower, exists to-day, though its designer did not live to witness the completion of his work.

ventured into the big cities, and was a lover of Nature.

His pictures are all of sacred subjects, and his angels are wonderfully beautiful, but his devils are not awe-inspiring. They seem to be ashamed of their unpleasant profession. He was the first to paint backgrounds with meadows covered with flowers, and the colours he used are bright and tender. Beautiful wall paintings of his are still to be seen in the Vatican at Rome and in Florence.

Fra Angelico died in 1455. Eleven years earlier there was born in Florence a boy named Alessandro Filipeppi, afterwards known as Botticelli. Young Sandro was apprenticed to a jeweller, but he loved painting and had the luck to become a pupil of the monk Lippi.

Pupil and Master

Botticelli became a much greater painter than his master, but the reason why we have chosen him out of many great Italian painters is that he ori-

Anderson.

MADONNA AND CHILD

After the death of Giotto, Fra Angelico and Fra Lippi carried on the development of art in Florence, and this painting of the Madonna and Child was the work of Fra Filippo Lippi, who was born in 1406 and died in 1469. It shows a fine feeling for feminine beauty and the figures are markedly human. Though this artist lived so long ago, some of his work may be seen in the National Gallery, London.

Anderson.

THE MAGNIFICAT

In the Latin tongue the word " Magnificat " means " doth magnify," and it is the title of that part of the Church of England service beginning: " My soul doth magnify the Lord." The title is given to this " Madonna of the Magnificat," which is regarded as the supreme masterpiece of Botticelli (1444–1510). The picture, to be seen in the Uffizi Gallery, Florence, shows intensely spiritual expressions, and has great decorative charm.

ginated a new style of painting. Almost all those before him had pictured only sacred subjects, but Botticelli broke new ground.

The Coming of Spring

His most famous picture, painted in 1477, is " Primavera," the Coming of Spring. In the centre is Venus, Goddess of Love, with Mercury, messenger of the gods, and the three Graces.

Figures and faces are beautiful, and flowers surround the figures. Here is beauty of a pagan type, and Botticelli's patron was not the Church, but the younger Lorenzo de' Medici.

Botticelli painted many religious pictures, yet he was the first great painter to break away from the old tradition, that all painting must be only for the service of the Church. He was a friend and follower of the great preacher and reformer, Savonarola, and may have been present at the marvellous " bonfire of vanities " at Florence, when women flung cards, dice, masks and carnival costumes, as well as costly ornaments, into a huge blaze in the public square. Later, Savonarola was excommunicated and was strangled and burned.

This was so great a blow to Botticelli that he fell into a state of melancholy and his later pictures show the change.

IN THE FLEMISH STYLE

These portraits of Jan Arnolfini and his wife were painted by John Van Eyck (1385–1440), and the original may be seen in the National Gallery, London. John and his brother Hubert Van Eyck worked the greatest revolution in painting, for they discovered (not in Italy, but in the Netherlands) how to paint in oils. Hubert was the elder of the two brothers.

The painters of whom we have been writing worked in " tempera," or distemper ; that is to say, their colours, ground in water, were mixed with some sort of thin glue or with yolk of egg beaten up with vinegar. They had not the great range of colours which are at the command of the modern artist, and did not know the art of oil painting.

Painting in Oils

This great discovery, namely, of oil painting, was not made in Italy, but in the Netherlands, and was due to the genius of two brothers, Hubert and John Van Eyck. Hubert was born about 1365 ; his younger brother, John, in 1385. These two men worked the greatest revolution in painting that the world has ever seen, but is is a sad fact that we know hardly anything about their lives or doings. Giorgio Vasari, a painter himself, wrote the lives of the early Italian painters, but there was no one to chronicle the lives of the Van Eycks, or tell us how they made the discovery which has meant so much to art.

The only story that remains to us, and we do not know whether it is true or a legend, is that John Van Eyck one day finished a picture, and after varnishing it with great care put it out in the sun to dry. When he came back he discovered, to his disgust, that the heat had cracked and ruined his picture. This started

THE MAN WITH THE PINKS

The original of this picture, which was painted about five hundred years ago by John Van Eyck, may be seen in the Berlin Museum. The work of one of the first artists to use oil paint, the picture astounds us to-day by its life-like realism. The identity of the sitter is quite unknown, but his patron saint was probably St. Anthony, because of the bell which hangs below the Cross on the twisted chain that the man is wearing.

Four and a half centuries ago the artist Hans Memlinc painted an oblong casket, the sides of which he adorned with six miniatures illustrating the Legend of St. Ursula. Here Ursula, on her pilgrimage, reaches Cologne.

In the above miniature the Saint is arriving at Basle. The casket upon which these paintings were made measures 3 feet in length, 2 feet 10 inches in height, and 1 foot 1 inch in breadth. It is to be seen at Bruges in the Hospital of St. John.

Photos: F. Bruckmann.

Here the Pope and the pilgrims are embarking at Basle. Even the roof-slopes of the casket are adorned with beautifully-painted medallions and four angel-musicians.

In this miniature is depicted the martyrdom of the pilgrims. St. Ursula was the daughter of a King of Brittany. The colours in the paintings are still bright.

F. Bruckmann.

By examining the above miniature, we can study the scene of the martyrdom of St. Ursula. Accompanied by a maiden and one of the Pope's suite, she stands undismayed before the General of the Huns, refusing to deny her Faith and calmly awaiting death by the archer's arrow. The object of Ursula's pilgrimage is believed to have been to escape her marriage to a pagan prince. She sailed up the Rhine to Basle, went to Rome, and was martyred on her return.

him on a series of experiments to find colours which should be more lasting, and after trying many things he discovered that linseed oil and oil of nuts dried more quickly than anything else, and that colours mixed with these oils were more brilliant than those blended with tempera, and—more than that—were proof against water. So came about the discovery of painting in oil, a discovery which rapidly spread to Italy, Germany, and other parts of Europe.

The Martyrdom of St. Ursula

John Van Eyck was as original a genius as Giotto himself, for he was really the first artist to paint what we call a picture. An example is his " Man with the Pinks," which, after 500 years, still astonishes all who see it by its wonderful drawing and perfect truth to life.

If you ever visit the Belgian town of Bruges, which is only an hour by rail from Ostend, you are sure to be taken into the ancient Hospital of St. John to see the pictures of Hans Memlinc. They are so brilliant, so beautiful, the colours so shiningly clear, that it is almost impossible to believe that they were painted more than four and a half centuries ago. By far the most wonderful of them all are the paintings on the Shrine of St. Ursula.

St. Ursula was the daughter of a King of Brittany, whose story is that she was persecuted by a pagan prince who wanted to marry her, and was told that in order to escape she must go on a pilgrimage to Rome with 11,000 virgins. Where she collected this army of young women the historian does not relate, but she did so and they all sailed up the Rhine to Basle and thence made their way to Rome. Unfortunately, on their way back they fell into the hands of the Huns at Cologne and were all massacred.

We may believe the story or not as we please; but, anyhow, it gave the great Memlinc an opportunity to paint a series of deathless pictures. Though the casket is only 3 feet long and less than 3 feet high, there are eight paintings and six medallions as well. Every tiny detail stands out as perfectly as on the long-past day when the artist still wielded his brush. They have the daintiness of miniatures.

The Genius of the Renaissance

Renaissance means re-birth. In the year 1452 there was born at Vinci, an Italian village not far from Florence, a boy who was destined to be the father

W. F. Mansell.

THE LAST SUPPER

This illustration is reproduced from a copy made by Marco d'Oggiono of a masterpiece by Leonardo da Vinci (1452–1519). Few pictures have stamped themselves on the imagination of the whole world as deeply as this one, which so dramatically recreates the Bible scene. The original picture was painted slowly and with infinite labour in Milan.

DA VINCI'S "MONA LISA"

W. F. Mansell.

This is probably the most famous picture in the world, and was the work of Leonardo da Vinci.
Not so many years ago the masterpiece was stolen from its place in the Louvre at Paris, and it
was many months before the canvas was recovered and put back. Mona Lisa was the third
wife of Francesco dei Giocondo, a Florentine official, and it is related that Leonardo hired
musicians to play whilst he painted, so that his subject should preserve her intent expression.

of the greatest re-birth of art that the world has ever seen.

Leonardo da Vinci was not merely a great artist, but also a great genius, a sort of superman of a type that appears in the world's history only at very long intervals. He was splendidly handsome; he had such immense strength that with his bare hands he could straighten out a heavy horseshoe. He was brave to a fault, and a brilliant talker. Of him the Italian writer Vasari says: " His every action is so divine that he outdistances all other men."

If he had not shone so greatly as a painter he would have gained world-wide fame as a sculptor; if he had never touched brush or chisel he would still have been celebrated for his inventions. In science and invention he was centuries ahead of his time. He was a clever chemist and the author of the first standard book of Anatomy.

In a word, he was a genius, and it is not surprising that he was the wonder of his own age and of those that have passed since his death.

While he was still a schoolboy his flashes of brilliancy astounded his masters, but he was oddly wayward. He would take up a thing, excel in it and fling it aside. The only subject in which he never seemed to lose interest was painting, and his father presently persuaded his friend, Andrea del Verrochio, a well-known artist, to take young Leonardo as a pupil.

Another Pupil excels his Master

Leonardo's master received a commission from the monks of Vallombroso to paint a picture of St. John baptising Christ, and the master allowed the boy to paint one of the angels in the picture. When Leonardo had finished there was a breathless silence, for his angel was so much more beautiful than any of the others that there was no comparison. Amazed that a mere boy could paint better than he, del Verrochio never again dipped a brush in colour.

Very soon Leonardo became known all over Italy. He was invited to Milan, where he painted his famous " Last Supper." He was so slow with this work that the Duke Sforza spoke to him about it and asked him why he wasted time mooning about. Leonardo gently explained that it was necessary for him to think out every head before beginning to paint it, and that it was very difficult to express the face of a man like Judas who betrayed the Master from Whom he had received so many benefits. " But," he went on, " to save time I will put in the head of the prior." The Duke was hugely amused and decided to let this clever youngster finish the work at his own price and leisure.

How the " Mona Lisa " was Stolen

The most celebrated of the paintings of Leonardo da Vinci is the " Mona Lisa," often called " La Gioconda," who in real life was the third wife of a Florentine official. Her strange smile has been the puzzle and admiration of all the many generations who have seen the picture.

This is the picture which was stolen from the Louvre in Paris in the year 1911, and the theft caused a sensation all over the world. The thief actually took the picture off the wall, frame and all, and since it is about thirty inches high by some twenty inches in breadth, the astonishing thing is that he was not seen. He must have crossed two rooms, descended a flight of stairs and walked across two courtyards, carrying the picture. The director of the Gallery and twelve attendants were dismissed, and hundreds of detectives and police were set to work. Yet no sign was found of either the thief or the picture.

Just before Christmas, 1913, a man went into a shop in Florence and offered to sell a picture. The owner of the shop, a dealer in antiques, immediately recognised it as the missing masterpiece. The man, whose name was Vincenzo Perugia, was arrested and confessed that he stole the picture to

Anderson.

One of the rulers of the city of Florence was Lorenzo de' Medici, and Michael Angelo carved the above statue of his patron. Angelo was the leading sculptor of the Renaissance (*i.e.*, re-birth of the arts) period. He was also a painter and an architect. Michael Angelo was only seventeen when Lorenzo the Magnificent died, so that the boy artist lost his position, and had to leave Florence.

avenge the art thefts of Napoleon when he invaded Italy more than a hundred years ago. So now "La Gioconda" smiles again from the wall of her home in Paris.

When Mona Lisa came to be French

It is an odd thing that the famous picture never came into the hands of the man for whom it was painted, for it was still unfinished when Leonardo accepted the invitation of the King of France to visit him. Leonardo had been none too well treated in Italy and he was growing old and was thankful for the refuge offered to him. King Francis was very kind to him and often visited him.

One day when the King was in the artist's studio, Leonardo, who had long been ill, was seized with a sudden attack, and the King, much distressed, sat down beside him and put his arm around him. Leonardo looked up with a smile into the King's face, then his eyes closed, he quivered and lay still. He had died in the arms of his royal friend, a fit ending to a wonderful life.

The World's Greatest Artist

Some years ago the *Strand Magazine* asked various great living painters to give their opinions as to the world's greatest pictures. Sir Lawrence Alma-Tadema chose "The Disputation as to the Sacrament," by Raphael, and Mr. G. F. Watts chose the "Sistine Madonna" by the same artist. Others picked pictures by Titian, Tintoretto and Velazquez. It is notable that Raphael was the only painter chosen by two separate judges. But Raphael was a painter pure and simple, while Michael Angelo was both painter and sculptor, and equally great in both arts. It is the general opinion of those best able to judge that Michael Angelo Buonarotti was the greatest artist who ever drew the breath of life.

Born in 1475 at Castel Caprese, Michael Angelo was the son of the chief magistrate of the town. Like all great geniuses, he showed his love for art while quite a small boy and haunted the premises of his nurse, whose husband was a marble worker. Time and again his father beat him, but this had no effect on young Michael, and at last his father gave in and apprenticed him to the well-known artist, Ghirlandaio. Before his three years were up the boy's wonderful modelling brought him to the notice of the great Lorenzo de' Medici, who put him into the famous "Garden School" of sculpture, and presently gave him special work in his own household at a salary of 500 ducats a month.

How Trouble Began

Michael Angelo was only seventeen when Lorenzo the Magnificent died, and the boy lost his position and salary. Piero de' Medici succeeded. He was a tyrant and a fool who forced young Michael to waste his time by modelling a statue in snow. Michael had a friend, a poet, who dreamed one night that Lorenzo appeared to him and told him to warn Piero that he would be driven from the city. The poet did give the message and got a fearful beating for doing so. He also told Michael, who had sense enough to see that trouble was coming, so he cleared out and went to Bologna. Sure enough, in 1494 Piero de' Medici had to fly for his life and Florence became a republic.

At Bologna, Michael Angelo carved a Sleeping Cupid so perfect that a dealer sold it to Cardinal San Giorgio as an antique dug up in Greece. Presently the Cardinal discovered how he had been cheated, but instead of being angry he sent for Michael Angelo, congratulated him on being able to do such wonderful work and gave him commissions for other statues. Michael Angelo carved a Bacchus, an Adonis and a Cupid, each more perfect than the last.

Suddenly he changed. He gave up producing heathen deities and for three years worked on a Christ with the Virgin, the wonderful "Pièta" at St.

Alinari.

This most impressive statue of Moses, to be seen at St. Peter's in Rome, was the work of Michael Angelo. Before he was thirty, Angelo had established his reputation as the greatest sculptor in the world, yet he turned from sculpture when he began to paint for the Pope a series of scenes on the ceiling of the Sistine Chapel. When Raphael, then at the height of his fame, was shown the work, he thanked God that he had been allowed to live to see such painting.

Peter's in Rome, a work so perfect that it established his reputation as the greatest sculptor in the world.

Enemies and Rivals

His family believed that their distinguished member was making his fortune, which was very far from the case, but Michael Angelo, too proud to tell them the truth, starved himself to give money to them all. They were not content with what they received, and went about saying how mean he was. No wonder that he became harsh and bitter.

In 1501, when Michael Angelo was only twenty-six years old, he returned to Florence to design a statue of "David," which had been ordered by the city to commemorate her delivery from her enemies. Here he met the great Leonardo da Vinci, and these two, who ought to have been the best of friends, became bitter enemies and rivals. It is only fair to da Vinci to say that it was none of his fault; the trouble was caused by stupid people who drove the two great artists into rivalry.

Michael Angelo was so unhappy in Florence that he was glad to be called back to Rome by Pope Julius II., who wished him to design a mausoleum. A rival sculptor, Bramante, who was bitterly jealous, whispered to the Pope that it was unlucky to build a tomb while you were still alive, and the Pope at once abandoned the idea and meanly left Michael Angelo unpaid for all his time and trouble and also in debt for the marbles he had obtained. When the great artist went to the Vatican to see the Pope he was driven from the doors by a groom. He hurried back once more to Florence.

The Sculptor Turned to Painter

Next thing was an urgent message from the Pope ordering Michael Angelo back to Rome. At first he would not go, but in the end he obeyed, and what do you think the Pope wanted him to do? That he, a sculptor, should paint the ceiling of the Sistine Chapel!

Michael Angelo tried to refuse. He begged that the work might be given to Raphael. What he did not know was that his old enemy, Bramante, was at the bottom of this absurd demand. He hoped that Michael Angelo would try and fail.

Michael Angelo did try, and on March 10th, 1508, the unfortunate man wrote: " To-day I, Michael Angelo, sculptor, began the painting of the chapel." The painting which the Pope had ordered was a series of scenes from the World's History, and the first upon which Michael Angelo set to work was " The Flood." He knew next to nothing of painting, and his initial work was hardly done before it became mouldy and had to be begun again.

Old at Thirty-seven

For four long years he worked desperately and alone. His relations kept writing, worrying him for money, while the Pope, angry at his slowness, made threats of throwing him from the scaffolding. Remember, too, that all this time the artist was forced to lie flat on his back, for the painting was done on the ceiling.

On All Saints' Day, 1512, Michael Angelo announced that the work was finished, and when the people were admitted even his worst enemies were left gasping with wonder at the amazing beauty and genius of the work. Raphael himself, then at the height of his fame, thanked God that he had been allowed to live to see such painting.

No praise, however, could repay the artist for his work. He was half blind, so that for some years he could hardly see to read; he had strained and injured the muscles of his neck and, though only thirty-seven years of age, was already an old man. Then came the cruellest blow of all. The Pope died and his successor had no work for Michael Angelo. Once more he went back to

"BALTHASAR CASTIGLIONE" BY RAPHAEL

Alinari.

The original of this lifelike portrait is regarded as the masterpiece in portraiture of the artist Raphael. The subject of the portrait was Count Castiglione, the intimate and lifelong friend of the painter, himself a scholar and author. Raphael was born in 1483 and died in 1520. He was the son of a painter, and no artist ever worked harder or accomplished more in a short life. He was made chief architect of St. Peter's at Rome.

2—2

Florence, where he worked upon the tomb of his old patron, Lorenzo de' Medici.

In 1527 Florence revolted and was attacked by the troops of the Pope. Michael Angelo was put in charge of the fortifications, but he felt it his duty to warn the governor that the general in command, Malatesta Baglione, might betray the city. His warning was laughed at, but events proved the truth of his prophecy, for Baglione did betray his city and Florence fell.

Michael Angelo's life was spared, and presently he was dragged back to Rome to begin another terrible painting task. This was " The Last Judgment," which covered an immense wall at the entrance to the Sistine Chapel. He was sixty-one when he started this work, and it took him five years and left him a wreck.

Yet, in spite of all his hardships and disappointments, he lived to be eighty-eight years old. It is a sad picture that the writer, Vasari, gives of the wonderful man in his last years. Unable to sleep, he made himself a kind of helmet in which he fixed a candle so that he could see to work at night with his chisel. He ate nothing but bread and drank a little wine. In February, 1564, he was seized with fever, yet refused to go to bed. Five days later he became too weak to move, and on the following afternoon breathed his last. It is pleasant to know that his old servants and a few good friends were with him to the end.

" Beautiful as an Angel "

If Michael Angelo's life was long, stormy and unhappy, that of Raphael, who lived at the same time, was short, but smooth and pleasant. Raphael Sanzio, or Santi, was the son of a painter, born at the small town of Urbino in 1483, and became a pupil of Perugino, who was himself a famous artist. The boy was amazingly handsome. His portrait painted by himself shows him almost as a beautiful

Anderson.

THE MADONNA DEL GRANDUCA

Italy's great artist Raphael painted a large number of pictures of the Madonna and Child (Jesus and His Mother), and his genius enabled him to impart the most divine expressions to his holy subjects. The above work is known as the " Madonna del Granduca," and its original hangs in the Pitti Gallery at Florence.

woman, yet he was no weakling, but a man with a strong character.

Indeed, no artist ever worked harder or accomplished more in a short life of only thirty-seven years.

Raphael's Retort

His personality was as charming as his looks; everyone admired and loved him. He was the favourite of two Popes in succession, and was made chief architect of St. Peter's and guardian of the ancient monuments of Rome. Everywhere he went people followed him. Meeting him once, surrounded by assistants and friends, stern old Michael Angelo said to him: "You look like a general at the head of an army"; to which Raphael retorted with a smile: "And you, sir, like an executioner on the way to the scaffold."

Alinari.

PORTRAIT OF A YOUNG MAN

This fine portrait hangs in the Louvre at Paris, and was painted by Raphael, whose name was Raphael Sanzio. He was a man of singularly sweet disposition, charming in manner and conversation and a favourite with everyone. He perfected his art by study in Florence, and then went to paint at the Vatican.

Raphael's pictures have fetched enormous prices, probably the greatest ever paid for paintings. For his famous Ansidei Madonna in the National Gallery no less than £70,000 was paid to its owner, the Duke of Marlborough, and that was so long ago as 1885. It was a three times higher price than any which had been previously paid for a picture. What the picture is worth now can only be guessed—perhaps a quarter of a million.

Yet this picture is not as beautiful as his Sistine Madonna, which Mr. G. F. Watts, R.A., considered to be the finest picture in the world. Raphael was equally great as a portrait painter, and his masterpiece in this direction is the portrait of his friend Balthasar Castiglione, which is now in the Louvre at Paris.

In 1520 Raphael was struck down by a malignant fever, which he had caught during his work among the ancient ruins of which he was guardian, and on Good Friday, which was also his own birthday, he passed out of this life. Few men have been more deeply mourned.

The Tailor of Padua

In the year 1441 a man named Francesco Squarcione was admitted into the Guild of Painters at Padua. The amusing part of it is that Squarcione could not paint: he was a tailor by vocation. But more clever than other tailors, Squarcione had by degrees turned his shop into a sort of old curiosity or antique store, where he had many fine old statues. This brought him into touch with the numerous artists who came to the famous city of Padua; and so, as we have said, at last, at the age of forty-seven, he qualified for the Guild.

The next step was to engage apprentices, start a studio and secure contracts for art work. Being a clever business man, Squarcione managed to get hold of Jacopo Bellini, a brilliant painter of Venice, to act as teacher in his school, and the result was that this school, opened by a tailor, became one of the most important art schools in Italy and trained no fewer than 137 pupils, among them some of the world's most celebrated painters.

An Orphaned Genius

One of Squarcione's first apprentices was Andrea Mantegna, a nameless orphan, so amazingly gifted that, when only ten years old, he was admitted to membership of the Guild. At twelve he was doing important work in the Chapel of the Eremitani at Padua, and at seventeen painted an altar-piece for the Church of St. Sophia, which, as the historian Vasari said, "might have been the work of a skilled veteran instead of a mere boy."

Mantegna married the daughter of Bellini and set up a school for himself—much to Squarcione's annoyance. Soon Mantegna's fame spread so far that he was called to Rome by Pope Innocent VIII. to paint the walls of the Belvedere. Pay days came round but salaries were not always forthcoming. One day the Pope himself arrived to inspect Mantegna's work and asked what the figure was on which the artist was working.

"One much honoured here, your Holiness," replied Mantegna. "It is Prudence."

The Pope smiled.

"You should associate Patience with her," he answered, but after that payments were more regular. In any case, Mantegna was able to retire to Mantua, where he built himself a fine house and lived to the good old age of seventy-five.

Several of his finest pictures are in England, but the finest of all, "Parnassus," is in the Louvre at Paris. This picture shows the ancient Greek Gods "at home" on Mount Olympus. Venus and Apollo are on the mountain-top, while to the right stands Mercury, Messenger of the Gods, with Pegasus the Winged Horse.

Where Correggio Charms

Squarcione had a pupil named Tura, who founded a new school of art at Ferrara, and one of his pupils in turn founded at Modena a school which produced one of the world's most charming painters. He was Antonio Allegri, better known as Correggio, famous not only for magnificent form and design, but even more so for the beauty and delicacy of his flesh tints.

One of his most celebrated pictures is of Ganymede, the beautiful Trojan boy, of whom the story is that he was carried off by an eagle to act as cup-bearer to Jupiter. The picture shows the immense bird lifting the boy into the air while a dog leaps helplessly to the aid of Ganymede.

Very little is known of the life of Correggio, except that he was of a very shy and retiring disposition and—perhaps—something of a miser. But this may have been because he had a large

W. F. Mansell.

The artist Raphael painted many Madonnas, but the picture here reproduced is regarded as his most famous and most favoured. Other pictures with the same sacred subject may rival it in formal beauty, but in no other does he reach the same height of spiritual expression. The Christ-child, so solemnly yet naturally gazing at the Infinite, and the majestic but entirely human Mother are figures which, once we have seen them, cannot be forgotten.

family to keep and the pay of painters in those days was small.

The story of his end is curious. He was at Parma and was paid sixty crowns for some work he had finished. The money was given him all in small change and made quite a heavy burden. With this on his back he set out afoot for home. It was very hot and he stopped at a spring and drank so much cold water that it brought on a fever from which he died at the age of forty years.

The " Great " George

Giorgione was the son of a peasant and was born at Castelfranco in 1477. He was christened Giorgio, but grew up so tall and fine both in body and mind that he was always called Giorgione, or the Great George. He seems to have been a charming and lovable person, with beautiful manners and a great passion for music. Critics tell us that you can see the *melody* of line and *harmony* of colour in all his paintings.

Alas, most of his paintings have been lost, yet among the score or so that remain are some of the world's best portraits. The finest is " An Unknown Man," still to be seen at Venice.

The end of this splendid painter was tragic. In 1510 he fell in love with a beautiful Venetian lady. She caught the plague and he took it from her and died at the early age of thirty-four.

A Grand Old Man of Italian Art

Born only thirteen years after his master, Giorgione, Tiziano Vicellio was a mountaineer from the Apennines. He was worthy to succeed his great master for, as Vasari has written, " not only in his art was he great, but he was a nobleman in person."

Indeed, Titian is one of the most splendid figures in all the history of painting. Deep-chested, clear-eyed, with magnificent health and a fine presence, he was admired by all. But if he had had none of these qualities he would still have been considered the

Alinari.

FROM THE SCHOOL OF BELLINI

The original painting of the above picture is in the Louvre at Paris, and it is credited to the School of Gentile Bellini, illustrating the arrival of a Venetian ambassador at Cairo. Nearly five hundred years ago a tailor established at Padua near Venice an art school, in which Jacopo Bellini, a brilliant painter from Venice, was a teacher. From this school came some of the world's most famous painters. Gentile and Giovanni were the sons of Jacopo Bellini.

CORREGGIO'S GREAT PAINTING

Alinari.

This wonderful painting of the Nativity, called " La Notte " (the Night), was painted by Antonio Allegri, better known as Correggio, the name of the place in which he was born in 1494. He was famous not only for his beautiful form and design, but even more so for the delicacy of his flesh tints, and the colouring and beauty of his paintings of children have never been surpassed. The lighting effects in the above painting come entirely from the radiance of the Christ-child. Correggio died in his native town in 1534.

Anderson.

Regarded as being the most beautiful conception of Christ in art, the original of this painting (now in a collection in the United States of America) is believed to have been either a study or else a fragment of a lost picture. It was the work of the artist Giorgione (1477–1510), and it is said that its loveliness performed miracles of faith among those who came to see it when it was hung in a church in Venice.

"CHARLES V" BY TITIAN

Anderson.

Charles V was both King of Spain and Emperor of the Holy Roman Empire, and this picture, painted by Titian, so delighted the monarch that he paid the artist a thousand crowns, a great price in those days. The picture represents the King riding at daybreak over the plain of Augsburg, just before the battle in which his troops were victorious.

Anderson.

The original of this picture was painted by the great Venetian artist, Paul Veronese, who was
born at Verona in 1528, and died in Venice in 1588. The figure work is especially beautiful.
Veronese painted for a time in Rome, and was rebuked for his worldly treatment of religious
subjects; the picture above, as an instance, relating to the taking of Moses from the water.

"THE TAILOR," BY MORONI

To be seen at the National Gallery, London, this picture is regarded as one of the world's great portraits and a splendid example of Venetian colour. It was painted by Giambattista Moroni (1520–1578), and shows an honest tailor at his work, in marked contrast to the portraits of nobles and their wives by whom the artists of the time were so largely employed.

wonder of his age because of the beauty of his work.

Before he was thirty years old he was elected official painter of Venice, and after that his life was a happy and splendid one. He lived in almost royal state and had none of the unhappy pinching which made Michael Angelo's life so miserable. It is said of him that he ennobled all his sitters with something of his own majesty. He certainly did this in the case of the Emperor Charles V., whose portrait on horseback by Titian so delighted the monarch.

Year after year he went on painting, and in his ninetieth year was still wielding the brush with the same wonderful vigour. He lived to the age of ninety-nine, and even then did not die of old age. It was the plague which killed him.

"The Little Dyer"

"The design of Michael Angelo and the colouring of Titian" was the sign which Jacopo Robusti set up over the door of his studio at Venice, and if it sounds sheer impertinence it was not so, for Tintoretto (as he was called, owing to his being the son of a dyer) lived up to his motto.

Once, when asked to compete with other artists in a design for a ceiling picture for the monastery of San Rocco, Tintoretto took the exact measurements and set to work. When the day came for the exhibition of the designs it was found that the artist had completed the entire work and—not only that—had fixed it in place. The other artists were furious and the Prior asked why Tintoretto had taken it on himself to complete the work.

"That is my only method of preparing designs," replied the artist. "It is the only way of making sure that the purchaser gets what he is paying for. If you do not care to pay me for my work and pains I will make you a present of it." The Prior looked again. He saw it was good work. He paid.

Tintoretto's industry was amazing. He seems to have decorated half the great buildings of Venice in his time. His "Paradiso," still to be seen in the Ducal Palace, is the largest painting in the world, being 84 feet long and 34 feet high. Tintoretto was the last of the great religious painters of Italy.

The Painter of Feasts

Paul Veronese lived in the same century as Titian and Tintoretto, and in his pictures can be seen the life and luxury of Venice in that age. He excelled in painting feasts and pageants.

Anderson.

THE WASHING OF THE FEET
Tintoretto, painter of the above picture, also belonged to the sixteenth century, and was one of the great Venetian artists who studied under Titian. He painted a picture 84 feet in width and 34 feet in height, said to be the largest ever produced. He is best known for his treatment of Biblical and other religious subjects.

DÜRER AND HOLBEIN

A LANDSCAPE BY DÜRER

Albrecht Dürer (1471–1528) was a German artist who arrived in Venice as a young student, and after a time went back to his native Nuremberg, where he made his great name in the world of art. He was an artist who loved Nature, and you will see from the above landscape how this love found its expression in his delicate and yet vigorous drawing of trees and clouds.

WHILE Bellini was still alive there arrived in Venice a young man named Albrecht Dürer. In those days a student of art made for Italy just as now he goes to Paris. Dürer was Hungarian by descent, but had been taught painting and wood engraving at an art school in Nuremberg, where his father was in business as a goldsmith.

Dürer and Bellini's Brushes

Bellini was full of admiration for young Dürer's work, especially for the way in which he painted hair. Dürer seemed able to show each separate hair on the head of a subject, and Bellini thought he must have a special brush for the purpose. Dürer picked up some of Bellini's brushes.

"Any of these will do if I may use them," he said, and when leave was given proceeded to paint a tress of hair in a way which made Bellini and the other students declare that they had never seen anything like it.

In 1494 Dürer went back to Nuremberg, married and settled down to a life's work which has made his name one of the best known in the world of art. His most magnificent design is a wood engraving, "The Four Horses of the Apocalypse." The four terrible horses of this picture are Conquest, War, Famine and Death. Prints of his engravings sold readily, and if he did not make a fortune, Dürer was able to live comfortably. He was, so a historian of the time says, "a modest working man," and when in the fulness of time he died, the great reformer, Martin Luther, wrote of him as follows:

"It is well for a pious man to mourn the best of men, but you should call him happy, for Christ . . . called him away in a good hour from the tempests

W. F. Mansell.

In the above reproduction we have a further example of the etching of Albrecht Dürer. The subject of the picture is St. Christopher carrying the Christ-child across a river. The legend here illustrated explains how St. Christopher came by his name, which means " Christ-bearer." You see the Head of Jesus glowing with light from Above.

W. F. Mansell.

This is St. George and the Dragon as conceived by the German artist Albrecht Dürer early in the sixteenth century. There seems to be real flesh and blood in the figure of the saint, and the horse is a masterpiece of drawing. The same artist gave the world "The Four Horses of the Apocalypse," a picture inspired by verses 2 to 8 in the sixth chapter of the Book of Revelation, the four riders representing Conquest, War, Famine and Death. The Feast Day of St. George is kept in England every year on April 23rd.

and possibly yet more stormy times, so that he who was worthy only to see the best might not be compelled to see the worst."

The Dance of Death

Although they are only little woodcuts and not to be compared as works of art with the wonderful pictures and portraits of Hans Holbein, no works of this great master have ever appealed more strongly to succeeding generations than the picture sequence, " The Dance of Death." Death is shown dogging the footsteps of Pope and prince, rich man and poor man.

Hans Holbein was born in 1497 in the German town of Augsberg. He came of a family of painters, but his genius was like that of a sun among planets. We do not know much about the youth of this great artist, but about

W. F. Mansell.

TWO SQUIRRELS OF FOUR CENTURIES AGO

In this beautiful etching we see a pair of squirrels that had their being in 1512. We have a connection with the happy lives of these little animals which lived centuries ago, because of the genius of the artist Albrecht Dürer. There is wonderful expression in the face of the squirrel which is so obviously enjoying his nut, and the work in the tail is marvellous. Students of the time declared they had never seen hair so perfectly presented as Dürer could paint it.

Anderson.

Even to our twentieth century eyes this is a really living picture showing clearly in every detail the touch of a master. It is a portrait of Albrecht Dürer when young, and was painted by the artist himself in his twenty-seventh year. One of its most striking features is the delightful rendering of the long wavy hair. The great Venetian artist Bellini believed that Dürer had a special brush for the painting of hair. The original of this portrait is at Madrid.

1517 Holbein was in Basle, where he painted a wonderful portrait of the merchant, Jacob Meyer. Three years later he became a citizen of Basle and married a widow with two children.

When Rome was Sacked

The world at that time was in confusion, the Middle Ages giving way to modern thought. In May, 1527, the whole of Southern Europe was horrified to see Rome sacked by an army of Christian troops.

Holbein, like a wise man, had foreseen some of these troubles, and in 1526 found a refuge in England, where he became a friend of Sir Thomas More and painted a picture of his household. Presently he became the favourite of the wealthy German merchants settled in London and in 1536 was made Court Painter to King Henry VIII.

As Sir William Orpen says: " No Sovereign ever did a wiser or better thing for himself than Henry when he made Holbein his painter, for not only

W. F. Mansell.

"THE AMBASSADORS," BY HOLBEIN

The original of this picture is in the National Gallery, London. The two figures represent the ambassadors Jean de Dinteville and the Bishop of Lavaur, and the work is said to have been painted to attract to the artist the patronage of foreign diplomats. Holbein was appointed Court Painter to King Henry VIII., and it is mainly due to this artist that we know what Bluff King Hal looked like, and what he and his courtiers wore.

W. F. Mansell.

In the reign of King Henry VIII, a corporation of wealthy German merchants settled and traded in London under one title, "The Merchants of the Steelyard," and George Gisze, the subject of this portrait, was one of the band. The picture shows us the minute rendering of every detail, and is a striking illustration of Holbein's capacity and industry. Holbein died in London from the plague in 1543.

did the artist present the king to posterity in a manner that mitigates our judgment of his cruelties, but he made that whole period of history live for us as no previous period of history lives by his series of portraits and drawings of the English Court."

It is very largely due to Holbein that we know what Bluff King Hal looked like and what he and his courtiers wore.

One of the most delightful of all his portraits is that of Robert Cheseman, the King's Falconer, with a falcon perched upon his fist.

W. F. Mansell.

THE KING'S FALCONER

This fine portrait by Holbein is at The Hague in Holland, and is regarded as being one of the most delightful this artist painted. The subject is Robert Cheseman, falconer to the King. The falcon is perched upon the man's fist, and his be-ringed fingers are touching the smooth plumage of the handsome bird. In days gone by, falcons were trained to catch birds on the wing, and hunting with the falcon was a popular field sport.

RUBENS' "RAINBOW LANDSCAPE"

Painted by the artist Paul Rubens, the lovely original of this picture forms part of the Wallace Collection in London. Rubens was one of the world's greatest painters, and also one of the first artists to produce landscapes, the above being an outstanding example. Rubens was born in 1577 and lived till 1640. He studied in many of the Italian cities, travelled widely, and was knighted in London by King Charles I. Upwards of 1,200 pictures are believed to have been painted by this giant of the brush.

ONE year after the death of Titian there was born in Siegen, Westphalia, a boy who was destined to become one of the world's greatest painters. His father, Dr. John Rubens, was a native of Antwerp; but, being a Protestant, had been driven out by the Spaniards who then ruled the Netherlands. The boy was christened Peter Paul. His father died while he was very young, and his mother took her family back to Antwerp.

Page and Painter

The next we hear of Paul Rubens is as page of honour to Princess Margaret de Ligne-Aremberg, but the boy was mad on painting, and at fourteen was allowed to begin work as pupil to his cousin, Tobias Verhaeght. In all, young Rubens had three masters, the best being Otto Vaenius, who filled him with love for Italian art and presently sent him to Venice.

Perfect copies made by Rubens of pictures by Titian and Veronese caught the eye of the Duke of Mantua, and since the young artist was handsome and well-mannered, the Duke sent him on a mission to Philip III. of Spain. Few young men had seen more of the world than Rubens when the death of his mother recalled him from Spain to Antwerp, where the rulers of Flanders made him Court Painter.

He lived at Antwerp, and here, in 1609, married his first wife, the daughter of John Brant. At Munich may still be seen a charming picture painted by himself of Rubens and his wife. Both are richly dressed in the style of the time.

For twelve years Rubens lived and painted in Antwerp. He had many collaborators and pupils, and the amount of work he turned out was immense. Rubens was one of the first artists to paint landscapes. A famous example is the Rainbow Landscape in the Wallace Collection in London.

The Painter becomes Ambassador

In 1622 Rubens was asked to go to France by the Queen Mother, Marie de' Medici, to decorate her palace of the Luxembourg. He painted a series of magnificent wall pictures now in the Louvre. With his fine presence and courtly manners, the great artist became a favourite at the French Court and was presently sent to The Hague to secure a renewal of the treaty between Holland and Flanders. He did his work so well that the King of Spain made him a noble.

We next hear of Rubens visiting Spain for a second time, where, in Madrid, he met that greatest of Spanish artists, Velazquez, and the two became friends. Then Philip IV. of Spain sent Rubens to England as ambassador to Charles I. to arrange terms of peace between Spain and England. While in England Rubens painted the ceiling of the Banqueting Saloon at Whitehall. Rubens was doing this work when some personage asked him:

Anderson.

THE CHILDREN OF KING CHARLES I.

Anthony Van Dyck, who painted the above picture, was a pupil of Rubens, and became eventually almost as famous as his master. After visiting Italy, he came to England and was appointed painter-in-ordinary to King Charles I., who knighted him. Van Dyck was in the first flight of the world's great portrait painters, and is said to have produced upwards of thirty pictures of King Charles. The artist died in London.

RUBENS AND HIS FIRST WIFE

F. Bruckmann.

In this beautiful portrait study we see Paul Rubens and his first wife, Isabella Brant, painted by the artist himself. Note the clearness of the drawing, the beauty of the hands, the expression of the faces, and also the wealth of detail. This was a comparatively early work of Rubens, and such treatment formed the foundation for his more dashing and later style.

W. F. Mansell.

After the execution of King Charles I, the original of this illustration was sold by the Puritans and taken to Bavaria, only to be purchased later by the great Duke of Marlborough and brought back to England. The painting shows King Charles in an impressively knightly pose, and brings out all the virtues of the royal figure. Note the attendant on the right with the King's helmet. Van Dyck was buried in the Old St. Paul's Cathedral, but his tomb was lost amidst the ruins after the Great Fire of London.

THE LAUGHING CAVALIER

W. F. Mansell.

No one knows who was the subject of this painting by Frans Hals, but the young officer represented had a smile which no one even to-day can resist, and there must be very few people to whom the picture or reproductions from it are not familiar. There is no need to be an artist to appreciate its high qualities to the full. This is undoubtedly the best-known work of Hals and is now in the Wallace Collection in London.

" Does the ambassador of His Catholic Majesty amuse himself with painting ? "

" No," said Rubens, " the painter amuses himself sometimes with being an ambassador."

Early in 1630 King Charles knighted the artist-ambassador and Sir Peter Paul Rubens returned to Antwerp. His first wife was dead and he married again and settled down on his country estate near Malines, where he spent the last years of his life very quietly and happily.

Rubens' Favourite Pupil

Rubens was one of the earliest of the Flemish painters to bring into his country the grace and gorgeous colouring of the Italian school, but all his work was robust. Though Anthony Van Dyck was the favourite pupil of the great Dutchman, and later became nearly as famous as his master, his style was utterly different. It was refined, almost spiritual.

By Rubens' advice young Van Dyck visited Italy, and it is an interesting coincidence that later in life he was, like Rubens, called to England, where he became painter - in - ordinary to Charles I. Also, like Rubens, he was knighted.

One of his most famous pictures is Charles I. on horseback, which was bought for the National Gallery in 1884 for £17,500. Someone has said of this picture that it represents all King Charles' virtues and none of his vices, but no one can deny that it is a very splendid painting. If, however, you wish to see a far more perfect example of Van Dyck's art you should visit the Wallace Collection and inspect the portrait of Philippe le Roy, Governor of the Netherlands.

Van Dyck was one of the greatest portrait painters who ever lived, but though his success was great his life was not a happy one. His health was poor and he

F. Bruckmann.

HALS' " NURSE AND CHILD "

Here is a small facsimile of another painting by Frans Hals, which is a perfect example of his skill because it is so intensely human. You feel almost certain that the half-smile on the child's face will soon become a full smile. The details of lace and embroidery are most strikingly executed. Hals died in Haarlem in 1666.

FRANÇOISE VAN WASSERHOVEN

The original of this picture is in the National Gallery, London, and so strikingly is it painted that it shows us how strength of character and features may last right into old age, and that there is great nobility and dignity in being "up in years." The painter was Rembrandt, who ranks among ten or twelve of the greatest artists in the world, and was probably the finest portrait painter who ever lived. The older Rembrandt grew, the finer his work became.

THE THREE TREES

This is an etching by the artist Rembrandt, known by the title " The Three Trees."   It shows us faithfully one of Nature's moods, and has a grandeur of its own, never surpassed in etching. In the distance, on the left, is a view of the city of Amsterdam, where many of Rembrandt's original pictures may to-day be seen.

Photos: W. F. Mansell.

The actual painting from which this reproduction was taken was sold for £100,000 by Lord Lansdowne to an American art collector. It is known as "The 'Lansdowne' Mill," and was the work of Rembrandt. Its charm and appeal lie in the veil of soft beauty cast over the landscape by the atmosphere.

A MASTERPIECE IN PORTRAITURE

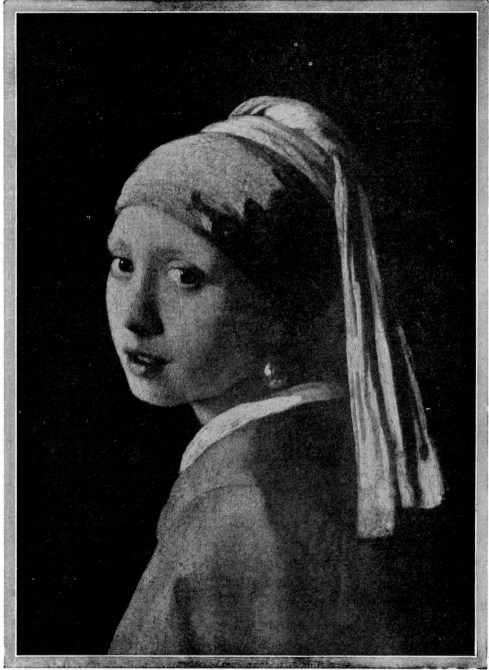

W. F. Mansell.

Known as the " Head of a Young Girl," the original of this picture is at The Hague, in Holland.
It was the work of Jan Vermeer, of Delft, whose pictures to-day command fabulous prices.
Vermeer counts as one of the " Little Masters " of Holland in the seventeenth century, and a
critic has referred to his works of art as " bottled sunlight." The twenty-six pictures which
Vermeer left when he died would not pay his trifling debts, but to-day their value would
probably be a quarter of a million pounds sterling.

was always going to quacks who poisoned him and made him worse. He suffered terribly from gout and was only forty-two when he died.

In 1580 there was born in the famous city of Antwerp a baby who was named Frans Hals, son of a burgher named Pieter Hals. We know very little of the life of Frans, but we gather that he was a cheery soul, fond of his pipe and his glass and of good company. Some have tried to make out that he was a drunkard, but, as Sir William Orpen says in " The Outline of Art," a drunkard would not have been able to paint beautifully at the age of sixty, and would certainly not have been chosen a director of the Guild of St. Lucas, as Hals was, at the age of sixty-four.

Frans Hals' most famous painting is the so-called " Laughing Cavalier," and truly this is one of the most delightful portraits ever painted. You do not need to know anything of art to enjoy it. The cavalier has such a jolly, devil-may-care expression. Hals' " Nurse and Child " is another example of exquisite skill. You can see the smile which in a moment will be a laugh rippling over the face of the wonderfully-dressed babe. His whole art is a reflection of the fine spirit of his country in its marvellous and successful struggle against an immensely stronger Power.

Art's Idle Pupil

Twenty-seven years after the birth of Frans Hals there arrived in the family of a corn miller named Hermon Gerritzoon van Rijn a boy who, as Rembrandt, holds place among the ten or twelve greatest painters of the world. At school he spent the writing hour making sketches on his exercise book, and no doubt was soundly beaten.

But his love for art was so strong that he was apprenticed to a fashionable portrait painter. He did not stay long, but soon went to Leyden to work for himself, and was only twenty when he painted his wonderful " St. Paul in Prison." In 1632 he fell in love with Saskia van Uylenburg, whose family thought a young artist no match for their daughter. But he married her and afterwards got even with the family by painting a series of pictures illustrating the life of Samson, in which Saskia is Delilah, he himself Samson, while the Philistines are members of his wife's family. He also painted a charming picture of his young wife and himself feasting together.

He flung his earnings about recklessly, and when his wife died in 1642 found himself poor and in debt. He wandered

W. F. Mansell.

THE COURTYARD OF A DUTCH HOUSE
Pieter de Hooch, who painted the above most realistic but homely picture, was born at Rotterdam in 1630, and died at Haarlem in 1677. He ranks high among Dutch painters, and was a master both of detail and of colour effects. The original of this particular picture may be seen in the National Gallery.

W. F. Mansell.

Another of the masterpieces to be found in the National Gallery, London, the title of this picture is " Lady Standing at the Virginal." The virginal was a musical instrument, something like a spinet, long since supplanted by the piano. The details of the interior of the apartment are perfect, and the lighting effects charming. Vermeer belonged to a great school of painters at Delft, in Holland, an ancient town where a famous porcelain was manufactured.

about the country painting many landscapes, always hard up and sometimes very unhappy. The relatives of his first wife had not forgiven him and they went to law with him to try to get his son, Titus, away from him.

Then he married again, a woman of humble birth, and this annoyed his aristocratic patrons, yet she proved a good wife, and started a business to sell the prints and pictures of her husband after he became bankrupt.

Rembrandt was perhaps the greatest portrait painter who ever lived, for he had the art or talent of seeing the true characters of his subjects and representing them on canvas. He learned constantly from experience, so that the older he grew the finer his work became. Sorrows piled upon him. His second wife died and then his dearly-loved son followed her to the grave.

The Little Masters

In 1669, worn out by hard work and misfortune, the great Rembrandt passed away. His pupil, Gerard Dou, a man with not a tenth of Rembrandt's genius, made a fortune, but, as Sir William Orpen says: "It is much easier to recognise industry than to understand inspiration."

All through the seventeenth century the Low Countries produced painters of genius. Those like Dou, who were content to paint every feather on a bird or

W. F. Mansell.

THE MILL AT AMSTERDAM

Jacob van Ruisdael, who was born in 1628 and died in 1682, delighted in painting foaming cascades and towering cliffs, but the above picture shows that he was equally at home with far less turbulent subjects. As a landscape the work is a model of sound composition, and the quaint old mill forms a strange contrast to the ornate and highly-finished building just beyond.
The original of this picture is at Amsterdam.

THE IDLE SERVANT

The National Gallery, London, houses the original of this lifelike picture, its meaning so well expressed in the title. The painting was the work of Nicolas Maes (1632–93), one of the pupils of Rembrandt. It is plainly the mistress of the household who has caught her servant asleep amidst the unwashed pots and pans. The incident of the cat stealing the chicken shows the artist's power of humorous observation. Maes achieved a great reputation as a painter of portraits.

every scale on a fish, flourished and made money, but others, who were really much greater artists, came near to starving. To-day the pictures of Vermeer fetch immense prices, yet when he died in 1675 he had nothing to leave his widow except twenty-six unsold pictures. The very least that such a collection would bring nowadays would be £250,000; then they were worth so little that they did not suffice to pay the small debts of the dead artist.

Painting for Pleasure

De Hooch and Albert Cuyp were great painters. Cuyp, in particular, had an amazing mastery of cloud and sky effects. Jacob van Ruisdael's pictures are austere and majestic. He delighted in painting foaming cascades and towering cliffs. In his picture

" The Mill " the spectator feels as well as sees the calm before the storm breaks.

" The Avenue " by Hobbema, who was a pupil of Ruisdael, is a delightful example of landscape and is one of the most prized possessions of the National Gallery. Yet Hobbema made so little by his brush that at the age of thirty he was driven to obtain a position in the Customs in order to be sure of his bread and butter, and afterwards painted only for his own pleasure.

The various Dutch painters of the seventeenth century have left to us every possible aspect of life of their period. We have portraits, interiors, landscapes, skating scenes, seascapes and shipping. Some of these paintings may even be called story pictures. " The Idle Servant " by Nicolas Maes is an example.

W. F. Mansell.

" THE AVENUE," BY HOBBEMA
The original of this picture is undoubtedly one of the most popular among visitors to the National Gallery, London. It shows a landscape which makes us all appreciate the delights of the countryside. Hobbema (1638–1709) was a pupil of Ruisdael; but though such a masterly painter, he could not earn a living by his brush, and was forced to take a small position in the Civil Service of his country. Thereafter he painted only for pleasure and as a hobby.

W. F. Mansell.

A Dutch artist of much more recent times was David Adolf Constant Artz (1837–90), the painter of the above picture. His works are wonderfully realistic, and he delighted in painting the fisher folk of Scheveningen (a popular bathing resort in Holland), especially on the sand-hills that fringe the shore thereabouts. One can almost feel the sun and hear the ripple of the calm water in this gem of art.

CHILDREN BY THE SEA

Among the school of modern Dutch painters must be included Josef Israëls, whose genius gave us " Children by the Sea," reproduced above, which was exhibited at the Paris Salon in 1857. Josef took secret lessons in painting from local artists and the youth was then allowed by his father to go to Amsterdam to study art seriously.

" Prince and Princess," is the title of this picture, which is the work of Matthew Maris, one of three artist brothers who were born in Holland. Matthew alone of the three had a romantic, poetic nature, and his pictures were like fairy stories in art. He went through the Siege of Paris, and eventually settled in London, where he lived the life of a hermit.

THE GREAT MASTERS OF SPAIN

Anderson.

THE LOAVES AND FISHES

This beautiful picture, which illustrates the Bible miracle of the loaves and fishes, was painted by Bartolomé Estéban Murillo (1617–82), the great Spanish painter, who was the most notable pupil of Velazquez. It was once thought that Murillo's pictures were better than those of his master, but the critics of our own time regard Velazquez as being the superior artist.

ON a day in March, 1914, a cruel and horrible outrage took place at the National Gallery when a woman named Richardson attacked with a chopper the exquisite Venus of Velazquez, and before anyone could stop her had slashed the lovely painting in seven pieces.

This picture, for which the price of £45,000 was paid, is one of the best-known examples of the art of Diego de Silva y Velazquez, who was born at Seville in 1599.

The King's Painter

Young Velazquez took to painting as a duck takes to water, and his father allowed him to become a pupil of de Herrera, who had himself been a student under the well-known El Greco. Herrera was an ill-tempered man, and the boy was glad to change a year later to the tutorship of Pacheco, whose daughter he afterwards married. A year or two later Philip IV. came to the throne of Spain and made Olivarez his Prime Minister. Olivarez was a native of Seville and a patron of painters, and in 1623 he persuaded the King to give a sitting to the young Velazquez. It is said that Velazquez conquered with almost the first stroke of his brush. He was appointed Court Painter, and the young King, who was only eighteen, made a friend of him and almost every day visited his studio.

Then came the visit of Rubens already mentioned, and Rubens not only made friends with Velazquez, but got on well with the King. In 1629 King Philip allowed Velazquez to go to Italy, where he visited Rome, Venice and Naples, met many painters and no doubt added to his knowledge of art. When he returned to Madrid he painted King Philip again and again. No fewer than twenty-six portraits of Philip by Velazquez are still in existence.

Rewarded—and Dismissed

The King and his artist lived and grew old together, and Philip, who was a kindly man, found the society of his friend a great relief from the horribly stiff etiquette of the Spanish Court. As an example, it may be mentioned that no man except the King might touch the Queen or a prince or princess on pain of death—even to save her life. A century and more later one

of the little Spanish princes fell downstairs and was saved from being badly hurt—perhaps killed—by a footman, who caught him in his arms. The footman was rewarded with a purse of gold but—he was dismissed from the palace service.

So many of the paintings of Velazquez are famous that it is hard to make a choice, but the finest is perhaps "The Surrender of Breda," in which you see Spinola, the Spanish leader, laying his hand kindly on the shoulder of the Dutch commander, Justin, who gives up the keys of the surrendered city.

Velazquez, like many great men, was far ahead of his times. Some of his

Anderson.

THE SURRENDER OF BREDA

There is a deep wealth of human sympathy in this picture by the great Spanish artist Diego de Silva y Velazquez, who was born at Seville in 1599. In the Dutch War of Independence, Spanish forces carried the day, and we see here Justin the Dutchman sadly, but yet with dignity, giving up the keys of the surrendered city of Breda. Meantime, Spinola, the Spanish conqueror, has laid his hand almost affectionately on the shoulder of his former opponent.

THE MAIDS OF HONOUR

Anderson.

Here is another picture by Velazquez. Its original is at Madrid. It is really an intimate painting of the Spanish royal family of the time, and possesses a wonderful sense of light and space. The story goes that Velazquez was painting the King when the little Princess came into the room with her attendants, so unconsciously setting the scene for a picture. The group itself is regarded as a brilliant triumph. Velazquez painted many portraits of King Philip IV. of Spain, and the artist and his royal patron were close friends.

MURILLO'S "THE MELON=EATERS"

F. Bruckmann.

Our reproduction is that of another picture which is known the whole world over. It was painted by Murillo in his early days, and we do not need to be told that the subject was taken from real life—almost a " snapshot," as modern photographers might say. Such a picture of two ragged youngsters, so human themselves and with everything round them realistic, is bound to appeal and to afford pleasure.

ST. JOHN AND THE LAMB

" Behold the Lamb of God, which taketh away the sin of the world," the words of John the Baptist, as quoted by the Apostle John, may be taken as the text of this beautiful painting by Murillo, who lived 300 years ago. The masterpiece hangs in the National Gallery. The lamb's foot placed on the arm of the infant St. John makes the animal seem almost human.

sketches from Nature anticipate the open-air landscape painting of the nineteenth century. Velazquez lived to the age of sixty and died suddenly. His funeral was the finest that was ever given to any artist. The whole Court attended, and scores of great nobles took part in the ceremony.

"The Melon-Eaters"

Two ragged youngsters enjoying a water melon between them is the subject of one of the finest paintings of Bartolomé Estéban Murillo. The colour is beautiful, the bloom of the fruit wonderfully rendered. Murillo was the greatest of the pupils of Velazquez, and one of his pictures, "The Immaculate Conception," was purchased by the French Government so long ago as 1852 for the large sum of £23,500. Murillo was very famous in his lifetime, and for two centuries his pictures were thought more of than those of Velazquez himself. To-day competent critics realise that Velazquez was, beyond measure, his superior.

During the latter part of the eighteenth century no country in Europe was in a more miserable condition than Spain. Public offices were sold to the highest bidder; the people were terribly taxed; and, as for art, it seemed to be dead.

The Bitterness of Goya

One day, in the year 1760, a Spanish gentleman, himself a painter, stumbled on a shepherd boy who, like the great Giotto, was drawing pictures of his father's sheep on a stone. Recognising the cleverness of the youth, he sent him to be a pupil to a painter in Saragossa. The boy's name was Francisco José de Goya y Lucientes, and he was the son of an Aragon peasant.

He grew up big, strong, handsome, brilliantly clever, but cursed with a fierce temper which was always getting him into trouble. At the age of twenty-two he was in Madrid, fought a duel, and would have been arrested had he not escaped with a band of bull-fighters and sailed to Italy. Here he got into fresh trouble and

W. F. Mansell.

FROM A PAINTING BY GOYA

Doña Isabel Cobos de Porcel was a Spanish beauty of high degree, and her portrait is here marvellously rendered. The artist was Francisco José de Goya y Lucientes, generally known more simply as Goya, and who was the greatest painter of his age (1746–1828). He was the son of a Spanish peasant.

Anderson

This portrait by the artist Goya shows a King of Spain who is stated to have been a " monument of serene and complacent stupidity." It is a matter of history that this monarch was a mere puppet in the hands of his wife, and the artist gave a perfectly truthful rendering of his sovereign —though some painters might have been more disposed to represent him on canvas as a man of high intellect.

had a narrow escape from being hanged. Again he had to make a hurried escape and in 1771 was back in Spain.

Held to Ridicule

The next we know of this eccentric genius, he was living quietly in Madrid, married and working steadily. A wonderful reformation, but it is not known how it came about. He was introduced to Court and painted a picture of the King, Charles III. Goya was what is called a realist, and his pictures mirror the rottenness of Spanish society of the period. His picture of Charles IV. on horseback portrays what has been called a " monu-

ment of serene and complacent stupidity." It is strange indeed that the artist managed to retain his popularity when he was plainly holding up his sitters to the ridicule of the world. He lived all through the conquest of Spain by Napoleon and painted several realistic pictures of unfortunate rebels being shot down by French firing squads. Another terrible picture of his is called " The Death of Truth," showing Truth suffering martyrdom at the hands of priests.

Poor Goya slowly became deaf; then his eyesight failed; but in the end it was a stroke of apoplexy that finished his tempestuous life.

Anderson.

THE SNOWSTORM

There is a great wealth of atmosphere and realism in this masterful painting by Goya. The discomfort of the human beings as they face the icy storm is amply suggested by the bending of the trees to the blast and by the sullen greyness of the clouds. One of the worst misfortunes that can befall an artist happened to Goya when, towards the end of his life, his sight failed.

THE MARRIAGE OF ISAAC AND REBECCA

W. F. Mansell.

The beautiful landscape reproduced above was painted by the celebrated French artist, Claude le Lorrain (1600–82). When this picture was painted (1648), people cared so little for landscapes that human figures illustrating the Bible story were included to impart interest. We know, however, that Claude's purpose was to show the beauties of natural scenery.

WE have talked of Italian, Spanish and Dutch art. Let us now turn to France. Painting came to France from two different directions, Italy and Holland, and the first French painters who can be called great were Nicolas Poussin, born in 1594, and Claude le Lorrain, born in the first year of the seventeenth century. Poussin learned his art in Rome and was one of the first great landscape painters, as well as a figure painter of ability. Lorrain, too, gained fame by his landscapes; but true French art, the kind of painting which we all recognise as purely French, did not begin until a later date. Antoine Watteau, born in 1684, was its first exponent.

How Watteau Starved

This boy was the son of a carpenter, and was never strong. His father was angry with him for his love of art. He could not understand it, and refused to pay the expenses of his son's education. A local artist named Guérin gave the lad some teaching, but Guérin died and young Watteau, afraid of his father, ran away to Paris with a scene painter named Metayer. Metayer deserted him and the boy was left alone, absolutely penniless and in very poor health. He found work in a wretched shop where religious pictures were produced by the score.

In these days such pictures are, of course, printed, but then all were turned out by hand. Watteau got a meal a day and about half-a-crown a week for working twelve hours a day. By happy chance, an artist named Gillot saw some of the boy's drawings and took him as assistant. Gillot was a decorative artist, but his pupil soon

TWO PICTURES BY WATTEAU

W. F. Mansell.

What we call to-day the pure style of French painting was introduced by Antoine Watteau, born in 1684, and the son of a carpenter. The above picture, entitled " The Music Party," is an excellent example of his style, and the original is in the Wallace Collection, London. Watteau's father was angry with him for being attracted to art, and the boy ran away.

F. Bruckmann.

The perfectly-painted children and the beautiful countryside that forms the background (we should refer to it as a " pastoral " setting), show us another type of picture painted by the French master, Antoine Watteau. Like so many other geniuses, Watteau suffered terrible hardships in his youth, and these undermined his health, so that he died at thirty-seven.

GILES AND HIS FAMILY

W. F. Mansell.

The Wallace Collection in London includes the original painting of this reproduction. It is considered a wonderful gem of art, and was the work of Watteau in the true French style. The Wallace Collection of pictures, miniatures, porcelain, etc., is at Hertford House, Manchester Square, London. The collection was bequeathed to the nation by Lady Wallace.

excelled him so greatly that Gillot grew jealous and the two separated.

Guardian of the Palace

But this time Watteau fell on his feet, for he got work with a man named Claude Audran, who was not only a painter, but a guardian of the Luxembourg Palace. Here for the first time in his starved life the young artist saw great pictures—those of Rubens—and in the wide, wild park he found many delightful subjects to paint. Without slavishly copying Rubens, Watteau adopted his style, but with a delicacy all his own.

Trouble loomed again, for Audran, in his turn, became jealous of his gifted pupil, but Watteau was too wise to quarrel. He left him and went back to Paris, where he competed for the Academy Prize and won second place. He was doing better now. Two of his pictures were hung in the Academy, and a well-known Academician named Fosse was so attracted by them that he called on young Watteau and was very kind to him. Presently, to his immense surprise and delight, Watteau was elected a member of the Academy, and after that he never looked back.

But, like many other geniuses, he had his health wrecked by his cruel hardships. In 1719 he visited London, but returned to France weaker than before. In 1721 he died at the early age of thirty-seven.

He was a man of great kindness and sweet disposition, and this quality shows in all his work. His colour was exquisite and his painting jewel-like in its beauty.

Rose du Barry

The famous Marquise de Pompadour was a great lover of good pictures and helped many of the French artists of the eighteenth century. The beautiful colour called Rose du Barry was invented by one of these artists and was originally called Rose Pompadour.

This painter was François Boucher, born in 1703, who won the first prize at the Academy when only twenty years old. He was a many-sided genius who painted portraits, designed tapestries, and,

W. F. Mansell.

THE MODISTE

We may inspect the original of this realistic picture in the Wallace Collection, London. It was painted by the French artist, François Boucher, who was born in 1703, and won the First Prize at the Academy when only twenty years of age. He invented the beautiful colour called " Rose du Barry."

into the bargain, was a very clever scene painter. He was famous for his bright, delicate colourings, pale blues and pinks, and was a favourite artist of Madame de Pompadour.

His pupil, Fragonard, is even better known than Boucher, and was extremely popular with the French nobility. But his work, lovely as it is, mirrors the times. Evil times they were, for it was the period when the under-dog in France, worn out with taxes and oppression, was beginning to growl and when the nobility pursued pleasure with a crazy blindness never before equalled.

The Greuze Girl

The pictures which Fragonard painted to please himself, such as "The Happy Mother," are far more pleasant and wholesome than his more elaborate works, such as "The Swing," painted merely to please his aristocratic patrons. "The Happy Mother" is to be seen in the National Gallery.

W. F. Mansell.

A LADY CARVING HER NAME

The painter of this picture was Fragonard, a pupil of Boucher, who came to be even better known than his master, for he was a great favourite with the French nobility. Fragonard painted in two styles—one to please himself, and the other to win the approval of his rich patrons.

There is a curious resemblance between the careers of Watteau and of another great French painter who lived in the same century. Jean Baptiste Greuze, born at Mâcon in 1725, was also the son of a carpenter: and, as in Watteau's case, the father was bitterly opposed to his son's desire to paint and beat him whenever he caught him drawing. Watteau, as we know, ran away to Paris, and so, too, did Greuze; and there, like Watteau, he nearly starved before he could find employment. At last young Greuze got a picture exhibited at the Salon and, all in a minute, became famous.

There the parallel ends, because, luckily for himself, Greuze was much stronger than Watteau and actually lived to be eighty years old. But his was not a happy life, and that was due to his wife. Her name was Anne Gabriel, and she was charmingly pretty. Indeed, it is her sweet and innocent-looking face which appears in the "Girl Looking Up" and

CHILD WITH APPLE

You would find the original of this most delightful painting in the National Gallery, London. The artist was Jean Baptiste Greuze, who was born in 1725. Like Watteau, he was the son of a carpenter, and faced very hard times when young, though he became famous " all in a minute."

many other of Greuze's famous pictures.

It would seem that Anne was not so good and sweet-minded as her pictures make her appear, for she led her husband a sad life and robbed him of his savings. Poor Greuze saw all the horrors of the French Revolution. Moreover, he outlived his great reputation and died at the age of eighty in great poverty.

A Painter of Napoleon

The French Revolution of 1789–95 changed more than the Government of France; it changed the whole art of that country. It is an interesting point that, while the French revolutionary mobs destroyed many fine old houses and monuments, their leaders did all they could to protect and encourage art. Large prizes were offered for painting and sculpture, and in 1793 the Louvre was opened as a museum. But the pretty romantic painting of artists such as Boucher, Fragonard and

Greuze was no longer popular, and the rage was all for the severe style of classic painting.

The first painter to satisfy the new taste was Jacques Louis David, born in 1748, who was appointed one of the two original members of the new Fine Arts Committee of the Institute of France.

David was a passionate admirer of Napoleon Bonaparte.

" Bonaparte," he said openly, " is my hero." He painted him again and again, but never very exactly, for Bonaparte had not patience to sit for more than a few minutes at a time. One of David's most celebrated pictures is " Bonaparte Crossing the Alps," but it is not one of his happiest efforts. His portrait of Madame Récamier, now in the Louvre, is a much finer picture.

There is a story connected with this picture. Madame Récamier left the artist

Photos: W. F. Mansell.

FROM A PAINTING BY GREUZE

The title of this picture (in the Wallace Collection, London) is " Espièglerie," a French word meaning a frolic, or a roguish or playful trick. This is precisely the spirit which the artist has caught on the dainty girlish face.

FIDELITY

W. F. Mansell.

In the above reproduction we see another striking picture by the artist Greuze. There is certainly fidelity and trustfulness in the lovely eyes of the subject. Greuze's wife Anne was a charmingly pretty woman, and her sweet face peers at us from many of her husband's pictures.

when the picture was only half finished but later repented and went back, begging him to go on with the portrait.

"Madame," he replied, "artists are as capricious as women. Suffer me to keep your picture in the state in which *we* left it."

Friend of an Empress

David was not a *great* painter, yet to him and his pupils all Europe owes the revival of the old classical style, and no artist of only moderate talent ever exercised so great an influence on the art of a continent. His picture of Madame Récamier is perhaps the best example of his work. Her dress, the couch on which she reclines and all the surroundings are in the severest Greek style, and in complete contrast to the work of Boucher and the artists of his school and period.

David's best pupil was Antoine Jean Gros. His master sent him to Italy to study, where he made the acquaintance of the wife of Napoleon Bonaparte (afterwards the Empress Josephine). She introduced him to Bonaparte, with the result that Gros painted the finest portrait of Napoleon that exists. He was on Napoleon's staff, and saw much fighting, with the consequence that his battle pictures are full of life and truth.

For a time his career was triumphant and he was made a Baron. But David, then in exile in Brussels, was troubled because his old pupil seemed to be giving up the sternly classical style. If David had realised how seriously Gros would take his reproaches he would probably have been more careful in his letters. Gros grew more and more despondent, and at last the poor fellow went away and drowned himself.

From the Greeks and Romans

One can have too much of a good thing, and the severely classical style

W. F. Mansell.

" MADAME RÉCAMIER," BY DAVID

This picture is a portrait of a French woman who was famous for her " salons," to which she invited the most eminent men of her time. The painting was done by Jacques Louis David (1748–1825), who adored Greek and Roman art, and worked in the classical style.

BONAPARTE AT ARCOLA

W. F. Mansell.

There is something quite poetical about this figure of Napoleon. It was the work of Baron Gros (1771–1835), and was painted when Bonaparte was at the beginning of his Italian campaign. The artist actually joined Napoleon's staff and saw much fighting, so that his battle pictures are full of life and truth. Eventually, because he could not paint in strict accordance with his master's ideals, Gros took his own life.

of the great painter David made French art so cold and chilling that a revolt started, headed by a brilliant young artist named Géricault. His picture of an officer on horseback shown in the Salon in 1812 created a sensation. It was so splendidly alive.

Then Géricault painted that terribly realistic picture "The Wreck of the Medusa," with its crowd of poor dying folk on a raft in mid-ocean. This was shown in 1819, and although the critics fairly foamed with rage it marked the turning point in French art.

Géricault himself died very young, in 1824, and was succeeded by one of the greatest masters of colour who ever lived, Ferdinand Delacroix. To begin with, Delacroix was so poor that he could not afford to frame his first picture, but surrounded it with laths painted yellow. Baron Gros was immensely struck with the picture and was kind to the young artist, yet thirty-five years passed before the splendid pictures of this talented painter admitted him to the Academy. So life and feeling came back into French art and a new school arose of what are called realist painters.

The Struggles of Corot

The name of Jean Baptiste Corot is now known all over the world, yet Corot had a harder struggle than Delacroix before he gained fame. He began painting at twenty-six, and his father made him an allowance of £60 a year.

W. F. Mansell.

"THE POOL," BY COROT

You will have heard of the artist, Jean Baptiste Corot (1796–1875). Here is one of his famous pictures, the canvas of which hangs in the Louvre at Paris. Corot's pictures are notable for their pale blues and greens, and soft, delicate colours, and he excelled at landscape. He was sixty years of age before he sold a single picture.

BY THE PAINTER OF PEASANTS

Jean François Millet (1814–75) loved to paint the peasants of his native France, and added a dignity to labour which appeals to everyone. The title of the above picture is "The Angelus," and it shows two simple toilers of the fields pausing in their work to utter a prayer as the Angelus bell in the distant church rings out its message. The Angelus is usually rung three times a day.

Photos : W. F. Mansell.

This companion picture (the original of which is in the Louvre at Paris) is entitled "The Gleaners," and gives a true presentation of harvest-home in France, where the fields have not the hedges to which we have grown so accustomed in this country. Millet himself came of peasant stock, and worked hard on a little farmstead in his boyhood.

For more than twenty years this was all he had on which to live. His pictures are noted for their pale blues and greens and soft delicate colours.

It was not until he was sixty that the greatness of Père Corot became known. His old age he spent happily as father of a little colony of artists in the forest of Fontainebleau.

Painter of Peasants

Jean François Millet will live for all time as the artist who painted the peasant true to life. "The Sower," "The Gleaners" and "The Angelus" are among the world's most famous pictures. Himself the son of a small farmer, he struggled for years against poverty, and it was not until the Great Exhibition in Paris in 1867 that Millet came into his own. By that time it was too late, for his health had begun to fail.

Another painter of the people was Gustave Courbet. Once a patron wished him to paint a picture of angels for a church.

"Angels!" said Courbet, "I have never seen angels, and what I have not seen I cannot paint." Courbet, son of a wealthy French farmer, was born in 1819, and in 1849 painted a picture which became famous. It was called "After Dinner at Ornans." It was thought so great that Courbet was placed "hors concours," that is, given the right to show at the Salon without submitting his works to the Selecting Jury.

Courbet hated the rule of Napoleon III. and refused the decoration of the Legion of Honour offered him. When the revolution broke out in 1871 he became President of Fine Arts and his first act was to pull down the column of Napoleon I. in the Place Vendôme. Yet he carefully preserved the artistic treasures of Paris against the fury of the mob.

When the Commune was suppressed Courbet was arrested and sentenced to pay 400,000 francs to reconstruct the Column. This ruined him and he died in exile.

Braun.

THE CHURCH AT VERNON

This well-known picture was painted by the Frenchman, Claude Monet, who was born in Paris in 1840. He was an artist who painted with broken touches, his idea being chiefly to give the most realistic effects of light. Such an artist is spoken of as being an "impressionist," meaning that he interprets impressions rather than hard outlines. You should study the way in which light falls on the water in this masterpiece.

W. F. Mansell.

THE BEGGAR'S OPERA

When John Gay first produced his play " The Beggar's Opera," at Lincoln's Inn Fields
Theatre, London, in 1728, the artist William Hogarth painted several pictures from its scenes,
one of which is reproduced above. It was Hogarth's association with the company playing in
this opera that indirectly led him to take up portrait-painting.

IT is time that we turn to England
and some of her great artists. The
Stuart kings had artistic tastes, particularly the two Charles, but when
George I. came to the throne all was
changed. These Hanoverian monarchs
hardly knew one picture from another,
and artists had no encouragement from
the Court. In the circumstances it is
rather wonderful that art flourished
as it did during the eighteenth century,
and that English painters arose whose
names stand in the highest rank.

Notes on his Thumb-nail

The first of these was William
Hogarth, who was born in London in
1697. His father was a schoolmaster,
and had the good sense to put no ob-
stacle in the way of his son's artistic
career. Young Hogarth was apprenticed to a silversmith, and when only
nineteen years old started business for
himself as an engraver. He worked
hard and in his spare time attended the
painting classes of Sir James Thornhill,

who was an artist favoured by Queen
Anne.

Thornhill's method of teaching was to
give his pupils pictures to copy, but
Hogarth despised this sort of work.
It was, he said, " like pouring water
from one vessel to another." He had
an original bent of mind and was
always on the watch for original subjects. It is said that, when he had no
paper at hand, he would make pictorial
notes on his thumb-nail. But if he did
not think much of Sir James, his
opinion of Sir James's daughter was
high, and in the end he ran away with
her and married her, much to her
father's annoyance.

Hogarth's first success was a set of
engravings published in 1724, called
" The Talk of the Town," making fun
of the way foreigners were lionised in
London. At first they scandalised
Londoners, but when Gay produced
his " Beggar's Opera," lashing the
same fashionable folly, Hogarth's engravings began to sell. Hogarth became

great friends with Gay's company, and this led to portrait painting. One of his first portraits was of Lavinia Fenton as *Polly Peachum*. She was the actress who afterwards became Duchess of Bolton.

Then came "The Rake's Progress" and other sets of engravings which made the young painter famous and brought him a good deal of money. Hogarth was the first great artist whose works were engraved in large numbers, and so he became the earliest to appeal to the masses as well as the classes. Sir James Thornhill was reconciled to his son-in-law, and from that time onwards Hogarth's career was successful. One often thinks what a marvellous *Punch* artist Hogarth would have made if *Punch* had then been in existence. There has never been anyone to surpass him in the art of showing up pictorially the follies of fashion.

With all his success, Hogarth re-mained the same simple soul to the end of his life. It is told of him that he once walked home to his house in Leicester Square in pouring rain, quite forgetting that he had a coach of his own waiting for him.

A Costly Joke

Richard Wilson was the son of a Welsh clergyman, and was born on August 1st, 1714, the very day on which Queen Anne died. From childhood he was mad on drawing, and he was sent to London to learn painting.

Though Wilson gained his fame by landscape painting, he was also a first-rate painter of portraits, and his portrait of himself, which is in the Royal Academy, is worth going a long way to see. Another beautiful picture of his is "The Thames near Twickenham."

Wilson was a sturdy sort of man, whose motto was "Art for Art's Sake," but he had the misfortune to

W. F. Mansell.

THE THAMES NEAR TWICKENHAM

This attractive landscape mirrors the sweet, natural beauty of the River Thames and gives us an idea of English scenery at its very best. The artist was Richard Wilson, who is known as the "Father of British Landscape." He was born in 1714, on the very day on which Queen Anne passed away. Though he achieved such fame, he died in poverty.

live during a period when Art was not appreciated. Yet for some years he managed to make, at any rate, a decent living. Then came disaster. In 1776 he sent to the Academy a picture of "Sion House from Kew Gardens," which attracted the notice of King George III., and which he thought of buying. The King told Lord Bute to ask the price, and the painter wanted sixty guineas. Lord Bute thought the price too high, whereupon Wilson smilingly said: " Tell His Majesty he may pay for it by instalments." Bute, who was perhaps the most pompous fool who ever held high position in the British State, took the laughing remark seriously and was profoundly shocked. Poor Wilson lost the little favour that the Court ever showed to artists, and for the last years of his life his income was no more than £50 a year. He died at Llanberis in 1782.

W. F. Mansell.

THE AGE OF INNOCENCE

This delightful picture is a portrait of the artist's little grandniece, Theophila Gwatkin, at the age of six. The original picture, now in the National Gallery, London, was the work of Sir Joshua Reynolds. It reveals in a charming manner the innocence of childhood.

Another Son of the Church

It is comforting to turn from the sad story of Richard Wilson to the happier one of Sir Joshua Reynolds. Born in 1723, Joshua was the seventh son of a Devonshire parson. He was a fine, handsome boy with manners that matched his appearance, and at quite an early age Lord Mount-Edgcumbe became his patron. Then a great piece of luck befell him. Commodore Keppel put into Plymouth for repairs, met young Joshua, took a liking to him, and offered him a free passage to the Mediterranean in his ship the *Centurion*. So Joshua went to Rome, where he saw the masterpieces of Michael Angelo and was able to copy and learn from them.

He was thirty when he returned to England ; then he made his home in London, and, painting steadily, became, by degrees, recognised as the greatest artist of his time. When the Royal Academy was founded in 1768 he was elected its first President. He was not only a great painter, but a distinguished gentleman, a friend of the great Dr. Johnson, of Burke and of Goldsmith.

The deep richness of his colours has never been surpassed, and he was one of the first successful painters of children in England. The sad part of it is that he was careless about the choice of his pigments, so that some of his greatest paintings, such as "The Tragic Muse," are wrecks to-day.

Life flowed on peacefully until he was sixty-six, when he had the misfortune to lose the sight of one eye. Three years later he died and was buried in state in St. Paul's Cathedral.

The Man who Robbed the Orchard

A little boy living with his father and mother at Sudbury in Suffolk saw a man robbing the orchard, and quickly made a sketch of him. So good was the likeness that the robber was recognised by it and arrested.

This boy was Thomas Gainsborough, afterwards to be known as one of the greatest of English painters. He was sent to school, but since he would work at nothing else but drawing and sketching, was dispatched to London at the age of fifteen to study under the French engraver, Gravelot. Afterwards he was a pupil of the portrait painter Hayman.

At the age of eighteen he came back to Sudbury and began to paint portraits. When he was only nineteen he married a charming girl called Margaret Burr, who had some money of her own, and the young couple settled down at Ipswich and lived very happily, Gainsborough soon making a name for his portraits.

Fortune at Bath

In 1760 he made up his mind to try his fortune at Bath, which had then become a very fashionable resort. He did well there; commissions poured in, yet even so he got only eight guineas apiece for portraits which have since sold for thousands. Personally he was very popular, but the rackety life did not suit his poor wife, who went out of her mind.

In 1768 Gainsborough was chosen one of the original members of the new Royal Academy, and went to live in London, where, it is

W. F. Mansell.

THE BLUE BOY

There is an interesting story behind this picture by Thomas Gainsborough. Sir Joshua Reynolds in a lecture to students remarked that blue should not be massed together in a picture. Gainsborough replied by painting his famous "Blue Boy" (here reproduced), so proving the statement by Reynolds to have been quite wrong.

said, duchesses besieged his studio.

He and Sir Joshua Reynolds were rather jealous of one another, and this led to a curious incident. In a lecture to Academy students Sir Joshua remarked that blue should not be massed together in a picture. Gainsborough heard and replied by painting his famous " Blue Boy," which proved Sir Joshua to be quite wrong.

His portraits brought Gainsborough a fortune, so that he was able to have two country houses as well as his town house. Early in 1788 he fell ill, and when the doctor told him his case was hopeless he calmly arranged his affairs. Before he died he sent a message to Sir Joshua to come and see him, and the two great painters made up their differences. " We are all going to Heaven," said Gainsborough at the last, " and Van Dyck will be of the party."

W. F. Mansell.

THE PARSON'S DAUGHTER

This picture is regarded as being the masterpiece of George Romney (1734–1802), who was the son of a Lancashire farmer. The painting displays the pensive beauty of an unknown subject, whose powdered, auburn hair is bound up with green ribbon. Romney died at Kendal.

The Painter of Lady Hamilton

There was not much love lost among the great painters of the eighteenth century, and Reynolds, kindly man as he was, became jealous not only of Gainsborough, but also of the other great portrait painter of the period, George Romney. Romney was the son of a small farmer in Lancashire and had hardly any education, but spent all his spare time in making sketches of the people around him. He fell in with a vagabond artist named Christopher Steele, and travelled with him. Steele treated him badly, and Romney was glad to get away from him and earn a living by painting portraits up and down the Lake country at two guineas apiece. By 1762 he had managed to save £100.

He had married, so now he left £70 with his wife, while with the other £30 he went up to London to try for a prize of fifty guineas, offered by the Society of Arts. He was at first awarded the prize, but afterwards the judges reversed this verdict, and he was awarded only the second prize of twenty-five guineas. Romney believed that this was the fault of Sir Joshua Reynolds and was greatly upset about it.

But slowly he gained success, and in 1767, when thirty-three years old, was able to visit his wife and daughter at Kendal. He then went back to London, where he soon was making £1,000 a year. In 1773 he visited Italy, where

W. F. Mansell.

BOY WITH BIRD'S NEST

We are indebted for this lovely work of art to the genius of
John Hoppner (1758–1810), who was born at Whitechapel,
London.   His mother had some form of employment at the
Royal Court, so that he was from childhood brought into touch
with the people of high degree whose portraits he was after-
wards to paint.

Perhaps no portrait painter who ever lived excelled Romney in the delicacy and sweetness with which he portrayed women. He died at Kendal in 1802.

A Methodical Genius

It is at school that nearly every great painter has first shown his love for drawing, and Sir Henry Raeburn, Scotland's greatest portrait painter, was no exception to this general rule. Henry Raeburn, son of a well-to-do manufacturer, was born in 1756. He was sent to Heriot's School, where his caricatures of his masters made other boys laugh, but did not please the subjects of these efforts.

At fifteen he was apprenticed to an Edinburgh goldsmith, but soon took to painting miniatures and portraits. One of his subjects was the young widow of a wealthy Frenchman named Leslie, and she and the artist at once fell in love and were married, so that at twenty-two Raeburn found himself a rich man.

Some men might have slacked off in these happy circumstances, but not Henry Raeburn. On the advice of Sir Joshua Reynolds, he visited Rome and stayed two years, learning much. When he returned he settled down to paint in Edinburgh, and there never was an artist whose career was a more unbroken success. He exhibited every year at the Academy; he was knighted by George IV., and became His Majesty's Limner for Scotland.

If Romney was the great painter of

he learned a great deal, and when he came back to London his charge of fifteen guineas for a portrait rose to £80.

He was forty-eight when he met the exquisitely beautiful Emma Lyon, known afterwards as Lady Hamilton, and for a long time would paint nobody else. One of his finest portraits of this lady is in the National Gallery. Later he painted the famous Mrs. Robinson, known as "Perdita," one of the greatest beauties of her time. The finest of all his pictures is "The Parson's Daughter" in the National Gallery, yet the strange thing is that no one knows who this lovely little lady was.

FLATFORD MILL ON THE RIVER STOUR, BY JOHN CONSTABLE

Constable is the greatest of all painters of the English landscape. He learned as a miller's son to watch the sky; and when he became an artist it was the effect of the light of the sky on the land, the trees, the rivers around his father's mill at Flatford, which gave him the subjects for very many of his pictures. When he painted this one, he was still putting in a lot of carefully drawn detail, but later he concentrated upon the broad effects of light and colour.

N.P.K. VII, p. 80.

TWO DANCERS ON THE STAGE, BY DEGAS

Edgar Degas was one of the greatest of the nineteenth-century French painters linked with the Impressionists. In his case the interest was not only in changing effects of light, but even more in transient alterations of form. He loved to draw jockeys riding, laundresses at work, women at their wash tubs, and especially the ballerinas rehearsing or on the stage. The poses of the dancers under artificial stage lighting created designs and colours which fascinated him. In this famous picture he catches an enchanting moment.

women, Raeburn excelled in his portraits of men, and his portrait of Sir John Sinclair is one of the finest paintings of its kind in existence. He was a methodical artist, working every day from nine in the morning to five in the evening. It is said that he spent more time in studying his sitters than in painting them. When he did start painting he worked with tremendous speed. In 1911 one of his portraits sold for the immense sum of 22,300 guineas.

Politics and a Painter

Though the first two Georges cared nothing for paintings or painters, it is not fair to tar George III. with the same brush, for he did occasionally buy a picture, and there is at least one case on record where he was kind to a struggling young artist.

W. F. Mansell.

BOY WITH RABBIT

This picture and the previous one form a splendid pair, but the original of the above small facsimile was the work of Sir Henry Raeburn, R.A., who is regarded as the greatest portrait painter Scotland has ever produced. Not many years ago a portrait by Raeburn was sold for a sum well in excess of £20,000.

This was John Hoppner, painter of the very beautiful portrait of the Countess of Oxford which is in the National Gallery. Hoppner's mother was employed about the Court, and her son became a chorister at the Chapel Royal. But the boy, like all great artists, soon showed his love for brush and pencil, and the King interested himself to get him admitted to the Academy Schools.

There, at the age of twenty-four, John Hoppner won the highest award, the Gold Medal, and settled down to a prosperous career of portrait painting. He painted the three princesses for the King and became fashionable.

Unfortunately for himself, he med-dled in politics. He turned Whig, and wrote some really excellent articles for the *Quarterly Review*. The result was that he lost all his favour at Court and all his commissions for painting Court beauties. Hoppner lived into the nineteenth century, and died in 1810.

A Child Prodigy

In 1769 a man named Lawrence kept the Black Bear Inn at Devizes, where smart people used to stay for the night on their way between London and Bath. Lawrence had a son named Thomas, who was such a handsome child that the visitors used to pet him greatly. He entertained them by drawing pictures; and, grown older, was allowed to copy paintings in the great houses in the neighbourhood.

His father, finding that his son was such a genius, took him to Bath and rented a studio, where Thomas, aged only fifteen, drew heads in charcoal at a guinea apiece. At sixteen the boy began to paint in oils, and presently his father brought him to London and rented a studio for him in Leicester Square. The amazing thing is that, at eighteen, young Lawrence was able to keep himself and his whole family by his painting, and at the same time attend the Academy Schools. He made friends with the great Joshua Reynolds, who was very kind to him.

No painter's career was ever more successful. His good manners and good looks helped him greatly, and at twenty-two (three years before the ordinary age limit) he was elected an Associate of the Royal Academy and became the King's portrait-painter-in-ordinary. He was able to put up his prices to a point never before reached, and merely for a head he received 200 guineas. For one portrait, " Lady Gower and Child," he was actually paid 1,500 guineas.

He visited almost every capital in Europe and painted a large number of royal personages. In character he was kind and generous, but weak and extravagant, and though he made a great income for many years, it is said that he was nearly always in debt.

A Girl in Boy's Clothes

Angelica Kaufmann, born in 1741, was the daughter of a Swiss portrait painter who settled in England, and at ten years old she was making a good deal of money by doing portraits in crayon. Two centuries ago there was such a prejudice against women artists that Angelica's father had to dress her in boy's clothes when he took her to the Academy to copy pictures.

" NATURE," BY LAWRENCE
W. F. Mansell.

For a charming study of two children this picture by Sir Thomas Lawrence, P.R.A., would be hard to equal. Lawrence was brought up at the " Black Bear," Devizes, Wiltshire, and passengers from the stage coaches which stopped at his father's inn used to pet him—whilst he entertained them by drawing pictures.

INTERIOR OF A STABLE   *W. F. Mansell.*

This is considered to be one of the finest paintings by the English artist, George Morland (1763–
1804). Though he is known to have produced upwards of 4,000 pictures, few of them attained
to the high standard of the one reproduced above. Morland was greatly addicted to bouts of
intemperance, and he went to the grave at a very early age largely as the result of his dissolute
habits.

When she was about fifteen her father went with her to Italy, and in Venice she met the wife of the British Ambassador, who took a great fancy to her and brought her back to England. Angelica was extremely clever. She spoke four languages fluently ; she was very sweet-looking, and she not only painted extremely well but was a clever musician. The Queen admired her and she became so popular that in 1769 she was nominated as one of the foundation members of the Royal Academy.

When she was thirty-nine she married the Venetian painter, Antonio Zucchi, and the two settled in Rome, where they lived and painted happily for many years.

All the early European artists painted figures or portraits, and up to the seventeenth century landscape painting was practically unknown. While in China and the East landscape had long been looked on as the highest branch of art, in Europe opinion was otherwise, and there was no one to appreciate the beauties of Nature.

The great Frenchman, Claude, born in 1600, was the first European artist to paint landscapes, but the people of his own time thought little of his beautiful work. In England Wilson, whom we have already mentioned, was the first landscape painter, but his finest work went begging.

Marvellous Morland

The earliest landscape painter to gain any success in England was George Morland, who was born in 1763. He was the son of a painter and, like many great geniuses, displayed his talent at a very early age. He began drawing when only three years old, and at ten a picture of his was exhibited at the Royal Academy. His father, who seems to have been pure brute, kept the wretched little boy shut up in an attic painting all day and every day, and lived on the fruits of his work, so it is not surprising that when the unfortunate George at last managed to escape he took to drink.

For years he rambled about the country painting rustic scenes and living in ale-houses. His pictures sold well and many were engraved, so that his name became known even in his lifetime. His industry was amazing, for he is known to have painted more than 4,000 pictures. Drink was his ruin, and Morland, who might have been one of the world's greatest artists, sank into a mere pot-boiler and died

in a debtor's prison at the early age of forty-one.

The Shakespeare of English Painting

In the year 1786 some drawings exhibited in the window of a hair-dresser's shop in Maiden Lane, Covent Garden, attracted the attention of passing artists. They were the work of Joseph Turner, the eleven-year-old son of the owner of the shop. The result was that Joseph was sent to the Soho Academy, and in 1789 was admitted to the Royal Academy Schools. So began the career of the greatest of all English artists, the man who has been rightly called the Shakespeare of British Art.

Young Turner had to make his own living while he learned. He sold a few sketches and used to do hack work for architects, as well as colouring prints for

THE FIGHTING TÉMÉRAIRE

W. F. Mansell.

The original from which the above reproduction was taken is in the National Gallery, London, and was the work of J. M. W. Turner, R.A. This fine picture is full of romance. The *Téméraire* was one of the towering battleships that took part in the Battle of Trafalgar in 1805. In this painting she is seen being towed to her last berth to be broken up. The old man-o'-war is almost spectral in the waning evening light, in contrast to the dark mass of the tug.

W. F. Mansell.

THE TRENT, NEAR BURTON

A typical hayfield figures in this fine picture, with a hay-barge floating lazily upon the placid river. The painting was the work of Peter de Wint (1784–1849), who was born at Stone, in Staffordshire, though belonging to an old and much respected Dutch family. De Wint loved painting flat stretches of river scenery under a summer sky.

engravers. He made a very good friend in the kindly Dr. Thomas Monro, who lived in Adelphi Terrace and had an evening painting club for a few young students. He fitted up a studio for the boys, and gave them oyster suppers besides many a shilling.

In 1797 Turner exhibited his first Academy picture and opened a studio of his own in Hand Court, Maiden Lane. In those early days he painted in water colours, and since he never had any difficulty in selling his sketches he was not half-starved as so many painters were in those times.

Two years later, in 1799, he was elected an Associate of the Royal Academy, and in 1803 painted his picture of Calais Pier, proving his amazing power of depicting rough seas and stormy skies. Of this picture Ruskin says it is " the first which bears the sign manual and sign mental of Turner's colossal power." From this time onwards Turner began to travel abroad, visiting France, Italy, Switzerland and parts of Germany. He became famous for his power of depicting the glories of the sky, especially the splendour of sunrise and sunset. His " Sun Rising

Through Vapour," painted in 1807, was his favourite picture. He sold it, but twenty years later bought it back in order to bequeath it to the nation.

To Greater Glories

Turner was never content to stand still. From year to year he advanced to greater and greater glories. He was able to see and reproduce Nature's own colouring in a way which no painter before or since has equalled. He was not without his critics. The novelist, Thackeray, accused him of " flinging a pot of paint in the public's face." Fortunately for the world, Turner was by that time independent of critics. He had made a comfortable fortune, for he was a good business man, and did not waste his money, so he painted as he liked.

In 1840, when Turner was sixty-five, he first met John Ruskin, then fresh from Oxford. Two years later Ruskin published his first volume of " Modern Painters," the real subject of which was Turner's superiority to all other painters, ancient and modern.

When Turner died in 1851 he left a fortune of £140,000, the bulk of which he willed for the benefit of art and artists. But his most magnificent bequest was to the National Gallery. It consisted of 362 oil paintings, 135 water colours, 1,757 studies in colour and thousands of sketches.

It is difficult to say which was Turner's greatest picture. In Mr. B. W. Leader's opinion, " Ulysses Deriding Polyphemus " is the finest. Turner chose for his subject the moment when Ulysses, having escaped from the monster by intoxicating him and destroying his one eye, has embarked in his ship and is mocking the impotent rage of the giant on the high cliffs above. The glowing colour of this picture, with its flaming sunrise, is beyond description.

Turner was not popular with his brother artists. He had a habit of visiting the Academy on Varnishing Day, and if his picture happened to be challenged by those hung near it he would put on a few extra touches of colour to heighten its effect. In so doing he simply " killed " the adjacent pictures. Yet he could be kindly. He had a great admiration for Sir Thomas Lawrence ; and once, when a landscape of his was hung between two of Lawrence's pictures, he deliberately darkened his own painting so that it should not clash with those of his friend.

Turner's Fellow Student

Though Peter de Wint's name is Dutch, and he was the son of a Dutchman, he was born at Stone, in Staffordshire, in 1784. He must have inherited his love of painting from some distant

"A WINDY DAY" BY DAVID COX   *W. F. Mansell.*
Here is another beautiful picture, the original of which hangs in the National Gallery. As one peers into the painting one can almost feel the wind sweeping across the common into the faces of the woman and her dog. David Cox (1783–1859) was one of the most remarkable landscape artists of his day and was an adept at portraying stormy weather. He was born near Birmingham, and was the son of a blacksmith.

LANDSCAPES BY JOHN CONSTABLE

This perfectly composed landscape painting, " The Hay Wain," came from the brush of John Constable, R.A. It was first exhibited at the Academy in 1821, where it occasioned no particular comment. Three years later, however, at the Paris Salon, it created a sensation and the artist was awarded a Gold Medal. Constable was born at East Bergholt in Suffolk, in 1776.

Constable, England's greatest landscape painter, devoted himself to three beloved sketching grounds—Suffolk, where he was born, Hampstead Heath, where he went to live, and Salisbury, where he stayed with his friend Archdeacon Fisher. He was thrilled by the beautiful building and spire of the Cathedral and painted them framed by the trees or across the water meadows. This is one of his finest studies.

ancestor, for though his father wanted him to be a doctor he cared for nothing but pencil and brush. He was sent to the engraver, John Raphael Smith, as pupil, and was for a time a fellow-student at the Academy School with the great Turner. By the time he was twenty-three he was exhibiting at the Academy.

Stormy Skies

He painted direct from Nature and was most successful in river scenes. His " Trent near Burton," a beautiful picture of typical English scenery, is at South Kensington.

While de Wint painted soft, quiet landscapes, David Cox, who lived and

painted at the same time as de Wint, was best in depicting stormy skies and wind-riven clouds. David, the son of a Birmingham blacksmith, was born in 1783. While quite a small boy he had a fall and broke his leg. Some kind person gave him a box of paints with which to amuse himself while in bed. He made such good use of them that when he got well again his parents apprenticed him to a painter of miniatures. This man committed suicide, and young Cox got a job with a scene-painter and went to London, where he painted scenes at 4s. a square yard at the Surrey Theatre. In his spare time he made sketches and sold them.

A clever water-colour painter named Varley was so taken with one of these sketches that he gave the boy free lessons. Cox improved so rapidly that he was able to give up his drudgery at the theatre and himself earn money by giving lessons. In 1805 he went to Wales, where he fell in love with the scenery, and this was the first of many visits to the country of mountains and passes. Almost every year of his life he visited Bettws-y-Coed and painted there.

Up to the age of fifty-six he painted in water-colours. Then a meeting with William Müller, a clever painter in oils, turned Cox's attention to that medium, and during the last years of his life he did almost all his work in oils.

One of his most celebrated pictures represents an old woman and

W. F. Mansell.

A WINDMILL ON MOUSEHOLD HEATH

The work of John Crome (1768–1821), this picture shows us a truly noble landscape. The artist devoted all his life to painting the beauties of East Anglia. He was born at Norwich, the son of a poor weaver, and began life as errand-boy to a doctor, afterwards obtaining a post with a sign-writer.

W. F. Mansell.

"GRETA BRIDGE," BY COTMAN

This picture of " Greta Bridge " is regarded as the masterpiece in water-colours of John Sell Cotman. It was painted during Cotman's visits to Yorkshire in 1803–5. The bridge seen is 3½ miles south of Barnard Castle, in Durham, and the buildings depicted in the background are much the same to-day. Cotman's pictures command high prices to-day, but he enjoyed little fame during his lifetime.

a dog struggling across an open common in the teeth of a strong breeze. The sky is full of wind, and looking at this painting you can almost feel the gale in your face.

Art from the East of England

At the time of Turner's birth a miller named Constable lived at East Bergholt, in Suffolk, where he owned two large windmills. In 1776 a son was born to him, named John, who was destined to take very high place among English painters.

His father wanted the boy to become a parson, but young Constable cared for nothing but brush and palette. Sir George Beaumont, a landowner in the neighbourhood, who was himself something of an artist, saw and liked the boy's sketches and was good to him. Through his advice and help John Constable was sent to London at the age of nineteen to study art, and was admitted to the Royal Academy Schools. He got on steadily, and in 1802 had a picture in the Academy.

He began as a portrait painter, but all his love was for Nature, and presently he went back to Suffolk and began to paint the country around his old home at Dedham. His pictures represent actual scenes, but they were so much in advance of his time that they did not meet with the appreciation they deserved. Constable made little money, but his tastes were simple, and he was not unhappy. It was not until 1819, when he was forty-three, that he was elected an Associate of the Royal Academy. Two years later his famous picture, " The Hay Wain," was exhibited in London, but attracted little attention. It was bought by a French collector, who exhibited it at the Paris Salon, where crowds collected to admire it. Constable was awarded a gold medal, and all French artists were loud in praise of his brilliant colouring. Although Constable had now a great reputation all through Europe, he was still without honour in his own country, and even after he had been elected an Academician, in 1829, his pictures did not sell.

Luckily his wife's father left Constable a comfortable sum of money, so he and his family were never reduced to the straits that have been the lot of so many great painters. When he died in 1837 his house was full of unsold pictures, yet the breath was hardly out of his body before the nation seemed to awake to the fact that it had lost one of its greatest sons.

Constable's character was summed up on the day after his death by a London cab-driver. When John Constable's great friend told the man that he would never drive Constable again, the cabby said with emotion: " I couldn't be more sorry if he was my own father. He was as nice a man as that, sir."

Old John Crome

Another great painter who arose out of the East of England was John Crome, born at Norwich in 1768. He was the son of a poor weaver, and began life as a doctor's errand boy, but he was so fond of paint and brushes that he got work with a sign painter. Just as Constable found a backer in Sir George Beaumont, so did Crome in Mr. Thomas Harvey, who lived at Catton, where he had a fine picture gallery. It was great good luck for the poor errand boy to be able to study great paintings, and Crome learned much from them.

Presently he fell in with another young

W. F. Mansell.

" THE BELOVED," BY D. G. ROSSETTI

This is a poetical illustration of the Bride in the Song of Solomon—" My beloved is mine and I am his." The original hangs in the Tate Gallery and was painted in 1865 by Dante Gabriel Rossetti. He was slim, dark, and the son of an Italian exile, and became one of Cotman's pupils at King's College School.

W. F. Mansell.

This very moving picture was painted by John Everett Millais. Both the pathetic tenderness of its principal subject and the lovely rendering of Nature are bound to appeal to everyone. When only nine years of age this great painter won the silver medal of the Society of Arts and at sixteen he was earning £100 a year from his work.

man, Robert Ladbrooke, who was as keen on painting as himself. These two married sisters, and formed a partnership. Ladbrooke painted portraits at 5s. apiece, and Crome sold his landscapes for what they would fetch— sometimes not as much as 5s. Luckily Crome was able to get pupils, and the money so earned kept the firm in bread and butter.

W. F. Mansell.

KING AND BEGGAR-MAID

The full title of this picture, the original of which is in the Tate Gallery, London, is: " King Cophetua and the Beggar-Maid." The king is about to lay his crown at the feet of the beggar-maid. This romantic painting is the work of Sir Edward Burne-Jones (1833–1898).

In 1805 Crome managed to form a school of artists in Norwich, and this school flourished greatly. Though Crome was still quite unknown in London, Norfolk appreciated him and bought his pictures. Within a few years Crome was able to rent a good house and keep a couple of horses. In 1806 for the first time one of his pictures was hung on the walls of the Royal Academy. After that about a dozen pictures of his were shown in London, but he himself only occasionally visited the capital.

His work rivalled that of the great Dutch artists, such as Hobbema. His " Mousehold Heath " in the National Gallery is a magnificent piece of work. When he was fifty-three Crome caught a chill from which he died. On the day before his death he said to his son, John, himself a fine painter:

" John, my boy, paint, but paint only for fame. If your subject is only a pigsty, dignify it." And this advice sums up in one sentence the aim and ambition of one of England's greatest artists.

He was called Old Crome to distinguish him from his son, who later became a well-known painter.

A Versatile Worker

In 1808 John Cotman contributed no fewer than sixty-seven pictures to the exhibition of the Norwich Society of Artists. He worked in oils and water-colours and did fine etchings as well; yet, in spite of his immense industry and the fine character of his work, was forced to give painting lessons in order to make ends meet.

He was son of a Norwich draper, and was, next to Crome, the greatest artist produced by the Norwich School. But, like Crome, he had no honour during his lifetime. The struggle to make a living told on his health and strength. Friends got him the position of drawing master at King's College School, but it was too late, and in 1842 he died.

W. F. Mansell.

"THE SCAPEGOAT," BY WILLIAM HOLMAN HUNT

This fine picture gives us a wonderful idea of distance and atmosphere. Its painter, Holman Hunt, was the brilliant artist who produced "The Light of the World." He was born in the City of London in 1827, and his father was opposed to his wish to become an artist. Yet, when barely sixteen, and at his own risk, the boy took up art as his life's profession, and bravely struggled through the trials of his early years.

When his pictures were sold the best price obtained for one was £8 15s., but that picture has since brought nearly £1,000, while his water-colours fetch large sums of money in any auction room.

The Pre-Raphaelites

One of Cotman's pupils at King's College School was a slim dark lad, son of an Italian exile. His name was Dante Gabriel Rossetti, and though no one could have guessed it at the time, this foreign-looking boy was destined to work a great revolution in English art, for later he joined with the famous Millais and Holman Hunt to found what they called the Pre-Raphaelite Brotherhood.

After the death of Constable and Turner, English art, which had been so great for a period, fell on bad days. Constable himself prophesied that within thirty years it would cease to exist. The cause of the temporary failure of English art was that her painters had become creatures of an orthodox rule, line and system. There was no chance for a painter to get a picture into the Academy unless he complied with these rules. In a sentence, originality was not wanted.

Rossetti realised this; so did Holman Hunt; so did Millais, who, at the age of only seventeen, had already won a gold medal of the Royal Academy. The three young painters consulted together, and decided that the only road back to greatness was a patient study of Nature.

Rossetti was at that time rather a poet than a painter, but he had all the driving force of a reformer. In spite of his hot temper, he was clear-headed and had great power of concentration. Though never so accomplished a painter as either of his associates, he was perhaps the greatest force of the three in bringing about a revolution in English art.

His painting began under the training of his friend, Ford Madox Brown, the historical painter, but though his work shows great beauty and richness of colouring, he never became a master of draughtsmanship. His paintings were all of a religious or classical type. " Beata Beatrix," in the National Gallery, and " Dante's Dream," in the Walker Gallery, Liverpool, are good examples of his work.

His life was not a very happy one. In 1851 he fell in love with a very beautiful girl named Elizabeth Siddal and married her. Only two years later she died of a chill, and the blow was too much for him. He became morbidly sensitive, his health suffered, and his eyesight was so bad that he was terrified of blindness. Yet he struggled bravely against his troubles and lived until 1882.

Holman Hunt

Born in the City of London in 1827, Holman Hunt was the eldest of the Brotherhood. At twelve he was placed in the office of an estate agent; but his one idea was to paint, and he spent all his pocket money on taking lessons. At sixteen he was already making a living by painting portraits, and presently he managed to get into the Academy Schools, where he met Millais. At nineteen he had a picture in the Academy, a simple little thing of a child holding a watch to its ear.

His first pre-Raphaelite picture was painted three years later, and is called " Rienzi vowing to avenge the death of his Brother." In this the principal figure is a portrait of Rossetti. " Strayed Sheep," painted in 1853, gives a remarkable sense of distance and atmosphere, but his most famous picture is " The Light of the World." He painted this subject twice, and the original picture, which is now in Keble College Chapel, Oxford, ranks as one of the finest works of its kind painted during the nineteenth century. Hunt survived both his great associates and died in 1910 at the great age of eighty-three.

A Medal at Nine!

The extraordinary talent of John Everett Millais may be gathered from the fact that he was only nine years old when he won

W. F. Mansell.

THE LAST OF ENGLAND

In this picture, by Ford Madox Brown (1821–93), we see emigrants taking their last look at the " Old Country," as they leave to seek fortunes overseas. It is a sad theme and the artist has brought out sympathetically the serious thoughtfulness of expression. Ford Madox Brown was born at Calais.

the silver medal of the Society of Arts. He came from Jersey and was two years younger than his friend, Holman Hunt. When he was twelve he painted his first picture in oils and at sixteen was earning £100 a year by his work.

In the Victoria and Albert Museum may be seen his first large picture, called "Pizarro seizing the Inca of Peru." It is difficult to believe that this was painted by a boy of seventeen, yet such is the fact. In the following year he was awarded a gold medal by the Academy.

We have spoken of his meeting with Hunt, but it was not until Rossetti joined these two that the Brotherhood was formed. It is said that the three young friends first met at the house of Millais' parents, where they spent the evenings examining engravings of early Italian painters. The term "pre-Raphaelite" originated as a nickname because the three declared that they preferred the painters before Raphael to those who came after him.

W. F. Mansell.

DIGNITY AND IMPUDENCE

Everyone knows this picture, which has been reproduced again and again. One does not need to be a student of art to appreciate the stateliness of the bloodhound and the cheekiness of the little Scotch terrier. The painting was done by Sir Edwin Landseer, R.A. (1802–73). He was Queen Victoria's favourite painter.

Denounced by Dickens

"Christ in the House of His Parents" was Millais' first great picture under the influence of the Brotherhood. In order to get his details absolutely correct, Millais took his canvas to a carpenter's shop and painted the figure of Joseph from the carpenter, to get the muscles absolutely right. He purchased sheeps' heads from a butcher. This wonderful picture, now in the Tate Gallery, provoked a storm of abuse. "Mean, odious, revolting, repulsive," were adjectives showered on it. Charles Dickens denounced it in "Household Words." The Brotherhood suffered bitterly, and Hunt himself was left so badly off that he was forced to take on the work of restoring the wall paintings in Trinity House. Millais suffered least, for he found a dealer brave enough to give him £150 for the picture.

Ruskin came to the rescue, saying that the pictures of the Brotherhood gave him hope that they might become the foundation of " a more earnest and able school of art than we have seen for centuries." Hunt, however, was unable to sell his pictures, but Millais came to his help. Then followed the news that the Liverpool Academy had awarded Hunt their £50 prize for his picture, " Two Gentlemen of Verona." The tide turned, and in 1853 Millais was elected an Associate of the Royal Academy.

Hunt always remained faithful to the tradition of the Brotherhood, but Millais drifted away. " Bubbles," that

picture so well known as an advertisement of a famous brand of soap, is an example of his later style. In 1863 Millais was elected Royal Academician, and in 1896, after the death of Lord Leighton, he became President of the Academy. He died in the same year, and his body was buried in St. Paul's by the side of his great predecessor, Sir Joshua Reynolds.

Rossetti's Pupil

Edward Burne-Jones had meant to become a clergyman, but after meeting Rossetti at Oxford, felt he must turn to art, and under Rossetti's teaching rose to greatness. His favourite subjects were taken from the legends surrounding King Arthur, and the best description of his paintings is that they are dream pictures. They are very beautiful, but his women are so tall and slender they have the appearance of being half starved.

In 1884 he exhibited his most famous picture, " King Cophetua and the Beggar-Maid," and a little later was elected Associate of the Royal Academy; but he seldom exhibited, and afterwards resigned his associateship. He designed beautiful tapestries and stained glass windows, and was the originator of the Arts and Crafts Society, to which we owe so much fine printing and so great an improvement in furniture, pottery and household decoration.

By permission of the Corporation of Leeds.   *W. F. Mansell.*
THE RETURN OF PERSEPHONE
Here is a splendid example of the work of Lord Leighton, who was born at Scarborough in 1830. He was particularly fond of illustrating stories from Greek history and legend. In this story Persephone was gathering wild flowers when she was carried off to the underworld by Pluto. The picture shows her being restored to her mother, Demeter, by Hermes, the messenger of the gods.

By courtesy of the Redfern Gallery.

AUSTRALIAN LANDSCAPE, BY SIDNEY NOLAN

Many of the more recent landscape painters in Australia have chosen to depict not the romantic scenery, the countryside with its characteristic gum trees under the bright light of the southern sun which attracted the earlier artists such as Arthur Streeton, but the realistic aspect of the rather desolate regions "out back." There the trees stunted by drought, or the broken stumps of the brittle cork trees sticking out of the sandy soil, the great ant-heaps, the rather ugly little townships, have made their subjects. Sidney Nolan is one of the foremost of these artists. He often exhibits in Britain, and has a growing reputation.

Specially painted for this work.

A MINSTREL IN A NORMAN CASTLE

From earliest times Music and Poetry have held a fascination for mankind, and this has been expressed in various forms in different ages. In England the Anglo-Saxon gleeman was followed by the minstrel who came from France with the Normans. Often they were both poets and musicians. Those who preferred the wandering life were welcome guests at the houses of the rich, while others were retainers of noble families, entertaining them with music and song as our artist has depicted here. The rise of the drama and the introduction of printing brought about their disappearance.

"OUTWARD BOUND," BY POYNTER

Sir Edward John Poynter, who gave the world this beautiful picture (now in the Tate Gallery), was one of the best-known artists of the Victorian Age. He painted in water colours and in oils, did illustrations for magazines, and designed mosaics for the Houses of Parliament. In 1902 he was made a baronet.

The First of Animal Painters

Edwin Henry Landseer came of an artistic family, for his father, John Landseer, was a well-known painter and engraver, and two of his brothers were also painters and engravers. Edwin Landseer had a great love of animals, and his earlier pictures were of the wild animals kept in the Menagerie at the Exeter Exchange, London, on the very spot where the Strand Palace Hotel now stands.

The first picture he exhibited showed the heads of two dogs. He was only fourteen at the time. His "Prowling Lion" was in the Academy of 1821, and created quite a sensation, for pictures of animals were still extremely rare at that date.

Landseer took his work very seriously, and carefully studied the anatomy of animals. When he was twenty-two he visited Scotland, stayed with Sir Walter Scott at Abbotsford, and for the first time saw wild stags. After that "The Monarch of the Glen" became his favourite subject. He loved dogs, and his "Dignity and Impudence" is one of the finest of all dog pictures.

The Man who Revived Greek Art

Queen Victoria was very fond of him, and he taught her to paint. He was sculptor as well as painter, and the great lions at the base of the Nelson Monument in Trafalgar Square are his work. They are made of gun-metal from captured cannon. He was knighted and offered the Presidency of the Royal Academy, but refused the latter honour on grounds of ill-health. He had a terrible blow on the head in a railway accident in 1868 which affected his memory and indirectly caused his death in 1873.

Frederick Leighton, born at Scarborough in 1830, had a great advantage over most artists of his time in that he went to Italy when but ten years old and studied there. He was only twenty-five when he exhibited his first picture in the Royal Academy. It was called "Cimabue's Madonna carried in Procession through the streets of Florence." Design, drawing and colour were all so fine that his painting created a great sensation. Queen Victoria herself greatly admired it, and at a bound the young painter's reputation was made.

His career was one of unbroken success, and he not only became president of the Royal Academy, but was the first British artist to receive a peerage. One of his most beautiful and popular pictures is "The Bath of Psyche." He painted many pictures illustrating Greek legends, and is considered to have recaptured the true spirit of Greek art more nearly than any artist since Raphael.

"Faithful unto Death"

One of the finest of what may be called "story" pictures is that of a Roman sentinel standing steadfastly at his post in the gateway of Pompeii while the fiery mountain above rains death upon the doomed city. He has not been relieved; he has no orders to go; therefore he remains. This picture, now in the Walker Gallery at Liverpool, was painted by Sir Edward John Poynter, who was the son of an architect and born in 1836.

One of the best-known artists of the Victorian age, Poynter was a many-sided man who painted in water-colours and oils, designed mosaics for the Houses of Parliament and did illustrations for magazines. He was Director of the Royal College of Art at South Kensington and Director of the National Gallery. In 1902 he was made a baronet.

A Dutch-English Painter

Another painter of the story picture was Lawrence Alma-Tadema, who, though born in Holland in 1836, became an English knight in 1899, and in 1905 gained the great distinction of the Order of Merit. A typical picture of his is "A Silent Greeting" in the Tate Gallery, in which you see a Roman warrior placing a bunch of roses in the lap of a sleeping lady.

Sir Lawrence had a prodigious store of knowledge about Greek and Roman antiquities, and great actor-managers such as Sir Henry Irving often consulted him when producing historical plays. No man ever painted marble more realistically than this artist.

Father and Son

George Frederick Watts was a Welsh boy who had the good fortune to have a father who did all in his power to help his son to become a great painter. Young Watts' first great success was a prize of £300 for a design for a fresco to decorate the House of Lords. In 1847 he won a second prize—this time of £500—for another similar design. He was employed for years on decorating the walls of public buildings. Then, when he grew older, he took to painting

"HOPE," BY G. F. WATTS

W. F. Mansell.

We should regard this famous picture as an " allegory," for it is a representation of the idea expressed in the title. The picture shows us a girl sitting blindfolded, lyre in hand, on the globe in the dim twilight of the world. She forms the figure of " Hope," which " strives to get all the music possible out of the last remaining string." George Frederick Watts was a Welsh boy whose father did all in his power to help his son along the hard road to success.

allegorical pictures such as "Love and Life," which is in the Tate Gallery, and "Mammon," in the same collection.

"Mammon" represents the God of Riches on a blood-red throne surrounded with skulls. With one huge, heavy hand he crushes a woman while a man lies prostrate beneath his feet. Watts lived to be full of years and honours. He refused a baronetcy, but accepted the Order of Merit. He died in 1904 at the age of eighty-seven.

"Every picture ought to tell a story" had become a sort of motto in art circles in England when James

W. F. Mansell.

SIR GALAHAD

This is another charming picture by G. F. Watts giving us a perfect representation of both knight and horse. Watts died in the year 1904, at the ripe old age of eighty-seven. He was most successful in decorating the walls of public buildings and in painting frescoes.

McNeill Whistler arrived in Europe and revised this saying into: "Every picture ought to sing a tune."

The First Great American Painter

Whistler was born at Lovell, Massachusetts, in 1834, but his father, a railway engineer, migrated to Russia when his boy was eight, and James learned to speak French fluently in that country. In 1849 the elder Whistler died and his widow returned to America, where her son was sent to West Point Military Academy in the United States. But James failed to pass his examination. Chemistry floored him. As he used to say, "If silicon had only been a gas I might have been a general in the United States Army."

Fate had better things in store for him. He learned to engrave and etch, and went to Paris as an art student. Whistler delighted in the crazy student life of Paris, and it made of him a "quaint original who could not fail to be remarked." Listen to the way in which a friend describes him later in life:

"His face is a remarkable one. It is covered with countless wrinkles, but is clear of complexion. He wears a well-curled grey moustache and imperial. His eyebrows are bushy and his brown eyes glisten under them. His hair is all arranged in separate curls. They are dyed black with the exception of one which remains quite white and is sometimes tied with a small ribbon. He wears a very long black overcoat and a French top hat with a straight brim. He carries a kind of wand 4 feet long. When he walks in the streets of London small boys follow and nearly everyone turns to look at him as he passes."

Whistler's art was based on that of Japan. It was remarkable, but so revolutionary that the critics and the Royal Academy were extremely hostile to him. Whistler cared nothing for criticism and gave as good as he received. One critic mentioned that there was a

" THE ARTIST'S MOTHER," BY WHISTLER

It must be very satisfying to be one of the world's great artists and to be able to paint a living picture of one's mother. We have above a reproduction of such a painting, done by James McNeill Whistler. When a representative of the French nation wished to buy the picture, Whistler replied that the painting was the one he could " most earnestly wish to see become the object of so solemn a consecration."

deal of colour in his " Symphony in White." To this Whistler retorted:

" Did this wise person expect white hair and chalked faces ? Does he then believe that a Symphony in F contains no other note, but shall be a continued repetition of F—F—F ? Fool! "

Maps on Copper

Whistler's masterpiece is his portrait of his mother, now in the Luxembourg at Paris. It is one of the great pictures of the world, and long ago confounded the critics. Before he died, in 1903, almost every country except his own had recognised his art.

Many amusing stories are told of Whistler. As a lad he was apprenticed to a firm who etched maps on copper. Whistler had finished a very fine map, and, having nothing to do, amused himself by etching in around the border some sketches of the different members of the firm, including an unkind caricature of the chief. Then he went away for a holiday and forgot all about it. Meanwhile the plate was bitten-in and printed, with all the horrid little caricatures which Whistler had forgotten to stop out.

Result, when Whistler returned he was promptly dismissed. Just as he was leaving the office he happened to catch sight of the chief's huge magnifying glass lying on his desk. It was the " old man's " most sacred possession. Whistler stopped just long enough to paint a sprightly little red demon in its centre and passed on his way with a smile.

Next day, when the great man lifted his glass to inspect something, he dropped it with a howl plainly heard in the outer office.

Seeing Beneath the Surface

Of Sargent's work the " Outline of Art " says: " Some of his male portraits have been merciless in their unmasking of the real minds of the sitters." John Singer Sargent, one of the greatest portrait painters of modern times, was American-born, but learned his painting under Carolus Duran in Paris, and finally settled in England.

His finest picture is the full-length portrait of Lord Ribblesdale, painted in 1902, and now in the National Gallery. Sargent's power of setting before us the real personality of his sitter is almost unequalled in the history of portrait painting.

" The Last Muster "

Hubert Herkomer was another fine artist who, born abroad, became naturalised and painted in England. He was born in Bavaria and was brought to England when he was eight. His parents were desperately poor, and he himself had a terrible struggle to get a start. He sold his first picture for two guineas and afterwards lived on £2 a week earned by doing woodcuts for a comic paper. Then he was driven to design carpets.

Yet later Herkomer painted many famous pictures, the best of which is that

W. F. Mansell.

A PICTURE FROM JAPAN

Painted by one of the greatest artists of Japan, Hokusai (1760–1849), this is regarded as an impressive example of the natural and highly decorative style of Japanese colour-work. The title is " River-Scene with Bridge and Fujiyama in the Distance," and the print is in the British Museum, London. The mountain, Fujiyama, as we read in our geography, is an object of adoration to every person in Japan.

OLD BATTERSEA BRIDGE

W. F. Mansell.

This picture is described as a " nocturne in blue and gold," the word " nocturne " in an art sense meaning simply a picture of a night scene. The subject is old Battersea Bridge, London; and the artist Whistler. The painting was purchased for the National Gallery for 2,000 guineas. It is interesting to compare the above picture with the Japanese reproduction on the left because, according to experts, Whistler was influenced by the methods of Japanese artists.

of Chelsea pensioners called " The Last Muster," and became a very rich man. He set up an art school at Bushey, where he built a most beautiful house worth, with its contents, £100,000.

Scenes at Sea

No living British artist has a wider fame than Sir Frank Brangwyn, who was born in 1867 and is of Welsh descent. His early paintings are all of the sea. " Burial at Sea," " Salvage," and " The Convict Ship " are famous examples. Then by degrees he turned to decorative art. His splendid panel " Commerce " is in the Royal Exchange; the Skinners' Hall was decorated by him; and he has been in great demand in America, where his work is highly valued. His colour is splendid, and all his designs glow with rich tints. He was knighted in 1941.

It is an interesting fact that Whistler found favour in Scotland long before he was appreciated in England. And during the past fifty years Scotland has produced more than her share of fine artists. Sir James Guthrie, who became President of the Royal Scottish Academy in 1902, has the strength of the great Raeburn in his work.

Many Scottish artists gathered together in comparatively recent times. They grouped themselves in the so-called Glasgow School, of which you will read in the next chapter.

W. F. Mansell.

THE CHILDREN OF MR. ASHER WERTHEIMER

The portraits included in this picture are those of the children of Mr. Asher Wertheimer, the famous art dealer. The artist was John Singer Sargent, R.A., who was born at Florence in 1856, the son of American parents. He was one of the greatest portrait painters of modern times, and his power of setting before us the real personality of his sitter is almost unequalled in the history of portrait painting. Sargent died in 1925.

THE IMPRESSIONISTS AND AFTER

A BAR AT THE FOLIES BERGÈRE

The Impressionist painters were concerned with light and its effects upon colour. They usually painted out of doors, but also found subjects in cafés and theatres, where the inter-play of gaslight was as exciting as the sunlight of Nature. Manet's picture of the barmaid at the famous café and music-hall in Paris is one of the greatest of these studies of light glinting and shining from surface to surface, the whole scene being reflected in the great mirror at the back.

MEANWHILE something of great importance to painting had happened in France with the coming of what we now call "Impressionism." A number of French painters had decided that the artist should be chiefly concerned with the effects of light upon the scenes, people and objects which he painted. They saw that sunlight out of doors and gaslight in the cafés and theatres where they sometimes worked made the actual forms of things indistinct with spots of intense brightness and reflections; and they saw that colours were different under different lights. They also realised that the so-called "shadows" were only different colour effects. The first of them, Edouard Manet, once said, "The chief person in a picture is the light," and when he painted his famous "Bar at the Folies Bergère," one of the famous Parisian cafés, it was chiefly a study of the gaslights reflecting into the surfaces of bottles and glasses, with everything reflected again in a mirror at the back. How difficult such an effect is to put down in paint! When we look at such a scene the eye gives us one impression because the lighting binds it all together and the actual individual forms of things are blurred by the interplay of lights and reflections. That is also true of a landscape in the sunlight. So these new men tried to get just that effect and found they could do it best by putting on the canvas innumerable little touches of brightly toned colour rather than by considering outlines.

VIEW OF VÉTHEUIL, BY CLAUDE MONET   *Copyright.*

Water, sky, trees, meadows, among them the hint of the village; but the artist's concern is still with
the shimmer of light and colour, and as in all these impressionist paintings it is that vibrating effect
of the light which is the subject of the picture.

Ever-changing Effects

Claude Monet was the greatest and most consistent of these Impressionists. It was a painting of his in an exhibition in 1863, which he called " Impression," which gave the whole school their name, for the critics thought it was a fault and seized on the word, but the artists accepted it as a title of honour. Monet would paint one subject a score of times, because the changing light showed it to him as a score of different impressions. The front of Rouen Cathedral, for instance, he saw to be quite different at dawn, at noonday, in the evening. The light changed the colour and, coming from different directions and so making different shadows, changed the forms. So he put down all these different impressions of the one object.

He came to London with another Impressionist, Camille Pissarro, to escape the Franco-Prussian War in 1870, and they were thrilled by Turner's pictures, for they realised that he had been out for the same idea as they had and had been an " impressionist " fifty years before " Impressionism " was practised. Monet painted pictures of the Thames with lovely effects of the sun on the fog, of St. Lazare Railway Station in Paris with exciting light on the steam escaping from the trains. These men aimed at brilliant colour in both the light and the shadows, and they rendered them with tiny flecks of pure paint. When they wanted, for instance, to make a purple they did not mix red and blue on their palettes and then put that mixture on the canvas; they put a little dot or streak of red next to one of blue on the canvas, and as we look at the pictures these vibrate together between the picture and the eye and create a brilliant purple. This loses the drawing of the forms but gains tremendously in colour.

A World Art Centre

Alfred Sisley was another of the group. He often painted snow scenes because of the dazzling light and the lovely reflections in the shadows of the snow. Almost all the French artists began to work in this style, and so did others all over the world. Renoir applied it to figures, particularly to the flesh colour of the women and children whom he loved to paint. Degas used the colour effects but was more concerned with the forms than some of the Impressionists. He found his subjects on racecourses, in the theatre, particularly with the ballet girls, with the nude forms of women at their bath-tubs, with the working laundresses of Paris.

Paris was accepted as the leading art centre of the world, and students such as Wilson Steer, from England, and Whistler, from America, joined the thousands of art students there. Some of them became dissatisfied with Impressionism because they felt that it neglected the form. First among the French themselves, Seurat and Signac began to use the colour spot method (people called it " Pointillism ") more carefully to build up the shapes of things. Seurat's large picture in the Tate Gallery of bathing boys by a river, " Une Baignade," is a notable example of this. Then came Paul Cézanne, who argued that, whatever the effect of light, things had their own definite colour: an apple was green and red and was a certain solid, recognisable shape. He thought that painting

should keep the strong colours of Impressionism but ought to get back to geometry. Cézanne became the next great influence on painting. After him in recent years some people began to build up their pictures simply of geometrical shapes of things and made a sort of jig-saw puzzle of those shapes. They were called Cubists and, like so many painters

THE UMBRELLAS

We think of Renoir as an Impressionist painter of sunlight and of pretty women and children warmly coloured by it. In this great picture, however, we have him in another mood. Obviously he has been intrigued by the shapes of the umbrellas and the crowd beneath them. This time the colour is predominantly blue and silvery-grey.

of the present century, they put down not just what their eyes saw but what their minds created.

Vincent van Gogh was another Impressionist who went beyond Impressionism. An over-sensitive Dutch boy, he sacrificed everything first for religion and then for art. His loving brother Theo kept him going with what little money he could afford (for Vincent's pictures did not sell during his lifetime though they are among the most valuable in the world to-day). He wrote to Theo the most wonderful letters, which we can now read. He painted in tremendously bright colours and tried to express the fierce life-force in the trees, the corn, the people he painted. We would now call him an Expressionist, because he was expressing his own emotions and feelings about the things he painted. This movement also has been greatly taken up and exaggerated. It is again painting of something (this time a feeling) inside the mind rather than only of the thing seen by the eye. Van Gogh so neglected himself for his art that he lost his health and then his reason and shot himself: a sad end to this great artist.

Creators of Modern Art

Gauguin was a third influence in the creation of what we call " modern " art. Originally a successful business man, he also threw up everything for painting. He left Paris and his family and went to live in the South Sea Islands, where he could paint the natives and the scenery in the strong colours which the Impressionists had introduced, but he made flat decorative forms. He hated the civilisation he had left and went all out for simplicity in his life and in art. There is a story that when the important French governor of the island asked to have his portrait painted Gauguin sent back the impolite answer that he did not paint animals!

All the modern art about which we hear so much in these days really derives from these " Post-Impressionists," i.e., after-Impressionists. You will find

that such a person as Picasso breaks up his shapes like a Cubist or expresses his furious feelings as an Expressionist, or creates decorative shapes. Sometimes an artist will be only interested to put down the form without much concern for colour; sometimes he will become an extreme Impressionist and put down the colour with hardly any concern for the form, sometimes he will only be expressing his ideas. We have to remember that these modernists are painting what they think about the scenes or things or people they paint rather than simply what these things look like. There are, however, still thousands upon thousands of artists who realise that the inexhaustible beauty of this world and the inexhaustible forms and characters of people and things are glorious enough subjects. Most of them will paint these rather more gaily and brightly because of what the Impressionists brought into European art.

The Glasgow School

About the beginning of the present century a vigorous group of young painters appeared in Scotland calling themselves the Glasgow School. They were at first fired by the art of Whistler and the French Impressionists. Their object was to go back to nature, and their endeavour to express the mysterious quality of their native landscape of mists, and the illusive aspect of sunshine and shower that distinguishes Scotland from so much of the country south of the Tweed.

They were, without proclaiming it, opposed to the Pre-Raphaelites; that is to say, they had no intention of painting the local colour of things but the colour of objects as influenced by atmosphere. They had learnt from their French brothers that the glory of nature abides in the sky and atmosphere and the reflection these elements cause. These young artists went in a body to live and work in the little village of Brig o' Turk in the highlands, not far from Glasgow.

BOULEVARD MONTMARTRE, BY CAMILLE PISSARRO

Another study of the effect of light which destroys the exact forms of the houses, the trees, the traffic and the people in this typical Paris street scene. Everything in this instance is united in the warm darkness of late evening, and the artist has been fascinated by the pattern of light made by the illumination from street lamps, shops, and passing carriages.

The chief of the group were, alphabetically, Joseph Crawhall, James Guthrie, George Henry, E. A. Hornel, John Lavery, W. Y. MacGregor, Alexander Roche, James Torrance and E. A. Walton. The movement caused a revival of art in Glasgow.

A Silent Memoriser

One of them, Joseph Crawhall, went from Northumberland to join the group, so strongly did he feel in sympathy with their ideals. Crawhall so trained his memory that he seldom, if ever, painted any picture from nature directly. His father, it is said, taught him to go out and watch his subject, then return home and draw it, and never erase his effort. If he drew it badly he had to make a fresh start.

This firm rule developed in him a unique method of working. R. B. Cunninghame-Graham wrote of him: " I hardly ever saw him draw direct from nature. When he had to draw a horse, a dog, a goat, or any animal he would go and look at them for a full hour, with a look so intense it seemed to burn a hole into their skin. Then perhaps, but rarely, he would take a pencil or a piece of coloured chalk out of his pocket, and on the back of an old envelope set down cabalistic signs or drabs of colour."

By this unusual method Crawhall arrived at spontaneity and clarity. His works " The White Drake " and " The Black Cock," together with his hunting scenes, are among the great art treasures of Scotland. He was known as " The

By permission of J. Craik Henderson, Esq.

THE SPANGLED COCK

Alex Reid and Lefevre.

Colourful and gay, this picture was painted by Joseph Crawhall, the well-known Scots artist. So highly prized are his works among collectors that they rarely find their way into the market or cross the Border to come southwards. Crawhall excelled all artists of his time in the rendering of birds and animals.

Great Silence," so quiet and observant were his ways.

James Guthrie began, as most of this Scots school did, by painting landscapes with figures among which his "Goose Girl" brought him immediate fame. Soon, however, he displayed a talent for portrait painting which clearly marked him for celebrity.

Although George Henry, John Lavery, Alex. Roche and E. A. Walton became fine portrait painters also, none of these ever forsook landscape. Even in later years George Henry's landscapes were to be seen at the R.A. annually, and in spite of the fact that he was over eighty, and the last of the Glasgow School alive, his scenes of Arundel had a vitality of colour and brushwork that led one to think

of them as the work of a young man.

An Irish-Scottish Londoner

John Lavery was a poor Irish boy whose parents settled in Scotland, where Lavery had a severe struggle to make a living and learn to paint. With the advent of the Glasgow School he quickly rose with that group until he was in the R.S.A. with the others. He then left Scotland for London, where he became not only the leading Scottish painter of his time in the capital but one of the most distinguished international artists of his day. He painted innumerable portraits of celebrities, Royal and otherwise, besides a large number of landscapes of London street life, Royal processions, landscapes in France, Tangier and the U.S.A.. in which last country he was received as our most renowned living painter.

After he had made his name with the group, E. A. Hornel retired to his native town of Kirkcudbright where he worked on his large canvases in the open. Besides possessing a commodious studio in which he painted most industriously, he had a small shed built in the woods where he could lock up his canvases, taking them out in turn to work direct from nature. His painting was mostly done with a palette knife and his paint laid on lavishly, a type of painting that requires great experience and dexterity.

Cathedrals and Mountains

Sir David Young Cameron, though not initially of the Glasgow School, was very much associated with it and rose to great fame as an etcher of all sorts of subjects ranging from the interior of cathedrals to what might be called the exterior cathedrals of the Grampian Mountains; and, in that latter subject, he has no rivals.

Of the Scots of that period who came south, Sir Muirhead Bone was certainly the most illustrious. His small drypoint (*i.e.*, fine lines produced with a sharp needle) of Ayr prison, done as a comparatively young man, marked him as a master of drawing fused with drama. In size it was only a few square inches, yet in dramatic and imaginative content it was Rembrandtesque.

In later years his large quietly coloured

W. F. Mansell.

THE GREEN PASTURES

The lovely landscape reproduced above, with its two groups of cattle, is a splendid example of the work of George Henry, one of the members of the Glasgow School. This artist, though a portrait painter also, is most famous for his landscapes, especially those painted in the neighbourhood of Arundel in Sussex.

By permission of Raphael Tuck and Sons Ltd.

IN THE FORE CABIN

Sir John Lavery, an Irish boy whose parents settled in Scotland, was a painter noted for his very dainty style. He painted innumerable portraits of celebrities, Royal and otherwise, as well as State processions, London street scenes and so on. The picture above shows the fore cabin of H.M.S. *Queen Elizabeth.*

drawing of " The Painted Room at Greenwich," with its hundreds of naval men at lunch, shows him completely at ease in depicting crowds. His " St. Bride's " which was " done on the spot," as he has written in the picture's corner, is a marvel of draughtsmanship that has to be seen to be believed. It is the ruin of Wren's church in the heart of London with a distant view of Ludgate Hill and St. Paul's.

So fabulous were his feats of draughtsmanship that legends are already told of him. One says that when Sir Muirhead wanted to draw a certain railway station in Glasgow from a street overlooking his subject he found his chosen spot completely barricaded by a wooden hoarding. He also found a knot in one of the planks which he pushed through with his thumb, thus enabling him to have a one-eyed view of the station. Actually, this was enough for him to make one of his spectacular drawings. Another legend relates that he made a large drawing of the interior of St. Peter's in Rome on separate sheets from a small sketch book. When these sheets were pasted together each was found to fit exactly.

The New English Art Club

In the last years of the nineteenth century the strongest influence in the art of painting in England was the New English Art Club. In 1885 the

MODERN ART

Any portrait painted by Augustus John, R.A., not only shows what his sitter looks like, but tells us something about the character of the person. In this portrait of "Lawrence of Arabia" we gain an understanding of the kind of man Colonel Lawrence really was. It is typical, too, of this artist's work, and of much modern painting, that no attempt is made to pretend that the paint is flesh or cloth; it remains simply and frankly paint.

HISTORY IN DECORATIVE ART

In this picture, showing the "Departure of Lancaster for the East Indies," we have a fine example of
the decorative skill of the artist, Sir Frank Brangwyn, R.A. It was painted to occupy a particular space
on a wall, and it is all exciting and romantic, as this painter's work always is, whether he is depicting
an incident from our past history or some scene of modern life.

We have an example in this picture "Cottages At Burghclere," by Stanley Spencer, of one of the two
very different ways of painting adopted by this artist. One is in simple, flat shapes, with little light
and shade; the other, as in this picture, is similar to the work of the pre-Raphaelites, with every leaf
and object carefully drawn and brightly coloured.

This picture of "Icknield Way" by Alexander Jamieson, gives us another kind of painting, generally known as Impressionism. The artist is not really interested in the individual details of the scene, but is mainly concerned with the effect of light on the whole. As with this great tree, the vivid light blurs the shapes of all the details and leaves us with the broad impression.

MENIN ROAD AND CANAL BRIDGE

"The Menin Road," by Paul Nash. After serving in the 1914-18 war, Paul Nash was invalided to London and appointed an official war artist. He had no romantic attitude to war; his pictures showed it as brutal, terrible and ugly, depicting the desolation and desecration of nature, the torn land, broken trees, shell-holes full of mud, the sky cut across by searchlights.

W. S. Lowry, painter of this picture called "The Canal Bridge," with its amusing design of upright chimneys and thin people, lives in the industrial north of England. He makes his pictures of unpromising material, putting it all down rather simply, and showing us there is an interesting pattern underlying a scene we would tend to call ugly.

Charles Ginner, A.R.A., who painted this picture "Salisbury Cathedral," builds up his pictures with little flicks of solid paint, very painstakingly, so that we are aware of the individual leaves on the trees, the stones or bricks of a building, and even the tiles on the roof. The result of this care is seen in a pleasing pattern and a sense of solidarity.

HORSES IN TWO MOODS

All lovers of spirited horses and of open, rolling country will appreciate this fine painting "Kilkenny Horse Fair," by Sir Alfred Munnings, President of the Royal Academy, 1944-49. Horses are the favourite subjects of this artist, and the busy, bustling scene blends wonderfully with the typical Irish background. This was Sir Alfred's diploma picture in the Royal Academy in 1925.

Robert Bevan belonged to an interesting group of artists called the Camden Town Group. His picture of an old-fashioned hansom-cab yard in the days before taxis entirely took the place of those romantic vehicles shows us how the effect of sunlight and its reflection into the shadows can make the simplest scene exciting and beautiful.

QUAYSIDE AND WATER HIGHWAY

Edward Seago is a contemporary artist who lives in East Anglia. He loves the sky, and the effects that clouds and sunlight have upon the world beneath them. He often goes to the Continent to paint, and here is "Quayside, Dieppe" on a cloudy day when the grey sky reflects itself in the water and the wet quayside flagstones.

Walter Sickert was an artist who brought Impressionism from France to England. He used its brilliant effects of light and pure colour for many purposes—portraits, interiors, landscapes. In Venice, where the buildings, the gondolas and their picturesque mooring-posts were held between the brilliant sky and its reflection in the water, he found lovely subjects.

ENGLISH AND ABORIGINAL ART

National Gallery of British Sports and Pastimes

All sports fascinate the artist who painted this picture, "Watching the Sailing at Hammersmith Mall."
It depicts a busy scene on the Thames at Hammersmith, with a number of youngsters looking on.
Cosmo Clark, the artist, is an impressionist, and is keenly interested, as can be seen, in the effects
of light on the white sails and on the water.

Pix-Camera Press

The magnificently sweeping curves of this picture make an irresistible appeal. It is a water colour
by Albert Namatjira, full-blood Aborigine artist of the Western Aranda tribe of Central Australia.
Namatjira became interested in "white man's painting" while acting as guide to an Australian artist,
who gave him paints and lessons in water colour. His work has been praised by art lovers and critics.

LANDSCAPES WITH FIGURES

W. F. Mansell.

THE GOOSE GIRL

This famous picture brought immediate fame to James Guthrie and may best be described as a landscape with figures. Sir James, as he afterwards became, early displayed a great talent for portrait painting and held office as President of the Royal Scottish Academy.

By permission of the Aberdeen Art Gallery.

GUIDING THE PLOUGH

The picture reproduced above is an excellent example of the work of that great British artist Sir George Clausen, who was born in 1852 and died 1944. He made a profound study of the countryside all his long life and painted landscapes in sun and shade, flowers, farmers and farm workers. Most of such subjects were found in Essex.

idea of a modern society of painters took root in the minds of a group of artists most, if not all, of whom had been to Paris.

Actually "The New English," as it was named familiarly, has been largely responsible for most of the notable figures in the realms of English painting up to the present day. Among the innumerable names connected with its early and even more recent years are: Clausen, Steer, Brown, Bramley, Bartlett, Stanhope-Forbes, Tuke, La Thangue, Greiffenhagen, T. B. Kennington, Sargent, A. G. Bell, Adrian Stokes, Alfred Parsons, Manson, Sickert, Tonks, Dodd, Condor, Rothenstein, and many others.

Clausen began as a painter of portraits and figures treated as indoor subjects; and, although he also excelled as a portraitist, he is best known to a larger public as the great English painter of the farmer and farm worker.

In his open-air labouring scenes he was at first strongly influenced by Bastien Lepage, a Frenchman of amazingly realistic ideas. Clausen's early rustic pictures were as unmistakably like those of the great French master as his later pictures were unmistakably pure Clausen. He soon learned that he had a poetry of his own with which he imbued all his immortal canvases. Bastian Lepage's peasants

By permission of Sir Muirhead Bone.

A SCENE IN STOCKHOLM

This is a beautiful drypoint (*i.e.*, fine lines produced with a sharp needle) by Sir Muirhead Bone. It shows the Strandvögen at Stockholm and emphasises the artist's wonderful capacity for draughtsmanship. Sir Muirhead's pictures record all the great manifestations of our time, its functions and processions; industrial and public life; the hubbub of harbours and the bustle of humanity in the streets.

ON SEA AND LAND

By permission of the Tate Gallery.

Here is another picture, the original of which can be seen in the Tate Gallery, London. It was painted by the " New English " artist Tuke, and the tall sailing ships in the background are as interesting as the group of boys who are so thoroughly enjoying their dip in the smooth sea on a hot summer's day.

By permission of Sir Arnesby Brown.

Milking-time as the mists of the new-born day are sent fleeting away by the first sunrays is the subject of this charming pastoral painting by Arnesby Brown. This artist was a member of the New English Art Club, which exercised so strong an influence on the trend of painting and produced a long list of famous names from among the artists who joined it.

8—2

W. F. Mansell.

ORANGE LILIES

The lovely garden study seen above, which appeared in the Diploma Gallery of the Royal Academy, was the work of Alfred Parsons. The garden is at Broadway, Worcestershire.

In that room he produced some of his fine interiors.

Perhaps most of his admirers like him best as a landscapist, for in that department he showed his gifts as a master of rich colour. He could bathe his landscapes in luscious golden light. His sky, land, and sea showed a complete unity of colour in all three.

Born Bohemians

Augustus John, O.M., R.A., is not only a born artist, but that rare man, a born Bohemian. Owing to his innate talent for drawing and painting he was revered even when he was a student at the Slade School. Then, when his drawings began to appear at the New English, Sargent declared him to be " the finest draughtsman since the Renaissance." His instinctive love of

seemed to pose for the painter, while Clausen's models were depicted as though unaware of being observed by him.

Wilson Steer was a painter by heredity, his father having been a portrait painter and teacher of painting. Young Steer studied at the Gloucester School of Art and later in Paris, where he learnt the message of light and colour from the Impressionists. At twenty-six he was one of the founder members of the New English, and seldom showed at any other public exhibition in London and never sought Academic honours.

As a painter his chief message was to show how gay in colour and light contemporary life could be. Although he occupied a house with a large studio on the Embankment at Chelsea, he had the odd habit of painting more enjoyably in his drawing room among the furniture and ornaments he so much liked.

W. F. Mansell.

SAVERNAKE FOREST

One of the long avenues of this Wiltshire Forest, bordered and overhung with beech trees. The artist is Paul Nash, who, with his brother John, renders nature in the most delicate of hues.

the gipsies, together with his gift for learning Romany, proved he was an inveterate wanderer. He spent much of his time, both in this country and abroad, with these nomads with whom he seems to be perfectly at home. Among them he has found many of his models. Thus, when on a visit to Granada in Spain, he tells of falling in with some gipsy dancers living in the cave-dwelling of a nearby suburb. Their caves were whitewashed and clean and in that natural Bohemia he spent a pleasant evening.

His work is completely his own. It is alive with vitality and originality, and possesses the appeal that all artistic realism has for dealing in contemporary life. His many drawings in line are beyond praise for their apparent careless freedom, but when studied they reveal an amazing knowledge and acute observation.

Walter Richard Sickert was another master of painting whose work caught the eye of a large number of the younger artists. Sickert had been a keen admirer of Whistler, but early in his student days he was introduced to Degas in Paris. In Degas' zest for life and movement Sickert found the artistic nourishment his nature demanded. On his return to this country he began his long series of pictures depicting people in the streets of London and at his favourite watering places. He also revelled in the life of crowds and performers in music halls, and in Dieppe, a much-loved resort of his, he often painted its café life.

The Painter and the Aeroplane

C. R. W. Nevinson was conspicuous by his methods of depicting modern

By permission of the Tate Gallery.   *W. F. Mansell.*

ORPHANS

The above masterful picture, to be seen in the Tate Gallery, London, was the work of T. B. Kennington. He belonged to the New English Art Club and his works are much sought after.

life in its many aspects and he achieved some remarkable pictures of the aeroplane. He made many flights in all sorts of planes in order to produce his novel pictures of landscapes seen from the air, and was the first artist to produce cloudscapes with those machines as his chief motif.

A group of the younger generation that have come very much to the fore of late years must be mentioned, such as Stanley Spencer, whose very large picture " Resurrection " at the Tate Gallery is a memorable performance that has been followed by many others. Duncan Grant is a painter whose landscapes and interiors are notable for their rich colouring, powerful handling of paint and strong constructional compositions. Paul and John Nash have rendered nature in most delicate hues, whilst Edward Le Bas is one of the A.R.A.s whose paintings show great distinction in pure colour.

Women Painters

Within the present century this country has been particularly rich in women painters, of whom Dame Laura Knight, R.A., is among the most conspicuous. Her many pictures of circus folk have won for her a place as one of the most vigorous woman artists that England has yet given us. Then there was Annie Louisa Swynnerton, the first woman since the eighteenth century to be elected a member of the Royal Academy.

Ethel Walker, D.B.E., A.R.A., was born in Edinburgh but went to London early in her career to study at the Slade School and at Sickert's evening classes. She was soon noticed for her fine colour in portraits, decoration and flowers. Her decorations won for her permanent fame, for their beauties are dependent on rhythm and arrangement, while her delicate perception was trained by not working from the model except in the initial sketches. Thus, in this way, she allows her imagination full play.

Gwen John, the sister of Augustus, was also a fine artist, painting quiet figures in delicate colours.

It would not be possible even to list the enormous number of good artists, both men and women, working to-day, holding one-man shows and exhibiting at the Royal Academy or other traditional or rebel societies. Academic, impressionist, post-impressionist, or wildly modern, they show art of all kinds, holding the mirror up to nature and to the wonder of contemporary life.

By permission of the executors of the late P. Wilson Steer, O.M.

THE GROVE AT BRIDGNORTH

Wilson Steer, O.M., is thought of as an outstanding landscapist and the painting reproduced above is an admirable example of his work. His aim was always to show how gay in light and colour a picture could be, and he bathed his landscapes in luscious sunshine. Steer's most prized paintings now are his water colours.

LANDSCAPE AND MODERN INDUSTRY

It is characteristic of many modern artists that forms are simplified in order to show us the rhythm of the lines and shapes they see. In this picture, " Winter Landscape," by John Nash, the artist found that the snow had simplified many of the shapes, but he emphasised this simplicity in order to make the pattern as he saw it.

By courtesy of Mrs. Nevinson.

Here, in this picture of " Power House, Battersea," by C. R. W. Nevinson, one of our modern industrial buildings becomes a delightful design. The artist depicts it at dusk across the river, with golden lights reflected in the water. The bare bough of the plane tree softens the hard lines, and the flight of the gulls gives life and movement.

THE MENDIPS AND THE COTSWOLDS

We have a good example in this picture, " The Mendips," of the work of Tristram Hillier, an artist who loves every detail, draws its outline with care, then gives it strong light and shade and its own bright colour. Everything in this lively scene is depicted in that spirit. Look at the heap of stones in the foreground and note the way in which the wind blows the woman's skirt.

Sometimes an artist so enjoys the shapes and colours of the objects he sees that he crowds his canvas with hundreds of different things, each one being, when examined, a little separate study in itself. Nevertheless, such a picture must still have one main object to attract the eye, and in this painting, " A Cotswold Farm," by Gilbert Spencer, the wagon forms the main point of interest.

ART IN THE BRITISH COMMONWEALTH

LAURENTIAN VILLAGE BY CLARENCE A. GAGNON

Gagnon saw the beauty of the little villages which lie among the Laurentian hills on the north shore of the St. Lawrence. Especially when the masses of snow simplified the forms, the wooden houses and squat sleighs made patches of brilliant colour between the whiteness of the foregound snow and the purple of the wooded hills.

WHEN we are thinking about the painting and sculpture of the world we must nowadays give some consideration to that of the great new countries which form the British Dominions and realms overseas, particularly to Australia, Canada and South Africa, for in all these places there are now fine artists, art galleries and art schools. We have to think of them rather differently, however, from the European and other older countries, because whereas our art goes back at least to about the time of William the Conqueror (whose date of 1066 we all remember so easily) the white civilisations of these Dominion lands dates only from about the eighteenth century.

Even when the early colonisation can be claimed as being established, the first task for the emigrants from England, France and other European countries was that of starting up agriculture, building homesteads—often with their own hands from the simplest materials—getting the first settlements going, and the first towns, roads, and eventually railways. Sometimes they were engaged in wars with the native populations; always they were at bitter strife with Nature. Every inch of their precarious foothold on the new soil demanded strenuous and dangerous work; and to establish themselves firmly in anything like civilised conditions, as we now understand them, took generations of pioneering effort.

Needless to say, the kind of folk who labour with the axe and the spade, the saw and the hammer, and who live by the gun and the trap, working through every hour of daylight, have no time to write books, compose music, or paint pictures. Usually they are not the kind who want to do so. They might receive a few of these luxuries from " back home " when they had settled in a bit, but otherwise they did without them. So roughly we may expect no art of their own in these new lands until approximately the nineteenth century, and then it had to start from scratch and to overcome enormous difficulties. Only a few of the wealthy governing people would be likely to be interested, people who came from fine houses and homes over here and took some of their treasures with them. The art, therefore, carried on from that of Europe. What we want to see, however, from these new lands are examples of their own art, something inspired by their landscape and their people and conditions. Perhaps something which was touched with the influence of the native art of the aboriginal folk. So, alike in Canada, Australia, New Zealand and South Africa, we have to wait for many years, even for more than a century after the first effective colonisation, before we have a real national art.

CANADIAN PAINTING

Canada, we must remember, was a French settlement until 1763, and its early architecture and crafts have marked French characteristics; but its painting, except for some rather amateur views of the scenery, had to wait another sixty years before its first artist of note even came to the country. This was Paul Kane, a Dublin lad, who was brought by his parents when he was nine years old, in 1819. He was an

SPRING ICE, BY TOM THOMSON
Thomson loved this beautiful wild nature in which he lived his solitary life and amid which he died a solitary death when his canoe overturned. He painted the scenery in brilliant decorative colour. In this picture the water is vivid blue, the foreground gold and orange, the background bright green with warm red hills beneath a blue sky with a golden cloud.

adventurous young-ster, who preferred to wander about with the Indians and the trappers rather than attend to his studies in the Grammar School at York, as Toronto was then called. As soon as he was able he himself took to the road, living as best he could, and beginning to draw and paint the pictur-esque Indian en-campments and the wonderful Redskin people. About 1840 he worked his passage to Europe and for four years, desperately poor but happy, he went round the European art galleries.

Back in Canada, he decided to make the perilous journey along the Great Lakes, by foot over the Rockies, and so to the Pacific. He wrote of that adventurous journey in a book called "Wanderings of an Artist among the Indians of North America," and, of course, he illustrated it with his sketches. That book and the pictures he painted tell us much of the wild life of the time, the scenery before the making of roads or railways, the Indians, the fur trappers and traders. The whole art of Paul Kane, now largely in Ca-nadian art galleries, is a fascinating record of that exciting life and people of the pioneering days.

Almost at the same time a young German from Dusseldorf, who had joined the American army, deserted,

By courtesy of the Royal Ontario Museum, Toronto.

PORTRAIT OF KEE-A-KEE-KA-SA-COO-WAY, BY PAUL KANE

Kane was one of the pioneer painters of Canada in the middle of the nineteenth century. He undertook a hazardous sketching tour with the Hudson Bay fur traders into the almost uninhabited wild west to paint the Indians and their encampments. His records of that trip, of which this forceful portrait is one, tell us much about the Red Indians of those days.

married a French-Canadian girl, and settled in Canada as an artist. His name was Cornelius Krieghoff, and he, too, painted the Indians in their camps, but also the townspeople, especially in Quebec, where he went to live in 1853. His best pictures are rather like those of the Dutch tavern painters, especially those he did of a tavern which he fre-quented called " Chez Jolifrou." With Paul Kane and Cornelius Krieghoff, therefore, Canadian art really com-mences, just before the middle of the nineteenth century. Kane died in 1871, and Krieghoff a year later, and for a time Canada seems to have been too busy on her material development to carry her art much further.

Maples in Autumn

Nevertheless a few painters—men born in the country now—began to realise that Canada had her own wild beauty. Her typical scenery of mountains, lakes, pine trees, villages of wooden houses; the brilliant colour of the turning maples in the autumn, and the snowy landscape of winter with the people going about wrapped in their bright woollen clothes and sitting in their little squat sledges, offered new and exciting things for an artist to paint. Homer Watson, born in 1855, was one of the first of these native-born artists and declared his intention " to make pictures of attractive moods of nature." The moods which he found attractive were often very fierce and wild, and he expressed them with bold simple forms, bright colours and rather heavy paint — qualities destined to become characteristic of Canadian painting.

Meanwhile, towards the end of the nineteenth century artists everywhere were looking to Paris and the great Impressionists for their inspiration and methods. Three Canadian artists in particular became disciples of these, and lived partly in Paris and partly in their native land. So with Maurice Cullen, James Wilson Morrice, and Clarence Cagnon, Canadian art entered its greatest period. The French Impressionists, we will remember, were chiefly interested in painting the effects of light and its reflection into the shadows, and when these Canadians went back home they found that their villages under snow and ice in the brilliant winter sunshine offered amazing effects of this kind. In the Laurentian Hills, on the north shore of the St. Lawrence river, were the most charming little villages of simple wooden houses set against backgrounds of the pine-clad slopes. When in the winter these were under snow, with the sturdy villagers travelling along the rutted roads on their little one-man sledges, it offered the painters something very simplified in form and excitingly beautiful in colour. So, though these men might spend their summers in France or elsewhere in Europe, the picturesque winters brought them home to paint typically Canadian pictures in a manner so bold that they might have been designs for posters.

A Lover of the Wild

Tom Thomson, the next important painter, was another adventurous and very Canadian personality. " Artist, Woodman, and Guide who lived humbly but passionately with the Wild ": that is what his friends inscribed on the cairn which they raised to his memory in 1917, when his upturned canoe floating on one of the lonely lakes told the world that this adventurous artist-naturalist had met his solitary death. He was born in 1877 near Lake Huron, and as a boy, like young Paul Kane before him, he had loved to wander off into the wild sparsely inhabited country, fishing and exploring and making friends with the folk he met. For a time he went to the Pacific coast and learned to be an engraver, and then he came back to Ontario and got a job with a firm of commercial designers, Grip Limited.

There he met a group of young men who were destined to play a great part in his own life and in the story of Canadian art, for they formed a comradely band who went off sketching on Sundays and holidays, chiefly in the vast Government nature reserve of lakes and river and forest called Algonquin Park. Thomson went with them, sketched a little, and played his mandoline a great deal. In 1912 he went off with one friend on a long sketching and fishing journey by canoe. He spent two months in absolute remote country, and it proved to be a turning point in his career, for the experiences of that long contact with unspoiled

Nature determined him that it was that sort of life he loved most. He happened, too, to lose his job at this time, and happily a wealthy doctor friend arranged to buy his pictures. So Tom Thomson turned to the Canadian wilds and lived as woodman, fisher, guide, and also as their first great painter.

When he painted such things as his " Jack Pine " in fierce colour and bold silhouette against a background of lake and hills, people thought it was too strong, not subtle enough, but Thomson would simply declare, " Yes, it was just like that." " Brother to all untamed things in nature " they wrote of him; and when he died in that accident to his canoe they rightly said, " It took him to itself at last."

In the Canadian Way

It was largely Tom Thomson's sketching friends from Grip Limited who took Canadian painting its next step along the road which he had opened. A famous Group of Seven artists began to work together and exhibit together. Though they were not all painting in quite the same style they were all doing the same thing: showing us Canada, and especially wild Canada. The snow-crowned Rockies towering into blue skies, the pine-girdled lakes, the forests, the far sea coast, everything was turned into brilliantly coloured boldly designed pictures.

The names of these men are important in this story of Canadian art. They are: James Macdonald, who was born in England but went to Canada as a

Collection—Art Gallery of Toronto.

WINTER, CHARLEVOIX COUNTY, BY A. Y. JACKSON

Canadian art in this picture, painted in 1933, is feeling out for the pattern which the snow has emphasised in the rising and falling ground. Jackson has added even greater emphasis so that we are keenly aware of the form of the landscape, as well as of the colour given to the snow by the sun shining on to it; gold, with complementary purple in the shadows.

GUARDIAN OF BRACHINE GORGE, BY HANS HEYSEN

It is claimed that Hans Heysen was the first man to show Australian trees as they really are and not to imitate European painters' visions of them. In this picture he has clearly emphasized the skeleton structure of the trees and the mountain behind, and with his fine colour has made a strong design of this rather cruel landscape.

lad of fourteen and eventually became principal of the Ontario College of Art; Alexander Young Jackson, one of whose fine pictures you will find in the Tate Gallery; Arthur Lismer, another English-born Canadian; Franklin Carmichael; Lawren S. Harris, the most modernist of them, for he painted his landscapes as very simplified patterns emphasising the forms; Frederick Varley, a portraitist; and Alfred Casson. Like many such chance groupings of painters, it came to an end because artists are individualistic fellows and seldom co-operate for long, but during its existence it had splendidly served the art of the country. Many of the pictures of the Group of Seven were bought for the fine art galleries which by this time flourished in Ottawa, Toronto, Montreal, Quebec and the other growing cities of the land.

When some of us saw these Canadian pictures for the first time in a special pavilion of the Franco-British Exhibition at Wembley in 1924, we realised that this was something different from European art. A real Canadian style had come to maturity. Another important exhibition, called " A Century of Canadian Art," was held at the Tate Gallery in 1938, and this time extended from Paul Kane to the newer men and women who in these days imitate the abstract and other advanced styles of Parisian painting. Alongside any experiments of this kind, however, there will henceforth always be a strong body of artists who paint their native Canada in a Canadian way.

ART IN AUSTRALIA

The story of Australia being so very

different from that of other lands, so, too, is the story of her art. Two events—one of its strange, remote beginning, and one of its history in the mid-nineteenth century—have to be taken into consideration. The first is that far back in 1788 Australia was thought of merely as the penal settlement for transported prisoners; the second that when gold was found in 1851 there was a tremendous rush of new emigrants, and that the folk already there tended to desert the established cities and go off to the remote, wild country where the treasure was. Neither sounds very helpful to the encouragement of art, but actually quite a number of the convicts at Botany Bay were men of education and of courage, and when freed made wonderful pioneer colonists; and the gold rush added enormously to the country's wealth and population, again of bold and courageous settlers.

The first pictures of Australia came from the scientific-draughtsmen, Sidney Parkinson, who went out on the expeditions of Captain Cook in the *Endeavour*, about 1770, and William Westall who was with Captain Flinders in the *Investigator* in 1801. These were scientific and geographical expeditions, and they included artists to make records as we would now send photographers and cine-matograph men. They drew the coast scenery at the landing places, and the curiosities of natural history. William Westall, for instance, has left 1,000 such pictorial records. In a way all the early art of Australia was in this spirit, local scenes and the strange things of the country put down simply in water-colour and later as engravings just to show what they looked like. Some would be sent home to Britain for this purpose. It is amusing to recall the sensation created by the first kangaroo exhibited in London in 1790 as a marvellous sight. This whole new country with its gum

PORTRAIT OF MARGARET OLLEY, BY WILLIAM DOBELL

Dobell is one of those artists who by painting in his own exciting way is continually causing an outcry. He has more than once received the coveted Archibald Prize. This painting was one which won it. Something of Renoir's fierce colour and over-rounded forms, and a realism which does not beautify but creates a strong impression, make an impressive picture.

trees and its blinding sunshine, strange animals and aborigines, was full of curiosities to English eyes.

The first really helpful thing in Australian art was the appointment of Lachlan Macquarie as governor. His work was largely concerned with the penal settlement at Botany Bay, but being a man of taste and initiative he took the chance of being a long way from London interference and ruled the whole colony like a prince. When he wanted good public buildings he found in Francis Howard Greenway, one of the convicts, a first-rate architect; and another of his official prisoners, Thomas Watling, who had been transported for forgery, was given a more useful direction for his skill by being allowed to exercise it as an artist.

Early Water-colours

Under Governor Macquarie, who ruled from 1809 to 1821, the fashion was set for collecting portraits and miniatures in the English manner of the period, for building country houses, and for having these drawn by the few artists whom the rising young colony boasted. Practically all this early Australian art was in water-colour, largely because of the difficulty of taking out there the more complicated paints and canvases of oil painting. Among these first painters a man named Frederick Garling claimed that he painted every ship which came into Sydney Harbour over a period of forty years. Another, James Wallis, largely devoted himself to the painting of the aboriginals and made a famous picture of a native festival dance, a " Corroboree at Newcastle." Another was Conrad Martens, who had been a pupil in England of the water-colour painter, Copley Fielding. Martens sailed to Australia in the *Beagle* with the scientific expedition which included the young Charles Darwin, but in 1835 he settled in Sydney and stayed there for the rest of his life.

The discovery of gold in 1851 influenced everything in Australia, including the art. The population trebled in ten years, and—what was important for both art and literature—a host of newspapers and periodicals came into being. The life at the gold diggings was news, and men like G. F. Pickering and T. Balcomber made drawings of it which were reproduced as engravings and lithographs separately and in book and newspaper illustrations. The most important of these men was Samuel Thomas Gill. He was a tough character, who took part himself in the gold rush, drank, gambled, was a brilliant horseman, and with a lively pen and pencil drew the equally tough characters around him. " Gold Digging at Victoria " he called one series of his lithographs, and they give us an exciting picture of the life of the diggers.

Gum Trees and Sunshine

When the gold rush itself died down Australia had entered the established life from which it had never turned back. There was wealth, a growing population, established cities, the first art galleries, and, not least, the newspapers with their policy of including artists' drawings and good writing of short stories, poems and sketches. There was also much more traffic with the Mother Country, and a deep interest in England itself in the flourishing young colony. All this was excellent for the growth of art.

Everywhere in the world during the second half of the nineteenth century the exciting thing in painting was Impressionism, and when the first important Australian artists got to work during those years it was an application to the Australian scene of the Impressionist idea that an artist painted the effects of light. The wonderful climate, the brilliant sunshine, were helpful to this idea. The ubiquitous gum trees, with their shapes so different from the European trees were an important factor. Abram Buvelot, a Swiss artist who settled in Victoria in 1865, was one of the first to appreciate this, and his

MASTER LAMBTON

The picture here reproduced is one of the finest examples of the portrait-painting of Sir Thomas Lawrence, P.R.A. The subject is the Hon. C. V. Lambton, son of the Earl of Durham. The portrait was painted in 1828. The little boy was seven years old at the time but died at the age of ten. On the death of Sir Joshua Reynolds, Sir Thomas Lawrence was appointed painter to King George III. Portraits by this great master are to be seen in most large private and public collections of pictures. Our reproduction is taken from the original etching in colour by J. Alphege Brewer.

THE MILLS CIRCUS

This spirited picture is reproduced from a large painting by Dame Laura Knight, R.A., and it depicts with a wealth of detail and character both human and animal performers awaiting their call to the sawdust ring. Like other famous paintings, this one has been found a place on a crack ocean liner, for it may be seen in a 1st Class Dining Saloon in the R.M.S. *Queen Mary*. The artist first exhibited at the Royal Academy in 1903. Formerly Miss Laura Johnson, she married Mr. Harold Knight, the portrait painter. She was made Dame Commander in 1929.

MOTHER AND CHILD, NORTH QUEENSLAND, BY RUSSELL DRYSDALE

Russell Drysdale is one of the new realistic artists of Australia. He does not sentimentalise either the people or the ugly little townships " out-back " where they live. He has chosen this unpromising material as the subject of his painting. Everything in his pictures is kept quite simple in form and almost crude in colour; but it has an air of absolute reality.

" Waterpool at Coleraine " in the National Gallery at Melbourne is an important early picture.

He was followed by that fine painter, Arthur Streeton. Streeton painted in the open-air rather than the studio; he used a heavy square-headed brush which boldly rendered the shapes of the gum trees, and he loved the fierce white sunlight and the light tones of typical Australian landscape. One other tremendous contribution he made to Australian art was the establishment of painters' summer camps at Heidelberg and elsewhere where the next generation of artists worked together under his influence. This " Heidelberg School," as it grew to be called, remains the most important influence in Australian art,

and Streeton the most important painter-teacher.

The story-telling artists must not be forgotten. If now they were not so naïve as those early men who sketched the crowds in the goldfields, they still gave slightly sentimental pictures such as Frederick McCubbin's " Down on his Luck," the study of a settler for whom Australia had proved not to be paved with gold; or " Bush Burial " with its pathos. Another story artist was Tom Roberts who in his work has left us a fairly realistic record of the life of the settlers in those days. " Bailed Up " gives a glimpse of the holding up of a coach, and reminds us that the Bushranger was an equivalent of the older English Highwayman. In 1889

VALLEY OF THE MARIBYRNANG, BY C. DUDLEY WOOD

A romantic and traditional artist, Dudley Wood shows us a more beautiful Australia than that depicted by such moderns as Nolan or Drysdale. He uses brilliant colour and by keeping his actual paint very thin, so that the canvas shows through, makes it feel full of light and air.

the *Melbourne Herald* organised a big show of Impressionist paintings from Europe which had a profound influence in switching Australian art in this direction of pure landscape under the bright Australian light, as the painters in the open-air Camp-schools had begun it.

In the Flinders Ranges

Hans Heysen has a special interest in that he pushed north from the comparatively tame scenery around the cities of the coast into the dry hinterland. It is important to-day because men like Sydney Nolan and Russell Drysdale have also turned to this " out-back " region and found in its bleak landscape of sand, marked only by the vertical shapes of enormous anthills and the jagged broken trunks of the brittle cork trees a brutal vision of Australia. Heysen had a wonderful eye for the earth masses of the hills and mountains in this arid region of the Flinders Ranges, as he had for the shapes of the gum trees.

George Lambert was another of the driving forces. He was born in 1873, and as a young man of 27 went to Europe and in the years after his return became a great influence as a teacher, especially in his insistence that good draughtsmanship was an essential to good painting—a fact which the Impressionists tended to overlook. Lambert was a good portrait painter and figure artist, and he was also a sculptor. Max Meldrum, who came to Australia from Scotland, was another fine portrait artist and art teacher who insisted on sound academic training for an artist.

In the twentieth century Australian art has inevitably followed something of the same road as European and American; that is, to experiment with all kinds of methods which do not depend upon the artist putting down what his eye sees but what his mind designs.

Towards a New Realism

There have been violent quarrels about the extreme work, and Sir Lionel Lindsay (an artist himself and one of a family of thrilling graphic artists led by the great Norman Lindsay) has attacked modern painting in swashbuckling style. Nevertheless Post-Impressionism flourished. Cubism turning everything to geometrical shapes; Surrealism painting things with the inconsequence of objects seen in dreams; Abstraction merely making designs of forms and colours. James Gleeson and Peter Purves Smith are among the many experimenters of this kind, but on the whole Australian art has tended to swing back to a new Realism based on the working people, the folk living " out back " in the drab settlements, the arid country where the drought has left only the giant ant-heaps and jagged cork trees amid the sandy soil. William Dobell has proved the outstanding artist. He has won many of the big prizes, and often the work getting the prize has created a tremendous rumpus, as when his strong and ugly portrait of another artist, Joshua Smith, received the Archibald Prize in 1943. His " Mrs. South Kensington " was another rather cruel satire on the sort of lady who amid the more realistic conditions of Australian life affected the modes and manners of London. This new realistic movement is tremendously vital and healthy, and the landscapes and pictures of the up-country remote corrugated-

By courtesy of Mrs. Florence Rutter.

A most remarkable exhibition was held recently in a London art gallery. The pictures shown had been drawn by the untaught children of one of the most backward races in the world, the Australian Aborigines. This picture above, " Trees and Undulations," was drawn by an under-fourteen boy who had neither tuition nor a sight of other pictures to guide him. Other drawings were equally remarkable.

iron townships of Russell Drysdale and Sydney Nolan have now become well-known at exhibitions in London. They do not convey a pretty picture of Australia, but at least they are truthful of one aspect of it.

England has one other cause to be thankful for Australian art in that some of her brilliant newspaper artists and cartoonists have settled in London. One of the first of these was that brilliant draughtsman, Phil May, whose book and magazine illustrations stand among the best. " Low," the best-known name in this field in England, is an Australian, David Low; and so was that marvellous satirical draughtsman, Will Dyson, who worked on the *Daily Herald*. The Australian genius for graphic art, which

in the earliest days of the national newspapers had received such encouragement from them, thus remains in these days when Australian art is firmly established in all departments.

Aboriginal Art

Finally a word must be said about the arts of the Australian aborigines. These primitive folk have a wonderful sense of decoration which they use in carvings on their spears and boomerangs, paintings on tree bark, and in the hollowed trunks of the trees themselves, on possum skins, and grave posts. For these designs they naturally choose the important objects of their own simple lives and make pictures of trees, kangaroos, turtles, birds and snakes, the shapes of spears and boomerangs set amid an abstract patterning of lines and dots. One of the strangest of their arts is the making of elaborate designs on the sandy ground itself. Grooves and holes are made in the sand and filled with different coloured ochres. All this has symbolic ritual meaning and plays a part in the initiation ceremonies of the adolescents and the burial ceremonies. Thus they are a practical part of the life of these people, but the elaborate sense of decoration entitles them to be given a real place in any consideration of Australian art—or, indeed, in world art, for we have grown to respect these arts of primitive people.

HUNTING SCENE: PAINTING BY ARNHEM LAND ABORIGINES

The Australian aborigines have their own strange sense of design, and, although they do not put things down in the visual way of the white settler, this picture of kangaroos, emus and their tracks among the trees tells its story just as clearly to the aboriginal mind. It is painted on specially prepared string bark.

Literature
Through
the Ages

The Lives
of the
Great Poets

By permission of the Corporation of Manchester. *Rischgitz.*

CAPTIVE ANDROMACHE

The central figure of this fine picture by the late Lord Leighton, the original of which is in the Manchester Gallery, is Andromache, the widow of Hector, chief defender of Troy against the Greeks. Homer's descriptions of her parting with her husband when he went out to fight Achilles, and of her grief over his death, are perhaps the most pathetic passages in all poetry. After the fall of Troy she was taken as a captive to Greece by Neoptolemus, son of Achilles. One of Euripides' plays has her name as its title, and her story as its subject.

IN GREECE AND ROME

ARISTOPHANES described Homer as the " Bard of Battles," and a worse description could hardly be imagined, for Homer's two great works, the " Iliad " and " Odyssey," throw a bright light on an age when civilisation was just dawning and when life was far more vivid and interesting than it is to-day.

Troy's Wooden Horse

Tribal life was ending and men were settling themselves into little nations; they were beginning to explore a world of which they knew practically nothing. Yet Homer gathered much knowledge from the old Phœnician traders.

Homer was of all poets the most simple and direct; he drew the characters of his heroes as no living man, with the one exception of Shakespeare, has ever been able to do, making them stand out before us with all their faults and virtues. It is true that in those days fighting was considered the highest form of employment for men, but the fighting described by Homer is only a small part of his wonderful work. Read and see how he describes the purity and loyalty of Penelope and the penitence of Helen, and you will realise how poor a description is " Bard of Battles." And his language is always so fine, direct and simple. You can almost see the scene as the Wooden Horse is drawn into Troy.

Is it not strange and sad that we know nothing of Homer as a man, except the legend that he was blind? We do not even know when he lived or where. The historian Herodotus places the date of Homer as 400 years before his own time—that is, in the ninth century before Christ—but it is fairly certain that the fall of Troy occurred not later than 1250 B.C., and it would seem likely that Homer lived not long after that date.

Actually we are fortunate to possess Homer's great poems, for it has to be remembered that for centuries these poems were not even written, but handed down from one generation to the next by word of mouth. Stranger still it is that, even after they were written, his works lay for at least 1,000 years unnoticed in dusty libraries.

All that is changed, and many of the greatest writers of English—Pope, Cowper, Chapman, William Morris, and others—have used their best efforts to translate Homer's flowing Greek into our own language, so that we all can read and appreciate the works of one of the very greatest and most gifted poets who ever lived.

A Passion for Poetry

The works of Sappho were divided by the scholars of Alexandria into nine books, but all of her poems that have come down to us are two odes and a few fragments. Yet even these are enough to prove that Sappho was one of the world's greatest poets.

Of this Greek woman of genius we

THE DEIFICATION OF HOMER   *W. F. Mansell.*

This allegorical picture, painted in 1827 by the great French artist, Jean Auguste Dominique Ingres, and now to be seen in the Louvre, Paris, shows us Homer surrounded by the great poets of all ages while a winged figure crowns him with a wreath of olive. The sword below his feet symbolises the battles of the Iliad, and the oar near it the sea-wanderings of the Odyssey. On the second step is a Greek inscription meaning: " If Homer be a god, I reverence him as one of the immortals; if he be not a god, then I pronounce him to be one." On Homer's right are figures presenting the lyre of the musician and the mallet of the sculptor; and Minerva, the goddess of art.

CIRCE AND THE SWINE   *Rischgitz.*

An English painter, Briton Rivière, illustrates in this famous picture an episode from Homer's
"Odyssey." During his wanderings Odysseus (Ulysses) came to the mysterious isle of Ææa,
where lived Circe, an enchantress. His companions, whom he sent first to her house, were
changed by her into swine, as the picture shows. Their leader, however, who had not gone
with them, was able to resist her spells, thanks to a magic herb given him by the god Hermes,
and to compel her to restore them to human form.

know hardly anything, except that she lived at the end of the seventh century before Christ and that she had a daughter called Cleis. It is said that she left her home in the island of Mitylene for Sicily, but returned and became the centre of a group of women with a passion for poetry. Hard things have been said about her character, but there is little foundation for these stories or for the legend that she flung herself into the sea.

The Greatest of Greek Tragic Poets

" Fortunate Sophocles! With wealth
  and wit
 Together blessed he lived and full
  of days
 He died——"

So wrote a friendly poet of the same date as that of the great Sophocles, and very true his words were. Sophocles, an Athenian, was born in 496 B.C., and lived to the great age of ninety-one years. He had the very best education of the time, and when only sixteen was chosen to lead the chorus of youths who celebrated the great naval victory of Salamis.

Sophocles rose to be a man of note in Athens and was sent as ambassador to other States, and in 440 was actually chosen as general in joint command with Pericles.

Of his many works only seven remain to us, but these are enough to put Sophocles among the world's great poets. His " Œdipus Tyrannus " is so terrible a tragedy that it makes one shiver to read it. There is far more plot in his plays than in any written before his time; the construction is almost faultless, and he has a wonderful way of contrasting characters who are intensely different.

The Slave who was Boiled

Of all the old Greek poets, Aristophanes is the favourite of most young folk, and of a good many older people as well. In his plays he pokes such delightful fun at the stupid and unpleasant people of his day.

His pet aversion was Cleon the Tanner, a cross, dull-witted old fellow who led the Athenian mob. In " The Knights " Aristophanes makes him a bullying slave who runs the whole household. Of course he is brought to grief and is renovated by being " boiled," after which he becomes quite youthful and sensible.

Another play of Aristophanes, " The Wasps," makes fun of the way in which the Athenians were always going to law about trifles, while in " The Birds " he ridicules the ease with which they are gulled by any imposter. But " The Birds " is much more than a mere comedy. Some of it is lovely lyric writing with a wild sweetness hardly equalled by any other poet except, perhaps, Shakespeare. In " The Peace," too, there are charming descriptions of country life.

" Lysistrata," or " The Strike of the Wives," is most amusing, and in " Plutus " Aristophanes writes in the most modern way of the unjust distribution of wealth.

Virgil, the Magician

The schoolboy best knows this greatest of Latin poets by his " Æneid," the story of " Æneas the Trojan " who is supposed to have been the founder of Rome. That was his last and, in some respects, his most wonderful work, but it was not the one he liked best. He preferred the " Georgics," those four books which set out the whole art of farming, the cultivation of trees and plants, such as olives and vines, and the breeding of horses and cattle.

This great poem occupied him for seven years and raised him to the position of the greatest poet of his age. As for the " Æneid," he was so dissatisfied with it that he wished to burn it and left this order in his will; but, fortunately, the Emperor Augustus disobeyed his directions and we still have the wonderful epic.

Virgil was born near Mantua, 70 B.C., and was partly of Celtic descent. He was tall, dark, quiet and not given to much talking. We know that he was always delicate. While he was still a boy his father's land was confiscated, but the governor of the province, Asinius Pollio, was a man of letters and had read some of young Virgil's verse; so he sent the boy to Rome with a letter to the Emperor. Though the property was not restored, a sum of money was given in compensation, and within a very short time Virgil was comfortably off. He had a villa at Naples, and was able to work in comfort.

Driven by Poverty

The Latin language is not nearly as suitable for poetry as is classic Greek, yet Virgil succeeded in writing in Latin some of the world's greatest poetry. He was a man of such goodness and character that the early Christians called him the Prophet of Christ among the Gentiles, and his works ranked as sacred books. They were actually introduced into the Liturgy of the early Church.

It was the fashion for Roman aristocrats to release slaves who could purchase their freedom. The father of Quintus Horatius Flaccus was a released slave, and he gave to Horace, his only child, an education such as few but the sons of rich men obtained. He finished at Athens, and was still there when the murder of Julius Cæsar caused civil war to break out in Italy.

Horace came back and joined up with Brutus and the Republicans. Though only twenty-one, he was made an officer. The Republicans were badly beaten, and although Horace got off unhurt, all his property was confiscated and he was left without a penny. He managed to get work in the Civil Service, but it was so poorly paid that, as he says himself, he was driven to make verses in order to live.

These verses attracted the notice of Mæcenas, the rich and powerful Roman,

Anderson.

This bust, the original of which stands in the Capitoline Museum, Rome, is a presentation of the head of Homer, the earliest poet whose works have come down to us. The portraiture is the fruit of the sculptor's imagination, for practically nothing is known about the poet himself, and even the period in which he lived is the subject of dispute. But his poems, the " Iliad " and " Odyssey," render his name as famous to-day as it was twenty-four centuries ago.

who was also a friend of Virgil. Mæcenas was never one to let a poet starve, and after this meeting, Horace's life became a pleasant one. He ripened slowly, and all his best work was done after the age of thirty-five.

Though it has none of the romantic greatness of Virgil's, it is beautifully and very carefully finished. His "Odes" are his finest poetry, and though they show a rather melancholy temper, yet Horace was capable of touches of bright and flashing humour.

The Exiled Poet

The first verse that the Latin scholar learns is usually Ovid's lament for his dead parrot, "imitatrix ales ab Indis," the talking bird from the East Indies. Publius Ovidius Naso was a many-sided genius who wrote verse about a variety of different subjects. One of his works is a practical poem on artificial aids to beauty, while another seeks to awaken his countrymen to a sense of their religious duties.

Ovid came of good family, for his father was an "Eques," or knight. He had a first-class education, and while quite young became a public speaker. But poetry claimed him, and soon he gave all his time to it. For years he lived and worked in the best Roman society and was a favourite at Court; then all of a sudden came disaster. Ovid was banished to the shores of the Black Sea which, in those days, was on the very edge of the known world. What his offence was we do not know, but he himself admits that his punishment was deserved. He died in that desolate country.

ODYSSEUS RETURNS TO PENELOPE　　　　　*Rischgitz.*

This picture was painted more than 400 years ago by Bernardino Pinturicchio, an Italian artist. It records the moment when, after ten years' wandering during his return from Troy, Odysseus at last reached home again, to find his wife Penelope working on her tapestry, the never-ending weaving of which had kept her many suitors at bay. The figures are clad in the costumes of Pinturicchio's own day; and the ship seen in the background would have seemed strange indeed to old Homer, whose "Odyssey" contains the incident illustrated.

FROM DANTE TO CHAUCER

By permission of the Corporation of Liverpool.   *Rischgitz.*

DANTE AND BEATRICE

When the great Italian poet Dante was only a boy, he fell deeply in love with a beautiful girl, Beatrice Portinari, who to his great grief, did not return his affection. Dante, nevertheless, made her an important character in his " Divina Commedia," the greatest epic poem of Christendom. This well-known picture, by Henry Holiday, shows us Dante gazing intently at Beatrice as she passes, accompanied by a friend.

ALL arts died in the Western world during those terrible centuries after the fall of Rome. There was no painting or sculpture worthy of note, and if there were poets, their writings have perished as well as their names. Almost the only exceptions are two British bards, Caedmon, who lived in the seventh, and Beowulf, in the eighth century.

France had Roland in the eleventh century, a maker of songs, of whom we know very little indeed. It was not until after Dante was born in 1265 that Europe could once more boast of a great poet. The house in Florence where he was born still stands. He was the son of a lawyer, and was baptised by the name of Durante, afterwards shortened to Dante.

The Maker of the Italian Language

Dante is famous for his devotion to the beautiful Beatrice, whom he first met when he was only nine years old. He loved her intensely, but she was married to a man named Simone di Bardi, and died at the age of only twenty-four. Dante himself afterwards married Gemma Donati, daughter of one of the great Guelph faction in Florence. The Guelphs and Ghibellines were fighting fiercely, and Dante was drawn into the savage feud and was present at the Battle of Campaldino. Part of this is magnificently described in his wonderful " Divina Commedia." Dante himself rose to the high state of being one of the six Priors of Florence, and as soon as he was in power, banished the heads of the warring factions.

In the next year, 1301, Dante was sent on an embassy to the Pope at Rome, and while he was away Charles of Valois descended on his native city, and Dante's friends were destroyed or banished. Dante himself was banished and condemned to be burned alive if he ever returned. So for the last twenty years of his life he was an unhappy wanderer. He lived in Verona, Ravenna and other towns, and some say that he visited France and England. He died in Ravenna in 1321, and his body was buried with honour by his friend, Guido Novello da Polenta. A cast of his face was taken after death, so we know exactly what this great man looked like.

His "Divina Commedia" is the greatest work in the Italian language and one of the greatest in any language. It may be truly said to have been the

REEVE, FRIAR AND PARSON

These quaint, but spirited, drawings are some of the many illustrations in the Ellesmere MS of Geoffrey Chaucer's "Canterbury Tales," which were written during the third quarter of the fourteenth century. The drawings represent three of the many characters who each told his Tale.

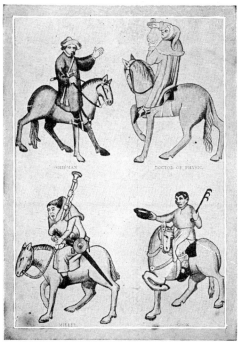

Photos : Rischgitz.

FOUR MORE CHARACTERS

Here you see the Shipman, the Doctor of Physic, the Miller, and the Cook, who took part in the famous pilgrimage to Canterbury described so amusingly by Chaucer, the Father of English literature. The Doctor carries a phial of medicine, the Cook a spit.

making of Italian. The "Commedia" gives us an insight into the whole knowledge of Dante's age, including morals, science and theology, and no work ever published, except the Bible, has been so widely translated, so frequently published in different editions, or been the subject of so many books.

A Poet Laureate

There is a curious resemblance between the careers of Italy's two greatest poets, Dante and Petrarch. Both belonged to Florence; Dante was driven from his home by his enemies, while Petrarch's father shared the same fate at the same time. Each, again, loved deeply a beautiful lady whom he was never able to marry, for Petrarch's Laura is only less famous than Dante's Beatrice.

CHAUCER AND HIS KING

Rischgitz.

When Geoffrey Chaucer was born, rather more than six centuries ago, England was only just beginning to have a language of her own. The poorer people and most of the merchants and tradesmen had spoken the Anglo-Saxon tongue; the upper classes spoke French or a language of French origin. But the two languages were gradually becoming merged into English, which adapted Norman, French, Latin, and even more Anglo-Saxon words into what was really a new language. Chaucer was the first person to use this English language for poetry and he devoted himself to making English an adequate instrument of literature. His greatest work was *The Canterbury Tales* which describes the pilgrims who set out from the Tabard Inn at Southwark to journey to the shrine of Thomas à Becket. On the road to Canterbury different members of the party tell their stories and Chaucer gives us twenty-four of these tales. This picture, painted by Ford Madox Brown, is in the Tate Gallery, London, and shows Geoffrey Chaucer reading his poems to King Edward III and members of his Court.

But there the resemblance ends, for, while the great Dante's last years were passed in exile and misery, Petrarch rose to great fame.

Petrarch's father was a lawyer. The boy was well educated, and afterwards travelled in France, Germany and Flanders. He was a friend of the Pope and of many kings and great nobles. He was actually offered the high post of Papal Secretary, but refused it. He had good looks and fine manners, and was immensely popular.

The climax of his career was on Easter Sunday, 1341, when he ascended the Capitol at Rome, clad in the robes of his friend, the King of Naples, and was acclaimed Poet Laureate.

Petrarch's fame rests chiefly on his Canzoniere, sonnets and songs, which were inspired by his love for the beautiful Laura. Yet Laura married another man.

"A Merry Heart"

Petrarch was born in 1304. Thirty-six years later a boy was born in England called Geoffrey Chaucer, who was destined to make an undying name as England's first great poet.

When Chaucer was born England was so much under the foreign yoke that French was still the official language. But the change was coming, for in 1362 it was ordered that English should be used in Courts of Law, and in the next year Parliament was for the first time opened by an English speech. England was changing, and it was into this changing England that Chaucer was born.

He was the son of an innkeeper, but we know nothing of his boyhood until 1357, when we find him as page in the service of the Duchess of Clarence. Two years later he was in France, fighting.

Truth and Honour

Again we lose sight of our poet, but eight years later find him not only writing verse, but becoming a very important personage, being sent on missions by the King to Italy, Flanders and France, and rising to be Comptroller of Customs for the Port of London. Later, in 1386, he lost his high position, and his last years were spent as a pensioner. But he never repined:

> " A merry heart goes all the day,
>   Your sad tires in a mile—a."

These lines seem to have been his motto. There was something very fine in Chaucer's character which shines out all through his writings. The age of chivalry had not yet passed away and you see it reflected among his pilgrims.

His knight, for instance:

> " . . . he loved chevalrie,
> Trouthe and honour, freedom and courtesie."

One feels that these were the traits that Chaucer himself most admired.

His writings are coloured by the Troubadour literature of France, which he knew well. He was also well acquainted with the works of Dante.

SHAKESPEARE AND MILTON

SPENSER AND SIR WALTER RALEIGH

Like Chaucer, Edmund Spenser was a courtier and moved in high places. In 1580 he was sent by Queen Elizabeth to Ireland, and while there had among his neighbours Sir Walter Raleigh, himself a poet of no mean order. This picture, from the brush of John Claxton, shows us Spenser reading his most famous poem, " The Faerie Queene," to Raleigh. Sir Walter persuaded Spenser to return with him to London and publish his poem. He did so, and at once became famous.

FOR a century and a half after the death of Chaucer no great poet arose in England. Then dawned the Elizabethan age.

Edmund Spenser

Men's imaginations were stimulated by wider travel and tales of the new world in the West; the master works of classical times were for the first time printed and spread abroad; and there arose a number of great writers, among whom was Edmund Spenser, who was the first to reveal the marvellous resources of the English language. His verses have been called " A labyrinth of sweet sounds that would cloy by their sweetness, but that the ear is constantly relieved and enchanted by their continued variety of modulation."

Spenser was a Londoner, born in Smithfield. He came from a noble family, " of which," he says, " I meanest boast myself to be." In spite of his genius, he lived and died in poor circumstances. He was one of the six poor scholars of Merchant Taylors' School and later went to Cambridge. His " Shepheardes Calender," published in 1579, was his first work and opened a new epoch in English literature. For a time he was secretary to the Lord Deputy of Ireland and was granted land in Ireland.

Much of his life was lived in Ireland, but his house was burned in Hugh O'Neil's insurrection and he ended his life in poverty. Yet even in his lifetime great fame was his, and after his death his body was laid in Westminster Abbey.

The Greatest of Poets

While opinions differ as to who was the greatest painter, there can be no doubt on the question of the greatest poet. Even Germans admit that Shakespeare has no rival. The more we read and learn about the early life of William Shakespeare the more amazing it appears that a boy brought up as he was, educated at the Free School at Stratford with "small Latin and less Greek," could have produced the mighty works we all know so well.

For Fear of Arrest

His father, well off at first, fell upon hard times when William was only fourteen, and we know that he did not attend church for fear of being arrested for debt. William himself fell into bad company and got into trouble for deer-stealing.

We know he went to London somewhere about the year 1585, but of what he did there we have no record. It is said that he held horses at the play house door. We have to skip seven years to 1592, when we know that he was already both an actor and a writer of plays.

In the following year, 1593, his "Venus and Adonis" was published. This he calls "the first heir of his invention." It is doubtful which of his plays came first. There is some evidence that it was the first part of "Henry VI." We know, however, that "Love's Labour's Lost," "The Comedy of Errors" and "Two Gentlemen of Verona" are among the first he wrote.

In 1593-94 came the wonderful "Midsummer Night's Dream," with its lovely fairy poetry. In that year Shakespeare himself acted before Queen Elizabeth. He became a shareholder in the Globe Theatre, which was on the south side of London Bridge, and made enough money to buy the house, New Place, in his native town. Later he bought land near Stratford for £320, then of much higher value than now.

It is said that it was by Queen Elizabeth's own desire that he wrote "The Merry Wives of Windsor," all done in fourteen days.

In or about 1600 his method of

WHEN TITANIA WAS ENCHANTED   *W. F. Mansell.*

Written in 1594, "A Midsummer Night's Dream" is an example of the wonderful imagination of Shakespeare at its best. It is a fairy comedy, and our picture, painted by Sir Edwin Landseer, shows the scene when Titania, having been enchanted by her husband, Oberon, King of the Fairies, while she slept, falls in love with Bottom the Weaver, to whom the fairy Puck has given an ass's head.

THE CANTERBURY TALES

Geoffrey Chaucer (1340–1400) was England's first great poet and there was much in his character that shines out through his writings. In his time pilgrimages were made to the shrine of Thomas à Becket, and such pilgrims inspired the Canterbury Tales, of which twenty-three were finished. In the verses twenty-nine people, including the poet, travel together, each to tell a tale on the way into Kent, and again on the way back. The picture above shows the company on the road, representing all types, and here are two lines taken from the prologue: " In fellowship, and pilgrims were they all, That toward Canterbury wolden ride."

SHYLOCK'S ANSWER TO SALANIO AND SALARINO

In the wide range of characters created by Shakespeare one of the most outstanding is that of the Jewish moneylender, Shylock. He plays an important part in that wonderful play "The Merchant of Venice," in which comedy hovers at times on the verge of tragedy. In the picture above, painted by Sir John Gilbert, R.A., Shylock is seen in a street in Venice, speaking to Salanio and Salarino, two friends of Antonio, the merchant from whom Shylock has demanded the fulfilment of his bond. Here he defends his conduct by comparison with their Christian code: "The villainy you teach me I will execute; and it shall go hard but I will better the instruction."

FALSTAFF AND HIS TWO LADIES

H. Dixon and Son.

Much of the fun of Shakespeare's " Merry Wives of Windsor " concerns the love affairs of the swashbuckling Sir John Falstaff with Mistress Page and Mistress Ford, and his escape from an awkward predicament by hiding in a basket of dirty linen. In this picture Sir John is literally in the hands of the two ladies, while in the background is seen the famous clothes-basket.

writing changed, and from comedy he turned to tragedy. " Hamlet " was written in 1602, " King Lear " in 1607. All through his life his work ripens and improves until it reaches heights hitherto untouched and never since equalled.

In March, 1616, Shakespeare fell ill of a fever, and on April 23rd his great spirit passed.

Thomas Carlyle has said, " The genius of Shakespeare is more potent than any other agency in binding together the scattered members of the British Empire."

" O Rare Ben Jonson ! "

These words are cut in the slab which lies over the grave of this great poet in Westminster Abbey. We might easily fill the whole space allotted to poets in this volume with records of the great

Elizabethans, and it is difficult to pick and choose among so many. We cannot, however, leave out Ben Jonson, in one of whose plays Shakespeare himself acted. Like Shakespeare, he was both actor and dramatist, and in 1598 Meres wrote of him that he is " our best for Tragedie."

He was educated at Westminster School and became a soldier. He fought in the Low Countries, where he distinguished himself by killing one of the enemy in single combat. He married, but says of his wife: " She was a shrew but honest." Once he went away from her on a visit to a friend and stayed *seven years*. He had a duel with another actor and killed him, for which he was tried and branded in the thumb. In 1598 his play, " Every Man in his Humour," was produced. This

FROM "MACBETH" AND "OTHELLO"

Macbeth and Banquo here meet the three witches on the heath, and Macbeth is hailed by them as future King of Scotland. Made ambitious by their prophecies, he became King after murdering his sovereign Duncan while he was asleep. Banquo later shared a similar fate.

Othello the Moor is here relating the story of his life and adventures to Desdemona and her father, the Venetian senator Brabantio. "She loved me for the dangers I had passed, And I loved her that she did pity them." (Act I., Sc. 3.) The artist, E. Becker, represents the recital.

The original of this picture hangs in the National Gallery, London. It was painted by John S. Sargent, R.A., and shows the late Dame Ellen Terry in one of her most powerful and also most successful parts as Lady Macbeth, wife of Macbeth. This is one of the greatest of Shakespeare's plays and was probably written in 1606.

THE TRAGEDY OF KING LEAR

" King Lear " is one of the noblest, and the saddest, of Shakespeare's tragedies. Lear, King of Britain, decides to abdicate in favour of his three daughters. Cordelia, the youngest, professes daughterly affection, but is disinherited by him, her portion going to her two sisters. This picture, by Ford Madox Brown, shows us Lear passing sentence on his daughter.

While her two sisters treat their father most cruelly, Cordelia remains faithful to him. She brings an army, entrusted to her by her husband, the King of France, to his aid. The same artist here depicts Lear asleep in his daughter's camp, and Cordelia pitying his fallen condition. Virtue in this case is not rewarded. Cordelia is murdered, and Lear dies of grief.

TWO FAMOUS COMEDIES

By permission of the Corporation of Birmingham.

Shakespeare was a master of comedy as well as of tragedy. This picture, by Sir John Gilbert, represents a scene in " The Taming of the Shrew," probably one of the poet's earlier plays. We see before us Petruchio, a gentleman of Verona, and his recently-wedded, shrewish wife Katharina, whom he has just brought home to undergo a course of " taming."

Photos : Rischgitz.

This is a scene in the Third Act of " Twelfth Night." Malvolio, the Countess Olivia's steward, is making himself ridiculous before his mistress and her maid Maria, in order to win Olivia's favour. He has been hoaxed by a letter concocted by Maria, but purporting to come from the Countess, in which yellow hose, cross-gartered, and a jaunty demeanour are admired— though really detested by Olivia. As a result of his prank he is locked up for a time.

is the one in which Shakespeare acted.

But he was greatest as a writer of songs. He wrote "Drink to Me Only With Thine Eyes," which has remained popular for more than 300 years.

The Blind Poet

Second only to Shakespeare in the roll of English poets is John Milton, born while Shakespeare was still alive, in the year 1608. His father, a Puritan, was a man of property and a clever musician. Young Milton had a thoroughly good education at St. Paul's School and at Cambridge. He took his M.A. degree in 1632, but instead of taking Holy Orders, went to live with his father at Horton, in Buckinghamshire, where he settled down and began to study with the object of becoming a poet. His is perhaps the only instance of a man deliberately dedicating his life to poetry.

There he wrote "L'Allegro" and "Il Penseroso," and, later, "Comus" and "Lycidas." This last resulted from the news of the death of his great friend, Edward King, drowned at sea.

He went to Italy and was made very welcome. Since his Italian friends could not, of course, appreciate his English verse, it would seem that he must have appealed to them as a man rather than as a writer. He married, but his wife left him. She could not stand the severe puritanism of Milton's character and home.

When the Civil War broke out Milton's pen defended the actions of the Puritans. The Restoration and accession of Charles II. drove him into retirement, but presently he was able to live in London, where he wrote his noble "Paradise Lost," the copyright of which he sold for £5.

Later in life he married again, this time more happily, and in spite of his blindness and the fact that the Great Fire of London nearly ruined him, his last years were not unhappy. He died November 8th, 1674.

Rischgitz.

THE MEETING OF MILTON AND MARVELL

This reproduction of a picture by the celebrated English painter, George Henry Boughton (1833–1905), shows us Andrew Marvell. the poet and politician, visiting the much greater poet, John Milton, at his country home. Though Marvell served Cromwell, he, unlike Milton, was a monarchist at heart, and after the Restoration was able to protect the author of "Paradise Lost" from reprisals by the royalists.

THE BLIND POET AT WORK

At the age of forty-four Milton became totally blind, and had to dictate his poems. The painter of this picture, John Calcott Horsley (1817–1903), has chosen for his subject the blind poet composing one of his latest works, "Samson Agonistes," a tragedy. It is thought that Milton used the story of Samson because it had strong resemblance to his own, which included much unhappiness and ended in blindness. Behind him is his Quaker secretary, Thomas Ellwood.

FROM DRYDEN TO BURNS

Rischgitz.

POPE'S INTRODUCTION TO DRYDEN

When John Dryden was sixty-nine years old he made the acquaintance of Alexander Pope, destined to succeed him as England's leading poet. This picture by Eyre Crowe records the incident of Pope, then a lad of twelve, being brought to the old poet as he sat in the seat of honour in Will's Coffee House, London. From the kindly reception given him by the veteran dated Pope's staunch admiration of Dryden and his works.

LIKE Milton, John Dryden was educated at Cambridge. He was at Trinity College, and in the records we find that he was punished for an offence against discipline on October 19th, 1652. His father died in 1654 and left him fairly well off, and the next thing we know of him is his marriage to Lady Elizabeth Howard, daughter of the Duke of Berkshire.

When or how he began to write is not known, but in 1670 he became Poet Laureate. For fourteen years he wrote only plays, and it was not until he was fifty years old that his full powers showed themselves. Then he wrote " Absalom and Achitophel " and " The Hind and the Panther." His rhymed translations of Virgil and Juvenal are very well known. He had a great power of writing splendid, if somewhat ungraceful, verse, and deserves to rank among great poets.

A Brilliant Wit

If Dryden's poetry can be compared to a broadsword, that of Pope resembles the flashing play of a light rapier. Alexander Pope had a brilliant wit and a command of English such as no Englishman had before and few have equalled since his day. It has been said of him that he was without rival as an artist in words. As a man he was not as great as in his art, for he was both vain and vindictive. On the other hand, he had lovable qualities, made many friends, and was always kind to those who were in want. In excuse of his less amiable qualities, it must be remembered that his health was wretched, and that he was somewhat deformed.

His father, a linen-draper, gave him a poor education, yet the boy showed his talent early and was only twelve when he wrote his " Ode on Solitude," a marvellous production for one so young. His "Essay on Criticism" brought him into the front rank, but it was his great translation of the Iliad that won for him not only fame, but a comfortable fortune, and he became the literary lion of London. He died in 1744 of dropsy.

Pope's Successor

While Pope was still alive a revolt had begun against the classical style of poetry, which aimed at perfection of form but failed in spirit or inspiration. James Thomson, a Scotsman, published his famous "Seasons" in 1730, in which, for the first time, we get descriptions of rural life told in charming verse.

Then came Gray, whose "Elegy Written in a Country Churchyard" has brought him imperishable fame.

Thomas Gray was at school at Eton, and a friend of Horace Walpole, son of the Prime Minister. He became a shy, studious man, who loved books, pictures, china and flowers. He was, perhaps, the first Englishman to realise the true beauty of the mountains of Scotland. He wrote little, yet his verse ranks very high among English poetry.

A third poet born in an age remarkable for its scarcity of poets was Oliver Goldsmith, born in Ireland in 1728. Young Goldsmith was sent to Trinity College, Dublin, where he got involved in a riot and fell into great disgrace.

Rischgitz.

DOCTOR JOHNSON AND OLIVER GOLDSMITH

Oliver Goldsmith was often in dire straits for money. One day his landlady called in the sheriff's officer to compel him to pay arrears of rent. At his wits' end, Goldsmith sent a messenger to Dr. Johnson, who had himself known the miseries of dire poverty and at once came to see him. Goldsmith had just finished a manuscript and the Doctor, after glancing at it, saw that there was good material in it. He sold it for £60 to a publisher, who for this small sum became owner of the famous "Vicar of Wakefield." This picture was painted by E. M. Ward, R.A.

In the end he ran away from College, but his elder brother patched things up and Oliver returned and took his degree.

"The Vicar of Wakefield"

No poet had a more adventurous youth than Goldsmith. He visited Scotland, Holland, France, Germany and Italy, wandering on foot and living goodness knows how. It was 1756 before he returned to England and became assistant to an apothecary. Then he turned proof-reader and finally became editor of the *Monthly Review*. He lost that work and was so hard up that he had to pawn his clothes to pay his landlady. But his essays had attracted the attention of booksellers and he began to write steadily. In 1766 " The Vicar of Wakefield " was published, and his reputation was made. In 1774 he wrote the famous play, " She Stoops to Conquer," and in the same year died of a fever. Of Goldsmith the great Dr. Johnson said: " He touched nothing that he did not adorn."

William Cowper, famous as author of " The Task," was born in 1731 and was sent to Westminster School, which he hated. He was a sensitive man and rather delicate. He was very fond of the country and animals, and in his letters there is a delightful description of the hares which he tamed and which roved round his study like cats or dogs.

The odd thing is that Cowper was middle-aged before he began to write, and nearly fifty when his friend, Lady Austen, persuaded him to write blank verse. No doubt he took Milton as his model, and though he had none of Milton's grandeur, his verse is charmingly sweet and serious. In 1794 a pension of £300 a year was granted him, but he did not live long to enjoy it, for he died in the year 1800.

Cowper was far in advance of his age. In a century when dumb animals had no rights under the law, and when bull-baiting and bear-baiting were common, he wrote:

" I would not enter on my list of
    friends,
Though graced with polished man-
    ners and fine sense
Yet wanting sensibility, the man
Who needlessly sets foot upon a
    worm."

Scotland's National Poet

" Is not ' The Task ' a glorious poem ? " wrote Robert Burns. " The religion of ' The Task ' . . . is the religion of God and Nature, the religion that exalts and ennobles man."

JOHN GILPIN'S FAMOUS RIDE   *Rischgitz.*

A certain haberdasher of Paternoster Row is said to have been the original of John Gilpin. The story of his adventures amused the serious-minded Cowper so much that he spent a restless night laughing and turning it into rhyme. His ballad appeared anonymously in a newspaper, was recited by a popular actor, and at once achieved an enormous success. The artist, Thomas Stothard, here depicts Gilpin riding at full gallop past the house in Edmonton where he was to dine with his wife, who is waving frantically to him from the balcony above.

Though Burns and Cowper never met, each enjoyed the work of the other. Burns was born in 1759, the son of a small farmer, who in spite of his poverty gave his son a good education. True, he had little Latin and no Greek, but he knew French and was well read for his day.

Verses of 1785

In 1784 his father died, and Burns had to try to farm for himself. He made a mess of it and turned to writing. " If," says a critic, " we had only the verses of 1785, Burns would remain the greatest of popular poets." He wrote of what he knew, sketches of what he saw around him. " The Cottar's Saturday Night," " The Twa Herds," " The Jolly Beggars." Burns had a passionate love of the beautiful, a keen sense of humour and a deep sympathy with all those around him. Many of his poems are songs, beautiful, tender and passionate. His work is the very essence of poetry, and could rise to great heights.

He proved that when in 1795 he

Rischgitz.

THE NATIONAL POET OF SCOTLAND

No writer is closer to the hearts of Scotsmen than Robert Burns, who has never been equalled as a poet in the use of the Scots dialect. Had he written nothing but " Auld Lang Syne," his name would still be a household word among English-speaking people.

wrote " A Man's a Man for a' that," two lines of which have been quoted perhaps more often than any other:

" The rank is but the guinea's stamp,
The man's the gowd for a' that."

Burns is by far the greatest of Scottish poets and one of the greatest of British.

FIVE GREAT ENGLISH POETS

THE HOME OF COLERIDGE

In 1909 the National Trust acquired this house at Nether Stowey, in Somerset, a few miles from Bridgwater, because for three years (1797–1800) it was occupied by the poet Samuel Taylor Coleridge, who wrote some of his best-known works there, including " Kubla Khan " and " The Ancient Mariner." While at Stowey, Coleridge had William Wordsworth as his neighbour and great friend.

IT was within sight of Derwent, " fairest of all rivers " in the poet's eyes, that William Wordsworth was born in the year 1770. He was educated at Hawkshead School and at Cambridge. In 1790 and again in the following year he visited France, and at first rejoiced in the liberation of France from its ancient tyranny. But the hideous anarchy and murderings that followed saddened him and turned his mind back to his own country. Of all our poets none had a more passionate devotion to England than William Wordsworth.

Although he was so entirely different from Burns, Wordsworth dearly loved his poetry and wrote of him:

" As him who walked in glory and in joy
    Following his plough along the mountain side."

For a time Wordsworth was badly off, but in 1795 a friend left him £900, a sum which was a small fortune to a man of Wordsworth's simple tastes. In 1802 he married Mary Hutchinson, whom he had known since they were both children together, and from then on lived a very happy and peaceful life in his much-loved dales. In 1839 Oxford gave him an honorary degree and in 1843 he became Poet Laureate. On his visit to London he met Tennyson, of whom he said: " He is the first of our living poets, and I hope will live to give the world still better things."

He lived to be eighty, was buried at Grasmere in the dales which he praised so often in beautiful verse. Of all our great poets Wordsworth's life was the happiest and that because his whole heart was full of love for God, for beauty and for his fellow men.

" Silas Tomkyn Comberbacke "

What possessed Samuel Taylor Coleridge to give himself such an amazing name as this, under which he enlisted in the 15th Dragoons, he only could have told. In any case his enlistment was a crazy business, for he never learned to ride or manage a horse. Luckily some of his friends found him and bought him out.

Coleridge, son of a Devonshire parson, was an eccentric genius who read the " Arabian Nights " when he was four years old, and a little later was reading Homer in the Greek for the mere pleasure of reading it. At school he used to swim in the river in his clothes and let them dry on him, with the natural result that he got rheumatic fever. Later he and others formed a plan for going to America and starting a sort of Socialist colony, but luckily that fell through.

" The Ancient Mariner "

He sold a volume of poems for thirty guineas, and on the strength of this got married. He met Wordsworth, and the two became friends. Wordsworth came all the way down to Somerset to stay with him. He wrote prose and verse for the *Morning Post*.

Coleridge was a brilliant genius, but eccentric and undependable, and in the course of his wanderings he acquired the habit of taking opium, which very nearly wrecked both his health and mind. Friends were good to him, especially Wordsworth, and by degrees weaned him from the drug habit, so that in his old age he did some fine writing.

That fragment of a poem, " Kubla Khan," is perhaps his best known work. It is said that he conceived it in a dream, and was writing it down when he was interrupted, and that then the

W. F. Mansell.

ENGLAND'S GREATEST PHILOSOPHICAL POET

This is a portrait, by F. R. Pickersgill (1820–1900), of William Wordsworth, who wrote so beautifully about Nature and simple things of everyday life. His poems teach us that beauty is not confined to what is rare or new, but lies all around for us to see, if we trouble to look for it.

rest of it passed from his mind. " The Ancient Mariner " is another of his works that will never be forgotten. Coleridge loved Nature, and wrote:

" No waste so vacant, but may well
   employ

Each faculty of sense, and keep the
    heart
Awake to love and beauty."

Peer and Poet

Lord Byron was another of the great
school of English poets who, like
Wordsworth, Coleridge and Shelley,
came under the spell of the French
Revolution, and hoped that it augured
a new dawn for humanity.

Of Byron, says his biographer, Professor Nicholls: " This scion of a long
line of lawless bloods . . . was specially
created to . . . smite the convention-
ality, which is the tyrant of England,
with the hammer of Thor and to sear
. . . the hollow hypocrisy, sham taste,
sham morals, sham religion of the
society by which he was surrounded."

Byron's life was a tragedy. Captain
Byron, his father, was a bad man, and
the boy's youth was made miserable
by quarrels between his father and
mother. Also he had a club foot,
which was a constant torture to him.
He was handicapped with an irritable
vanity, and his life at Harrow and
Cambridge was not a happy one.

His first book, " Hours of Idleness,"
was written in 1807. It was poor stuff
and was savagely criticised in the
Edinburgh Review.

" English Bards and Scottish Re-
viewers " was Byron's answer, and was
better work. His first great success was
" Childe Harold's Pilgrimage " in 1812,
which ran through seven editions. It is
said that he wrote " The Corsair " in ten
days and " The Bride of Abydos " in four.

At this date he was the darling of
London society, but this brought him
little happiness. He went to Italy and
lived there and later joined the movement for the independence of Greece.
He went to Greece in 1823, struggled
hopelessly against all sorts of difficulties, caught rheumatic fever, and
died on April 19th, 1824.

Sad Shelley

Descendant of an old and honourable
family, Percy Bysshe Shelley was
educated at Eton and Oxford, but was
sent down from the University for
publishing a pamphlet called: " The
Necessity of Atheism." While still at
Eton he had begun to write, but his
early efforts were very crude. Then he
married Harriet Westbrook. He was
nineteen and she only sixteen. She
was pretty but foolish, and the marriage
was a terrible failure which clouded the
whole of Shelley's life. For a long
time most of Shelley's work consisted
of revolutionary pamphlets. It was
not until 1815 that he produced his
first work of note, the poem " Alastor."
In the following year his wife Harriet
was found drowned in the Serpentine,
and the shock to Shelley was a heavy
one.

Lost in a Storm

Later, he went to live in Italy, and
there his greatest and best work was
done. His last great poem, " The
Triumph of Life," was written in his
boat near Casa Magni, his home close
to the Gulf of Spezia. It was never
finished, for while still at work he
heard that his friend, Leigh Hunt,
with his family, was arriving, and he
and Lieutenant Williams set sail for
Leghorn to meet them. A storm came
on, the boat upset, and later the
bodies of the poet and his companion
were found on the shore.

Like many great poets, Shelley was
far ahead of his time. He wrote:

" Never will peace and human nature
    meet
Till free and equal man and woman
    greet
Domestic peace."

That was a century before women
were granted the vote.

A Poet of Beauty

John Keats' first volume of poems
was published in 1817. Only four years
after, the poet died at the early age of
twenty-five. Yet in his short life he

found time to write so many beautiful things that he will always hold a high place among English poets.

John Keats was born in London, at Moorfields, and on leaving school he was apprenticed to a surgeon; but he disliked his work and soon gave it up to devote himself entirely to poetry, and it is our gain that he did so. For although he was to live but a few more years, his genius developed rapidly.

Magical Words

Keats was a poet of beauty. To create beauty was his aim, and no one can say that he did not succeed in this. He had no lesson to convey in his writing, unless it was that of the magical power of words. It is this idea of his, that poetry should be written for its own sake, and without any thought of a moral lesson or secondary purpose, that gives his work something in common with the poetry of the Greeks. One of the finest things he has left us is his ode " On a Grecian Urn."

Keats was a great lover of Nature, and a keen observer, and this is revealed in such beautiful poems as his

W. F. Mansell.

OUR MOST PICTURESQUE POET

George Gordon Byron became a peer by inheritance and the writer of romantic poems by genius and inclination. Of a restless nature, he travelled extensively, and he died in Greece, whither he had taken a brig equipped at his own expense to aid the Greeks against the Turks.

odes " To a Nightingale " and " To Autumn."

" Writ in Water "

At his own request, he had his tombstone inscribed with the words: " Here lies one whose name was writ in water." But we may say of Keats, as he said of the nightingale: " Thou wast not born for death, immortal Bird! "

John Keats died in Rome in 1821, and was buried there in the old Protestant Cemetery.

FAMOUS VICTORIAN POETS

By permission of the Corporation of Liverpool. *W. F. Mansell.*

ON THE ROAD TO CAMELOT

You have at least heard of Tennyson's well-known poem about " The Lady of Shalott," who lived on an island of that name. This picture, by G. H. Boughton, the original of which is in the Walker Art Gallery, Liverpool, illustrates the lines of the poem : " Sometimes a troop of damsels glad, Sometimes a curly shepherd-lad, Or long-hair'd page in crimson clad, Goes by to tower'd Camelot."

IT is the fate of many poets to die before the world has roused to the fact that they were great; but, happily, Alfred, Lord Tennyson never suffered in this way. His genius was recognised while he was still a young man, and though many critics pelted him with abuse, at any rate he was never ignored.

" In Memoriam "

Alfred Tennyson was the fourth of seven sons of a Lincolnshire rector, and these brothers seem to have been amazingly fond of one another. To Frederick and Charles, his two elder brothers, Alfred was devoted. It was Charles who, when Alfred was a tiny boy, gave him a slate and told him to write some verses about the flowers in the garden.

" Yes," said Charles, when he read what the little lad had written, " you can write, Alfred."

Alfred went to Cambridge, where he made many friends, among them Arthur Hallam, who, had he lived, might have been one of the greatest men of the nineteenth century. Tennyson's first poems appeared in 1830 and brought him much praise and some blame. For years the poet worked hard and lived hardly, for he was very poor. It was not until 1847 that his work, " The Princess," written in blank verse, brought him real fame and led to his becoming Poet Laureate in 1850. In the same year he published " In Memoriam," as a tribute to Arthur Hallam. " Maud," with its passion and beauty, was published in 1855. Ten years later appeared the " Idylls of the King."

Some men, once they have secured their fame, slacken off, but Tennyson never did so, and his works are spread out over a period of more than half a century. In 1884 Queen Victoria made him a baron of the United Kingdom. When he died, in 1892, his body found sepulchre in Westminster Abbey.

THE LADY OF SHALOTT

Threatened with a curse if she looked out through her window, the Lady of Shalott watched passers-by in a mirror. One day the gay Sir Lancelot rode past on his way to Camelot. Forgetful of the curse, she stepped to the window to watch him. "The curse is come upon me," cried the Lady of Shalott." Embarking in a boat, she floated, singing, down the river, but before she reached Camelot she was dead. This picture, painted by J. W. Waterhouse, R.A., shows her making her fateful journey.

Tennyson, perhaps more than any other poet, realised the great truth that " Love is the fulfilling of the Law." He wrote:

> " And he that shuts out love, in turn
>   shall be
> Shut out from love, and on her
>   threshold lie
> Howling in outer darkness."

He believed, too, in human brotherhood as:

> " The one far off divine event
>   Towards which the whole creation
>   moves."

The Difficult Poet

Robert Browning's style is often so obscure and difficult that the ordinary reader turns away from his poems with a feeling that they are too hard to read. Yet few, if any, men ever had more intense human sympathy or greater gifts of imagination than Browning. " The Ring and the Book," an immense work of more than 21,000 lines, is a marvellous achievement and full of splendid passages.

Browning was born in London in 1812 and was educated by a private tutor. Before he was twenty years old he had a threefold reputation as poet, musician and modeller. In 1846 he married Elizabeth Barrett, herself the most distinguished of modern women poets. The two took up their home in Florence, where they lived in the greatest happiness.

If you want to know what was Browning's belief, you have it in these lines of his:

> " But evil on itself shall back recoil
>   And mix no more with goodness;
>   if this fail
>   The pillared firmament is rotten-
>   ness
>   And earth's base built on stubble."

By permission of the Corporation of Liverpool.   Rischgitz.

THE LILY MAID OF ASTOLAT

In one of his Idylls of the King, entitled " Lancelot and Elaine," Tennyson tells the sad story of Elaine, the " Lily Maid of Astolat," who fell deeply in love with Lancelot and died of a broken heart when her love was not returned. Her body was laid on a barge steered by a dumb attendant, and carried down stream to Camelot, where King Arthur gave it a royal burial. Our illustration is reproduced from a painting by Mrs. Sophie Anderson, in the Liverpool Gallery.

Rischgitz.

THE POET-PEER

Alfred Tennyson was both the most popular poet of the Victorian era, and a very learned man. He treated an astonishing variety of subjects and adorned most of them with very beautiful language. The author of the splendid " Idylls," the haunting " In Memoriam," the touching " May Queen " and " Enoch Arden," and the stirring " Ulysses " and " Charge of the Light Brigade "—to mention but a few of his works—was a poet indeed. He only of our poets laureate received the honour of a peerage. Our portrait is from a painting by G. F. Watts, R.A.

Browning died on December 12th, 1889, and his body was buried with those of other great poets in Westminster Abbey.

The Poet of the Sea

Born in 1837, Algernon Charles Swinburne belonged to an old North Country family and was educated at

Eton and Oxford. He was a great friend of Dante Rossetti, whose story is given in our series of famous painters, and he began writing while still quite young. He was only twenty-seven when his " Atalanta in Calydon " was published, a masterpiece which proved that the world was richer by another great poet.

Swinburne was, above all writers, the poet of the sea. He knew the sea in every mood and could describe those moods in language which stirs the blood of every sea-lover. He wrote plays and prose as well as poetry, but it is as a poet that he will be remembered.

Though in his writing a rebel, Swinburne's life was on the whole a quiet one, and the last thirty years of it he spent in the house of his friend, Theodore Watts Dunton.

Rischgitz.

THE PIED PIPER OF HAMELIN

Though Robert Browning's poems as a whole can hardly be regarded as popular, most children are acquainted with two of them : " How they brought the Good News from Ghent to Aix " and " The Pied Piper of Hamelin." In the second of these, Browning versifies the legend of the piper who in 1284 freed Hamelin of a plague of rats ; and, when the promised money reward was not paid him, drew away all the children of the town by his piping and led them through an opening in a hill, which closed behind them. This picture of the Piper and his following is reproduced from a painting by J. E. Christie.

LONGFELLOW, EMERSON AND WHITMAN

Rischgitz.

THE RETURN OF HIAWATHA

The " Song of Hiawatha," published in 1855, is probably the most popular of the poems written by the American poet, Henry Wadsworth Longfellow (1807–1882). It ran through thirty editions in one year. In it Longfellow describes human character and life and natural objects from the point of view of an Indian minstrel, not from that of a white man. Our illustration, reproduced from a painting in watercolour by Houghton, shows us Hiawatha returning home with Minnehaha, who became his bride.

OF all American poets the most popular among English-speaking people is Longfellow. " The Courtship of Miles Standish," " Evangeline " and " Hiawatha " are read in every school where English is taught, and many young folk who have not much love for poetry will read " Hiawatha " for its story and the delightful word-pictures of Red Indian life.

A Poet of the People

Henry Wadsworth Longfellow was born in the State of Maine in 1807, and his parents, who were well off, gave him a good education. At college he gained such distinction in languages that he was sent to Europe to continue his studies. When he returned he married, but his charming wife did not live long, and after her death Longfellow became Professor of Modern Languages at Harvard University.

In 1841 appeared his ballads, " The Skeleton in Armour," " The Village Blacksmith," " The Wreck of the Hesperus," and others, and the reading world awoke to the fact that a new and very gifted poet had arisen.

" The Building of the Ship " is, of all his poems, the best loved in America, but " Hiawatha " is most popular on the Eastern side of the Atlantic. Longfellow was a splendid-looking man. With his high forehead, massive head, full beard and silvery hair, he attracted the attention of everyone. And his nature was as fine as his looks, for he was always calm and amiable. Everyone loved him and when he visited England he was received with the greatest honour.

He was charmingly modest. He did not consider himself fit to stand among those whom he describes as:

"The bards sublime
Whose distant footsteps echo
In the corridors of time."

Yet there are poets with greater genius than his whose works we could more easily spare than those of this notable American writer.

By permission of the Corporation of Preston.   *Rischgitz.*
THE COURTSHIP OF MILES STANDISH
This picture illustrates the close of Longfellow's charming poem named above. Priscilla is riding to her new home on a "milk-white steer," holding the hand of her young husband, John Alden, to whom she has just been married. Readers who have not read the poem are advised to read it. The original painting from which this engraving was made is the work of L. J. Pott.

The Boy in Blue Nankeens

Somewhere about the year 1815 a boy attending the grammar school at Concord, Massachusetts, told his parents that there was a newcomer to the school, "a spiritual-looking boy in blue nankeens," whose looks he liked very much.

This boy was Ralph Waldo Emerson, destined to great fame as poet and essayist. He came of a good New England family, and showed his genius early, for at ten years old he was turning Virgil into English verse for his own amusement. He went to Harvard University and afterwards became a schoolmaster. He was much liked by his pupils and, it is said, never had need to punish them. Afterwards he became a minister, but his views on religious matters led to a difference with his church and he left the pulpit and began a new career. He took to lecturing and soon made a name. He visited England and made friends with the great Carlyle, and these two men, utterly different in temper, began a correspondence that lasted for forty years.

His Earliest Poems

In 1836 Emerson's first book of poems appeared. It was called very simply "Nature," and it took twelve years to sell 500 copies. But this was followed by "The American Scholar," a lecture delivered at Harvard, the echoes of which rang round the English-speaking world. It was a new event in the history of American literature and made a great reputation for Emerson.

PIONEERS! O PIONEERS!

Specially drawn for this work.

Walt Whitman, the great American poet, cared nothing for the rules of verse-writing, and it was a long while before his work was widely read. Now, however, he stands in a class by himself, and the picture above illustrates his poem, " Pioneers! O Pioneers! " The drawing reminds us of the words: " We to-day's procession heading, we the route for travel clearing."

Walt Whitman

The son of a carpenter, who was also a farmer and later a house-builder, Walt Whitman, the great American poet, was born at Long Island in 1819. He has written of his " perfect mother " who much impressed her son by her sound sense and deep affection. After an elementary education until he was twelve, Whitman worked in carpentry, printing, teaching and journalism and wandered through many parts of the United States. He was a voracious reader, but it was his wide experience among different classes of people during his wander-years through the West and South that gave him his understanding and sympathy with all sorts and conditions of men.

The Spirit of America

His poems and writings were not widely popular in his own country for quite a long time, yet to-day he is recognised as the most powerful literary force in American history and as one who expressed the spirit of his country as a great democracy that would give the world a free society welded together by love and equality.

Sometimes his poems are not easily understood; he was not a writer of smooth rhyming verses which tripped easily from the tongue. He was the imaginative poet anxious to give a vision of a larger life for mankind. It was of another outstanding leader of democracy and mighty fighter for freedom, President Lincoln, that Whitman wrote his lines: " O Captain! My Captain! "

" O Captain! my Captain! our fearful trip is done,
The ship has weather'd every rack, the prize we sought is won,
The port is near, the bells I hear, the people all exulting,
While follow eyes the steady keel, the vessel grim and daring."

Walt Whitman died in 1892 and to-day his poems are read in twenty-five different translations, while his influence on writers of our own time has grown steadily.

SOME MODERN POETS

THE LAKE ISLE OF INNISFREE *Specially drawn for this work.*

William Butler Yeats, the Irish poet, was born in Dublin and devoted part of his early life to the study of painting. Soon, however, he turned to literature and wrote poems, plays and essays, though his memory is most respected for his beautiful and often mystical verses. A good example of this poet's work is the Lake Isle of Innisfree, an incident from which is illustrated above.

BRITAIN has always been rich in poets and it is not unreasonable to say that during the first fifty years of the present century there have been more good poets than at any time since the early part of the seventeenth century. Perhaps there are no dominating figures such as Tennyson and Browning in the last century, but there have been many fine writers of poetry, among them such outstanding poets as W. B. Yeats (1865–1939), the Irish writer whose verses combine the beautiful with the mystical and even fantastic. Among the honours Yeats received was the Nobel Prize for Literature in 1923.

Robert Bridges

There are writers and poets who never really attain wide popularity and yet have great influence on other writers who follow them. It is to this class that Dr. Robert Bridges belongs.

Born in 1844 and educated at Eton and Oxford, he studied medicine at St. Bartholomew's, London, and became a doctor at the Great Ormond Street Children's Hospital and later at the Great Northern Hospital.

It was not until after he had retired from medical work in 1882 that he really began to write and slowly made a name among all lovers of good work as the most classical and artistic of modern poets. "He gave to lyric poetry a new cadence," W. B. Yeats wrote of him, "a distinction as deliberate as that of Whistler's painting." There is a restful calm about many of his poems which charms the ear and soothes the mind as in "The Storm is Over":

"While silver mist upstealeth silently,
  And the broad cloud-driving moon in the
    clear sky
  Lifts o'er the firs her shining shield,
  And in her tranquil light .
  Sleep falls on forest and field.

See! sleep hath fallen; the trees are asleep:
The night is come. The land is wrapt in sleep."

He was made Poet Laureate in 1913 and on his death in 1930 was succeeded by John Masefield.

John Masefield

Born at Ledbury, in the West of England, in 1878, John Masefield spent his youth and early manhood in wandering in many parts of the world, earning a living as best he could in any job that came his way. It was his experiences as a sailor before the mast that inspired his earlier poems, published in 1902 under the title "Salt Water Ballads." The boy at school and the older man by the fireside feels something of the call of the sea when he reads even the opening lines of "Sea Fever":

" I must go down to the sea again, to the lonely sea and sky,
And all I ask is a tall ship and a star to steer her by,
And the wheel's kick, and the wind's song and the white sails shaking,
And a grey mist on the sea's face and a grey dawn breaking."

His success as a poet and writer led him to give up his wandering and devote his whole time to literature. Yet in his writings he shows the same versatility as he did when he was a wanderer ready to take on any task on sea or ashore. "The Everlasting Mercy" and "The Widow in the Bye Street" are narrative poems of stern realism, while "Reynard the Fox" and "Right Royal" give vivid pictures of sporting life in the English countryside.

He has written, too, fine novels in prose such as *Jim Davis*, *Captain Margaret*, *Lost Endeavour* and *Sard Harker*.

Another fine poet who may well be remembered in the years to come when much of his other work is forgotten is Sir Henry Newbolt (1862–1938). Who has not heard that great and popular poem " Drake's Drum " sung or recited and felt thrilled by the lines:

Specially drawn for this work.

A POET AT THE WHEEL

John Masefield's early life at sea in sailing ships gave him inspiration for many of his poems. Often as an apprentice he would have to take his " trick " at the wheel on a moonlight night in the tropics and must have been impressed by the beauty of sky and sea.

" Take my drum to England, hang et by the
      shore,
   Strike et when your powders runnin'
      low;
   If the Dons sight Devon, I'll quit the port
      o' Heaven,
   And drum them up the Channel as we
      drummed them long ago."

It was largely of British seamen and
their stirring deeds that Newbolt has
sung in his well-known volumes
" Admirals All " and " The Island
Race," and for that we owe him our
gratitude. He was knighted in 1915 and
made a Companion of Honour in 1922.

Like Masefield, the Welsh poet, W. H.
Davies (1871–1940) spent his early years
as a wanderer, and his powers of observation and description are shown in
his exquisite poems on Nature as well as
his love of the simple things of life.

" They Shall Grow Not Old . . ."

Laurence Binyon (1869–1943) won
early fame as a poet while at Oxford,
where he was awarded the Newdigate
Prize. Later, while he held a position
at the British Museum in the Oriental
Prints and Drawings Department, he
gained a high reputation for his cultured and scholarly verse. During the
Great War of 1914–18 he wrote some of
his most memorable poems, among
them those lines " For the Fallen ":

" They shall grow not old as we that are left
      grow old:
   Age shall not weary them, nor the years
      condemn.
   At the going down of the sun and in the
      morning
         We will remember them."

Rupert Brooke (1887–1915) had
written several volumes of poems of
great beauty and promise, revealing
his own intense joy in living, when he
died on active service in the Mediterranean early in the first World War.
The lines from his poem " The Soldier "
will long be quoted and were prophetic
of his own fate:

" If I should die, think only this of me:
   That there's some corner of a foreign field
      That is for ever England."

Did you ever read a truly noble
poem entitled " The Hound of Heaven " ?
It appeared in the first volume of
poetry issued by Francis Thompson
(1859–1907) and is notable for its
majestic lines and brilliant conception.

" I fled Him, down the nights and down the
      days;
   I fled Him, down the arches of the years;
   I fled Him, down the labyrinthine ways
   Of my own mind . . ."

Thompson was born at Preston and
planned first of all to enter the priest-
hood. Changing his mind, he sought
to follow his father as a doctor, but
failed to secure the necessary qualifica-
tions and fell to the lure of London's
lights. In the Great City he made no
progress, however, and roamed the
streets in rags. Eventually, it was
another poet, Mrs. Alice Christiana
Meynell, and her husband who helped
him to get his earliest efforts published.

Thomas Stearns Eliot, O.M. (born
1888) ranks to-day as the outstanding
poet of our times. He wrote " The
Waste Land " and a play of exceptional
quality, " Murder in the Cathedral," as
well as " The Family Reunion." His
essays and lectures on poetry and
literature have given him a high place
and he has been honoured by the
universities of Britain and America.

At the Bluecoat School

First at Christ's Hospital and then
at Oxford, Edmund Charles Blunden
(born 1896) is another modern poet
who served in the Great War of 1914–
18. His " Undertones of War " was a
powerful piece of prose writing, but
it is upon his own beautiful verses, his
life of Leigh Hunt and his connection
with poetry generally that he has
built up his reputation.

Walter De La Mare (born 1873),
himself in the forefront of modern
poets, compiled an anthology or collection of poems specially for children.
He, too, is a writer of prose. Ralph
Hodgson (born 1871) is an outstanding
poet and through all his work there
runs his deep love of birds and animals.

The Lives
of the
Great Composers

A Story of
Music
and Musicians

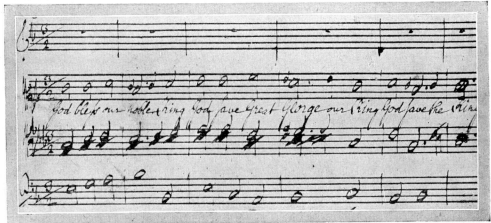

British Museum.

AN EARLY VERSION OF OUR NATIONAL ANTHEM

The above reproduction shows us a very early version of our National Anthem, as performed at Drury Lane Theatre, London. It is believed that the air was composed by Dr. John Bull (born in 1562), but the above version was written by Dr. Thomas Augustine Arne, who was born in 1710, was educated at Eton and died in 1778. He composed "Rule, Britannia." The precious score by Dr. Arne, from which our illustration is taken, is in the British Museum.

THE GOLDEN AGE

FROM the time of the Middle Ages up to the eighteenth century, when music was for the most part a vocal and not an instrumental art, musicians led either a wandering or a secluded life. First, there was the travelling musician, the minstrel or troubadour, who moved on foot from village to village and from castle to castle, singing songs and playing tunes, and even reciting narrative poems, entertaining his listeners for the price of a good meal and a night's lodging, or for a few pence.

Sometimes he became a member of the staff in the service of royalty or the nobility. In Germany there were the Minnesingers, the knightly counterparts of the troubadours and minstrels, who mostly sang of love and heroism. Then came the Mastersingers, guilds of tradesmen and craftsmen who took their subjects mostly from the Bible, and met in places of worship.

The church encouraged all forms of art, and there a man could devote his life to music usually under the most congenial conditions. This service of the church produced some of the greatest composers, from Palestrina to Bach, whilst the earliest MS. extant is "Sumer is icumen in," written by a monk of Reading Abbey named John of Forneste, who died in 1289.

Written for Choirs

The music of the fifteenth and sixteenth centuries was brought to its greatest heights by composers such as Palestrina and Vittoria in Italy, and William Byrd and Thomas Tallis in England. It was chiefly written for choirs which were divided into anything from four to sixteen parts. This music was called polyphonic, and had no instrumental accompaniment. It is both as ingenious and as expressive as any pieces written for the modern orchestra.

Although Byrd (1543–1623) was not the only great British composer of that time, he represented the highest peak in what is known as " The Golden Age " of English music, which flourished during the Tudor period. Church music, madrigals and instrumental music of the very finest quality were produced by such composers as Wilbye, Tallis, Dowland, Weelkes and Gibbon. The " Golden Age " came to an end with Henry Purcell (1658–1695), and

British Museum.

SUMMER IS A-COMING IN

This is probably the first English song to be written down. It was composed nearly 700 years ago by a monk of Reading Abbey, who gave it the title: " Sumer is icumen in." The music and words were prepared as a " round " for six voices. The parchment on which they are written is still preserved in the British Museum.

Dr. Arne (1710–1778), who wrote the early version of our National Anthem which is in the British Museum, and " Rule, Britannia." The original air of the National Anthem is believed to have been composed by Dr. John Bull (1562 ?–1628), but Dr. Arne's version was the one performed at Drury Lane Theatre.

Ten years before Purcell died two of the greatest German composers in the history of music were born: John Sebastian Bach (1685–1750) and George Frederic Handel (1685–1759).

Born at Eisenach, Thuringia, Bach led a comparatively uneventful life. Except for a period of six years as Prince Leopold's Kapellmeister (director of music) at Cöthen, he spent his life in the service of the Church, an occupation that kept him hard at work and more or less free from financial worries.

From the middle of the sixteenth century until 1845 the Bach family flourished in considerable numbers, the majority of them being either amateur or practising musicians. John Sebastian himself, essentially a family man, had no fewer than twenty children! Seemingly unharassed by this huge responsibility, Bach, in the course of his routine duties, composed for purely practical purposes a stream of masterpieces : cantatas, the Mass in B minor, Passion Music of St. Matthew and St. John, orchestral and instrumental pieces, including the six Brandenburg Concertos, the Forty-eight Preludes and Fugues for clavier (a forerunner of the piano), and a host of compositions for the organ.

Buried and Forgotten

Bach came at the end of a great period and summed up all for which it stood. It was because of this that his music found little favour with younger contemporaries and immediate successors. For nearly two hundred years after his death the greater part of his works lay buried and forgotten. Their style was considered old-fashioned. It was not until 1829 when Mendelssohn revived the St. Matthew Passion that Bach really came into his own.

Indeed, it was chiefly Bach's skill as an organist that secured him fame during his lifetime. He was described as the prince of organists. Throughout his life his thirst for knowledge and experience was insatiable. There was little music, from that of Palestrina to that of his contemporaries, which he did not study. Much of it he copied in script and kept for reference.

Bach was a man of strong will and set purpose. He had his own ideas on how his work should be carried out and if they ran counter to those of his patrons so much the worse for them. He could be obstinate and aggressive and show a bad temper that brooked no defiance, yet though he knew his own strength as a musician he was not without humility. Once when asked the secret of his organ playing he said: "There is nothing wonderful about it. You just strike the right note and the organ does the rest."

Rischgitz.

THE " SHAKESPEARE OF MUSIC "

You can see the original of this fine picture in the National Portrait Gallery, London. The artist was Closterman, and his subject Henry Purcell, who was born in 1658 and died when he was only thirty-seven. Purcell wrote a great many anthems and much church music, in addition to operas, and is regarded as the greatest composer England ever had. He was once a choirboy.

Playing in the Attic

Handel was born at Halle, Saxony, in the same year as Bach. Halle was an obscure provincial town in which his father, a barber-surgeon, was held in some esteem. At a very early age Handel showed such an interest in music that his fond mother secretly installed a clavichord (another small keyed instrument, a forerunner of the piano) in an attic where the child used to play at night until he was discovered by his angry father who forbade him to play again. However, his parent apparently relented later, for when Handel was seven he was taken to play the organ to the Duke of Saxony, who was so impressed with his genius that he persuaded the boy's father to let him study under the local organist. Handel's fame as a child genius spread, and after the death of his father he studied music in earnest.

He went to Italy, then the centre of the musical world, where he made three important friendships. These were the famous Italian keyboard composer Scarlatti; Prince Ernest of Hanover (by whom he was afterwards taken to Hanover to serve under Elector George, who later became George I of England);

and the Duke of Manchester, a rich music and opera lover who was the means of persuading Handel to come to London in 1710. When Handel arrived in England the conditions in London were deplorable, the streets being filthy and infested with robbers.

Handel entered into this turbulent world when he wrote his opera "Rinaldo," which was presented at the Queen's Theatre, Haymarket, in 1711 and captured the London audiences. He made many friends (and enemies as well) before he left to resume his duties at Hanover. Two years later he returned to London, where he remained more or less for the remainder of his life, writing operas and oratorios.

Rischgitz.

GEORGE FREDERIC HANDEL

This is a portrait of Handel, the great German musician, who is remembered specially for " The Messiah," composed in 1741, a sacred work often performed at Christmas and at Easter. We think of Handel as a great master of " oratorio," the name applied to a dramatic musical composition of religious character.

The Most Popular Oratorio

His most widely popular work, " Messiah," was composed when he was under a cloud of misfortune and bitter disappointment. His last two operas had failed, largely through the plots of his opponents, who even hired ruffians to prevent people reaching the theatre where his operas were being given. " Messiah " was first performed in Dublin in April, 1742, and had a magnificent success. When it was given in London it was practically a failure.

Only when it was performed in the Foundling Hospital in 1750 did it win its way to the hearts of Londoners, and since then it has been the most popular of all oratorios in every part of the country.

Handel's life was one long series of adventures. In turn, he touched the highest peak of success and the lowest level of failure. In 1751 the lamp of

A MUSICIAN'S SITTING=ROOM

James's Press.

Like so many great composers of music, John Sebastian Bach was a German. He was born in 1685, and died at Leipzig in 1750. Bach's pieces are all noble and learned. This photograph shows us the musician's sitting-room, with its clavichord, the instrument used before our present-day piano was perfected. Bach also composed music for the organ.

Rischgitz.

George Frederic Handel first saw the light in 1685, in Saxony, and died in 1759, when he was quite blind. In Germany he was in the service of the royal personage who afterwards became King George I. of England. When he was about twenty-five years old, Handel came to England, where he stayed for the remainder of his days; and, in the above picture, we see the composer in the company of his patron, George I., in a State barge.

life began to flicker. Handel was no longer seen walking in Bond Street. He reclined in a carriage, exhausted by the iron grip of gout that was undermining his already weakening constitution.

A Blind Old Titan

Worse was to come, however, for his sight began to fail, and a visit to Guy's Hospital told him the terrible truth. At first he was crushed under the blow, but his powerful will and dogged courage soon asserted themselves. He sent for a secretary and once again took up the threads of his work with increased energy. He practised and played his harpsichord for hours on end, and insisted upon presiding at the organ in performances of his oratorios. He played from memory and extemporised: giving sound to that wonderful music endlessly passing through his mind. He even played concertos at Covent Garden; and the crowds came in their thousands to enjoy the emotional spectacle of the blind old Titan defying Fate.

In 1746 he was a pauper, broken by his enemies and by adversity; in 1759 he died a national hero, leaving £20,000 and all his debts paid in full.

Handel's influence during his life and after his death became so overwhelming in this country that a fashion for foreign music and musicians completely killed our own school of composers, and at the end of the eighteenth century English music finally petered out into something which was hardly more than nondescript.

The year 1750 is roughly the dividing line between the close of the great polyphonic school and the beginning of the schools which exploited one dominating melody accompanied by chords. Bach and Handel successfully fused the two styles, but the most outstanding composer to write more or less pure music of this type was Bach's third son Carl Philip Emanuel.

Instrumental music was now waiting for a really great and original mind to establish these new principles, and the first on the scene was Franz Joseph Haydn (1732–1809). Haydn, whose father was a wheelwright, was born at Rohrau, a village in Lower Austria, near

James's Press.

HAYDN PLAYS ONE OF HIS COMPOSITIONS

The year 1732 saw the birth of Franz Joseph Haydn near Vienna. He composed more than 150 symphonies before he died in the city of Vienna in 1809. In the above illustration we see Haydn playing one of his own compositions before an enraptured circle of friends and admirers. The great composer loved country life, and wrote down much of his music on scraps of paper during walks through fields and woodlands.

Rischgitz.

A MUSICIAN CROSSES THE CHANNEL

Joseph Haydn paid at least two visits to England. On one of his journeys to this country
the ship passed through a terrible storm. In the above picture, after the artist Hamman, the
incident is realistically illustrated. It is interesting to note that this adventure afloat so affected
the composer that it afterwards found expression in the powerful piece " The Seasons," and
in his oratorio " The Creation."

the Hungarian border. Very early in
life he began to sing, and at the age of
six sang in performances of Masses in
the church choir and played the clavier
and the violin. He also created a great
sensation at a local festival when he
gave an impromptu performance on
drums strapped on the back of a hunch-
back boy, so that he could reach
them!

Quartet and Symphony

He joined the choir of St. Stephen's
Cathedral, Vienna, and studied under
Porpora, a celebrated Neapolitan composer and teacher of singing. Haydn's
parents were too poor to support him
and he had a hard struggle to make
both ends meet until, in 1755, a

wealthy Viennese music-lover invited
him to take charge of his private
orchestra at Weinzil. For the orchestra
he wrote a series of eighteen works
called " Divertimenti," scored for strings
with parts for oboes and horns, which
were the forerunners of the Quartet
and Symphony.

In 1763 Haydn accepted the post of
Kapellmeister to Prince Esterházy at
Eisenstadt, where he remained until the
death of his patron in 1790. His output
of music during these years was enormous. Haydn's finest works were
produced during the last years of his
life. In 1791 he paid his first visit to
London, where he produced six new
symphonies at the Hanover Square
Rooms. Three years later he again

came to England and produced another set of six symphonies. Among numerous other works Haydn composed 153 symphonies, 77 string quartets, 31 concertos for various instruments, 35 sonatas for the piano, and the oratorios " The Seasons " and " The Creation." He died in Vienna during Napoleon's bombardment of that city in 1809.

Haydn's friend Wolfgang Amadeus Mozart (1756–1791) was the most precocious genius in the history of music. His father was a violinist in the Archbishop's band at Salzburg, where Mozart was born. At the early age of six he was not only a brilliant harpsichord player, but he had already composed a set of five minuets and an allegro for that instrument. Indeed, at the age when most little boys are playing in the nursery Mozart was being dragged round Europe showing off his remarkable gifts as a musician.

Composer and Teacher

When he arrived at manhood the fickle aristocrats who had once pampered and petted him and showered him with gold pieces and snuff boxes took no further interest in him. Until his death, when real success was almost within his grasp, he eked out a livelihood as a composer, virtuoso and teacher, earning little more than a fiddler in a modern music-hall. What with incessant work, lack of money and, in later years, ill-health, Mozart had little about which to feel happy. The remarkable thing, however, is that through all these vicissitudes his kindly nature and lively spirits were never damped.

Mozart's entire output, like Haydn's, was very considerable: 41 symphonies, 26 string quartets, 7 string quintets, 42 concertos (25 of which are for the piano), operas and Masses.

Photographische Gesellschaft.

MOZART PLAYING IN PARIS

Born at Salzburg in 1756, Wolfgang Amadeus Chrysostom Mozart was one of the most gifted boys who ever lived. When he was only six years of age he could compose original music for the harpsichord. In the above picture we see this great Austrian composer delighting an audience in Paris, for he toured many of the chief cities of Europe, and also visited London.

Rischgitz.

MOZART THE COMPOSER AT THE POINT OF DEATH

This picture, after the artist O'Neill, shows us the great composer Mozart in the final hours of his life, when his keen interest in music was in no sense dimmed, as we can tell from the people grouped round his bed. He died in Vienna in 1791, whilst still a young man. It is sad to relate that, despite his fame and the fact that he composed so much fine music and played for the entertainment of kings and queens, Mozart passed away in a state of poverty.

12—2

BEETHOVEN AND SCHUBERT

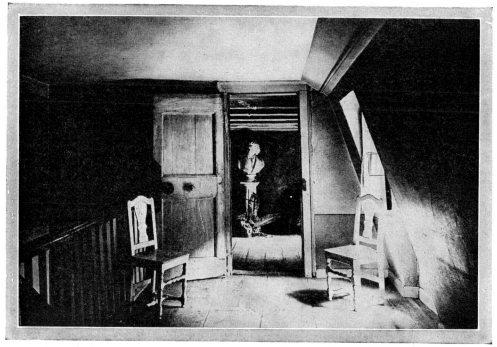

L.E.A.

THE BIRTHPLACE OF THE COMPOSER

Here is a photograph, taken at Bonn, in Germany, of the very room in which Ludwig van Beethoven was born in 1770. Beethoven is regarded as the greatest composer of music the world has ever known. It is a very strange fact that, at the time when he was producing some of his finest scores, he was stone-deaf.

IT was Ludwig van Beethoven (1770–1827) who brought instrumental music in the forms of the symphony, sonata and string quartet to its highest state of development. Beethoven was born at Bonn, where he passed the first twenty-two years of his life. His youth was spent in poverty and misery, for his father hoped to turn the boy into an infant prodigy like Mozart, and kept him hard at the piano and violin as well as at his schoolwork. At eleven Beethoven was taken away from school to study music. After his mother's death in 1787 he was even more unhappy owing to his father's thriftless habits.

When Deafness Came

For years he was compelled by lack of means to accept the patronage of wealthy men, which must have been galling indeed to a man of his character, for he was the first composer to break away from the established custom of patronage. He rightly insisted upon the dignity of the artist, but was sometimes, perhaps, rather too forcible in his way of doing it. Once when he and Goethe passed the carriage of the Duke of Weimar, Goethe doffed his hat and bowed low. Beethoven, however, only drew his hat more firmly upon his head with the remark: "When two men are together such as Goethe and myself, these fine gentlemen must be made conscious of the difference between ourselves and them."

In 1798 Beethoven began to suffer from deafness, which increased as he grew older. Not once, however, did he allow his infirmity to interfere in the slightest with what he felt himself

A DREAMER OF WONDERFUL MUSIC

Hanfstaengl.

Beethoven was fond of the countryside, and especially of woods; and, before his sense of hearing failed, delighted in listening to the song of the birds. This great German composer is described as being a very ugly man, but the face in the portrait reproduced above gives one the impression of tremendous strength of will and force of character. Beethoven died in 1827.

destined to accomplish, always showing an indomitable will and an incredible power of concentration.

From the first to the last he never stopped producing masterpieces: nine symphonies, 32 piano sonatas, 17 string quartets, the opera "Fidelio," the Mass in D, among a host of other works. Of course, not all of his enormous output was on the same supreme level of his best works, but, unlike many of the great composers, age did not weaken his creative powers. He went from strength to strength, as the Ninth Symphony and the last group of string quartets testify.

Much of Beethoven's music was symbolical of himself. His nature, by turns volcanic, tender, thoughtful, playful, tragic and noble, is reflected in his music. His music was his life and his life was his music.

His Retreat in the Country

Almost every summer he left the hot and dusty streets of Vienna for some country retreat, because his love of the country was intense, second only to his

James's Press.

BEETHOVEN BEFORE HIS PIANO

In this illustration we see the composer Beethoven sitting, lost in thought, before his piano. It was not always in this attitude, however, that he carried out his compositions. Sometimes he would pour cold water over his hands as he strode up and down the room, shouting almost at the top of his voice.

SYMPHONY B MINOR

Franz Schubert, Op. posth.
(1797-1828)

By courtesy of Messrs. Boosey & Hawkes, Ltd.

Schubert's " Unfinished " is one of the most famous symphonies in the world; here is the first page of the score of this great work. The two movements were written in 1822 and there is no indication why the work was left uncompleted. The manuscript was discovered only by accident and the first performance took place in Vienna on December 17th, 1865.

art, and because his deafness drove him more and more to seek refuge in communion with Nature.

The last twelve years of his life were lonely and unhappy ones. In 1815 his brother died and left him joint guardian with the boy's mother of his nephew Carl. Although Beethoven was passionately fond of his nephew, they did not get on at all well together, and to make things worse, Beethoven became involved in a series of law-suits with his sister-in-law. On December 2nd, 1827, he caught a chill which developed into inflammation of the lungs. After some four months of intense suffering, Beethoven died, appropriately enough, in the midst of a violent thunderstorm.

Beethoven showed in many of his works such as the overtures "Coriolanus" and "Egmont," and the "Pastoral" Symphony, that he was a romanticist as well as a classicist, and that he was striving to express profound thoughts and deep emotions in his music.

This can also be said of his contemporary Franz Schubert (1797–1828), who was a classicist in his instrumental works but a romanticist in his songs. He was the founder of what is known as the German Lieder, a style of songwriting in which the music is intended to be a direct interpretation of the words rather than merely a means of showing off the singer's voice.

Photographische Gesellschaft.

THE COMPOSER AMONG HIS FRIENDS

The original picture from which this illustration was taken was painted by Carl Röhling, and gives us a glimpse of the composer, Schubert, among his intimate friends. How wonderful it must have been to hear some of these old-time masters playing their own works! Schubert's life was but a short one, spent wholly in the shadow of hard times.

Schubert composed, during a period of seventeen years, 630 songs, including such masterpieces as the " Erl-King," and " The Miller Maid " and " Winterreise " cycles.

Although Schubert was a great composer, he was quite undistinguished outside his music. Physically he was a squat, stout, clumsy little man with an unhealthy complexion and rounded shoulders. But if you observed his features closely enough you would be somewhat struck by the strength of his jaw, the luxuriousness of his black hair, and those bright eyes that looked so penetratingly through his powerful glasses.

For facility of invention Schubert's only rival in the history of music is Mozart. Music simply poured from Schubert without any apparent conscious effort. Sometimes he forgot what he had written as soon as he had put it on paper. He once applauded one of his own songs and asked the singer the name of the composer!

Schubert was a romantic lover of nature, and it was one of his chief delights to wander among the little wine-producing villages around Vienna.

Although he was essentially a lyricist, he was hardly less successful with the larger forms. His instrumental works are full of melodic beauty, orchestral colour, and romantic expression. The most important of these works include the " Unfinished " Symphony, the " Trout " Piano Quintet, the Piano Trio in B flat, and his last three String Quartets.

W. F. Mansell.

AN EVENING WITH SCHUBERT

This picture, painted by a Viennese artist, gives us a good idea of an evening party arranged for his friends by the great Austrian composer, Franz Peter Schubert, who was born not far from Vienna in 1797, but lived only till 1828. Schubert wrote operas, symphonies, works for orchestras, and some hundreds of songs.

THE BIRTHPLACE OF SCHUMANN

Robert Schumann was a German composer who was born at the town of Zwickau, in Saxony, in the year 1810. The room that was his birthplace is illustrated above. He is best remembered for his beautiful and romantic music for the piano. Because of an accident to one of his hands, the composer himself could not become a pianist.

ET us return for a moment to the sixteenth century, which saw the beginning of opera. The earliest composers modelled their operas on Greek lines and sang them to a kind of musical chant. This chant, or rather recitative, was called the " New Music," and found an ardent supporter in Claudio Monteverde (1567–1643), a highly original Italian composer of great knowledge and technical skill.

He was a viol player in the Duke of Mantua's orchestra, later became Maestro di Cappella, and was commissioned to write an opera to be performed at the marriage of the Duke's son. Unhappily, this opera " Ariadne," except for one small fragment, has been lost. In 1607 he wrote his famous opera " Orpheus," which was a great advance upon anything of this kind that had been previously composed.

In these works and elsewhere Monteverde was the first to exploit the individual character of the instruments of the orchestra to intensify dramatic feeling.

In the Italian Style

Opera continued to thrive and develop in Italy during the seventeenth and eighteenth centuries, but it became very formalised and hardly more than a means of showing off the talent of great solo singers. The real foundations of opera as a true dramatic art were laid by the Austrian composer, Christoph Willibald Gluck (1714–1787). He was taught the violin, harpsichord and singing at a Jesuit school in Bohemia, and later studied in Milan.

Within the next few years he wrote seven operas in the Italian style which won him great popularity. As a result of this success he was invited to London, where he produced two operas in 1745, which were a complete failure. Next he went to Paris, where he was so impressed with the operas of the great French composer, Rameau, that he resolved to reform German opera.

In 1762 Gluck produced "Orfeo," an opera in a new style. This was followed five years later by "Alceste," to which he wrote a preface setting out his ideals. Among other things he "resolved to avoid all those abuses which had crept into Italian opera through the mistaken vanity of singers and the unwise compliance of composers which had rendered it wearisome and ridiculous."

The Viennese public did not approve of Gluck's innovations, so he returned to Paris in 1774 and wrote a version of Racine's "Iphigénie en Aulide," which was accepted by the Académie Royale on condition that he wrote a further "six operas of the same kind." Meanwhile he was challenged by Italian opera enthusiasts to compete with Piccinni (1728–1800) in setting the same libretto "Iphigénie en Tauride." Gluck was the first to finish his setting, and he produced it in 1779. Not only was it his finest work but it was unanimously admitted that his version was far superior to that of Piccinni. Gluck died in Vienna after a series of strokes.

Italian and German Opera

The two main styles of opera, the Italian and the German, were exploited by Mozart. His earlier operas were written in the Italian style to Italian words, but with "Il Seraglio" he established real German opera with German words. His greatest opera in the Italian

Copyright.

FRANZ LISZT AND HIS FRIENDS

This charming sketch, made by the artist Kriehuber, shows us a most historic group. At the piano is Franz Liszt playing Beethoven's Sonata in C Sharp minor. His friends are Berlioz, the French composer, Czerny, Ernst and the artist himself.

James's Press.

THE HOUSE WHERE BRAHMS WAS BORN

Johannes Brahms was a very famous German musician who was born at
Hamburg in the year 1833, in the quaint old house here illustrated. He
died at Vienna in 1897. He was devoted to children and always kept a
box of tin soldiers for his young visitors to play with.

Gluck stressed the importance of the poetry and drama of the opera, while Mozart regarded the music as being of chief importance.

By the end of the eighteenth century music in all its aspects, and, in fact, all the arts, had become extremely formalised and composers laid the accent on perfection of form rather than expression of emotion. Towards the end of the century, however, the two great German poets, Goethe and Schiller, started a new movement which later became known as the ''romantic'' movement. It was a revolution against formality, the expression of strong emotion and the description of picturesque scenes becoming the chief purpose of art.

style was "The Marriage of Figaro," and his finest effort in the German style was "The Magic Flute."

With the exception of Mozart's work, Viennese composers did not take opera very seriously. Mozart, however, excelled in opera as he did in all other branches of music, and wrote "La Finte Semplice" when he was twelve. The chief difference in the outlook of Mozart and Gluck was that

One of the first and greatest of romantic composers was the Frenchman, Hector Berlioz (1803–1869), who was born at La Côte St. André. His father was a country doctor who wanted him to follow his profession. However, at the first sight of the operating theatre Berlioz fled, and decided that music was preferable to medicine, so that despite parental opposition he entered the Paris Conservatoire in 1823. Here he proved a far from satisfactory student as he found theory irksome and loathed any kind of restrictions.

After two unsuccessful attempts he won the Prix de Rome, which entitled him to three years of travel, two of which had to be spent in Italy. Two years previous to this Shakespeare began to be widely read on the Continent, and the great English actor, Charles Kemble, took an English company to Paris.

Thus Shakespeare became the rage, and Berlioz fell violently in love with Harriet Smithson, who played the parts of Ophelia and Juliet. He could neither speak her language nor pronounce her name, but he was literally madly in love, and poured out his passion in his settings of Moore's Irish " Melodies "—Miss Smithson being Irish by birth. It was not until she was leaving Paris that she even heard of Berlioz's infatuation and then she declared that it was quite hopeless.

The Fantastic Symphony

Berlioz's immediate reaction to this was to write the Fantastic Symphony, which is concerned with the story of a young musician (himself). He has poisoned himself with opium in a fit of despair, but the dose is too weak to do more than put him to sleep. His dreams take the form of musical imagery and even his beloved (Harriet Smithson) becomes a melody—the recurring theme that runs through the work.

Six years after Berlioz fell in love with Harriet he met her for the first time, and, although she had lost her good looks and was heavily in debt, he still saw her through the haze of the youthful romance and married her in 1833. Money being scarce, he was compelled to take to literary work to support himself and his wife, and had little time for musical composition.

Photographische Gesellschaft.

FRÉDÉRIC CHOPIN AT THE PIANO

Like so many other great pianists, Frédéric François Chopin was a boy prodigy, and played confidently before grown-up audiences when barely eight years of age. In the above reproduction of the painting by L. Balestrieri we see the composer in his later years playing one of his own compositions to a circle of friends, whose rapt attention shows how they are enthralled.

Rischgitz.

FELIX MENDELSSOHN

The portrait above, after the painting by the artist Magnus, shows us the composer of those very charming piano pieces, " Songs Without Words," and of music which takes us into the realms of the fairies. Mendelssohn was a German, born at Hamburg in 1809. He died before he was forty years old.

Luck changed for him, however, when Paganini (the famous Italian violinist) sent him 20,000 francs for his Childe Harold Symphony, the solo viola part of which had been composed for the great violinist.

Berlioz now began to arouse interest in the public, and eventually came to London, where he conducted various concerts (including those of the Royal Philharmonic Society). With his striking appearance and mass of red hair, Berlioz was a true romantic in every way; indeed, he has been called the " Byron of Music."

A few months before he died he was invited to Russia, and his last birthday banquet (at which 500 guests were present) was a scene of great triumph. He was a sick man, however, and the excitement proved too much for him.

Weak and exhausted he spent the rest of his life in bed, where he received his friends sadly and silently, scarcely able to show by signs that he was pleased to see them.

Berlioz's place in the history and development of orchestral music is important because his innovations had a far-reaching effect on the modern orchestra. He exploited the full resources of each instrument and explored the endless possibilities of instrumental combinations. Thus he produced an enormous range of tone colours and increased the emotional and descriptive possibilities of orchestral music.

The first half of the nineteenth century saw innovations in every direction: the widening of the harmonic vocabulary, the extension of musical forms, such as the symphony and symphonic poem, as well as the improvement of the mechanism of instruments in general and the piano in particular. The piano

Mondiale.

VON WEBER

Carl von Weber was a pupil of Michael Haydn and a cousin of Mozart. At the age of seventeen he was made conductor of the Opera at Breslau.

became the most popular instrument, and this produced a wonderful line of players and composers, headed by Schumann, Chopin, Liszt and Brahms.

Robert Schumann (1810–1856) was the most literary-minded of all the great composers. In fact, there was a time in his life when literature nearly claimed him for its own, but instead he became the perfect exponent of the German romantic movement in music. Nurtured in the atmosphere of books, he came under the compelling influence of the romantic poets and novelists.

An Unhappy Ending

He was born at Zwickau, in Saxony, and his father was a bookseller and a writer. He went to Leipzig University to study law, but when he met Professor Wieck (who taught him the piano) he gave up law for music. He fell in love with Wieck's daughter, Clara, but their projected marriage met with much opposition from Clara's father.

During the years they were engaged Schumann wrote some of his loveliest and most inspired piano music, such as " Papillons," " Carnival," " Fantasie-stücke," " Kreisleriana," " Scenes from Childhood," and " Arabesque." The courtship and marriage of Robert and Clara Schumann was as near perfection as is possible in this imperfect world. Owing to an accident to one of his fingers when a young man, Schumann was forced to give up playing the piano, but Clara Wieck was a distinguished pianist, and did more than anyone to make her husband's music known.

Schumann's end was an unhappy one. He developed strange noises in his head

Rischgitz.

THE FIRST CONDUCTOR WITH A BATON

Carl Maria Friedrich Ernst von Weber, if not born with a silver spoon in his mouth, at least came of a distinguished family, and we think of him in our day as Weber the Composer. He was the first conductor of an orchestra to use a baton, as is shown in the caricatures reproduced above. 1786 was the year of his birth, and he died in London in 1826 after producing " Oberon," for the purposes of which opera he learned to speak the English language.

THE TWILIGHT OF THE GODS

Hanfstaengl.

The opera, " The Twilight of the Gods," lasts for close upon five hours if played at its full length. It was written by Richard Wagner. The scene illustrated above shows us the last journey of Siegfried after his death from Hagen's treacherous spear-thrust. Gunther follows the bearers as they carry Siegfried's remains over the rocky heights towards the Hall of the Nibelungs.

Hanfstaengl.

This is a scene from the opera " Siegfried," by Richard Wagner. The man who plays the name-part is stretched comfortably under a tree and falls into a reverie, wondering what the father and mother he never knew were like. Sighing gently, he leans still further back, and a deep silence settles upon the scene till the song of a bird in the branches overhead seems to bring to him a message that he understands.

and one day walked out and attempted suicide by throwing himself into the Rhine. He was rescued and put into an asylum where he died two years later.

Schumann's greatness as a composer rests chiefly on his piano music and songs. In the songs the piano accompaniment is often as important as the vocal part, as seen in those lovely song cycles " Dichterliebe," and " Frauenliebe und Leben." Schumann's larger works, symphonies and otherwise, contain much beautiful music, but on the whole do not reach such heights as his songs and piano pieces. He was essentially a miniaturist. Among his most satisfactory large-scale works are the Piano Concerto in A Minor, the 'Cello Concerto in A Minor, the Piano Quintet, Overture " Manfred," and his Symphonies Nos. 2 and 4.

A Tour of Germany

Frédéric Chopin (1810–1849) was born near Warsaw, Poland. He was a delicate child, but his parents were cultured people who brought him up in a refined and gentle atmosphere. He studied for six years at the Warsaw Conservatorium before going on a short tour to Germany and Austria, where he made his first appearance as a virtuoso before he finally settled down in Paris in 1831.

Paris was the home of romanticism, and Chopin met and made friends with all the poets, painters and musicians who were living there. His most important friendship was with George Sand, the novelist, a most remarkable woman who took Chopin to Majorca in 1837, where she mothered him and tried to nurse his delicate health back to normal. But although she saved his life during the months they were there, consumption had set in and the remaining years of his life were one long struggle against the disease, until, in 1848, it was said that he " came into the room bent double, and with a distressing cough . . . but when he sat down to the piano he played with an extraordinary strength and animation."

Nocturnes and Preludes

Although Chopin was essentially a romantic composer, he never gave his pieces picturesque and descriptive titles. His romanticism expressed itself in the finest shades of emotional feeling, the very essence of poetry, with which he imbued his music. From first to last he was the perfect miniaturist, and left behind him the rich heritage of some of the finest piano music the world has ever known. The Nocturnes, the Preludes, and the Waltzes, in particular, show his inventive genius and lyrical style at their best.

Franz Liszt (1811–1886) was perhaps the greatest pianist of all time, and as a composer he displayed a most original mind, particularly in his twelve symphonic poems, the Dante and Faust Symphonies, and his Piano Sonata in B minor.

Few great artists have led such a full and spectacular life as Liszt. As a child he was the pet of the aristocracy of Vienna, Paris and London, and was hailed as the " eighth wonder " of the world.

His life falls into three definite periods. First that of the virtuoso, who swept Europe to and fro like a hurricane, driving his audiences into frenzies of admiration. He humbled kings and queens with the keen edge of his tongue. If he dropped his handkerchief women tore it to shreds and triumphantly carried away the pieces to keep as mementos.

Friendship with Wagner

The second period begins when, having sickened of his life as a showman, he went to Weimar as Music Director of the Court. For ten years or more Weimar became the centre for the " new music," with Wagner as the great figurehead. His friendship for Wagner is a wonderful story of supreme generosity and self-denial. What little leisure he had he devoted to his own compositions, some of the finest of which were written at Weimar.

The third period of his life Liszt spent in teaching the piano, without any remuneration, to those whose gifts were worthy of fostering. Both his practice and his teaching embraced all the chief characteristics and qualities of his contemporaries and predecessors. As most of the leading pianists of his time studied under him, his influence was therefore enormous.

Indeed, the extent of Liszt's combined influence as composer, conductor and pianist has no parallel in the history of music. There is hardly a composer of the nineteenth century, from Mendelssohn to Mackenzie, and Berlioz to Borodin, who did not benefit in some way or another from Liszt's advice or practical assistance.

A Boy Composer

Felix Mendelssohn-Bartholdy (1809-1847), to give him his full name, was born at Hamburg. The son of a wealthy Jewish banker, he received a first-class education in literature, music and drawing. His first public appearance was made as a pianist at the age of nine, and at fourteen he was already the composer of a considerable quantity of music, including songs, sonatas and symphonies. He came to London in 1829, where he was received with great enthusiasm; after which he made an extended tour through Austria, Italy, Switzerland and France, at the end of which he was the idol of Europe.

Mendelssohn was a man who never had to suffer poverty, for he lived in affluence all his life—which he spent in conducting and playing the piano. He was a frequent visitor to England, Queen Victoria being one of his biggest patrons, rarely losing an opportunity of hearing him play. He modelled his music on the strict classical lines to be

THE MASTERSINGERS OF NUREMBERG
" Die Meistersinger," as the title of Richard Wagner's famous opera is usually written, was composed round the old-time German contests of song, which were conducted on very strict lines. The picture above shows Eva pouring out her heart to the old mastersinger Sachs. Walther stands by her side, and Magdalena and David, both dressed for the festival, are entering. They join in singing a fine quintet.

Rischgitz.

GIACOMO PUCCINI

This great Italian composer of opera was
born of a musical family in 1858. He died
at Brussels at the age of sixty-six.

but he was helping to support his family by playing the piano at cafés in the neighbourhood.

At the age of twenty Brahms was introduced to Schumann, who on the evidence of a handful of manuscripts hailed him as a "new master." This was the beginning of a life-long friendship between Brahms and Schumann and the latter's wife, Clara Schumann, the pianist.

Piano Music and Songs

For the best part of his life Brahms spent his time composing, conducting and producing his works at various cities all over Germany and Austria. His home was in Vienna, where he died in 1897, a rich and distinguished composer. Brahms was a master in all branches of music excepting opera. His orchestral works include four symphonies, Variations on a Theme of Haydn, and the "Academic" and "Tragic" Overtures. His superb chamber works have never been surpassed by any composer, and his piano music and songs—to say nothing of his choral music—are a monument to his industry and genius.

The first great German composer of romantic opera was Carl Maria von Weber (1786–1826). He was a delicate child, who owing to a diseased hip-bone was not able to walk before he was four years old, and limped all his life. He was taught to play and sing almost before he could speak, and was at first a very unpromising pupil.

At the age of seventeen he was made the conductor of the Opera at Breslau. He spent several years wandering from one city to another writing and producing operas and other works, and in conducting. In 1817 he married a young singer who had played the principal part in his opera "Silvana" when it was first produced at Frankfort in 1810. He then settled down in Dresden as conductor of the opera. In 1811 Weber's opera "Der Freischütz" met with a wonderful success

found in Haydn, Mozart and early Beethoven, and he had no interest in the innovations of the later Beethoven nor in the romantic movement.

However, it would not be true to say that he was quite unaffected by it, for he gave romantic titles to some of his works. In these he set out to write poetic music in strictly classical forms, such as the overtures "A Midsummer-Night's Dream" and "Fingal's Cave," and the "Scotch" and "Italian" Symphonies.

Johannes Brahms (1833–1897), also born at Hamburg, was a great admirer of Mendelssohn and Beethoven; and like Mendelssohn he was equally unaffected by the romantic movement.

Brahms was the son of a theatre double-bass player, and when he had been taught music for some time by his father he studied under various local musicians. At the age of fourteen he was not only the conductor of a small choral society of a near-by town, all over Europe, and was performed simultaneously at three London theatres.

He was then invited to come to London and write another opera to be produced at Covent Garden. Although Weber had been warned by his doctor that he should go away for a few months to a warmer climate, he was so anxious to make money for his family that he accepted the offer. He reached London in March, 1826, when he immediately set to work on his new opera " Oberon," which was performed about five weeks later. As well as working on his opera, Weber had given several concerts in London, but his already delicate constitution could not stand up to the strain and he died in June, 1826, barely forty years old.

Another distinguished romantic composer of opera was the German-Jew, Giacomo Meyerbeer (1791–1864), who spent the greater part of his life in Paris (although as Royal Director of Opera at Berlin much of his time was spent in that capital) writing for the Paris stage, and therefore he may be said to represent French opera rather than German. Like all other romantics, he chose weird and picturesque subjects as seen in his operas " The Huguenots " and " Robert the Devil."

Weber's follower, and the greatest of all German composers of opera, was Richard Wagner (1813–1883), who was born at Leipzig at a time when that city was struggling to free its country from Napoleon. Young Wagner was fascinated by Greek mythology and worshipped Shakespeare, but, unlike many of the great composers, he displayed no very special gifts as a young man. In fact, when he began his career as a humble theatre conductor he had to learn the job as he went along.

From the first, however, he dreamed of accomplishing wonderful things. After experience and study had equipped him with the necessary technique to execute the projects of his ever-vivid

Stage Photo Co.

A SCENE IN VERDI'S OPERA " IL TROVATORE "

Scene I., Act II., of " Il Trovatore " is set in a gipsy encampment in the Biscayan mountains. The picturesque and colourful surroundings are such as to impress any audience, as can be understood from the above illustration. Giuseppe Verdi was born in 1813, and lived till 1901. " Il Trovatore " was first performed as long ago as 1852.

and active imagination, he never once swerved from the path that led to " Tristan," " The Ring "—and Bayreuth.

Both Money and Advice

All through his life Wagner was in financial difficulties, and from more than one town he was forced to flee from his creditors. His friends—and he had many—were for ever lending him money and making other sacrifices, in return for which they were treated to extravagant pleasantries and often abuse. However, the greatest friend he ever had was Liszt, who not only gave money and advice, but dedicated his life to the propagation of Wagner's art.

In the operas " Tannhauser " and " Lohengrin," and in the music dramas, as Wagner called them, " The Mastersingers," " Tristan and Isolde," " Parsifal " and the " Ring " cycle (consisting of " The Rhinegold," " The Valkyries," " Siegfried " and " The Twilight of the Gods ") he gave the highest manifestations of the romantic ideal. It was the application of the symphonic idea to opera which made these works so important, and Wagner's innovations in harmony and orchestration influenced almost every composer that came after him.

From a dramatic and intellectual point of view the innovations of the German composers made little impression on Italian opera. On the whole the Italian composers had a greater sense of the theatre, but, as Weber said, " the pleasure of the sense is what is aimed at." The first important Italian composer of opera during the nineteenth century was Gioacchino Rossini (1792–1868), who was born at Pesaro, his father being the town trumpeter.

Rossini composed his first opera in 1810, and then followed a series of operas until he made a great success with " Tancredi " in 1813. He composed " The Barber of Seville " in 1816, while he was musical director of the San Carlo Theatre in Naples.

Rossini was an excessively lazy man in his habits, and did most of his composition while he was in bed. He is reputed as being too lazy even to pick a piece of paper up from the floor, preferring to write another song, or whatever he happened to be working on, to replace it.

Rossini's output consisted of about fifty operas, fifteen cantatas and a few sacred and secular vocal works. His best-known operas are " The Barber of Seville," a sparkling comedy; and " William Tell," a serious romantic work influenced by the French school.

The greatest opera composer that Italy has ever produced was Giuseppe Verdi (1813–1901), who was born at Parma. As early as seven years old he showed musical ability.

His Life for Music

In 1836 he married, but in less than four years he lost his wife and two children in very tragic circumstances, and, after overcoming his first impulse to throw up his work, he devoted himself entirely to music. He became one of the most popular and famous composers in the world and his twenty-eight operas include " Rigoletto." " Il Trovatore," " La Traviata," and " Aïda." " Aïda " was finished in 1871 and then came sixteen years of silence. At the age of seventy-four, Verdi suddenly produced " Othello," a tragic opera in a new style, and six years later " Falstaff," a comedy-drama, both of which are two of the greatest operas.

Another great Italian opera composer was Giacomo Puccini (1858–1924), who was born at Lucca of a musical family which originally came from Celle.

After leaving Milan Conservatoire he met a young librettist, Fontana, and wrote his first opera " Le Villi " in 1884. From that time onwards he produced at fairly regular intervals a succession of operas, which included " Manon Lescaut," " La Bohème," " La Tosca," " Madame Butterfly," and " The Girl of the Golden West."

EDVARD GRIEG AND HIS WIFE

In this picture we see Edvard Hagerup Grieg, the great Norwegian composer, who was born in 1843 at Bergen. His family was of Scottish origin. Grieg is best known for his piano music and pieces composed for orchestras. His " Peer Gynt " suite is a classic. He was a true musician of the Northlands, which have given the world far fewer composers than Germany.

A DIRECT result of romanticism was the development of national music, and the most fertile soil was in such countries as Russia, Scandinavia and Bohemia. Thus Smetana and Dvořák in Bohemia, Glinka, Rimsky-Korsakov, Borodin and Mussorgsky in Russia, and Grieg in Norway, saturated themselves in the folk lore and folk song of their respective countries and produced a " national music," which repudiated the German and Italian influences which had dominated the world of music for so long.

Music of the Czechs

Frederick Smetana (1824–1884) was the founder of modern Bohemian or Czech music. He was an avowed follower of Liszt, and his early symphonic poems show Liszt's influence. He was keenly interested in politics and joined various national and artistic movements. Among his compositions are eleven operas, of which " The Bartered Bride " is the best known, and a cycle of six symphonic poems entitled " My Country."

Anton Dvořák (1841–1904) was one of the greatest composers of the nineteenth century. He was born in a Bohemian village where his father was a butcher and a publican. As he showed signs at a very early age of musical ability, Dvořák was allowed to study the violin, piano and organ under a local musician. In 1857 he went to the Organ School at Prague, where he only just managed to make both ends meet, as his parents were **too**

Rischgitz.

ANTON DVOŘÁK

Born 1841, Dvořák was one of the greatest
composers of the nineteenth century. For a
long while he was viola player at the Prague
National Theatre. He died in 1904.

poor to help him. From 1862–1873
he was viola player at the Prague
National Theatre, and during that time
Dvořák composed a great number of
works.

In 1892 he went to America as Principal of the New York National Conservatoire, where he interested himself
in negro folk music, which strongly
coloured such works as the " New
World " Symphony, and the " Nigger "
Quartet.

Edvard Grieg (1843–1907), having
received his first lessons in music from
his mother, and started to compose at
the early age of ten, was trained at the
Leipzig Conservatoire under professors
who believed the German tradition to
be the universal tradition. Grieg
showed little individuality as a creative
artist, and he was dissatisfied because
he could not free himself from German
influences.

However, by chance he met a young
Norwegian composer named Rickard
Nordraak, who showed him his collection of Norwegian folk songs. They
immediately fired Grieg's enthusiasm,
and he and Nordraak decided to use
Norwegian folk music as a basis for the
creation of a style that would be
distinct from the German tradition.
Unfortunately Nordraak died a year
or two later, and Grieg was left alone to
establish a national school of music,
which he did with signal success.

Grieg was essentially a miniaturist
and most of his best work was accomplished in the lyrical forms of short
piano pieces and songs. The writing
for the piano is always beautifully
calculated, if not as brilliant and
inventive as that of, say, Chopin or
Schumann. His music is strongly
impregnated with the spirit of Norwegian folk song and legend, the
fundamental characteristics of which
are mysterious gloom and deep melancholy contrasted with wild and un-
restrained gaiety.

Unfortunately Grieg wrote comparatively few works for the orchestra,
although he treated it with mastery
and understanding, as shown in the ever-
popular Piano Concerto in A minor and
the two " Peer Gynt " Suites.

A Literary Revival

Apart from folk song, which has
always flourished in Russia in rich
abundance, art music, chiefly in the
form of opera and sentimental
" romances," was a weak and undistinguished imitation of the Italian
style up to the nineteenth century,
when Glinka (1803–1857) came on the
scene.

Two important influences prepared
the way; the growth of patriotic
feeling inspired by the Napoleonic
Wars and the national literary revival
brought about by the great Russian
poet and novelist, Pushkin, whose
writing later inspired some of the finest
music of the leading Russian composers.

Glinka was the first to create a distinctive national style in Russian music—a style coloured with certain characteristics of folk song. Another composer working on similar lines was Dargomizhsky (1813 – 1869), whose operas " Russalka " and " The Stone Guest " are important landmarks.

The Music of Russia

Russian music now bloomed into full flower with a group of five composers who became known as " the mighty handful ": Balakirev (1836–1910), Cui (1835–1918), Borodin (1834–1887), Mussorgsky (1839–1881), and Rimsky-Korsakov (1844–1908). With the exception of Cui, these composers were real masters of their art, and many of their best works have become established in the world's repertoire.

A fact about many of the Russian composers of this period—in particular " the mighty handful "—is that they were not what we call professional musicians, for to some of them composition was always a sparetime occupation. Cui, for instance, became a general in the army and an authority on fortifications, Mussorgsky was first a guards' officer and later a civil servant while Borodin was a doctor of medicine and professor of chemistry.

Russian music undoubtedly reached its greatest heights with the best works of Balakirev, Mussorgsky, Borodin, and Rimsky-Korsakov. For richness of harmony and orchestral colour, attractive and novel melodies and rhythms, and unconventional methods of construction, the tone-poems and symphonies of these composers stand in a unique class of their own.

Tchaikovsky, who has been generally accepted in England as the greatest representative of Russia, is the least national of all the great Russian composers.

Peter Ilyich Tchaikovsky (1840–1893) was born at Kamsko-Votinsk, and describing him as a child, his French governess said that his " sensitiveness was simply boundless and one had to handle him very carefully. A mere trifle would wound him. He was a *porcelain* child. There could be no question of punishing him; he would take to heart the least criticism—a single word of reproof, such as other children would take no notice of—and be alarmingly upset by it. . . ." He was moody, imaginative, impressionable, nervous and excitable. As he grew older his moods alternated between happy and exuberant spirits and black depression. In the midst of a lively conversation with his friends suddenly a look of abject suffering would pass over his features and he would relapse into silence.

The greatest emotional upheaval that he sustained during his life was his marriage to a singer whom he did not love and with whom he had no intellectual sympathy. He married her

Rischgitz.

CLAUDE DEBUSSY

At the age of twenty-two this French composer won the Prix de Rome. He was born in Paris in 1862 and composed some of the most beautiful music of modern times. He died in 1918.

because he was afraid she would commit suicide if he refused her. After nine weeks they separated and Tchaikovsky suffered such mental torture that he became unconscious. "A few days more," he said, "and I swear I should have gone mad." Then he himself attempted suicide by standing in a frozen river in the hope of getting pneumonia.

From then onwards the strain of melancholia gradually got the upper hand of him, and his music became increasingly an outlet for his thoughts and feelings.

His Game of Patience

In May, 1892, Tchaikovsky moved into the country near the little town of Klin, some distance from Moscow. He went there because he wanted solitude, finding that his friends and the distractions of town life took up too much of his time, but when he settled down he missed his friends, whose custom it was to play whist with him. Alone, he therefore lapsed into a solitary game of patience.

Although he had said he was "worn out" and "done for," he was conceiving in his mind the "Pathetic" Symphony, and it is curious to note that after he had completed the symphony his mind remained serene and cheerful up to his death. This fact also disposes of the idea that he committed suicide. The truth is that he was merely unfortunate in drinking some unboiled water which brought about a fatal attack of cholera.

Some French Composers

Except for the great figure of Berlioz during the first half of the nineteenth century, French composers achieved little or nothing of distinction. But after Berlioz's death an important school of composers re-established French music on a firm and lasting basis.

The first composer to unite the German classical tradition and the romantic ideals of Liszt with the gracefulness and purity of style of the early French keyboard writers and opera composers was Camille Saint-Saëns (1835–1921). His opera "Samson and Delilah," the symphonic poems "Omphale's Spinning Wheel" and "Danse Macabre" continue to remain popular to-day. More individual but less grandiose in style was Gabriel Fauré (1845–1924), whose songs, piano pieces and chamber music are among the finest in French music.

César Franck (1822–1890) was perhaps the most solid of the French composers, and he modelled himself on the German tradition. Like Bach he was a wonderful improviser at the organ, and all his spare time he spent in composition. His was a very uneventful life, but although he had a singularly sweet and patient disposition, he was not treated very well by his colleagues. Among his greatest works are his Symphony in D minor, Violin Sonata in A, String Quartet in D, and the large-scale choral work "The Beatitudes." His outstanding works for the piano are the Prelude, Chorale, and Fugue, and Prelude, Aria, and Finale.

There were numerous lesser composers, such as Massenet, Gounod, Lalo, Bizet, and later Vincent d'Indy, Chabrier, Chausson and Duparc, who all contributed beautiful and distinctive works to the repertoire of French music.

Claude Achille Debussy (1862–1918) was born at Paris, and won the Prix de Rome at the age of twenty-two. After three years in Rome he went to Russia and came under the influence of the Nationalist composers, Mussorgsky in particular. In his early years Debussy was also strongly influenced by Wagner, whose music he afterwards disliked very much. When he returned to Paris he frequented the salon of Mallarmé, where he met all the leading poets.

Debussy experimented with various Greek modes, the whole-tone scale, and with the overtone of bells. His attitude towards the purpose of music thus became completely changed. He developed a system of harmony and orchestration that was entirely new and eminently suitable for obtaining " impressionistic " effects.

In his early days Maurice Ravel (1875–1937) flirted with impressionism, but never made it the sole purpose of his art. After such impressionistic masterpieces as the lovely " Daphnis and Chloe " and " Mother Goose " Suites, he became essentially a classicist, as shown in his Sonatina for piano and Piano Concerto.

The Waltz King

Johann Strauss senior was one of the first musicians to devote himself entirely to light music, and his son, Johann Strauss (1825–1899), the " Waltz King," carried on this tradition. He composed some four hundred waltzes and swept the world of opera off its feet with a score of operettas and the immortal " Die Fledermaus."

Brahms himself had a great admiration for Strauss, and once when asked to sign a fan belonging to Strauss's wife, he wrote the first few bars of the " Blue Danube " Waltz with the words: " *Not*, I regret to say, by your devoted friend, Johannes Brahms."

Some of the best light music to be written outside Vienna and Paris is to be found in England. It started with the wonderful partnership of Gilbert and Sullivan which resulted in their immortal operas. Sullivan's music from an orchestral point of view was far superior to anything written in England at that time.

Sullivan was succeeded by Edward German (1862–1936), who wrote a quantity of incidental music including the ever-popular Henry VIII and Nell Gwynn Dances, and the light operas " Tom Jones " and " Merrie England." Coleridge-Taylor would have been German's greatest rival had he lived.

WHERE THE GREAT RUSSIAN COMPOSER WAS BORN

This house at Kamsko-Votinsk, in Russia, was the birthplace in 1840 of the composer of sad and strange music, Peter Tchaikovsky. In 1848, when his parents left the district for Moscow, the boy musician could already read scores at sight and play them easily. We think of Tchaikovsky as the " sad musician " because his works are in many cases tinged with melancholy.

MUSICIANS OF MODERN TIMES

THE great tradition founded by Sullivan and German is carried on to-day by Eric Coates, composer of the famous "London" Suite and "The Three Bears." Coates was a distinguished chamber music player and principal viola of the Queen's Hall Orchestra before he gave up playing for composition.

Since the beginning of the twentieth century England has produced a school of composers that is worthy of taking up the golden threads that were broken after the time of Purcell. The first two really great composers who came on the English scene were Sir Edward Elgar (1857–1934) and Frederick Delius (1862–1934).

SIR EDWARD ELGAR   *L.E.A.*

Sir Edward Elgar, whose portrait appears above, was born at Broadheath, Worcestershire, in 1857, and is regarded as the greatest modern English musical composer. His music was written mainly for orchestras.

curious mixture of the visionary and of everyman: the visionary in his music; everyman in his fondness for pageantry. Thus he was able, as Ernest Newman says, "to express the very soul of our race in the military marches, in the 'Cockaigne' Overture and in 'Falstaff.'"

Elgar's greatest works, such as the "Enigma" Variations, the two symphonies, concertos, the symphonic study "Falstaff," and the "Dream of Gerontius," show us the complete man and musician.

A Self-Taught Musician

Elgar, a native of Worcester, was virtually a self-taught musician. His father kept a music shop, and at a very early age Elgar learned to play various instruments. He had a great struggle to gain recognition, but he was fortunate to marry a wife with an income. He developed an extraordinarily personal style in his music that characterised the very spirit of England and Englishmen.

His enormous vitality, humour and sensitiveness, his love of animals and of the countryside are a few of his essentially English qualities. He was a

Frederick Delius was born at Bradford, and was intended for a business career. Music, however, occupied his mind to such an extent that he was a failure as a business man. After considerable opposition from his father, he finally went to Florida, and later to Leipzig Conservatoire, where he met Grieg, who influenced him a great deal. In 1888, Delius settled in Paris, and later bought a small estate at Grez, near Fontainebleau.

Delius was a true romantic and in some ways an impressionist; perhaps it would be more accurate to say that he is a fusion of the two. He was inspired by the beauties of Nature and romantic poetry, especially if the latter had a philosophic appeal. His harmony is essentially chromatic, always changing and blending into beautiful and varied colours, as in the " Brigg Fair " variations.

Delius, perhaps, will always remain for the few. The appeal of his music is so essentially personal and intimate. His colours are the tints of autumn; his melodies the expression of throbbing emotions. In his music he weaves sad but beautiful dreams, as witness the tone-poems " On Hearing the First Cuckoo in Spring," " Summer Night on the River," " A Song Before Sunrise," and " In a Summer Garden."

Delius, however, rises to his highest flights when he writes for chorus and orchestra—in " Sea-Drift " (words by Walt Whitman), " Songs of Sunset " (words by Ernest Dowson), and " A Song of the High Hills." That Delius could handle a large canvas with great imagination and skill is seen in his " Mass of Life " and his delicate and moving opera " A Village Romeo and Juliet."

Two composers whose names rarely figure in programmes to-day, although they once enjoyed considerable reputations, are Sir Granville Bantock and Joseph Holbrooke, both of whom have been prolific composers. For his period, Bantock was bold and original in outlook, particularly in his treatment of choral music. His development as a composer shows the successive influence of Wagner, national folk song, and the music of the Orient.

A Woman Composer

Dame Ethel Smyth (1858–1944) is another English composer whose work has been unduly neglected, possibly on account of her sex. She was born in London and studied at Leipzig.

Although to an extent a follower of Brahms, she developed a highly individual style, which is to be found in her operas " The Wreckers " and " The Boatswain's Mate," and her fine Mass in D. When she died at the age of eighty-six a link with the Brahms tradition was broken.

During the early years of the present century another school of English composers sprang up whose ideals were similar to the nationalists in Russia, Czecho-Slovakia, Norway and elsewhere. Cecil Sharp and Barclay Squire ransacked the country for folk songs and dances, taking them down in their notebooks before they should vanish for

Central Press.

DAME ETHEL SMYTH

Her opera " The Boatswain's Mate " contributed largely to the fame of this great English composer and conductor. She died in 1944 at the age of eighty-six.

Rischgitz.

DELIUS AND HIS WIFE

Frederick Delius was born at Bradford in 1862 and was intended for a business career, but music claimed him. He rose to his greatest flights when he wrote for chorus and orchestra. He died in 1934.

Symphony No. 5 in D, the Mass in G minor, and " Dona Nobis Pacem " and " Sancta Civitas," there are mystical qualities of rare distinction and beauty. Vaughan Williams's study and love of early church music has also had a strong influence in the formation of his very individual harmonic and polyphonic style.

Vaughan Williams's most distinguished colleague was Gustav Holst (1874–1934), who startled English musicians with his brilliant set of orchestral tone poems " The Planets." But Holst's gifts chiefly lay in the direction of choral music, and the " Hymn of Jesus " deserves to be considered one of the outstanding landmarks in British music. However, Holst's outlook is austere and uncompromising, and so his music is very limited in its appeal, although his many skilful arrangements of folk-songs will always remain popular.

The rich store of Irish folk-songs and dances inspired and influenced E. J. Moeran and Sir Arnold Bax, who died in October, 1953. Bax was essentially a romantic, and wrote an enormous quantity of music of every kind excepting opera. His seven monumental symphonies have yet to become as popular as they deserve. His tone poems, such as the " Garden of Fand," " Tintagel " and " The Tale the Pine Trees Knew," show the utmost fertility of invention, poetic feeling, and a rich sense of harmonic colouring. His innumerable songs and works for piano solo (there are four sonatas) include some of the best examples in British music. But nowhere did Bax reach greater heights than in his chamber music; his Piano Quintet, Viola Sonata,

ever by dying out with the old farmers and labourers who had handed them down through generations. These folk-songs were collected and published, and they fired the enthusiasm of a number of young composers, who at that time were studying at our colleges and academies, notably Vaughan Williams and Holst.

Of the many composers who followed the Folk-Song Movement the most gifted and the most individual is undoubtedly Vaughan Williams. He excels as a composer of songs and choral, chamber and orchestral music. In his " Sea," " Pastoral " and " London " Symphonies he seems to express the very heart and atmosphere of England; in such works as his new

Nonet, and Oboe Quintet, are all masterpieces.

John Ireland has remained practically uninfluenced by the folk-song movement. He is one of the most self-critical composers of all time ; he puts pen to paper only when he is genuinely moved, and scraps everything that does not conform to his high ideals.

In his symphonic works like " The Forgotten Rite," " Mai-Dun " and the Piano Concerto, everything is calculated with the utmost precision—every note, phrase, chord or effect of orchestral colour is an integral part of the whole conception. Perfection of form, which in his case is always compact and closely knit, is his constant ideal.

Ireland has written some of the most beautiful songs of any British composer, settings of some of the cream of English poetry. But as a composer of piano music he is perhaps unequalled, and the most striking characteristic of his music is its wealth of melody and rhythm which gives it vitality and power.

One of the most alert and vigorous figures among British composers is Arthur Bliss, an artist of outstanding skill and high ideals. He is completely unaffected by folk-songs and his approach to music is essentially classical. Among his later works " Morning Heroes " is a splendid exception; his chamber music, Introduction and Allegro for Strings, and Piano Concerto

may be classed among some of the finest achievements of British music.

Orchestral Writing

Of the younger school of composers, William Walton is dazzlingly brilliant: there is no problem that he does not surmount with the utmost ease—the Overture " Scapino " is one of the finest feats of orchestral writing in the twentieth century. As an essay in musical wit, " Façade " is a scintillating example; as a profound piece of musical thinking and self-expression the Viola Concerto is undoubtedly a landmark; as an example of ingenious, colourful and graphic choral writing,

Rischgitz.

SIR GRANVILLE BANTOCK

Sir Granville was a bold and original composer, his work showing the influence of Wagner, national folk songs and the music of the Orient. He was a most prolific worker.

"Belshazzar's Feast" stands out almost alone after the works of Elgar and Delius.

While English music was once again coming into its own, the great German tradition came to an end with the works of Richard Strauss, who was born at Munich in 1864, and began his musical career as an orchestral horn player. Later he distinguished himself as a conductor.

As a composer he followed in his symphonic poems the tradition of Liszt, and up to the year 1899, when he produced "Ein Heldenleben," he had written a series of masterly symphonic poems, some of the most notable of which are "Death and Transfiguration," "Till's Merry Pranks," "Don Quixote" and "Don Juan."

Windmills and Cowbells

In his operas, notably "Electra,"

B.B.C.

ERIC COATES

A native of Hucknall, Notts., Eric Coates won a scholarship at the Royal Academy of Music. He composed the famous "London" Suite and "The Three Bears."

"Salome" and "Der Rosenkavalier," he carried on the Wagner tradition. Strauss's use of the orchestra is as brilliant as it is ingenious. He delights in realistic effects for their own sake, such as the windmills in "Don Quixote" and the cowbells in the "Alpine Symphony." Among other compositions Richard Strauss produced a number of songs, such as "Morgen" and "Cradle Song," which belong to some of the best things in German "lieder."

Space will not permit mention of the many composers of to-day who, although they have yet to be assessed at their true worth, have already accomplished fine and important work—such composers as Hindemith, Schönberg, Béla Bartók, Poulenc, Milhaud, Honegger, Benjamin Britten, Prokofiev, Stravinsky and Shostakovich.

A Finnish Composer

One composer, however, must be mentioned—the Finnish composer, Jean Sibelius. In his seven symphonies and seven tone-poems, such as "Tapiola," Sibelius has shown himself to be one of the greatest masters of the present century.

Sibelius lives, as Grieg did, among the hills and woods of his country. He has a beautiful house, in which he . composes all his music, and, although he sometimes travels about giving concerts, he is always glad to return to his home in the country, where everything is normally so quiet and peaceful.

Perhaps you have heard some of Sibelius's music? One of his most famous pieces is called "Finlandia." It gives us a charming musical picture of the country to which Sibelius belongs. Another of Sibelius's works is his "Valse Triste," and there are many others.

Sibelius has also written many beautiful songs and orchestral works. His music somewhat resembles that of Grieg.

Literature
Through
the Ages

Great Books
and
Their Writers

Rischgitz.

JOHN BUNYAN'S WIFE INTERCEDES FOR HIM

John Bunyan was a great writer of the Stuart period, though but the son of a tinker and so little educated that in his youth he could scarcely read or write. He was born at Elstow, a village near Bedford, in 1628; and, after his conversion, persisted in holding forbidden religious meetings. For these offences he was sent to gaol. We see in the above picture, after Duvall, how his wife interceded for his release. The first part of " The Pilgrim's Progress " was written in prison.

JOHN BUNYAN—AND AFTER

DURING the Stuart period, when England was in great distress because of quarrels over religion, two great writers arose from the Puritan party.

John Milton, the gifted poet, was in every way a contrast to John Bunyan, the author of " The Pilgrim's Progress," yet these two earnest writers both sought to turn the thoughts of their readers away from worldly pleasures towards a higher life.

John Bunyan

Milton's studious youth was spent among books and cultured people. He was educated at Cambridge, where the future poet got a good education for his life work in Literature. But Bunyan, born in 1628, and the son of a poor tinker, was scarcely taught to read and write. Bunyan served a year in Cromwell's army and was the father of two children, whom he supported as best he could by tinkering. The powers which the one achieved through happiness, care and study, the other developed through poverty and agony of mind. For Bunyan thought himself the greatest of all sinners and became terrified at the idea of the punishments God would have to inflict upon him for all his sin.

He even thought his delight in music and ringing the church bells was a temptation of Satan. His wife, a godly woman, encouraged her husband to improve his reading by the help of the Bible and a few books they possessed about religion. He became a preacher, and, as preaching the Puritan doctrines was then forbidden, Bunyan was imprisoned in Bedford gaol, where he continued to preach to his fellow prisoners, and began putting his thoughts into writing.

The Pilgrim's Progress

If he had promised not to preach, he would have been freed, but his conscience forbade that, and, with short intervals of liberty, he actually lived twelve years in prison. He wrote three books before he began his famous allegory or parable called " The Pilgrim's Progress." This is really the story of any Christian's life, as a journey beset with troubles, dangers and temptations to stray from the right path. Christian sets out to travel from the City of Destruction along the Valley of Humiliation and the Valley of the Shadow of Death, to the Celestial or Heavenly City. Like Milton's " Paradise Lost," the tale is concerned with Earth, Hell and Heaven, but Bunyan keeps to simple names and easy descriptions of rivers, mountains, bogs, gardens and houses. Each is used to represent some spiritual experience, and the definite names clear up any difficulties as to the meaning of the Slough of Despond and Doubting Castle. The people whom Christian meets are labelled in the same clear way, according to their characters— Obstinate, Mr. Worldly Wiseman, Mr. Greatheart, Hopeful, and so on.

With Simple Truths

Everybody can understand this story; nobody can argue about the simple truths of its religious teaching. No book has ever found so many readers, except the Bible itself, upon which the story was founded. Three thousand copies were sold in Bunyan's lifetime; and Americans have always appreciated its Puritan teaching.

Bunyan became head of the Baptist Church when the law allowed freedom of preaching, and he travelled about teaching, honoured and beloved wherever he went. He died in 1688.

Samuel Pepys [1633-1703]

Pepys and John Evelyn were friends, yet neither knew that the other was keeping a diary. Pepys reveals much more of his personality and private life. He was a vain man, fond of gossip, and very fond of his food. Parts of his diary are most amusing to read.

Details of serious Government affairs are found side by side with trifling matters such as: " Being washing day, dined upon cold meat."

The book is a most interesting commentary on the manners and customs of the seventeenth century. Pepys was Secretary to the Admiralty, and had exceptional opportunities for gathering information. His first-hand records of the Plague and the Great Fire of London are very vivid.

In Secret Shorthand

The diary covers nine years. It was written in a kind of secret shorthand, so that for many years after Pepys' death nobody could read it. Then by accident the clue to his cypher was discovered. The six carefully bound volumes had been left to Magdalene College, Cambridge, where he had been educated.

" *Sept.* 4, 1666. I after supper walked in the dark to Tower St. and there saw it all on fire, at Trinity House on that side and the Dolphin tavern on this, which was very near us, and the fire with extraordinary vehemence. Now begins the practice of blowing up of houses, those next the Tower, which at first did frighten people more than anything; but it stopped the fire where it was done, bringing down the

SAMUEL PEPYS THE DIARIST

Rischgitz.

This portrait of Samuel Pepys is reproduced from the painting by J. Hayls in the National Portrait Gallery, London. Pepys (pronounced as though it were spelt Peeps) was an Admiralty official. We know him best because for over nine years he kept a most intimate diary in a curious form of shorthand. It took three years to translate the shorthand. The diary gives us a wonderful insight into the manners and customs of the seventeenth century and contains in detail accounts of the Plague and Fire of London.

14—2

IN THE DAYS OF CHARLES II

The original of this picture, which is in the South Kensington Museum, was painted by Seymour Lucas. It shows us a naval architect describing a model of a new warship to the Navy Board in the time of Charles II, when the Dutch fleet threatened us. In the background, bending over the model, is John Evelyn. Near him is another famous diarist, Samuel Pepys.

Photos: Rischgitz.

The Rijks Museum in Amsterdam is the home of the above picture, which was painted by Jan Peters. It illustrates the burning of the English Fleet off Rochester in the year 1667. We notice that towering vessel, the *Royal Charles*, in the foreground. The incident occurred in the Dutch War, and John Evelyn the diarist records how he gazed upon the Dutch Fleet—" a dreadful spectacle as ever Englishmen saw, and a dishonour never to be wiped off! "

THE FIRE OF LONDON

Rischgitz.

The great Fire of London began on September 2nd, 1666, and raged for five days. Nearly 400 acres of houses were destroyed. The above illustration is taken from the painting by Stanhope A. Forbes in the Royal Exchange, London, and shows people escaping from the doomed city by water. Our knowledge of the great Fire of London is considerably enriched by the diaries of Samuel Pepys and John Evelyn, and by the writings of Daniel Defoe.

houses to the ground in the same places they stood, and then it was easy to quench what little fire was in . . . and Paul's is burned and all Cheapside. I wrote to my father this night, but the post-house being burned, the letter could not go."—*The Diary of Samuel Pepys*.

Daniel Defoe [1659-1731]

We are so used to the daily newspaper giving us details of all that is happening in the world, that it is difficult for us to realise that once there were no newspapers. Indeed, Daniel Defoe, the author of "Robinson Crusoe," was one of our earliest journalists. He improved upon the very meagre news-bulletin which was issued during the Civil War of Stuart times, and which merely recorded events. He began commenting upon what was happening and gave his own opinions so that articles were included in the bulletins as well as news.

He published a journal called *The Review*, by himself, while he was in prison in Queen Anne's reign. He had got into trouble through writing a satire against the High Church party, who were then persecuting dissenters. He was first put into the pillory for punishment, but the people protected him and pelted him only with flowers, while they drank his health. He was, however, imprisoned, and had to depend upon his pen for a living. After a time, *The Review* was published three times a week, Defoe writing all the articles himself. He had an imaginary club which he called *The Scandalous Club*—this was supposed to discuss

Rischgitz.

ROBINSON CRUSOE EXPLAINING THE SCRIPTURES TO FRIDAY

The reproduction above is taken from a painting by Alexander Fraser in the Walker Art Gallery, Liverpool. It shows Robinson Crusoe reading passages from the Holy Bible to Man Friday. The idea of Robinson Crusoe was probably borrowed by Daniel Defoe from the experiences of a Scottish sailor named Selkirk, who quarrelled with his captain and was set ashore on an uninhabited island.

DANIEL DEFOE IN THE PILLORY

Rischgitz.

The pillory was an instrument of punishment. Evildoers condemned to stand in it were often pelted with garbage and savagely insulted by the mob which gathered round. Daniel Defoe was condemned to the pillory for some of his writings, but the sympathy of the populace was with him and he was pelted only with fragrant flowers, whilst people came to Temple Bar (where the pillory stood) to drink his health. The above picture is reproduced from Eyre Crowe's painting.

swearing, drinking and gambling, and similar evils, in the columns of the journal.

Robinson Crusoe

After a year and a half in prison he was employed by both the Whigs and Tories in writing political pamphlets, but it was not until he was nearly sixty that his famous "Robinson Crusoe" appeared. The story of the lonely man on the island has been popular ever since, with grown-ups and children. Every detail is described; exact accounts of every happening are given; clothes, savages, tools—all are carefully noted; and the reader need imagine nothing. Defoe pretends it to be a true story of adventure, but he probably borrowed the idea from the experiences of a Scottish sailor named Selkirk, who quarrelled with his captain and was set ashore on an uninhabited island, where he was left alone for four years. Crusoe spent twenty-eight years on his island before he was delivered by pirates. Defoe had wonderful powers of description. In his "Journal of the Plague Year" he gives a vivid account of the terrors of the plague as though he had seen it all himself, though at the time he was only a small boy. He was carefully educated, though never at a college, and had a splendid command of the English language. Like "Pilgrim's Progress," his great adventure story has been translated into many foreign tongues.

Jonathan Swift [1667-1745]

Although of English parentage, Swift was born in Ireland, educated in Dublin, and connected with that country for many years. There he wrote the famous "Gulliver's Travels," his most popular book.

Swift had a proud disposition and was naturally inclined to resent authority over him and any patronage. He was hardly grateful to the uncle who educated him, and while secretary to Sir William Temple and enjoying his confidence and friendship, he hated to feel his position as being something between a servant and a friend. This attitude rather embittered his whole life; but one great influence kept him sweet, and that was his love of Esther Johnson, a child of seven whom he first met in Temple's house. He taught her to read and write, and from " The Journal to Stella " we can tell by his letters how much she meant to this lonely man. He called her *Stella*, which meant the same as " Esther," a star, and there was no bitterness in his writing to her. The letters give a splendid picture of the times of Queen Anne's reign—they are full of everyday interests, politics,

DEAN SWIFT AND STELLA   *Photographische Gesellschaft.*

Jonathan Swift, of whom we most often think as Dean Swift, was private secretary to his mother's kinsman, Sir William Temple. In Sir William's house Swift became tutor to Esther Johnson, the little girl seen with him in the above picture. Swift called his young friend Stella, which means a star, as does the name Esther; and Stella figures in his Journal and in his Sonnets. Swift's writings show how much Stella meant to him.

gossip, friendships, jokes and charming nonsense, and afford us a peep at the inner nature of a man whose writings could sting and lash unmercifully.

Satire was his strong point; the books for which he is famous were all satires. One called "The Battle of the Books" arose out of a quarrel as to whether ancient or modern books were the better. He pretended that the books left the shelves and fought.

Against Evil

The arguments on both sides were so cleverly put that the question was left unsettled. "A Tale of a Tub" was written to show up the Church. It was the story of evils in three brothers, Peter (the Catholic Church), and Martin and Jack, the English and the Presbyterian Churches. He wrote very fiercely and the book lost him his chance of promotion in the Church, for he was only offered the post of Dean of St. Patrick's, Dublin. He hated Ireland, but helped the cause of Irish politics with his usual force.

By courtesy of George G. Harrap & Co. Ltd.

AMONG THE LILLIPUTIANS

You may remember the incident in "Gulliver's Travels" where Gulliver says: "I walked with the utmost circumspection, to avoid treading on any stragglers." The illustration is by Willy Pogány. We can all enjoy the adventures of Gulliver in Lilliput and elsewhere. "Gulliver's Travels" is the most famous of Jonathan Swift's books, and the only one for which he received payment.

His gloomy outlook increased as he grew older. "Gulliver's Travels" began quite playfully; in the first voyage he laughed at the follies of his fellow men quite gently, but the book ended in a savage attack on the whole of the human race. We can all enjoy Gulliver's adventures in Lilliput, where he ridicules the mean ways of men, although the laugh is against our ancestors of the eighteenth century.

THE LAY OF THE LAST MINSTREL

This poem is in reality a most absorbing romance told in rhyme. It was Sir Walter Scott's first success and brought him immediate popularity when it was published in 1805. The story is related by an aged minstrel and deals with life on the Border between England and Scotland in the sixteenth century. The minstrel tells his tale at Newark Castle. Our illustration is a facsimile of the painting by R. Beavis.

SIR WALTER SCOTT, born in the year 1771, was contemporary with Wordsworth, Coleridge and Lamb, and belongs to the Age of Romance. His memory is endeared to Scotch and English alike, not only by his work as poet and novelist, but by his lovable nature. Thousands throng the streets of his native Edinburgh every year to do him honour and admire the dignified monument erected to him in Princes Street.

His work as a lawyer took him to the Border, dear to his ancestors, and all his life he never tired of collecting legends, books and armour connected with the history of the Tweed country.

He wrote poetry while a barrister, and spent his holidays on long walking tours, making the acquaintance of humble folk and listening eagerly to their traditional tales.

During college life at Edinburgh he had studied Spanish, Italian and French hurriedly, in order to get at the stories in those languages. He was familiar with Chaucer, Spenser and Shakespeare. He first became famous as a poet, though his poetry is not of the highest quality. It was popular then because it told a good tale in simple verse which was easy to grasp, free from digressions and unhampered by any deep character study. The tales told were exciting and attached to actual places and events in history. "The Lay of the Last Minstrel" was his first success, and made him popular at once. "Marmion" described in detail the defeat of the Scots at Flodden; and "The Lady of the Lake" drew the attention of every reader to the beautiful "Trossachs" country.

The Waverley Novels

Scott was well paid for his work, even before it was written. He bought Abbotsford, beautifully situated on the Tweed. Here, amid horses, dogs, visitors and his own children, he lived

SIR WALTER SCOTT

Rischgitz.

The original of this fine picture hangs in the National Portrait Gallery, London, and shows us the great Scottish poet and novelist, Sir Walter Scott. The portrait was painted at Abbotsford on the Tweed by Sir Edwin Landseer, who was Queen Victoria's favourite artist. Sir Walter was born in Edinburgh in 1771 and became a lawyer after leaving Edinburgh University. He was a poet first and afterwards became our leading writer of historical novels. He died at Abbotsford in 1832.

happily and busily. Byron was attracting notice as a poet, and Scott began to write romances in prose. " Waverley " came first, published anonymously, and immediately successful. Scott was the first writer of historical novels, and was eminently fitted by nature and study for the task. Some, like " The Heart of Midlothian " and " Old Mortality," interest us in Scottish history. " Ivanhoe " and " Kenilworth " are English in setting, while " Quentin Durward " was the first of those to deal with Continental affairs. All are based upon his own research work and careful study of the times. He introduces imaginary characters as well as historical personages, and excels in descriptions of people and scenery.

Facing Disaster

Suddenly Scott found himself involved in the failure of a big publishing firm—Ballantyne Brothers. He refused to become bankrupt, and set to work to earn by his pen enough to pay off his share of the debt—£130,000. He wrote desperately — novels, histories, and essays, giving up every moment possible to the struggle.

The death of his wife and overstrain led to a breakdown in health. He was persuaded to take a sea voyage, but it was too late, and he returned to Abbotsford to die.

Dr. Brown has told us in " Pet Marjorie " about a clever little girl friend of Scott, in whose witty chatter he delighted. Like his own grandson, she never grew up, but the great novelist rejoiced in the companionship of both children.

Jane Austen [1775-1817]

Jane Austen was liked by everybody, and loved by those who knew her intimately and brought their joys and sorrows to her instinctively. Her daintiness and lively charm attracted young and old, and these qualities were enhanced by a clever wit and cheerful outlook upon the world.

A sheltered life at her father's rectory of Steventon, near Basingstoke, did not bring her into contact with many people; she was the youngest of seven. Yet when she was old enough to go to dances at the neighbouring houses of well-to-do folk, she began at once to describe the county squires, their wives and daughters, the officers they met, and the clergymen and fashionable ladies who attended these assemblies. She was very like the heroine of her first novel, Elizabeth Bennet, in " Pride and Prejudice," for, although she loved fun, " I hope I never ridicule what is wise and good. Follies and nonsense, whims and inconsistencies do divert me I own, and I laugh at them whenever I can." She called her book " First Impressions," and it was rejected under that title.

For the sake of Mr. Austen's health the family moved to Bath, and the scene of " Northanger Abbey " was laid there. She revelled in the fuller opportunities for social enjoyment at this fashionable resort, and this book has a strong local interest. Her father's death led to further changes of home, first to Southampton, then to Chawton, near Winchester.

" Pride and Prejudice " Accepted

At Chawton Jane Austen felt inspired to write again, and enjoyed finishing " Sense and Sensibility," begun thirteen years before. That was accepted, and she began " Mansfield Park," and sent " Pride and Prejudice " in again under its new name. This was both her first and favourite novel. She had lived herself among the characters, and it was her masterpiece. The book is full of mischievous fun and minute observation of people. The reader feels he knows intimately every one of the characters, because they are so naturally presented by their creator.

There is no rhetoric, no exaggeration or striving after effect. She keeps her characters well in hand, they share her

Rischgitz.

By permission of the Corporation of Sheffield.

ROB ROY AND THE BAILIE

Taken from the original picture by J. Watson Nicol, this illustration shows us one of the many dramatic incidents in Sir Walter Scott's sixth Waverley novel, "Rob Roy." The hero of this romance is Robert MacGregor, a robber and cattle-stealer, who is presented to the reader as a Jacobite. Bailie Nicol Jarvie is one of the chief characters in the story which is related by another well-drawn character, Frank Osbaldistone.

own peculiar reserve. Scenery is a mere background to the human interest, which is all-compelling, in spite of the limitations of the author's environment.

Jane Austen had been very well educated for a girl of the period— French and Italian were included in her studies—and she was familiar with the works of Richardson, Johnson, Cowper and Scott. She possessed also a power of criticising her own work. She knew her books to be " rather too light and bright and sparkling," and certainly, compared with the tempestuous " Jane Eyre " of Charlotte Brontë, Jane Austen's books are almost devoid of human passions and the deeper problems of life. Yet she had earned the fame of a great writer by describing in her own minia-

ture style the life she saw around her, drawn perhaps from fewer than a dozen country families. " Persuasion " and " Emma " were written during the last three years of her happy, uneventful life. The unusually warm tribute on her tomb in Winchester Cathedral reads: " The benevolence of her heart, the sweetness of her temper, and the extraordinary endowments of her mind obtained the regard of all who knew her and the warmest love of her immediate connexions."

Charles Lamb [1775-1834]

Many of us as children made our first acquaintance with the plays of our greatest dramatist through Lamb's " Tales from Shakespeare." He and his sister, Mary, set themselves a labour of love in popularising the great dramas, telling the stories in language easily understood by the young reader, and quoting often Shakespeare's own lines. Lamb was a critic too; he commented upon the early Elizabethan dramas. But the book that endears him to most people is his " Essays of Elia." Here may be found the record of Lamb's life and friendships, precious to all who admire this lovable creature. Read " Old Benchers of the Inner Temple," where Lamb's father and his employer are referred to as Lovel and Salt. The essay on " Christ's Hospital " introduces Coleridge, with whom he was at school there. " Mackery End " gives a real idea of Mary, his sister (whom he calls " Bridget " all through the Essays), and his elder brother. The characters in " South Sea House " he actually met when a clerk there. His absorbing interest in the theatre led him to write " Barbara S—," the tale of the little child-actress.

CHARLES LAMB

Rischgit..

Charles Lamb, of whom we think as a great essay writer, was born in the City of London in 1775 and gave us " Tales from Shakespeare " and the " Essays of Elia." In his work he was closely assisted by his sister Mary. Our portrait is after the painting by Meyer.

Specially drawn for this work.

RUMPELSTILTSKIN, FROM THE BROTHERS GRIMM

The two Brothers Grimm, to whom the world of girls and boys owes Grimms' Fairy Tales, were both German professors and men of great learning. The above picture illustrates the story "Rumpelstiltskin." You will remember how the hobgoblin appears before the miller's daughter and asks why she weeps. " Alas ! " says she, " I must spin this straw into gold, and I know not how."

The Gentle Elia

In " Old China " we have Lamb at his best; the excellent picture of Mary Lamb, his love of the quaint and old, his regret for the past pleasures, known only in his days of poverty, make this essay a masterpiece, second perhaps only to the inimitable " Dream Children." This betrays his love for children, his disappointed hopes as a lover, his understanding sympathies and loyal devotion to his unfortunate and talented sister; for Lamb sacrificed his own wishes to the needs of Mary; who, subject to fits of insanity, became the object of his lifelong care.

William Hazlitt [1778-1830]

A prominent writer but one who fell into quite a different category was William Hazlitt, best known as an essayist and a sincere critic of the times in which he lived. He was born at Maidstone, studied art for a while and then turned to literature on meeting such giants as Wordsworth, Coleridge and Lamb. He became a contributor to various magazines and newspapers; and, as you read Hazlitt, you are bound to be struck with the admirable and most cultured style that runs through all his works.

The Brothers Grimm [1785-1863, 1786-1859]

These two clever German students have made their family name famous throughout the civilised world. They were both educated at Cassel and, later, at Marburg University, and both were concerned with books all their lives. Jacob became professor and chief librarian at Göttingen, where he lectured on the German language and literature; his brother was also a professor there. Both were exiled for a while because, with six other professors, they opposed the King of Hanover, but later both became professors in Berlin. The elder wrote a famous German grammar book and a history of the German language.

Hansel and Gretel

The younger, Wilhelm, devoted himself to German mediæval poetry, but worked with his brother at a great dictionary. Together they made their collection of fairy tales in three volumes, issued at different times. These caused people to become interested in studying the folklore of different countries.

In reading " Hansel and Gretel," " The Frog-Prince " and " Rumpelstiltskin," one would hardly connect such entertaining stories with two solemn learned gentlemen devoted to literary study! Yet what they probably considered the least serious part of their life work has brought them fame, not only in England and America, but in all the chief countries of the world, and made for them firm friends among the children of many nations.

The stories of the fairies were actually collected from the country folk of Germany.

James Fenimore Cooper [1789-1851]

Most boys and girls have enjoyed the adventure stories of this American writer ; perhaps " The Last of the Mohicans " is the favourite, but " The Pathfinder " and " Deerslayer " are almost as popular.

Born at New Jersey, into a wealthy Quaker family, the boy had the advantages of a good education at Yale.

His first adventures were on the sea; from a midshipman he became a lieutenant, but resigned on his marriage to live a life ashore.

" The Big Serpent "

Of his thirty-two stories, the best were those concerned with the sea or with the life of the Red Indians. He had great powers of description, and some of his characters—" Long Tom Coffin " and " The Big Serpent "—deserve to be remembered with those of "Treasure Island."

Records of his sea experiences found more serious expression in " The Two Admirals " and " Lives of Distinguished American Naval Officers."

Captain Marryat [1792-1848]

Frederick Marryat, perhaps better remembered as Captain Marryat, is still popular with the young people of to-day, though the majority of his stories are laid in the eighteenth century. In writing so realistically of the sea, he was dealing with a subject he knew well, for he entered the Royal Navy as a midshipman and saw much service. By the year 1830 he was both a captain and a C.B. and he carried the bluffness, the stern discipline and the lighter moments of seafaring into " Peter Simple," " Jacob Faithful " and, what is perhaps his best-loved work, " Mr. Midshipman Easy."

By courtesy of Messrs. George G. Harrap & Co. Ltd.

THE TOURNAMENT AT ASHBY

One of the most fascinating of the famous Waverley novels by Sir Walter Scott is " Ivanhoe," the first in which the scenes are laid outside Scotland. The period is just after the return of Richard I from the Holy Land, and the story gives a vivid picture of feudal England and the days of Chivalry. Our illustration, from the painting by Rowland Wheelwright, depicts one of the most thrilling moments in the tournament at Ashby-de-la-Zouch in Leicestershire when Ivanhoe and Brian de Bois-Guilbert were engaged in desperate combat.

AN INCIDENT FROM " WESTWARD HO!"

Specially painted for this work.

The picture illustrates an incident towards the end of Chap. IX of " Westward Ho!" where horse and rider roll into a bog-hole. This story, which introduces Elizabethan seadogs, their struggle with the Armada and adventures on the Spanish Main, is considered by many to be the best work of Charles Kingsley (1819–75), who was rector of Eversley, Hampshire. A native of Devon, this clergyman worked and preached in crowded parts of London, helping people who were very poor. Another favourite story by Kingsley is " Hereward the Wake," and he will always be remembered for his children's book " The Water Babies."

DICKENS AND OTHERS OF HIS TIME

Rischgitz.

THE GRAVE OF LITTLE NELL

This illustration, after the drawing by George Cattermole, shows us the old, old man sitting near the grave of " Little Nell " in the scene from Charles Dickens' great story, " The Old Curiosity Shop." " And thenceforth, every day, and all day long, he waited at her grave for her. . . . How many glimpses of the form, the fluttering dress, the hair that waved so gaily in the wind . . . rose up before him in the old, dull, silent church ! "

THE eighteenth century gave us many writers whose names and works will always live, and the ensuing hundred years were in no sense less fruitful. To start at the beginning, October, 1800, saw the birth of Thomas Babington Macaulay, one of our greatest essayists and historians. After taking up the law he went to India as a member of the Supreme Council, and it was when he returned to the Motherland in 1838 that he commenced his famous " History of England," which opens at the accession of James II. Ten years later the first two volumes of this work appeared, but the author was dead before the fifth and last volume came out. A brilliant statesman, raised to the peerage in 1857, Lord Macaulay was always torn between politics and writing. His grave is in Westminster Abbey.

In the year 1805, a few months before Nelson won his great victory at Trafalgar, a little Danish boy was born, who was destined to give delight to thousands of children.

Hans Christian Andersen belonged to a poor family of Odense. His father was a cobbler, and could only send his boy to the charity school until he was nine, at which early age he was obliged to earn money in a factory. The father was a learned man in his way, and used to read far into the night with his son Hans, who was perhaps inclined to dream and waste his time.

Seeking his Fortune

After his father's death the boy continued to be interested in ballads and poetry, and began to compose plays himself. He thought perhaps some of them could be acted if he went to Copenhagen, so he set out thither with his small bundle and thirty-seven shillings to seek his fortune. He became a joiner. Nobody seemed to want his plays until he came under the notice of an influential man, who procured for him a free place at a good school, from which he passed quickly to the University. He had very little money and could not marry, so no children of his own listened to those delightful tales we have all enjoyed. In 1835 some were published at Christmas, and were so popular that he continued to write more every Christmas for several years. These, and not his plays, have made him famous, although his ambition was to become a great dramatist.

Who could ever forget " The Fir Tree " or " The Little Match Girl " ?

" In her numb little hands she carried a bundle of matches, which all day long she had offered for sale in vain. Now she feared to go home, for she had earned no money, and perhaps her cruel father would beat her. Besides, her home was little better than the streets. It was a bare garret, through the crazy walls of which the keen wind blew and whistled, and whose roof let in the rain and snow, although she tried to stuff up the crannies with rags."

William Harrison Ainsworth [1805–1882]

What lover of history has not revelled in Ainsworth's romances ? Not long ago the tale of Dick Turpin and his famous ride from London to York, which he described in " Rookwood " in 1834, was republished under the title " The Bold Highwayman— Dick Turpin." The modern schoolboy can still find pleasure in " Old St. Paul's " with its thrilling tale of the Plague and The Fire. This was first published serially in the *Sunday Times*, as was " The Lancashire Witches." His " Tower of London " has been read eagerly for half a century in French, German and Dutch translations.

On both the Harrison and the Ainsworth side of his family, the writer came of scholarly Manchester people with a love of learning. William's earliest ambition was to make a real firework rocket ; then he became keen on a theatre he had made for himself in the cellar, writing the plays in spare time.

William Makepeace Thackeray [1811–1863]

A novelist of quite a different type was William Makepeace Thackeray. He was born at Calcutta, for his father was in the service of the East India Company, and came home to go to school, first at Chiswick and afterwards, in 1822, at Charterhouse. Thackeray's earliest important contribution to English literature was " Vanity Fair," which appeared in monthly parts, and then came the work by which he is best remembered, " Esmond," with its sequel " The Virginians."

If you take up some of Thackeray's many novels you will find them simple in style and full of deep human interest, whilst you cannot fail to realise that they are faithful mirrors of the times in which the writer lived.

Charles Dickens [1812–1870]

When the story of " David Copperfield " was appearing month by month in a magazine throughout the summer of 1849, nobody, except his friend Forster, had any idea that Dickens was relating his own life experiences.

Painful though it was to the author to recall the agonies which his sensitive nature had suffered during those impressionable years of neglected childhood, yet it was those actual experiences of the underworld that gave Dickens the opportunity of meeting all sorts and conditions of men, women and children, who like himself were battling with hard Fate. His first-hand knowledge of the back streets of London, its debtors' prisons, lodging-houses and factories came from this background; his own wanderings and privations taught him what no study of books could have done in easier circumstances.

He set out to fit himself for his life work and to use every talent he possessed in showing up the abuses which existed in workshops, factories, private schools and prisons.

By permission of Messrs. Hodder & Stoughton.

The Pickwick Papers, first published under the title " The Posthumous Papers of the Pickwick Club," was the earliest of the novels of Charles Dickens. Upwards of 300 characters appear in the book, the central figure being that of Mr. Pickwick, illustrated above by Frank Reynolds. Indirectly, the name is taken from the village of Pickwick, on the Great Bath Road between Bath and Chippenham. The work first appeared in monthly parts.

It was the children who appealed most to this author; he rarely sees the funny side of life in their misery. Almost all his child characters are little old grown-up folk with responsibilities far beyond their years. Little Nell watching and planning, caring with uncanny wisdom for her grandfather, remains always a pathetic figure. Oliver, David, Pip, Smike, Paul and Florence Dombey, are all hopelessly at the mercy of authority in some form. Young Traddles and The Artful Dodger get a good deal out of life in spite of circumstances, and Kit cuts quite a manly figure with his family.

The Old Curiosity Shop

It was perhaps " The Old Curiosity Shop " that endeared Dickens to the English-speaking race, though " David Copperfield " was his masterpiece. He began his literary work by writing " Sketches by Boz " in his spare time while reporting for a newspaper, and " Pickwick Papers " followed in monthly parts. This was hardly a story, but a series of incidents, yet it is the characters in the Club that we remember rather than their doings.

Dickens himself loved light, colour and movement, and the characters he created overflowed with abundance of life, like himself. He appealed to his readers with his jollity almost as much as with his intense sympathies.

Nobody has written of the English Christmas like Dickens. His " Christmas Carol " and " The Chimes " breathe its very atmosphere of outdoor fog and chill contrasted with indoor comfort, appetising odours and cheery fires. It was the latter book, written in Italy, which tempted the novelist into reading his work aloud to audiences. He was always dramatic; from a child he had been encouraged to act and recite, and into these public readings of his own work he put far more energy than was good for him, for he was never robust. He worked too hard at his writing and was subject to fits of fatigue and depression. After giving up the editorship of the *Daily*

Specially drawn for this work.

FROM " DAVID COPPERFIELD "

Regarded as the best of all the works of Charles Dickens, " David Copperfield " first appeared in monthly parts, publication beginning in May, 1849. The incident depicted is the one where David is interviewed by Mr. Creakle, who grasps the boy by the ear. " When I say I'll do a thing, I do it," says Mr. Creakle; " and when I say I will have a thing done, I will have it done."

News he went to Switzerland. "Dombey and Son" and "David Copperfield" were his next ventures. "Bleak House" dealt with the injustice of delaying lawsuits; perhaps Inspector Bucket and the pathetic crossing sweeper, Poor Joe, helped to account for its enormous sales. "Little Dorrit" showed Dickens' scorn of bad government in public offices, just as "Oliver Twist" and "Nicholas Nickleby" had exposed the workhouse system and the wretched schools.

Sir John Martin Harvey's play "The Only Way" is based upon Dickens' story of the French Revolution, called "A Tale of Two Cities."

Dickens' last years were spent in the house at Gadshill, outside Rochester, which as a small boy he had longed to possess.

Specially drawn for this work.

OLIVER TWIST ASKS FOR MORE

" Child as Oliver Twist was, he was desperate with hunger, and reckless with misery. He rose from the table; and advancing to the master, basin and spoon in hand, said, somewhat alarmed at his own temerity: ' Please, sir, I want some more.' "

Another notable author of the Dickens era was Charles Reade (1814–1884). Like so many other literary men, he was called to the Bar, but his heart was in writing and he began his long career by producing dramas. Among his novels, "The Cloister and the Hearth" ranks very high, but "Peg Woffington" is still widely read, and so is "It is Never too Late to Mend." A year after Reade's birth there appeared in a London family a baby boy who was destined to become a delightful writer of English. His name was Anthony Trollope (1815–1882), and he gave us "Barchester Towers" and "The Claverings" among at least fifty novels, which it is said brought him in a very substantial fortune.

The Brontës [1816–1855]

Away on the great moorlands of Yorkshire, situated among lonely hills and barren ridges, lies the village of Haworth. There, at "The Parsonage," now preserved as the Brontë Museum, can be seen the childish work of the three clever sisters, Charlotte, Emily and Anne Brontë, whose lives were spent almost entirely among these wild surroundings.

Stories, poetry and essays contributed by each of these children were cleverly illustrated by their artistic brother Branwell.

Tastes in Common

Their father, the Rector, an Irishman, was moody by nature, and became more depressed and short-tempered as his troubles came. Less than a year after the family had come to Haworth from Bradford, where his six children had been born, he lost his wife, and the two elder girls contracted consumption while at boarding school, and died shortly after.

Charlotte Brontë, now the eldest, felt keenly the responsibility of her position; her only brother was a great worry to them all. Every spare penny had been spent to send him to London to study art, but he was a failure in every way. After his death in 1848, Mr. Brontë grew bitter, and the three sisters had to depend upon themselves to make the best of their lives. They had many tastes in common; all loved books and longed to write. They could only be educated at a second-rate boarding-school, and Charlotte helped the family finances by acting as part governess during her last years at Cowan Bridge School. This is probably the " Lowood " she describes so minutely in " Jane Eyre."

Currer, Ellis and Acton Bell

On her return to Haworth, the three sisters collected the poems they had written. They published under the names of " Currer," " Ellis " and " Acton " Bell (using their initials), as they did not wish to be known. The book was not a success, neither was Charlotte's first novel. Still she did not give in, but sent in another she had been writing from her own life experience.

This was the famous " Jane Eyre,"
one of the strongest novels ever written. Pathetic, emotional, vivid, full of life as she had encountered it, the book made a direct appeal to its readers.

" Wuthering Heights "

Both her sisters wrote. Emily had even more talent than Charlotte. She was very imaginative; her tale called " Wuthering Heights " was largely autobiographical, and very cleverly written. She was also the most poetically gifted of the sisters. Anne produced " Agnes Grey " and " The Tenant of Wildfell Hall."

After the death of both her sisters, within two years of her success, Charlotte married one of her father's curates, yet even that happiness was short-lived. In less than a year she died.

The tragic story has been written by loving hands. Mrs. Gaskell, the author of " Cranford," was her friend. She wrote " The Life of Charlotte Brontë," and this, like all her works, is stamped with infinite skill. Elizabeth Cleghorn Gaskell (1810–1865) is widely known if only for her first work " Mary Barton," which portrayed Lancashire life so realistically. She was brought up at Knutsford, in Cheshire, and it is of this place she wrote in her famous " Cranford."

Another woman writer of the same period was George Eliot (1819–1880), for that was the pen-name of Mary Ann or Marian Evans. She was born near Nuneaton and kept house for her widower father, whom we meet in " Adam Bede." Though she was interested in literary subjects early in life, George Eliot had reached forty years of age before she wrote " The Mill on the Floss " and " Silas Marner." Her works are unsurpassed for the living characters they contain and rank very high among English fiction.

Charles Kingsley [1819–1875]

While Dickens was writing novels to induce people to realise that many public institutions needed improvement, Charles Kingsley also was writing

Specially drawn for this work.

AMYAS LEIGH OF " WESTWARD HO ! "

The central character in Charles Kingsley's enthralling adventure story, " Westward Ho ! " is Amyas Leigh, a youth of his own county of Devon. Amyas was big and strong, though of most equable temper, and we meet in the book Raleigh, Drake, Hawkins and other heroes of the stirring days of Good Queen Bess. The sub-title of the book is " The Voyages and Adventures of Sir Amyas Leigh, Kt., of Burrough, in the County of Devon, in the reign of Her Most Glorious Majesty Queen Elizabeth."

stories with a purpose. The text of his sermon was perhaps " Those who wish to be clean, clean they will be." In his famous " Water Babies " he teaches us through a fairy story much about " cleanliness of mind," for while sympathising with Tom's wretched life as a sweep, he insists that Tom needed many a lesson before he could become a real Water Baby.

Against Dirt and Disease

The book is full also of interesting information about Nature, especially water animals and plants, for Kingsley was a scientist as well as a clergyman. All his life he carried on a crusade against dirt and disease, and called upon people to rid themselves of such evils as bad drinking-water, unclean houses, and infectious diseases. His " Alton Locke " is a clever novel, calling attention to many hardships among the working classes in London.

He loved his native Devon, but worked among the crowded London

Specially drawn for this work.

THE CORAL ISLAND

" To my horror I saw the shark quite close under the log, in the act of darting towards Jack's foot. . . . The monster's snout rubbed against the log as it passed, and revealed its hideous jaws, into which Jack instantly plunged the paddle and thrust it down its throat." This is a thrilling incident from " The Coral Island," the third of R. M. Ballantyne's boys' books, which was first published in 1858.

streets, preaching, and helping the poorer folk. In his historical novel, " Westward Ho! " he introduces the Elizabethan sea-dogs and their struggle with the Armada into a very exciting story. " Hereward the Wake " and " Hypatia " deal with English and Roman times respectively, while " The Heroes " narrates old Greek stories. Kingsley's life has been written by his wife: she includes most interesting letters revealing not only the novelist's lovable nature, but his wonderful influence over all with whom he worked.

Robert Michael Ballantyne [1825–1894]

Robert Louis Stevenson once called this splendid writer of boys' stories, " Ballantyne the Brave." Both men were born in Edinburgh, and R.L.S. succeeded Ballantyne as a master writer of adventure and travel. Few people realise, however, that Ballantyne's thrilling stories were almost all based on his actual personal experiences.

Early Work

As a child he loved reading and story-telling, but showed no special talent; the great gift he afterwards possessed of writing a straightforward tale like " The Coral Island " with ease and fluency developed with practice.

Family difficulties forced Robert to begin work early, and a relative managed to get him a post in the Hudson Bay Company. At sixteen he was on his way to the wilds of North America, a venture well suited to his disposition.

He described his life in Canada as " hard, rough and healthy." He and his friends did very little office - work. Most of their time was spent in fur-trading, canoeing and fishing; but it was a very lonely existence. It was to relieve the loneliness that young Ballantyne wrote long letters to his mother, full of his doings, and as the mail left only twice a year, we may imagine how full of adventure these budgets became. It was in this way the author began to feel his power of composition, although the idea of writing a continuous narrative did not occur to him until his six years in Canada were almost at an end. He enjoyed writing, but the book was only written on paper and was passed round among his friends on his return to Scotland.

However, a cousin promised to get it printed, and " Hudson Bay " became an immediate success. Several years passed before the author took to writing seriously but he was at last persuaded, and "The Young Fur Traders" and "Ungava"—a tale of Eskimo life—gave further details of his doings in Canada. After that he got into touch with travellers who could give him first-hand information, and few writers of fiction have been so exact and careful in collecting their material.

Before he wrote "The Lifeboat," Ballantyne went to Ramsgate and made friends with the coxswain of the lifeboat there. He spent three weeks on the Bell Rock Lighthouse itself before beginning "The Lighthouse." While planning "Fighting the Flames," he actually joined the Fire Brigade and rushed through London streets in uniform on the fire engines. His married life was spent in Edinburgh until 1873. After that he settled in London.

In the Doone Valley

Turning from a boys' writer, we can consider next Richard Doddridge Blackmore (1825–1900), and there are very few young people who do not take up that long, romantic story "Lorna Doone." The author was a lawyer (and later a market-gardener) who took to writing, and it may surprise you to know that he wrote poems also. He did not consider "Lorna Doone" his best book, but through all his works there runs the same deep sympathy with nature.

Jules Verne [1828–1905]

Every schoolboy has at some time or other been thrilled by the work of this imaginative Frenchman.

Verne, after studying law, and writing comedies and librettos for opera, suddenly struck an entirely new vein

Specially drawn for this work.

ON THE BRINK OF DISASTER

The above picture illustrates a stirring passage from "Hudson Bay," by R. M. Ballantyne. The description reads: "The canoe got into a strong current, and almost in an instant was swept down towards the fall. To turn the head of the canoe up the stream, and paddle for their lives, was the work of a moment; but before they got it fairly round they were on the very brink of the cataract."

in fiction. Like H. G. Wells, he foresaw the possibilities of science in the near future, but he exaggerated these into the wildest narratives of adventure, carried out by means of inventions.

The stories were cleverly thought out, the exciting escapades are made natural, and all kinds of "mechanical" characters necessary to the progress of the tales are introduced and accepted by the reader.

"Around the World in Eighty Days" is a remarkably clever story, which leads us on to read "Five Weeks in a Balloon."

"Twenty Thousand Leagues under the Sea" stirs up every imaginative mind, and in the weird "Hector

ALICE AND THE WHITE RABBIT

" Alice felt so desperate that she was ready to ask help of anyone; so, when the Rabbit came near her, she began, in a low, timid voice, ' If you please, sir. . . .' The Rabbit started violently, dropped the white kid gloves and the fan and skurried away into the darkness as hard as he could go." From " Alice's Adventures in Wonderland," by Lewis Carroll.

Servadac," the author actually gives an account of a voyage on a comet!

Though born in the same year, George Meredith (1828–1909) must be placed in a very different category from that of the ingenious French writer. He ranks very high indeed among English novelists and poets, and those who have not read any of his books have missed the masterly work of one of the great Victorians.

With Portsmouth as his birthplace, George Meredith started out in life in a solicitor's office, but soon took up writing and began by producing a poem on the Battle of Chillianwallah for one of the magazines. Then he turned to journalism and was for a time a war correspondent. Among his outstanding stories, which all should read, are " The Ordeal of Richard Feverel," " Evan Harrington " and " The Adventures of

Harry Richmond." This novelist lived and died at Flint Cottage, Boxhill, Surrey.

Lewis Carroll [1832–1898]

Few of us would associate the clever nonsense of " Alice in Wonderland " with a professor in mathematics, yet Charles Dodgson, a learned student and tutor at Oxford, was the author of that delightful book and its sister story, " Through the Looking Glass."

He was a bachelor who loved being with children, and the story was actually told to three sisters one summer afternoon while resting on the shady bank of the Thames. Alice in a kind of dream goes down a rabbit-hole in pursuit of the White Rabbit, and has weird adventures among the animals.

Nonsense rhymes add to the general muddle, and make the book a delightful problem. " The Hunting of the

Drawings by permission of Messrs. Macmillan & Co., Ltd.
THE KING AND QUEEN OF HEARTS

This picture and its two companion illustrations are from the drawings of Sir John Tenniel. Above we see the grand procession, when the Queen demands of the Knave of Hearts the identity of the little girl. " My name is Alice, so please your Majesty," said Alice, very politely.

Snark" and "Sylvie and Bruno" are still favourites, even with the modern child, "Through the Looking Glass" has been dramatised with great success, and is now also a ballet.

Mark Twain [1835–1910]

This was the pen-name of a famous American writer, known all over the world for his humorous books. He was Samuel Langhorne Clemens, born in Florida, Missouri, and he adopted the name of "Mark Twain" from the call which the pilots make on the Mississippi River, when sounding the depth of the water. The words actually mean "by the mark, two fathoms," and while a pilot on that river, Clemens had used that call hundreds of times. One of his books described his experiences at that time—"Life on the Mississippi."

Once he went silver mining in Nevada, then for two years he was editor of *The Virginia City Enterprise*. In 1867, he visited France, Italy and Palestine, gathering material for his book, "Innocents Abroad." This made his reputation as a humorist.

He became an editor again at Buffalo, and married a wealthy lady, but the publishing firm with which he was connected failed, and he began lecturing and writing in earnest to pay off debts.

By permission of Messrs. Macmillan & Co., Ltd.

WHO STOLE THE TARTS ?

This delightful pen and ink drawing shows the trial of the Knave of Hearts in the story "Alice's Adventures in Wonderland." The King of Hearts, who acts as judge, wears his crown over the wig, and it is the strangest court of justice imaginable. The White Rabbit reads the accusation, which originates from the familiar nursery rhyme: "The Queen of Hearts, she made some tarts, all on a summer day."

A later journey gave him experiences of which he made the most in "A Tramp Abroad." The best known perhaps, of his famous books are "Tom Sawyer" and "Huckleberry Finn." These two books are full of real humour, fine writing and sound philosophy of life. We all know the cute, mischievous Tom and his equally intelligent Aunt—"She talks awful, but talk don't hurt—anyways it don't if she don't cry!"

Once Tom had been set to whitewash a fence as punishment; Ben Rogers, whose ridicule he dreaded, hove in sight, eating an apple. Tom went on with his work, taking no notice.

"'Hello, old chap; you got to work, hey?'

"'Why, it's you, Ben! I warn't noticing.'

"'Say, I'm going in a swimming, I am. Don't you wish you could? But, of course, you'd druther work, wouldn't you? 'Course you would!'

"Tom contemplated the boy a bit, and said:

"'What do you call work?'

"'Why, ain't that work?'

MARK TWAIN   *James's Press.*

Here is a portrait of Samuel Langhorne Clemens, who was born in the United States of America in 1835. He is best known among young people for his famous books, "Tom Sawyer" and "Huckleberry Finn." He adopted the pen-name "Mark Twain" from the call which pilots used to make when taking soundings in the Mississippi River.

"Tom resumed his whitewashing and answered carelessly:

"'Well, maybe it is, and maybe it ain't. All I know is, it suits Tom Sawyer.'

"'Oh! come now, you don't mean to let on that you like it?'

"The brush continued to move.

"'Like it? Well, I don't see why I oughtn't to like it. Does a boy get a chance to whitewash a fence every day?'

"That put the thing in a new light. Ben stopped nibbling his apple. Tom swept his brush daintily back and forth—stepped back to note the effect. . . .

"'Say, Tom, let me whitewash a little.' . . .

"The retired artist sat on a barrel in the shade close by, dangling his legs, munched his apple and planned the slaughter of more innocents . . . boys happened along every little while; they came to jeer, but—remained to whitewash. . . ."

Richard Green [1837–1883]

It is delightful to read Mrs. Green's introduction to her husband's masterpiece, "A Short History of the English People." We note that word "people," for it was the aim of this clever student of our country's story to trace the development of the people themselves from earliest times, and not merely to chronicle events or give the records of successive reigns.

The book has such a personality behind it, that we cannot separate the work from its author. From earliest schooldays, Green was an historian in the truest sense, piecing together the past from what he could see and trace for himself in the present. He reconstructed the history of

Oxford, his native city, by joining in its old rites and traditional processions, studying brasses in churches, tablets and records of the market places, colleges and city boundaries. St. Giles' Fair was fraught with interest to the young student of humanity. "In a walk through Oxford," he wrote, "one may find illustrations of every period in our annals." His youth was connected with Magdalen College School.

Everything associated with his training was conservative, but so independent a thinker soon began to unravel problems in his own way. When a school essay was set on "Charles the First," he devoted much study to the subject, and won the prize for a most original outburst of conviction that the king was in the wrong!

From that time he became rather a rebel in his opinions, and "Man and Man's History" became the chief interest of his life.

He had few friends or advisers, he read enormously, and his brilliant history book is founded on a conscientious study of original parchments and records.

Thomas Hardy [1840–1928]

Novelist, poet and dramatist, Thomas Hardy began his career as an architect and his first actual appearance in print was with an article "How I Built Myself a House" in 1865. In 1871 his first novel "Desperate Remedies" was published and in the following year came the first of those great stories known as the Wessex series. All of these fine novels give vividly intimate and life-like delineations of the people of Dorset and the neighbouring counties. Most of them are, in the main, tragic stories, with characters taken from among the yeomen and the tradesmen,

Specially drawn for this work.

TOM SAWYER AND HUCKLEBERRY FINN

Do you remember this incident in Mark Twain's "Tom Sawyer"? While Joe is slicing bacon for breakfast in the camp "Tom and Huck asked him to hold on a minute; they stepped to a promising nook in the river bank and threw in their lines; almost immediately they had reward. . . . They fried the fish with the bacon and were astonished; for no fish had ever seemed so delicious before."

set against a background that at times seems to play a dominant part in the story, for Hardy was a master of descriptive writing.

The first of the Wessex novels, "Under the Greenwood Tree," has more humour than most of them and tells of the loves of a rustic boy and girl against a background of village life, with the carrier's family and the members of the parish choir forming a cheerful chorus.

On Egdon Heath

"The Return of the Native," first

published in 1878, is set amid the wild and even sinister scenery of Edgon Heath, with Clym Yeobright, his mother, and the strangely fascinating Eustacia Vye standing out as great characters against a grim and sombre background. In what is probably the most famous of all his novels " Tess of the D'Urbervilles," which appeared in 1891, Hardy told his most challenging and tragic story; while in " The Trumpet Major," a more genial and happy story written eleven years earlier, we have a picture of the anxiety prevailing in the English southern counties at the time of Napoleon's threatened invasion. There is, too, a glimpse of George III and his family at their favourite watering-place of Weymouth.

The Napoleonic Wars are the background again in his great epic-drama " The Dynasts " which appeared in three parts from 1904 to 1908. This amazing and wonderful work is not a novel but poetry, drama and history, and is justly regarded as a noble contribution to the great literature of the world.

Many honours were bestowed on Hardy and in 1910 he was awarded the Order of Merit and the gold medal of the Royal Society of Literature. He died in 1928 and stands to-day among the immortals as one of the greatest of English writers.

Joel Chandler Harris [1848–1908]

There are few of us who have not laughed over the antics of Brer Rabbit and the Tar Baby in that delightful series of tales told by " Uncle Remus." The American author, who began life in a printing office, studied law and abandoned it for journalism, made his most distinctive contribution to the world's literature in these quaint tales, told in dialect and dealing with negro life and its folklore. Uncle Remus, the principal character, is a remarkably vivid and real creation, and the homely philosophy and poetic feeling in his stories

appeal just as much as his humour to both children and grown-ups.

It was in 1880 that the book " Uncle Remus: his Songs and his Sayings " was published; then followed " Nights with Uncle Remus," " Free Joe," and other sketches of life in Georgia.

What the Brothers Grimm did for German folk stories, Harris did for American negro literature of his country.

Brer Rabbit and the Tar Baby

" Brer Rabbit was mighty pert and spry, and he never let Brer Fox catch him. So Brer Fox pretended to be friendly, and asked Brer Rabbit to come to dinner with him. But Brer Rabbit did not come; he knew what was going to be eaten at that dinner. Brer Fox then thought of something else. He went to work and got some tar and some turpentine and fixed up a thing which he called a Tar Baby. He set up this Tar Baby by the road near Brer Rabbit's house and laid low beneath the bramble-bushes near by to watch what would happen."

Robert Louis Stevenson [1850–1894]

In one of his books, this most charming of authors wrote: " To travel hopefully is a better thing than to arrive." The life of R.L.S. was, indeed, one of much wandering; his courageous spirit, full of the keenest enjoyment of life, carried him victoriously through forty-five years of wretched physical weakness, and led him to experience far more adventure in his search for health than hundreds of robust citizens, who, with wealth and strength but far less vital energy, are content to remain at home.

Even as a child, the wander-lust was there.

" My bed is like a little boat:
Nurse helps me in when I embark."

So many of the poems in " A Child's Garden of Verses " recall the longings of an imaginative, lonely child to

THE KIDNAPPING OF DAVID BALFOUR

This picture by W. R. S. Stott catches perfectly the frenzied moment when David Balfour, hero of
" Kidnapped," by Robert Louis Stevenson, realises that his Uncle Ebenezer is leaving him to his
fate. " I gave a piercing cry, so that both sides of the anchorage rang with it, and my uncle turned
round where he was sitting and showed me a face full of cruelty and terror. . . . A thunderbolt
seemed to strike me; I saw a great flash of fire, and fell senseless."

explore the world, " so full of a number of things."

His journeyings by canoe with a friend on the canals and streams of Belgium and France are delightfully described in " An Inland Voyage," while his happy vagrant wanderings with the obstinate Modestine for his sole companion have given us as record " Travels with a Donkey in the Cevennes." While in a very low state of health he made a wonderful attempt to reach the woman he loved, and who needed him, by crossing America in an emigrant train, travelling with offensive companions, and putting up with hardships that would have tried even a healthy man.

Yet he could recall the pathetic and humorous incidents of that journey with intense pleasure in " Across the Plains."

What trace is there in " Treasure Island " of the boredom of an invalid's life ? Who could guess that the creator of Long John Silver and Ben Gunn was racked by a consumptive cough ? The eternal spirit of youth out for adventure riots through the book. It was written to please a boy (his stepson); and which of us cannot recognise Robert Louis Stevenson in young Jim Hawkins, the irrepressible hero ?

Exiled from his native Scotland year after year in winter months, and driven even from the sheltered Bournemouth air after a grim fight with severe illness, Stevenson and his wife, during a visit to the United States, decided to try the effect of a yachting cruise in the warm Pacific Seas.

In the South Seas

The death of his father, son of a famous lighthouse engineer, had made the final parting with Scotland a little easier, for his mother accompanied him in the new adventures. For three years the Stevensons wandered from island to island, staying at times in one group for several

Specially drawn for this work.

MY KINGDOM
And all about was mine, I said,
The little sparrows overhead,
   The little minnows too.
This was the world and I was king;
For me the bees came by to sing,
   For me the swallows flew.

Taken from " A Child's Garden of Verses," by Robert Louis Stevenson.

Specially painted for this work.

HOW THEY BROUGHT THE GOOD NEWS

Robert Browning (1812–89) wrote many beautiful poems during his long life, much of which was spent in Italy. One of his best-known works, popular because it is so spirited, is " How They brought the Good News from Ghent to Aix." It deals with no particular incident in history and is entirely imaginative, yet it has made a lasting place for itself. This lilting poem begins: " I sprang to the stirrup, and Joris, and he; I galloped, Dirck galloped, we galloped all three . . ." and the scene as they depart, with the watchman wishing them " God speed ! " is depicted above.

Specially painted for this work (and included by permission of the late Mr. Rudyard Kipling).
THE MEETING AT THE COUNCIL ROCK
As a writer Rudyard Kipling possessed a many-sided genius, writing of soldiers and Army life, of ships and the men who sail them, in both verse and prose. In another phase he dealt with technical things, machinery and steam engines, as an engineer might have done, and with equal skill depicted the work of the Civil Service in India. Yet it is his stories of animals which most endeared him to readers all over the world, and in our picture above is shown an incident in the life of Mowgli, who plays a part in the Jungle Book stories. Father Wolf has brought his cubs and Mowgli to the Council Rock for the Pack Meeting and Baloo, the sleepy brown bear, is addressing the animals.

weeks, finding everywhere fresh experiences, wonderful natural beauty and eternal sunshine. In the famous "Vailima Letters," penned from time to time to friends at home, R.L.S. writes:—

"This climate, these voyagings . . . new islands, new forested harbours; new interests of gentle natives—the whole tale of my life is better to me than any poem."

His book "In the South Seas" gives his impressions of these happy visits to the various islands and conveys some idea of his intense sympathy with the native mind, which made his life so rich in interest and power at Samoa. For it was agreed that for Stevenson's sake a definite home should be made there in the Samoan group of islands, where, with the least possible strain upon his delicate health, he could pursue his beloved work for literature. Many of his books

LONG JOHN SILVER *Specially drawn for this work.*

The eternal spirit of youth looks out from Robert Louis Stevenson's classic adventure story, "Treasure Island." In the above illustration we see Long John Silver. His "left leg was cut off close by the hip, and under the left shoulder he carried a crutch, which he managed with wonderful dexterity, hopping about upon it like a bird. He was very tall and strong, with a face as big as a ham . . . plain and pale, but intelligent and smiling."

had become popular and more were in demand. His friends arranged to have his work published as he produced it, and as the island was well served by calling steamers, R.L.S. was able to keep in touch with home. His stepson, Lloyd Osbourne, returned to England to bring out to Samoa the house furniture from Bournemouth.

At Vailima

At first, Stevenson and his wife lived in a small wooden house, while the natives cleared the ground of bush growth. He delighted in adding to the new home and was often tempted to overwork physically. His position among the native chiefs was of real importance; they loved and respected "Tusitala," as they called him, and in return for his help during a political crisis, they made him a great cutting in the forest, called "the Road of the Loving Heart." In the "Life of R.L.S.," written by his cousin Balfour,

or in the "Vailima Letters," which he sent to Europe regularly, one may read delightful accounts of the author's last three years at Vailima. There he died in 1894, working at his books to the end.

His Samoan friends hacked a path up the steep hill-side, so that he could be buried as he wished on the mountain top.

Later a tomb was erected, inscribed both in English and Samoan. His own "Requiem" was written there:—

> "Under the wide and starry sky
> Dig the grave and let me lie.
> Glad did I live, and gladly die,
> And I laid me down with a will.
>
> This be the verse, you grave for me:
> 'Here he lies where he longed to be;
> Home is the sailor, home from sea
> And the hunter home from the hill.'"

W. F. Mansell.

A MEMORIAL TO ROBERT LOUIS STEVENSON

In this fine memorial we see the author of "Treasure Island" lying on his invalid couch in Samoa writing the prayer of cheerfulness which is inscribed above. It was for his health's sake that Stevenson went to live in the South Sea Islands, where he was loved and respected by the native chiefs. "R.L.S.," like Ballantyne, was a native of Edinburgh, but even in his early years the Scottish winters were too severe for his delicate constitution.

THE COMPLEAT ANGLER

Specially drawn for this work.

The picture above, so characteristic of Izaak Walton's great book, the work upon which his whole fame rests, breathes the very spirit of his writings. " I will walk the meadows, by some gliding stream . . . and be quiet; and go a Angling," wrote Walton, whose later days were spent in leisure with brothers of the fishing rod.

IT is not going too far to state that British girls and boys are more whole-heartedly interested in animals and birds and their ways than the children of any other nation. It seems an outstanding characteristic of our race and it may be that this genuine love of all dumb creatures has been fruitfully fostered by the nature writers in which our literature is singularly rich. In the following pages, therefore, we shall consider both the lives and the works of some of these particular authors.

Izaak Walton [1593–1683]

" You are assured, though there be ignorant men of another belief, that Angling is an Art," wrote Izaak Walton in dedicating his book " The Compleat Angler " to " my most honoured Friend " John Offley. But it is his gifts in the art of writing that have earned Izaak Walton his place among the immortals. Of this book Charles Lamb

said " It breathes the very spirit of innocence, purity, and simplicity of heart; it would sweeten a man's temper at any time to read it; it would Christianise every angry, discordant passion."

Walton was born at Stafford in 1593 and settled in London as a draper. He held the lease of a house in Chancery Lane, but retired from business at the age of fifty when the Civil War broke out. For his retirement he bought land at Shallowford, near Stafford, but spent most of his time visiting his friends, who were mostly eminent clergymen " of whom he was much beloved." Thus the last forty years of his long life were spent in ideal leisure, travelling here and there and visiting his clerical friends and brothers of the fishing rod. Apart from his famous book on Angling he wrote the lives of John Donne, Hooker, George Herbert, and Bishop Sanderson, but it is " The Compleat Angler " on which his fame rests.

J. Dixon-Scott.

" THE WAKES " AT SELBORNE

Here is the charming old house in which Gilbert White, the great writer on natural history, was born. He became curate of Selborne in 1784 and lived there until his death in 1793.

no care, and those very many other various little living creatures that are not only created, but fed, man knows not how, by the goodness of the God of Nature . . . and let the blessing of St. Peter's Master be with mine. . . . And upon all that are lovers of virtue; and dare trust in His providence; and be quiet; and go a Angling."

He died at Winchester in 1683 at the age of ninety. To his memory London anglers erected a window in the Church of St. Dunstan, Fleet Street, in 1895.

Gilbert White
[1720–1793]

There were and have been, since the middle of the eighteenth century, writers on Natural History who were more learned and more scientific than the modest and gentle curate of Selborne, Gilbert White. Yet none can claim to have made so

The first edition was published in 1653, but was added to regularly during the next twenty-five years. The original thirteen chapters grew to twenty-one, and a second part dealing with fly-fishing was added by his friend, Charles Cotton. Additions made to the original edition were happy quotations, new turns of phrase, songs and poems, and through the whole book there breathes Walton's own gentle disposition and piety. At the close of " The Compleat Angler " he writes: " I will walk the meadows, by some gliding stream, and there contemplate the lilies that take

great an appeal to all classes and types of readers as the man who recorded his observations on his country rides and walks round his native village of Selborne in Hampshire.

Other great writers on Natural History were at work in White's day; there was Linnaeus in Sweden as well as Buffon in France, compiling great works, classifying and recording; arranging the plants and animals in due order and dividing them into classes. Gilbert White scarcely belonged to this scientific school and his work did not compete with theirs but was complementary to it. His one written work by which he became world-famous consists chiefly of letters to his two friends, Thomas Pennant and Daines Barrington. These letters are the most important part of the book now known as "The Natural History of Selborne," and in many editions his "Naturalist's Calendar" is included as well as "Observations on Various Branches of Natural History." The very first edition to be published contained the "Letters" and "Antiquities of Selborne," but it is the Letters which have attracted and fascinated succeeding generations of readers.

In these Letters we have delightful glimpses of White's full and happy life. He was a modest little man, 5 feet 3 inches in height, devoting himself to his work as curate among the villagers, but fond of walking or riding round the countryside and patiently watching and studying the habits, homes, ways and times of all the plants and animals in that district of Hampshire in which he lived. Selborne was his native village. His grandfather was vicar of that parish and Gilbert was born in the vicarage on July 18th, 1720. After school at Basingstoke he went to Oxford and in due course became a Fellow of Oriel. Later he held several different curacies, one of which was at Faringdon, the next parish to Selborne. Then in 1784 he became curate at Selborne and here he lived until his death in 1793.

He had begun his Natural History diary in 1751, but it was not until 1767 that he wrote his first letter to Thomas Pennant and in 1769 his correspondence with Daines Barrington began.

The British Countryside

It is in these letters that he reveals not only his keen interest in all the

Specially drawn for this work.

GILBERT WHITE AT HIS DESK

In this illustration we see the gentle curate of Selborne at his desk. Much of the written work for which he became world-famous consists of letters which he wrote to two friends, and in this correspondence we have delightful glimpses of the naturalist's full and very happy life, spent chiefly in his native village.

Specially drawn for this work.

PAYING CALLS IN THE PARISH

Gilbert White was a very modest little man, 5 feet 3 inches in height, and he never failed in his duty as curate of Selborne, visiting the villagers and making friends of the children. Most of all, though, he loved walking or riding through the countryside.

were chiefly concerned in classifying the plants and animals of the world.

All that he wrote in his full life amounts to little more than a hundred thousand words, not much more than one ordinary modern novel in length. Yet of his work, there have been published well over one hundred editions of all sorts and sizes since his brother's firm, Benjamin White & Son, of London, first issued " The Natural History and Antiquities of Selborne " at the end of 1788. Its style is simple, yet direct and graphic, but there is something more in his writing that has made its appeal to generations of readers; it is the atmosphere of the English countryside, recorded with gentle humour and quiet contemplation by a kindly, tolerant, scholarly Englishman, that gives this Natural History its abiding charm.

His work is valuable as a contribution to our knowledge, but there have been other works on

teeming life of the countryside, but the endearing charm of a sweet, kindly personality. He was not a specialist, collecting specimens to classify and index, but mainly an observer, content to sit quietly by and watch the birds or the field mice without disturbing them. Yet he made a number of very important original discoveries and was probably the first in the field with his ideas of bird territory. He was always discovering things for himself and had little use for second-hand knowledge, though he did not neglect all that was being done by those workers who

Natural History which added more. Gilbert White's " Natural History of Selborne " is something different from the specialised knowledge of most writers on this subject. It is the charm and fascination of the atmosphere of the world he describes, and it is not so much what he tells us as the pleasant and delightful way in which he says it.

Henry David Thoreau [1817–1862]

One of the most scholarly and yet unusual books ever to be written is *Walden, or Life in the Woods*. It deals with the animals and birds, with trees and grasses, with the woodland and the pond, but is not a nature book in the accepted sense, for it tells of a man who built a hut for himself in the very heart of the woods and lived there alone for two years, during which time he jotted down in the most perfect English his inmost thoughts.

Henry David Thoreau, author of *Walden*, was born at Concord in Massachusetts. His grandparents had crossed the Atlantic from Jersey but he was actually far more Scottish than French. An adoring sister helped a great deal in meeting Henry's fees at Harvard University and for a short while he was himself a schoolmaster, though success did not attend his efforts in this direction.

His Love of Nature

From that time a love of nature claimed him entirely, and he was about twenty-eight years old when he set up his hut in the wood and tried to carry into effect his own ideas and opinions. Thus, he had little or no money, but was not above setting up a fence or performing some other manual work to bring him in a few dollars if there was something he wished to buy. He grew much of his own food and was never idle, but he made friends of the birds rather than of human beings. If you would read what it is like to live in solitude for two years you should study *Walden* and it will surprise you to know what a lot Thoreau got out of his existence and the wonderful thoughts he was able to put into his book as the result of this experiment in leading the truly simple life.

Thoreau wrote several books and some poems but the greatest of all his works was *Walden*. He was a friend of Emerson and for a while these two American authors lived together.

William Henry Hudson [1841–1922]

For over thirty years William Henry Hudson, field naturalist as he described

Specially drawn for this work.

HUDSON IN SOUTH AMERICA

William Henry Hudson described himself as a field naturalist. Here we see him studying wild life in South America, where he was born, not far from Buenos Aires. It was here that he first became a keen student of Nature and he wrote of the animals, birds and flowers of his native pampas.

WILLIAM HENRY HUDSON

Our own land provided much of the material for Hudson's nature books but it was not until his later years that full appreciation and success came to him.

himself, lived on the pampas of South America not far from Buenos Aires. He was born on his father's farm on August 4th, 1841, and did not come to England until 1869. It was this part of his life that provided the material for some, but not all, of his finest writing, since it was among the birds and flowers of the pampas that he first became a keen student of nature. One of his earliest books, "The Purple Land," written in 1885, is a romance of Uruguay, and one of his last was "Far Away and Long Ago," written in 1918, in which he gives the story of his early life.

It was not solely of South America he wrote; England provided the material for some of his best-known books: "A Hind in Richmond Park"; "Nature in Downland"; "Afoot in England" and "Hampshire Days" tell of the beauties of Southern England, and while he wrote on the "Birds of La Plata," there is also "British Birds" to keep it company.

The Wild Birds' Melody

He was a naturalist first and foremost, yet it is not just his profound knowledge of Nature that gives his books their abiding charm, but his deep understanding of human joys and sorrows and his ability to bring to his readers not only the joy and beauty he himself felt but the pleasure of discovering the interesting facts for oneself. His own feelings, too, are described at times as when he writes of "Birds in Town and Village," and tells of a girl with whom he talked on one of his walks. Rapturously she exclaimed, "Oh, I do so love the birds!" and the picture remained in his mind until he felt he must go on again as he could no longer keep away from the birds that he, too, loved. "For now all at once it seemed to me that life was not life without them; that I was grown sick and all my senses dim; that only the wished sight of wild birds could medicine my vision; that only by drenching it in their wild melody could my tired brain recover its lost vigour."

It was many years before the world recognised Hudson's genius as a writer on Nature. For the greater part of his life after he came to London he lived in poverty, marked by frequent ill-health. His wife kept a boarding-house and Hudson lived there, known only to a small circle of friends who appreciated his work. He was granted a Civil List pension in 1901 but gave this up later when a wide public wakened to the beauty of his writing and so brought success to him in his later years.

One cannot choose any single book of Hudson's and say that it represents him at his best since each of them has a character of its own. His friend, Edward Garnett, has recorded the tribute paid to Hudson by another great writer, Joseph Conrad, who said of him: "One can't tell how this fellow gets his effects; he writes as the grass grows." Apart from his South American Nature books and those dealing with the English countryside and birds, he wrote a number of romances. Among these are "Green Mansions," written in 1904; "A Little Boy Lost" (1905); "An Old Thorn" (1911) and "Dead Man's Plack" (1920).

A Girl of the Woods

It was in "Green Mansions," that wonderful story of strange adventure in the vast forests of South America, that we meet Rima, the girl of the woods, who was at times like a humming-bird: "now dark, a shadow in the shadow, seen for an instant, and then—gone, oh, little thing! And now in the sunshine standing still, how beautiful— a thousand times more beautiful than the humming bird. Listen, Rima, you are like all beautiful things in the wood —flower and bird, and butterfly, and green leaf, and frond, and little silky-haired monkey high up in the trees. When I look at you I see them all—all and more, a thousand times, for I see Rima herself."

After Hudson's death on August 8th, 1922, his friends decided to erect some permanent memorial to him, and it was the great sculptor, Jacob Epstein, who carved the statuary of Rima which decorates the bird sanctuary in Hyde Park. It was erected in 1925 and dedicated to the memory of that great lover of birds and master-writer on all the varied beauties of Nature, William Henry Hudson.

Richard Jefferies [1848–1887]

It was at Coate Farm in the hamlet of Coate in North Wiltshire that

Specially drawn for this work.

A LINNET FOR SIXPENCE

Not so many years ago, happy, carefree little birds, such as linnets, were exposed for sale in Club Row and other street markets. Hudson, who would buy and release such captives, helped to get this traffic stopped by the Bird Protection Act.

Specially drawn for this work.

A VOYAGE OF ADVENTURE

"Bevis," the Story of a Boy, is quite unique in juvenile literature and is a famous book by Richard Jefferies. In this incident, Bevis, Mark and Pan the dog are setting off on the raft.

which reason he was accused, not altogether unjustly, of indolence. But he had to work and did reporting for a local newspaper as well as some sensational stories and local histories. Then he began to write short sketches of country life and these were published in London newspapers and magazines.

Some of these sketches were issued in book form under the title of "The Gamekeeper at Home" in 1878. In describing what he hoped to do before these papers were written, Jefferies said: "I should not attempt a laborious, learned description, but rather choose a chatty style. I would endeavour to bring in some of the glamour—the magic of sunshine, and green things, and calm waters—if I could."

It is in this he succeeded and in the pages of this book one feels the sun and the wind and the rain and open country.

"It's indoors, sir, as kills half the people, being indoors three parts of the day," says the gamekeeper. "There ain't nothing like fresh air and the smell of the woods. . . . There's the smell of the earth, too, specially just as the plough turns it up, which is a fine thing; and the hedges and the grass are as sweet as sugar after a shower. Anything with a green leaf is the thing, depend upon it, if you want to live healthy."

It is this smell of early morning and

Richard Jefferies was born on November 6th, 1848. For the greater part of the first thirty years of his life he lived there just as his ancestors had dwelt there or in that neighbourhood for generations. And it was of this ancient countryside, its downs and its people, that Jefferies largely wrote.

He was something more than a writer on Natural History, for his outlook embraced the farmers, the labourers, the gamekeepers and poachers, and he wrote of the fields and the woods and the sky above them. He was a dreamer, and work on the farm had no appeal for him, for

Specially drawn for this work.

The illustration above depicts a well-remembered incident from " Wild Life in a Southern County " by Richard Jefferies. It depicts how thieving jackdaws visit the poultry run and steal food put down for the fowls. " Four or five jackdaws will perch on the post and rails," one may read, " intent on the tempting morsels; sitting with their heads a little to one side and peering over. Suddenly one thinks he sees an opportunity. Down he hops and takes a peck."

Specially drawn for this work.

STUDYING WILD LIFE

Richard Jefferies was never so happy as when he was in close communion with the animals and birds of the countryside. Sadly enough, for all his joy in the open air and the health-giving powers of the sun and the wind, this nature writer suffered much from ill-health.

of the woods and the sweet land that permeates Jefferies' writing on the countryside. " Wild Life in a Southern County "; " The Amateur Poacher," and " Round About a Great Estate," published in 1879 and 1880, are three other books all rich in this atmosphere of the countryside he knew and loved.

" I used to take a gun for nominal occupation," he wrote in a letter to his editor, " and sit in the hedge for hours, noting the ways and habits even of moles and snails. . . . The secret of all living creatures is— quiet."

Nature near London

For some years in his early 'thirties Jefferies lived in or near London, and in " Nature near London " appeared sketches which had been published in a London newspaper. They were different from his country books ; it was not the countryman and sportsman who was writing, but a sensitive Londoner taking his walks abroad from the city and recording all that he saw as an artist acutely observing the loveliness and beauty around him.

Jefferies wrote fiction, too, but in most of these books it is the background of the countryside that dominates the story. " Amaryllis At The Fair," published in 1886, may not be a great novel, but its pages glow with its writer's own joy in the country life. In " The Story of My Heart," published in 1883, is a description of the stages through which he passed rather than a diary of his life, though he called it an autobiography. As he lay under a chestnut tree feeling that the whole of existence is permeated with reverent love, he conceives a vision of what the human race may become, a pure and noble race of demi-gods.

" The Life of the Fields " and " The Open Air," published in 1884 and 1885, were essays contributed to different newspapers and magazines. In some of them he goes back to his native Wiltshire, but in others he writes of

London or Sussex or takes Somerset for his scenes. He did not write solely for grown-up readers ; two of his books, " Wood Magic " and " Bevis : the Story of a Boy," were written for children and it might be said that he wrote as a child.

He is back again in his native Wiltshire and in " Wood Magic " the little boy, Bevis, talks with the birds, the animals, and even with the wind blowing around him. A dreamy, adventurous, impatient little boy is Bevis as he plays about the farm just as Jefferies himself had done. The birds are real persons with their own names: Kapchack the magpie; Tchink, the chaffinch; Choo Hoo, the wood pigeon, and they talk to Bevis, explaining many strange things to him. In " Bevis : The Story of a Boy," the child of " Wood Magic " has grown to be twelve or fourteen years old and with his companion, Mark, they set forth on strange adventures in the fields and the woods and around the ponds. They " bathed in air and sunbeam and gathered years of health like flowers from the field."

Life in the Country

Yet, sadly enough, for all his joy in the open air and the health-giving powers of the sun and the wind, Jefferies himself suffered from ill-health, and this at times, because of his inability to go on with his work, brought the threat of poverty. Illness came to him but he was still able to continue with his work though under difficulties. In 1887 he wrote a Preface to the work of another great writer on Natural History, Gilbert White of Selborne.

Sir Charles G. D. Roberts, [1860–1943]

Among the great nature writers there are few whose animal and bird stories are better known than those of this Canadian author and poet. The

By permission of Messrs. J. M. Dent & Sons Ltd.

BIG BEAR AND LITTLE BEAR

The incident depicted above is taken from " Heart of the Ancient World," one of the popular nature books written by Sir Charles G. D. Roberts. Sir Charles is best known for his works on the wild life of Canada.

son of a clergyman, he was born in New Brunswick and became first of all a schoolmaster and then a university professor, though he was also a novelist and historian. In the War of 1914–18 he enlisted as a private soldier, rising to the rank of major, and he is best known for such books as " The Forge in the Forest," " Wisdom of the Wilderness " and its sequel " They That Walk in the Wild," and so on.

As an observer of wild life Sir Charles wrote with such a wealth of sheer descriptive power that one cannot fail to be thrilled as one reads and it is not going too far to say that the animals in his tales are so humanised that we at once regard them as we should men and women or boy and girl characters in a novel.

Henry Williamson [born 1897]

Among those writers from Gilbert White to Richard Jefferies who have loved the English countryside and all its creatures, Henry Williamson will surely take a high place. His love of Nature, combined with his poet's imagination and his skill as a writer, enables him to bring to all who will read the charms of the moor and fen and meadow, and to follow him in the adventures over land and water of some creature of the wilds as in " Tarka the Otter."

Yet the actual writing of this book was done under many handicaps. Williamson himself has told us in " Devon Holiday " how he had difficulty in paying the small rent of his cottage in Devon. His wife was ill and during the day he did the housework and cooking then carried on with his writing in the kitchen " while the baby cried in the crook of my left arm." Much of the work was written after midnight and after the writing came revision. Not until he had completed the seventeenth version of " Tarka " was he satisfied.

It was the magic of this book that brought him fame in 1927; in the following year this story of Dartmoor and Exmoor was awarded the Hawthornden Prize for Literature. Most of his earlier books were written around the country of the Two Rivers, the Taw and the Torridge in Devon, but he has also written in recent years a more practical book, "Story of a Norfolk Farm," published in 1941. A few years ago he moved from his beloved West Country and went to Norfolk.

TARKA THE OTTER

Specially drawn for this work.

This is a picture of Tarka, who figures in one of Henry Williamson's earlier works. This otter is himself a prime favourite and the book itself was re-written and revised many times before its creator was satisfied.

WRITERS OF YESTERDAY AND TO=DAY

Specially drawn for this work.

THE NIGGER OF THE " NARCISSUS "

The famous story by Joseph Conrad, the title of which is quoted above, gives an account of the voyage home from India in an old-fashioned sailing ship, and is full of the romance and poetry of the sea. Of the incident illustrated we read: " We pressed round Jimmy, bothered and dismayed; sheltering him we swung here and there in a body."

LOOKING back to the time of your grandparents we may say that their particular period in our history was both fruitful and progressive in the interesting realms of literature. During the later years of Queen Victoria's long reign many writers came to the fore in an age when inexpensive books and expanding education promoted a taste for good reading.

The great majority of these authors have so well weathered the test of time that they are widely read to-day, and will be for a very long time to come. Let us therefore consider some of yesterday's writers, taking them in order according to the respective years in which they were born.

Sir H. Rider Haggard [1856–1925]

Born at Bradenham Hall in Norfolk, Rider Haggard spent several years of his early manhood in official posts in South Africa. It was his experiences and the legends he heard here which on his return to England led him to write a story suggested by a visit to the Zimbabwe ruins. The result was his most famous book " King Solomon's Mines," written in 1885, a romance of adventure in the wilds of Central Africa in quest of King Solomon's Orphir. Critics may say that it is a fantastic and highly-coloured story, but its thrills and perils, its hair-breadth escapes and desperate fights have held countless readers enthralled and it is rightly numbered among the classics in the world of adventurous fiction.

" Allan Quatermain " is a sequel to " King Solomon's Mines " and was written some two years later. " She " is the story of a mighty Queen and enchantress in an imaginary African country, while " The People of the Mist " is another great adventure story. Among his other works of fiction

Specially drawn for this work.

FROM " KING SOLOMON'S MINES "

A visit to the Zimbabwe ruins of South Africa suggested to Rider Haggard his most famous book " King Solomon's Mines," from which the subject of this picture is taken. " Greeting!" the tall newcomer cries to the white men. " The King's greeting!"

settlement of ex-soldiers in British dominions. For his many public services he was knighted in 1912.

Joseph Conrad
[1857–1924]

Born in the Ukraine of Polish parents, Joseph Conrad resolved early in life to join the British merchant service. He succeeded in landing at Lowestoft in May, 1878, not knowing a word of the English language of which he was later to become so great a master. From 1878 to 1894 he was a deep-water sailor and for the last ten years of that period he was a master-mariner. Eventually for health reasons he had to leave the sea, and his first novel, " Almayer's Folly," was accepted in 1895.

It was followed by some of the finest stories of the sea ever written. " An Outcast of the Islands " came in 1896, and in the following year appeared " The Nigger of the Narcissus," an account of the voyage home from India in an old-fashioned sailing ship. In it are given wonderful and realistic descriptions of seafaring life by one who had both knowledge of the sea and a poetic imagination. The story of the storm and the striking characters of the crew are portrayed with a deep sense of humanity and with quiet touches of humour.

" Jess " deserves special mention for the fine picture it gives of home life among the Boer farmers on the African veldt.

In addition to the goodly number of adventure stories and novels that he wrote, Rider Haggard was a practical farmer and gardener in Norfolk, and wrote a highly valuable work " Rural England," which was published in two volumes in 1902. He also penned other practical books on agricultural questions and visited every part of the British Empire in connection with the

In " Typhoon," too, there is a description of a ship in a storm that is one of the greatest pictures of the sea ever written. " Lord Jim," written in 1900, tells the story of a young officer of the merchant navy who rebuilt his broken character among the savages of Malaysia.

Conrad's other works include " The Secret Agent," a new kind of detective story; but it is as a writer of sea stories, including " The Mirror of the Sea " and " Some Reminiscences," both of which tell largely of his own experiences, that Joseph Conrad takes his place in the gallery of famous English writers.

Sir Arthur Conan Doyle
[1859–1930]

" Well, I never! " says one of Sherlock Holmes' clients. " I thought at first you had done something clever, but I see there was nothing in it after all."

It was this capacity of the great Sherlock Holmes to read a man's history from trivial clues and then to make it all appear so simple that made his name a household word throughout the world. The creator of the redoubtable Holmes, Conan Doyle, was the son of an artist and grandson of the famous cartoonist, John Doyle. Born in Edinburgh, he studied medicine and practised as a doctor for eight years before his success as a writer led him to abandon medical life in favour of literature. It was while he was a student at Edinburgh that he was greatly impressed by the methods of his tutor, Dr. Joseph Bell,

who insisted on the importance of careful observation and deduction in medical work.

Conan Doyle built up the character of Sherlock Holmes chiefly on this power of deduction and the capacity of creating an exact picture of the true facts from the observation of small and trivial details. For Sherlock Holmes' companion in his many adventures Doyle chose Dr. Watson, and it was in the pages of the *Strand Magazine* in 1892 that the adventures of Sherlock

SHERLOCK HOLMES
This is a reproduction of the first drawing of Sherlock Holmes, one of the most famous characters of fiction. He was the creation of Sir Arthur Conan Doyle.

Holmes made their first appearance. Within a comparatively short time these detective stories had brought their author world-wide popularity. They began, too, the era of the detective novel, though no other hero of detective fiction has ever quite reached the stature of the redoubtable Holmes.

It would take much more space to tell of all Conan Doyle's literary work whether as war correspondent, historian, or writer on public affairs. Yet, when much of the fine work of a great, big-hearted author has gradually faded from public memory, the name of his greatest character, Sherlock Holmes and of his good friend " My dear Watson," will be remembered and quoted.

Sir James Barrie [1860–1937]

It is impossible to describe that whimsical indefinable charm known as " The Barrie Touch." One must read " A Window in Thrums " and " Margaret Ogilvy " to appreciate the genius that sprang from the little Scottish village of Kirriemuir and that most fascinating of mothers, who knew her son could not keep her out of his stories. " When you looked into my mother's eyes, you knew as if He had told you, why God had sent her into the world—it was to open the minds of all who looked—to beautiful thoughts, and that is the beginning and end of literature."

As a playwright Barrie stood apart, writing of a world of charm and unreality. He dared to deal with sentiment in this material age as a thing of beauty. There was no bitterness, no cynicism in his fun. He never tired of finding loveliness in the simple things of life. His women were charming, from Margaret Ogilvy and Tibbie to the little group of charladies in " The Old Lady Shows Her Medals." His novels came first and influenced public opinion at a time of Victorian prejudice against novels and theatres. In " Sentimental Tommy " he is laughing at himself, and " Tommy and Grizel " is delightful.

" A Kiss for Cinderella "

In 1894 " The Professor's Love Story," his first play, was produced, followed by " The Little Minister," " Quality Street " and " What Every Woman Knows." During the 1914–18 war " A Kiss for Cinderella " and " Dear Brutus " drew large audiences, and in 1920 " Mary Rose " crowned his success. Of " Peter Pan " there is no need to speak; and the world was the poorer when his creator passed away in London in June, 1937.

" Quality Street " is a comedy of the manners of England in Napoleonic times; its air of decorum and " artificial " atmosphere, which might so easily have been merely old-fashioned, made the play a brilliant success. Like all true classics, it proved to be of the quality that will not age.

W. W. Jacobs [1863–1943]

Some writers impress by their wide range and versatility, but it has been wisely said of William Wymark Jacobs that he cultivated a small garden to perfection. No one can forecast the judgment of future generations, but it is safe to say that for many years to come W. W. Jacobs will stand as one of the foremost humorous writers of Britain. Until 1899 he was a clerk in the Post Office Savings Bank, but his first novel, " The Skipper's Wooing," had been published in 1897. He had become known as a writer of short stories by his contributions to the *Idler*, then edited by another famous humorous writer, Jerome K. Jerome.

Jacobs created a whole world of Thames-side characters and told his stories with an artistry and use of language that made him a master of style in his own sphere of joyous laughter. He left his Civil Service post to devote himself to his writing and during the next thirty years a long series of short stories and several novels came from his pen. Some of the

FROM "THE LITTLE MINISTER"

Stage Photo Co.

Sir James Barrie was born in 1860 and died in 1937. Young folks think of him very affectionately as the author of "Peter Pan." His novels made people far more broad-minded and tolerant than they had been. The scene illustrated above forms part of "The Little Minister." We see the Rev. Gavin Dishart on the left and the woman Babbie, seemingly a gipsy, but really the daughter of an earl.

17–2

FAMOUS CHARACTERS OF W. W. JACOBS

It has been said that W. W. Jacobs cultivated a small garden to perfection. By this is meant that his literary work was confined almost exclusively to one style for which the author created a whole world of Thames-side characters, such as those illustrated above, which brought laughter to thousands of readers all the world over.

characters he created will live long in humorous literature: Bob Pretty, Peter Russet and Ginger Dick, to mention only a few of them, brought laughter to many thousands of readers throughout the world. For many years month by month, Jacobs' yarns made their first bow in the pages of the *Strand Magazine*, and then later in book form under such titles as "Many Cargoes," "Sea Urchins," "Light Freights," "Captains All," "Ship's Company," "Night Watches" and "Deep Waters." At least thirty-eight editions of "Many Cargoes" have been published.

He wrote, too, stories of the macabre such as "The Monkey's Paw," "The Well" and "The Ghost of Jerry Bundler." "Beauty and the Barge" appeared as a stage play, and other stories were filmed, while Dame Ethel Smyth's opera, "The Boatswain's Mate," was founded on one of his stories.

Sir Arthur Quiller-Couch [1863–1944]

Who, when he first began to use a public library, did not seek out and read with avidity "Dead Man's Rock"? Though it was so irresistible, it was a first novel signed merely with the pen-name "Q," but it became the forerunner of many other novels all of which enhanced the high literary reputation of Arthur Thomas Quiller-Couch. Most of these stories have a Cornish setting, for the novelist was born at Fowey, and he did much to enhance the appeal and claims of his native county.

Knighted in 1910, Sir Arthur became Professor of English Literature at Cambridge. Apart from his novels, he was well-known as a critic of literature and had a wide repute for his lectures, some of which have been published in book form.

Rudyard Kipling [1865–1936]

Rudyard Kipling was engaged in writing short stories for more than forty years, and, towards the end of his life, delighted his admirers with a tale for everybody, "Thy Servant a Dog." Perhaps it was through his animal stories that most of us made our first acquaintance with this great writer, and which of us who revelled in the "Just So Stories" did not find ways and means of getting at both the "Jungle Books" somehow? Then perhaps we learnt that our author was connected with India, claiming that country at birth, and returning later as assistant editor of *The Pioneer*. His experience of Anglo-Indian life on the frontier has given us that graceful group of child studies in the "Wee Willie Winkie" volume—"Baa, Baa Black Sheep" and "His Majesty The King." "Stalky and Co." ranks with "Tom Brown's School Days" as a favourite school yarn.

Kipling loved England as most men do who come back to her from the ends of the earth. On Empire Day, children in schools sing his patriotic verses, and recite his stirring poetry—"God of our fathers, known of old," and the solemn "Land of Our Birth" —the Children's Song.

At the outbreak of the 1914–18 war his was the voice that challenged the men of the nation—

"For all we have and are,
For all our children's fate,
Stand up and meet the war
The Hun is at the gate.

There is but one task for all
For each our life to give.
Who stands—if freedom fall?
Who dies—if England live?"

Many a small child has gained his first idea of world geography from his "Big Steamers," written during the same war, too—

"Oh where are you going to, all you Big Steamers
With England's own coal, up and down the salt seas?"

Kim

Most of the finest poems are now available in a small volume called "A

Specially drawn for this work.

THE TREASURE AT LAST

Here is an incident from Sir Arthur Quiller-Couch's stirring story "Dead Man's Rock." The scene is laid on the Cornish coast and Culliver has found the chest of treasure and opened it. "As he stretched out his hand towards the Great Ruby, I laid mine heavily on his shoulder," says the narrator.

Choice of Songs " (Methuen), while his soldier poems are collected in " Barrack Room Ballads." " Kim " is perhaps the greatest of his Indian stories; it is so much more than a tale of India, just as " They " and " The Brushwood Boy " are to be read and not talked about in cold print.

Kipling understood India and the life of its people as few others do. His stories reveal his knowledge of its mysterious power, its isolation from the world outside and its special character. He also realised the great influence of splendid Englishmen who as civil servants went out to administrate in India, and tried to work in sympathy with the Eastern mind and its outlook. The story of " William the Conqueror "—in the volume called "The Day's Work "—illustrates this point.

Another side of Kipling's genius deals with technical things—pistons, bridges, bolts, bars, steam engines, and men's skill in managing the machinery of the world. For most of us, though, the author of " Purun Bhagat," the first of the " Second Jungle Book " tales, holds our affections, and we would rather follow the fortunes of Mowgli at the Council Rock than those of an ambitious locomotive.

By permission of the late Rudyard Kipling and Messrs. Macmillan & Co., Ltd.

THE LAMA

The above illustration, by J. Lockwood Kipling, is taken from " Kim," by Rudyard Kipling, and shows Kim and the lama. " They ate together in great content," says the book, " clearing the beggar's bowl. Then the lama took snuff from a portentous wooden snuff-gourd, fingered his rosary awhile, and so dropped into the easy sleep of age, as the shadow of Zam-Zammah grew long."

Arnold Bennett
[1867–1931]

Born at Shelton, near Hanley, Arnold Bennett spent his early years in this district of Staffordshire, and it was the " Five Towns " of the Potteries which formed the background of those earlier novels that made his fame. " Anna of the Five Towns " established his reputation by its appealing study of simple, self-effacing womanhood, ignorant of worldly wisdom, but capable of great heights of renunciation.

It was, too, among the smoke and commercial activities of the Potteries that the scenes of " Clayhanger " (1910), " Hilda Lessways " (1911), " The Card " and " The

Matador of the Five Towns" as well as other novels were laid.

Bennett was essentially a modern writer, with wit and humour in his style. During his busiest period he lived mainly at Fontainebleau in France, and the influence of French literature is marked in many of his books. Apart from his novels he wrote fluently and wisely upon wider subjects and his obvious sincerity gave his opinions considerable weight. Several highly successful plays came from his pen, including "What the Public Wants," "The Great Adventure"; and, in collaboration with Edward Knoblock, that fine play "Milestones."

By permission of the late Rudyard Kipling and Messrs. Macmillan & Co., Ltd.

MOWGLI LEAVING THE JUNGLE

Our print, by Maurice and Edward Detmold, is taken from "The Jungle Book," by Rudyard Kipling. There are few people who cannot follow the adventures of Mowgli with the closest interest. Kipling, who was born in India in 1865 and died in January, 1936, knew our vast overseas Empire as few men have done. In particular, he had a close understanding of and sympathy with the minds of Eastern people.

John Galsworthy [1867–1933]

Educated at Harrow and Oxford, John Galsworthy was called to the bar in 1890, but never really practised as a barrister. Instead, he travelled widely and devoted himself to writing, but it was not until 1890 that his first notable book appeared—"The Villa Rubein,"

a volume of tales. After that he produced a constant succession of books and plays.

All his work is marked by a high technical skill, but above that quality is its sincerity of purpose and scrupulous fairness. Joseph Conrad said of him that the foundation of his talent lay in a remarkable power of

G. K. CHESTERTON

Chesterton was a very active figure in
the world of literature during his lifetime.
Famous as a critic, he also wrote verse and
even detective fiction.

ironic insight and a keen and faithful
eye, adding that his style was that of a
man whose sympathy with mankind
is too genuine to allow him the smallest
gratification of his vanity at the cost
of his fellow creatures.

Some of the most famous of his novels
are those included in the Forsyte saga:
" The Man of Property," " Indian
Summer of a Forsyte," " In Chancery,"
" To let," and others, all dealing with
the history of the Forsyte family.
" The Country House " and " The
Freelands " are among his other works
dealing with the English landed classes.
A literary artist, Galsworthy wrote pure
and unaffected English, always calm,
restrained and judicial. He painted a
faithful picture for us to look at and
form our judgment upon.

As a dramatist he ranks high in
modern stage history, and here, too, he
turned a searching light on conventions
and on the administration of justice as
in " The Silver Box " (produced in
1906), or on the relations of Capital

and Labour in " Strife " (1909), or on
prison problems in " Justice " (1910),
or on political principles in " The Mob "
(1914).

G. K. Chesterton [1874–1936]

In his day there was no more outstanding and active figure in the literary
and journalistic worlds than Gilbert
Keith Chesterton, born and educated in
London, and winner of the " Milton "
prize for English verse at St. Paul's
School at an unusually early age.
Much of his work, however, at one
period was in the journalistic rather
than literary sphere. He had a daringly
original point of view and both delighted and startled his readers with his
criticisms on social questions, art,
politics and literature.

Yet it was in fiction that his fanciful
imagination found free play. " The
Napoleon of Notting Hill," published
in 1904, gives a fantastic history of
civil war between London suburbs,
while in " The Club of Queer Trades "
(1905) he showed his inclination for
detective fiction which was more fully
developed later in " The Innocence of
Father Brown " (1911), a new type of
amateur detective story.

He wrote both poetry and light verse
of a very high order. " Lepanto " is a
wonderful short poem that will be
quoted and read aloud for the beauty and
colour of its lines for as long as poetry
appeals to the human ear: " Where
the grey seas glitter and sharp tides
shift, And the sea folk labour and the
red sails lift"; or " The Rolling English
Road " with his final note: " For there
is good news yet to hear and fine things
to be seen, Before we go to Paradise
by way of Kensal Green."

He was, too, a great critic and writer
on English Literature, and it is probable
that it will be by his critical work and
his poetry rather than by his fiction
that the lovable personality of " G.K.C."
will live longest among the great names
that have added new lustre to English
literature during the past century.

John Buchan [1875–1940]

In this section we are dealing entirely with books and literature, but John Buchan must be rather an exception because he was a very wonderful man not only as a writer but in many other ways. The son of a Scottish Minister, he studied at Glasgow University and afterwards at Oxford, later going to South Africa.

We hear of him next as a Member of Parliament and in 1935 he attained to the very high office of Governor-General of Canada, being created Lord Tweedsmuir.

Turning to his writings, the stories of mystery and adventure which he told in the most perfect English and yet with a very full measure of plot and clear characterisation rank high indeed. "The Thirty-Nine Steps" (published in 1915) may be described as pure adventure, but "Greenmantle" is regarded as being one of the finest of this author's many novels.

Leaving fiction now, John Buchan gave us fascinating biographies, each bearing the hall-mark of most patient research and a deep wealth of knowledge, when he re-told in his own inimitable way the stories of Sir Walter Scott, Oliver Cromwell, Julius Cæsar and others.

Sir Hugh Walpole [1884–1941]

Among all the excellent novelists who made their mark in English literature during the first forty years of the present century, Hugh Walpole deserves special mention. A son of the Bishop of Edinburgh, he was intended for the Church, but after a time as a schoolmaster turned to literature and produced many notable books, the first of which, "The Wooden Horse," was published in 1909. "Fortitude" was

Specially drawn for this work.

ARNOLD BENNETT'S CHARACTER, "THE CARD"

This modern writer was born in the Potteries district of Staffordshire and began his working life as a journalist. He soon turned to fiction, however, and two of his finest novels, "The Old Wives' Tale" and "Clayhanger," deal with his native county. "The Card" (published in 1911) is highly amusing and an incident from this story is depicted above.

published in 1913 and "The Dark Forest" in 1916. Then came, among others, "The Secret City," "The Young Enchanted" and the three "Jeremy" novels.

Perhaps his finest and most mature work is to be found in the great series of novels dealing with the Herries family, set against the background of the Lake District of Cumberland; here Walpole himself lived in later years. "Rogue Herries," "Judith Paris," "The Fortress," and "Vanessa" are all written in that charming and satisfying style that gave distinction to everything that Hugh Walpole wrote.

In this section mention may be made of two remarkable books which have long retained their popularity. The first of them is "Vice Versa," by F. Anstey (Thomas Anstey Guthrie, 1856–1933) and it tells of a well-to-do father who changes bodies but not minds with his schoolboy son. The tale is fantastic, but it has a marvellous sequence of laughable situations.

The second outstanding book is "Three Men in a Boat," which first saw light in 1889, the work of Jerome Klapka Jerome (1859–1927). Though written more than sixty years ago, this humorous story is still widely read.

T. E. Lawrence [1888–1935]

Then, among the writers of yesterday, Thomas Edward Lawrence may well be included. He produced a remarkable book in "The Seven Pillars of Wisdom," first issued on a limited scale in 1926 and more fully in 1935. Meanwhile, a shortened version, "Revolt in the Desert," came out in 1927.

Lawrence of Arabia, a colourful and romantic figure, spent much time unearthing the secrets of Syria and he wrote of this interesting work in "Crusaders' Castles." The fascinating story of his life and leadership is told elsewhere in this work.

Specially drawn for this work.

THE THIRTY-NINE STEPS

First issued in 1915, this is one of the stirring adventure and mystery stories written by John Buchan, who was created Lord Tweedsmuir for his great services to the Empire. A stirring episode in "The Thirty-Nine Steps" is illustrated above.

FROM THE GREAT DRAMA 'SAINT JOAN"

In this photograph we can study a scene from George Bernard Shaw's beautiful drama, " Saint Joan." The drama has as its central character Joan of Arc. The left-hand figure above is the chaplain, John de Stogumber. In the centre comes Cauchon, Bishop of Beauvais. On the right is the Earl of Warwick, Governor of Rouen when Joan was burned at the stake.

George Bernard Shaw [1856–1950]

Someone described Bernard Shaw as " a modern Don Quixote who must be a-tilting." It is true that the Irish blood in this brilliant wit made him a fighter, but he was more than the cynic and the jester. Perhaps he represented cold intellectualism as opposed to senti-ment in life. He was certainly out to destroy romance, from a conviction that it was closely allied to the shams of this world and was hindering moral progress.

All his keen critical and artistic powers were used in propaganda work; he felt that the stage should be able to uplift the people, and hoped to use it to bring about a reformation in our social system.

His dialogue is clever, original and witty; the plays make better reading perhaps than drama, for his plots are less important than his theories. The men in them are definitely useful types, and his women only are allowed to be individuals; indeed, the stage is merely a platform for the author.

In an early play, " Widowers' Houses," he tackled the slum question. " I do not love the poor, but I hate poverty."

The " Devil's Disciple " teaches that soul alone can produce noble action, while " Captain Brassbound's Conver-sion " shows the uselessness of revenge. " Back to Methuselah " is too long for acting, but intensely interesting to read as the drama of life itself.

In " Saint Joan " there is perhaps less of Shaw himself; history has tied him down to facts. He allows very little of the real romance of her story to inspire his Joan of Arc; she is robbed of personal magnetism, yet the play is a masterpiece. Here Shaw has no axe to grind, but has written a beautiful drama on a plane of emotion quite unusual to him.

GEORGE BERNARD SHAW

Born in Dublin in 1856 Bernard Shaw came to London at the age of 20. Between 1879 and 1883 he wrote five novels, but it was as a playwright that he achieved world fame. In 1925 he received the Nobel Prize.

Maurice Maeterlinck [1862–1949]

Quite the most famous Belgian writer of his day, the son of a lawyer of Ghent. His two delightful plays " The Blue Bird " and " The Betrothal " have not only been translated into English, but acted in our English theatres. Because his plays are mystic and do not deal with ordinary ideas, they are difficult to stage. The scenery, for instance, in " The Blue Bird " was most beautifully thought out, in order that nothing should spoil the symbolistic character of the play—" such stuff as dreams are made on."

Maeterlinck's quiet life amid the winding canals and brooding skies of the peaceful slow-moving Flemish town encouraged a natural tendency to solitude and silence. Reserved by nature, he fled before any public notice of his work, though he confessed himself encouraged and warmed by the appreciation of his dramas shown in Paris when he was young. He had gone there to study law, but like our own Scott and Stevenson he preferred literature, and lost no opportunity while in the capital of reading and learning from the museums and public galleries. He even began contributing to *La Jeune Belgique* before he definitely abandoned law as a profession.

The Life of the Bee

In 1890, a glowing criticism of " La Princesse Maleine," which showed clearly the influence of Hamlet and Macbeth, brought him publicity, from which he escaped. In 1892, he wrote " Pelléas and Mélisande," for which the music was afterwards written by Debussy. The influence of the brilliant Georgette Leblanc, whom he afterwards married, was very marked. They lived in an old ruined Abbey in Normandy, and it was the garden of this lonely place that inspired him to write " The Life of the Bee." He found mystery even here in " The Spirit of the Hive " as he called it.

He translated Macbeth for his wife to act, with the gloomy atmosphere of the Abbey as a background. He modernised the story of Bluebeard in his play " Ariane," advocating freedom of thought for women.

He believed physical fitness to be necessary to soul development, and was most keen on exercise and outdoor life. The body in health is able to help the mind to realise the significance of inward things, of which outward material things are only the symbols—for real happiness is that of the wise, thoughtful man and not the adventurer.

In 1911, Maeterlinck was awarded the Nobel Prize; this marked his European reputation. He also contributed largely to French, English and American magazines.

A. E. W. Mason [1865–1948]

It was his power of creating character and giving his stories a sense of movement that won for A. E. W. Mason his popularity among all classes of readers. His name was made with " The Courtship of Morrice Buckler," first published in 1896, but his greatest success was " The Four Feathers " in 1902, a story which brings into play the moral ideas by which high character is forged and tempered. It tells of the son of a long line of soldiers, a man brave in the highest sense of the word yet mistrusting his own nerve. He is branded as a coward but eventually proves his real heroism when as a captive at Omdurman in 1898 he expiates whatever errors he has made in the past.

Other books such as " The Broken Road " (1907) are laid in India, while " At the Villa Rose," a very fine detective story, is set on the Continent. " Running Water " (1907) was later produced as a play, while another of his famous stories, " The Witness for the Defence," was first written as a play and then turned into a novel. Other well-known books which have come from his versatile pen include " The House of the Arrow " (1924); " No Other Tiger " (1927); " The Prisoner in the Opal " (1929) and " Fire Over England " (1936). " The Drum " was one of the successful films shown in 1937.

By permission of the artist and Messrs. Methuen & Co. Ltd

THE BLUE BIRD

This is a typical scene from Maurice Maeterlinck's delightful play " The Blue Bird," reproduced from a picture by E. Cayley Robinson. The two children, Tyltyl and Mytyl, seen above, go in search of the Blue Bird (the symbol of happiness) and then find " it was here all the time."

Howard Coster.

H. G. WELLS

This well-known author was a draper's assistant, chemist's apprentice and schoolmaster before he took to writing and gave the world not only stories but also historical and scientific works.

During his varied career he served as a captain in the Manchester Regiment and then as a major with the R.M.L.I. in 1914–18, and from 1906–1910 sat in the House of Commons as M.P. for Coventry.

H. G. Wells [1866–1946]

If the French writer of scientific romances, Jules Verne, began the fashion of using inventions as " plots " for exciting tales, H. G. Wells brought that type of story almost to complete perfection.

Not only had he a trained scientific mind, but he had also a gift of introducing real living characters into his tales of adventure.

" The Time Machine " was the first of these scientific stories; then came " When the Sleeper Awakes," " The First Men in the Moon," and " The Food of the Gods." He studied science under Huxley, and gained his B.Sc. at London University, hoping to become a teacher of science, but ill-health compelled him to give up teaching. He had already had experience as a draper's assistant, and had been a chemist, before he began to study for a profession. At the age of twenty-seven he had produced nothing of literary importance, yet he stands to-day in the front rank of English prose writers.

Fame from Short Stories

His short stories were peculiarly successful, even in an age when many great writers, such as Barrie, Kipling, Stevenson and Conrad, were perfecting the art of writing little masterpieces. The best of his short stories can be read in " The Country of the Blind." His longer novels show him to have been a thinker of vast imaginative insight into character. " Tono-Bungay " and " Ann Veronica " have always been popular; " Kipps " recalls his life as a draper's assistant, and " Love and Mr. Lewisham " reminds us of his teaching days.

Hilaire Belloc [1870–1953]

We think of this versatile writer, who was born in France, as the accomplished creator of books of history, poetry, fiction, travel and adventure and even books for children, such as " The Bad Child's Book of Beasts," published in 1896. He is also an exceptional biographer, as his lives of Charles I and Wolsey prove; for, as character studies, they are amazingly vivid and alive.

From a literary point of view " The Path to Rome " (published 1902) is an outstanding effort. It is the narrative of a tramp afoot, and this author has a knack of depicting scenes and people, the humour and the gay philosophy of life just as he meets it. Indeed, if you read the book, you will feel you are really Belloc's companion throughout the fascinating trip.

Specially drawn for this work.

" Could you find the house again ? " asked the Greek. This is a tense incident from " The Four Feathers," published in 1902. The story was written by A. E. W. Mason and ranks as one of his best. It shows how high character is forged and tempered, for the hero mistrusts his own nerve and is at first branded as a coward.

H. M. Tomlinson [born 1873]

For H. M. Tomlinson it is mainly the sea or the Thames waterfront which form the background of his books. He has written of " London River " in which colourful pictures are given of life on the Thames and the days when Poplar was famous for the building of clipper ships. Then in " Gallions Reach," his chief character, Jim Colet, boards a ship on London's waterfront and, after many adventures, including shipwreck, returns again to the Thames. In " The Sea and the Jungle " he gives us a vivid account of a voyage on a tramp steamer from Swansea to Brazil and then along the Amazon forests, back to Jamaica, and so home again. About all Tomlinson's books, whether stories or essays, there is the charm and fascination of one who chooses his words as an artist selects his colours to gain just the right effect.

Winston Spencer Churchill [born 1874]

To write of the statesman whose name will live in history among the greatest leaders of our nation and to touch just briefly on one aspect of his many talents is almost an impossibility. Yet it was as a writer that Winston Spencer Churchill first came into the public eye and his name must be in any list of great writers of the twentieth century. Whilst serving as a soldier in the 4th Hussars he was granted permission to go to Cuba in 1895 where Spain was at war with the United States. It

Specially drawn for this work.

AN INCIDENT FROM THE STORY " KIPPS "

The intensely human story " Kipps " recalls a wearisome life actually led by H. G. Wells when he was a draper's assistant, the young man Kipps meeting with all sorts of strange adventures and being constantly nagged by the old fellow to whom he is apprenticed. It is not surprising that he commonly went to bed exhausted and footsore.

was the fine descriptive letters he wrote to the Press at this time that first gained him his reputation as a brilliant writer.

Historian and Biographer

Then as a young politician he was not content to rely upon notes or upon the inspiration of the moment when he was speaking. He wrote and re-wrote his speeches, polishing and pruning with the instinct of the born writer. Indeed, the man who is to-day regarded as one of the greatest of world orators was not a ready speaker but depended upon his written words. Wherever he served as a soldier he managed to combine his military duties with those of a war correspondent and represented famous British newspapers in several campaigns. His books on this period of his life include " The Story of the Malakand Field Force " (1898); " The River War " (1899) and " London to Ladysmith *via* Pretoria."

Later he wrote the Life of his father, Lord Randolph Churchill, one of the most interesting political biographies in our language, while his magnificent Life of his famous ancestor, the great Duke of Marlborough, would itself have given him a high place as historian and biographer. " The World Crisis " tells of the war of 1914–18. His successive volumes of history of the last war have won world-wide fame.

Always in his writing there is a glow and colour in his words—" purple

McLeish.

THE AGE-OLD CITY OF LUCCA

Lucca, capital of the Tuscan province of the same name, is known to have existed in 218 B.C. and to have been colonised by the Romans under the name Luca. This Italian city figures in Hilaire Belloc's charming book " The Path to Rome."

patches " as someone has called them. There are, too, such phrases written and spoken by him as that famous testimony to the R.A.F. in the Battle of Britain: " Never in the field of human conflict was so much owed by so many to so few," or his words in praise of the people of our cities who had fought the air raids: " I see . . . quiet, confident, bright and smiling eyes, beaming with a consciousness of being associated with a cause far higher and wider than any human or personal issue. I see the spirit of an unconquerable people."

Somerset Maugham [born 1874]

Few writers can have had such a varied training for their art as William Somerset Maugham. Born in France in 1874 he was educated at King's School, Canterbury, Heidelberg University, and then as a medical student at St. Thomas's Hospital, London.

Some of the experiences gained during this phase were used in " Liza of Lambeth," published in 1897. After his medical education he went to live in Spain and later travelled a great deal in the East. The scenes of many of his novels are set in the East, while his adventures when he served in the Secret Service during the War of 1914–18 were used in his novel " Ashenden." For a time during that war he was a medical man and then on the staff of the Intelligence Department.

His plays, however, have dealt with problems far different from those of the medical profession or the Secret Service. " Our Betters," rightly regarded as his most brilliant play, is a witty and cynical piece of social satire. Other plays which have added to his fame include " A Man of Honour," " East of Suez," " The Camel's Back " and " The Letter." They are as varied in theme as his novels.

G. M. Trevelyan [born 1876]

Few men have been honoured with the Order of Merit, since its membership is limited to twenty-four, but this distinction has been conferred on George Macaulay Trevelyan for his distinguished historical writings. His reputation was made with his volumes on Garibaldi and the Making of Modern Italy. During the War of 1914–18 he served as commandant of the first British Ambulance Unit for Italy and later published a vivid account of his three years' experiences.

He has also written "England in the Age of Wycliffe" and "England Under the Stuarts" as well as a "Life of John

Specially drawn for this work.

ON THE " LONDON RIVER "

The spirited and realistic author Henry Major Tomlinson was actually born in the dockland of London and he writes of ships and their romance as one who knows them intimately. The above scene is typical of the waterfront which forms the setting for so many of Tomlinson's books and he can always paint a colourful picture of life on the Thames

Bright." For some years he was Professor of Modern History at Cambridge University.

E. M. Forster [born 1879]

Another scholar is E. M. Forster, a former Fellow of King's College, Cambridge, and an LL.D. of Aberdeen, who was awarded the Benson Medal of the Royal Society of Literature in 1937, besides being Rede Lecturer at Cambridge in 1941. It is as a novelist, though, that his chief contributions to literature have been made, and all his work has distinction, a clear and easy style, combined with accuracy of observation. It is his sincerity and understanding of changing class distinctions which give " Howard's End " and " A Passage to India " their compelling interest. " A Passage to India " brought its author two of the treasured awards in Literature, the Prix Femina Vie Heureuse and the James Tait Black Prize in 1925.

Francis Brett Young [1884–1954]

This latter distinction has been gained also by another author whose work has earned popularity among both literary critics and the ordinary reader who is more concerned with a good story than any other quality. Francis Brett Young's fine novel " Portrait of Clare " was also awarded the James Tait Black Prize. Like several other authors who have distinguished themselves by their acute understanding of human nature, Francis Brett Young was a medical man and served in the R.A.M.C. in war time. One of his books, " Dr. Bradley Remembers," reminds us of his expert knowledge as a doctor, while others, such as " The Black Diamond," " Woodsmoke," " White Ladies," " Cold Harbour " and " Mr. Lucton's Freedom," range over wider fields, but all of them have that distinction of style which gained their writer his high place in contemporary fiction.

Bassano Ltd.

PROF. G. M. TREVELYAN, O.M.

This is a studio portrait of one of our greatest British historians, great-nephew of Lord Macaulay. His " History of England " contains in one volume the most vivid account that has been written of our land.

Arthur Ransome [born 1884]

Here is an author very much after the hearts of modern girls and boys, for he writes thrilling stories of adventure and tells in a most human style of lengthy cruises. Well known also as a British expert on the literature of Russia, Mr. Ransome illustrates his own works.

" Swallows and Amazons," " Peter Duck " and " Secret Water " are among Arthur Ransome's popular titles, and he has a way of carrying his lovable characters from one book to another so that we can keep on following the adventures of youngsters with whom we have already made firm friends. This author may, further, be regarded as an adept in making island plans and treasure charts which add to the delights of his books.

Frank Swinnerton [born 1884]

The gifted author of " Nocturne " (1917), Frank Arthur Swinnerton, writes largely on the lives of simple, middle-class people and there is always a welcome touch of humour. We think of him also as one of our present-day men of letters, for he is an outstanding critic and may be taken as an inspired and inspiring guide to the literature of our time.

One of his most fascinating books is " Harvest Comedy," published in 1937, whilst " The Georgian Literary Scene " is a review of the writers of this century and their contributions to our literary wealth.

J. B. Priestley [born 1894]

" The Good Companions " is the title of the book that first brought fame to J. B. Priestley, and it might be taken as the broad motto which inspires a great deal of his writing and radio talks. It is as though he says " Let's all be good companions, whatever our fortune in life, and pull together for the common good." That is the spirit behind " The Good Companions " in which Jess Oakroyd, the worker from Yorkshire, Miss Elizabeth Trant, the lady with a small fortune of her own, Inigo Jolifant, the young schoolmaster, Susan Dean and her fellow-artistes of " The Dinky Doos," all join forces in the touring company known as " The Good Companions," a delightful, robust, humorous story in which many widely varying types are portrayed with keen insight and kindly understanding.

Records of Travel

Since its publication in 1929, John

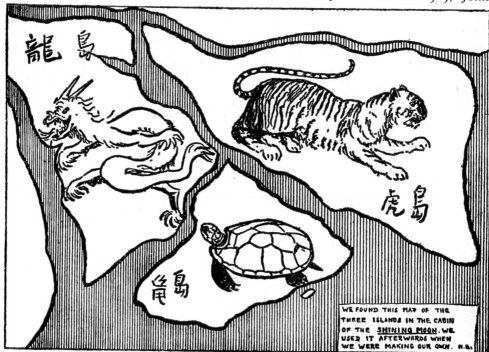

By permission of Messrs. Jonathan Cape Ltd.

A MAP OF THE THREE ISLANDS

This is one of the intriguing plans to be found in " Missee Lee," a book by Arthur Ransome. Mr. Ransome ranks very high as a writer for girls and boys and pens mostly tales of travel and adventure. His family characters, " Swallows and Amazons " appear in many of his works, growing older from book to book.

Boynton Priestley, the young journalist who joined the Army in 1914 and, after nearly five years as an infantry officer, went to Trinity Hall, Cambridge, has written many books and plays, all of which have added to his reputation. Some of his books have been more in the nature of travel records, but it is the people who interest him—the man he meets in the train or the bus. Yet, as in " English Journey," he is interested in the places, too, and where men work and live and play and how these places affect the people. " It is little England I love. . . . Not until I am safely back in England do I ever feel that the world is quite sane. Never once have I arrived in a foreign country and cried: ' This is the place for me.' "

C. S. Forester [born 1899]

Among our modern novelists, here is one widely known for his splendid tales of action and adventure, particularly stories of the Royal Navy. One of his earliest books was " Brown on Resolution," published in 1929, and he has since given us " Captain Horn-blower," noted for its brilliant characters and swift movement in a number of books, including " The Happy Return," " A Ship of the Line " and " Flying Colours."

Peter Fleming [born 1907]

This present-day author, who was educated at Eton and Oxford, is one of our brilliant travel writers and has made some strange journeys in South America and parts of Asia. His book " Brazilian Adventure " contains some wonderful descriptions of places and personages and is by no means lacking in humour.

" One's Company," published in 1934, is the story of travel in China, travel that at times became beset by peril and was always thrilling and adventurous.

Women Writers

Even in the days when women had no vote and in most spheres of work no one had yet thought of claiming equal

Howard Coster.

FRANK SWINNERTON

As well as writing novels about simple, middle-class people, Swinnerton is an outstanding critic. In " The Georgian Literary Scene " he reviews the writers of this century with great shrewdness.

rights for them, women had made names that ranked equally with their brother writers in the world of literature. Jane Austen, George Eliot and the Brontë sisters, for example, stand in the gallery of the great writers of the past.

Among the notable women writers of to-day Sheila Kaye-Smith is one of those authors who have placed their stories against the familiar background of some English county. Just as Thomas Hardy wrote of Wessex or Hugh Walpole set some of his finest stories in the Cumberland Lake District, it is mostly of her native Sussex that Sheila Kaye-Smith has written. The daughter of a surgeon of St. Leonards-on-Sea, Sussex, her novel, " Tamarisk Town," is an original and striking story of how a Sussex seaside village rose in importance. As it rose so did its leading character rise to fortune. He helped to make the town and eventually to mar it, and in so doing brought about his own fall.

"Sussex Gorse" is another story of a man with an urge to acquire something, and his character is shown against the familiar Sussex background from early youth to old age. "Challenge to Sirius," "The George and Crown" and "The Village Doctor" are others, but perhaps her finest work is in "The End of the House of Alard" which tells the story of an English squire struggling to hold his large estates in the face of post-war difficulties. "Green Apple Harvest" is set in rural Sussex, while another fine story, "Iron and Smoke," shows the contrast between the industrial North and the agricultural South, where farms and ancient estates mould a different breed of people.

"The King Waits"

Clemence Dane, the pseudonym under which Winifred Ashton writes, has produced both books and plays. In "The Babyons" there are four stories of compelling interest dealing with four generations of the same family, set in 1750, 1775, the Victorian era and the present day. Other books by this distinguished writer include "First the Blade," "Regiment of Women," "The King Waits," while among the plays she has written are "William Shakespeare" and "Naboth's Vineyard."

Bearer of a famous name in literature, Rose Macaulay has written brilliantly witty books of which the best known are "Potterism," "Crewe Train," "Told by an Idiot," and "They Were Defeated."

G. B. Stern (Mrs. G. L. Holdsworth) has also written both books and plays that have earned high praise. Among her novels are "Tents of Israel," "The Dark Gentleman," "Thunderstorm," and "Monogram."

Specially drawn for this work.

AN INTERESTING TRAVEL BOOK

This is an incident taken from Peter Fleming's "One's Company," a travel book dealing with China. The coolie thrashing the pig is not nearly as cruel as he would appear because he is only waiting for a passer-by to intervene.

CAPTAIN HORNBLOWER, R.N.

Specially drawn for this work.

The illustration reproduced above depicts one of the stirring events that are recounted in " A Ship of the Line " by C. S. Forester. " Cleared for action, sir," comes the clarion call as everyone stands to his post. This story, and several others, centre round Captain Hornblower, R.N., and the same author gave us " Brown on Resolution " as one of his earlier works.

Lord Peter Wimsey

Dorothy Sayers' character, Lord Peter Wimsey, is in his own way almost a rival of the famous Sherlock Holmes, and although she has written other books and plays it is as a writer of mystery stories such as " The Nine Tailors," in which Lord Peter plays the leading part, that Dorothy Sayers has earned world-wide fame.

The Fascination of Books

It can certainly be said that there is to-day no scarcity of distinguished writers, both men and women, and it is as well that we should know as much about them and their books as possible, because it is an essential part of our education to do so. We should know of good poems, of good histories, biographies, essays and travel books and, of course, of stories, because from well-written fiction there is always so much to learn.

Another interesting point to consider is the number of great writers of our own time who have given us works specially for children. John Masefield, Howard Spring and Walter de la Mare are just three examples. To-day's young people are as fortunate in their writers as were those of the last generation who had Rudyard Kipling's " Jungle Books " and " Just So Stories."

It is good, too, that we should read all the nature books we can, such works as those of Henry Williamson and many other living authors. In these books there is sound knowledge to be obtained and they are no less satisfying than fiction, however temptingly it may be penned.

British Council.

DEVIL'S DYKE AND THE SUSSEX DOWNS

This spacious view of the Downland of Sussex makes us think of " Sussex Gorse," " Green Apple Harvest " and other delightful books by Sheila Kaye-Smith. Daughter of a Sussex doctor, she has used her native county as the background for many of her tales, and in one of them strikes a contrast between the industrial North and the agricultural South.

Specially drawn for this work.

In all pioneer lands the people who were struggling to win an existence in hard conditions were at first too occupied in establishing themselves to turn their thoughts to the cultivation of the arts. But gradually a literature emerged, and we may imagine that perhaps it had its roots in the occasional hours snatched by a few men to write down the wonders of their experiences.

CANADIAN WRITERS

ALTHOUGH Canada is an " older " country than Australia—older, that is, to the European settler, for it was colonised first by the French in the seventeenth century, then by the British to whom it was ceded in 1763— her literature, like that of Australia, practically does not begin until the nineteenth century. True, there were some early writers in French and English back in the eighteenth century, and even earlier such travel books as Cartier's " Voyages "; but all the writing which we can consider literature belongs to the last hundred years. Before that the same conditions of the hard life prevented the cultivation of fine writing, as it did in all pioneer lands. There was magnificent material to write about but little time or encouragement to use it; and the type of person who was opening up the vast Northern country and trying to win an existence from hunting, fishing, trapping and early agriculture was not the type to turn it into art.

Two early books belonging to the older days ought to be noticed. One was "The Sayings and Doings of Sam Slick," by Thomas Chandler Haliburton (1796–1865), which was published in book form in 1836 but had previously appeared in the newspaper *The Novascotian.* Sam Slick was a clever character creation, a seller of very bad clocks, a sayer of very meaningful remarks, touching on life, politics, law and much else of the Nova Scotia of his day, where he was a lawyer and judge. Haliburton, his creator, hated shams and hypocrisy and attacked them with delightful irony. The fun is often rather exaggerated, but it remains good fun and always has a purpose behind it: the purpose of debunking nonsense and pompousness.

The other book was " Wacousta," by John Richardson (1796–1853), which was really the first Canadian novel, though a woman writer, Julia Beckwith (1796–1867), had published a rather crude and melodramatic story, " St. Ursula's Convent, or The Nun of Canada," eight years before. " Wacousta " appeared in 1832, and is a thrilling story of the chief of the Red Indians, Pontiac, and his fight against the British. It breathes the love of Canada and is the beginning of the historical novel there.

The next outstanding writer and work were also historical. The man was William Kirby (1817–1906), and the book was " The Golden Dog " (1877), a thrilling romance of life in Quebec in the mid-eighteenth century. It is a kind of Dumas story, full of colour and excitement, if a bit over-wordy in its dialogues; but it recreates those great days of the French colony at Quebec. Actually Kirby was a Yorkshireman, who was taken as a child by his parents to Cincinnati, and then, as a young man of twenty-one, went to Canada with a trunk full of books and a rifle, because he wanted to live under British rule. Rather a dandy, he nevertheless set up in trade as a tanner, but later became a Customs officer. His first publications were of long poems, rather in the Goldsmith manner ; but his lasting fame depends upon " The Golden Dog."

By the time this was published a group of writers born in the late 'fifties and early 'sixties were getting into their stride. Chief among them was that other historical novelist, Gilbert Parker (1859–1932), Canada's best-known writer. Parker left Canada for England in 1889, but he remained Canadian at heart and his most famous works were such books as " When Valmond came to Pontiac," " Seats of the Mighty " and " The Power and the Glory." Sir Gilbert (for he was knighted in 1901) is also a fine historian and wrote a history of the 1914–18 War. Most of his writing being done in England, it is rather more that of the professional European literary man than the colonial putting down his direct experience of life in a new land; but he remains a splendid story-teller.

More truly Canadian in feeling is that writer of animal stories, Charles G. D. Roberts (1860–1943), whose work is referred to in the section on Notable

This fine picture, " An Indian Encampment along the Islands of Lake Huron," was painted in 1845 by Paul Kane, whose portrait of Kee-A-Kee-Ka-Sa-Coo-Way is reproduced on page 123. It was among scenes such as these that the earliest Canadian writers found their inspiration.

Nature Writers. He has gained fame as poet, historian and novelist, but nothing he has done is so good as the animal stories in "The Kindred of the Wild." Canada is a land of splendid wild animals, moose, deer, wolf and a host of others, and it is not surprising that these have given rise to much sensitive writing. Not only Charles Roberts, but Ernest Thompson Seton, Miss

By courtesy of Messrs. Thomas Nelson & Sons (Canada) Limited.

A delightful illustration from " Canadian Verse for Boys and Girls " to " Ships of Yule," a poem by Bliss Carman. Born in New Brunswick in 1861, Carman became a journalist; he published many books of poetry in which he expressed his philosophy of nature-worship. He was crowned Canadian poet laureate shortly after the first World War.

Marshall Saunders—who writes about dogs, canaries, ponies and other domesticated pets—and, nearer our own time, Mazo de la Roche, one of Canada's finest and best-known novelists, also wrote animal stories. Charles Roberts has been called the " laureate of the animal world " and has always stood for the idea that men are kin to the wilder creatures. Even his titles grip one—" Feet of the Furtive," " The Secret Trails "—and he seems to understand what animals feel without sentimentally making them " think human." He said that he wanted the animals to " state their own case," and his stories and sketches have beautifully done just this. With him we must consider Thompson Seton, who changed his name around and wrote as " Seton-Thompson." He is a fine artist and illustrated his own books, a naturalist who for a time held an appointment as official naturalist to Manitoba, and a scientist. One of his earliest books— and still one of his best—was " Animals I Have Known " (1898), and that title might well cover all his works. Another classic by him is " Lives of the Hunted ";

once again the title tells his sympathy for the creatures. If the name of Mazo de la Roche is best known as the novelist who created those great family cycles of " Jalna " and the Whiteoaks family it should equally be remembered for her volume " The Sacred Bullock." This fine collection of animal stories carried on the distinctly Canadian tradition of good writing about animals. We have grown used now to this attitude to the kindred forms of life, but we must remember how great and how early a contribution Canada made to it.

Meanwhile a slightly later generation of prose writers and poets, born towards the end of last century, came to maturity in the early years of this. Robert Service can be claimed a little doubtfully as a Canadian writer because as the " Poet of the Klondike " he made his name; but he was born in 1876 in Lancashire, educated in Scotland, went to Canada when he was twenty-one, left to drive an ambulance in France in the 1914–18 War, married a French girl and lived in France thereafter. The gold rush to the river and district of Klondike in Yukon in Western Canada from 1896 onward directed the eyes of the world to that part; and if Service found in it the gold of ballad poetry, he turned that into a fortune. His " Songs of a Sourdough " (1905) became world famous. They were galloping Kipling-esque and often sentimental ballad poetry, but people read them and recited them for the joy of their rhythm and verve:

" There are strange things done in the mid-
        night sun
    By the men who moil for gold;
And Arctic trails have their secret tales
    That would make your blood run cold;
The Northern Lights have seen queer
        sights,
    But the queerest they ever did see
Was that night on the marge of Lake
        Lebarge
    I cremated Sam McGee."

" Rhymes of a Rolling Stone " he called one of his books, and that title tells its own tale. His novels, such as " The Trail of the '98," are not really as good as the poems, but that one is probably his best and is a rousing yarn of the Yukon in the gold rush days as Service knew it, because he lived there at that time. Another tale of the same hard-living kind is " The Frontiers-man," by H. A. Cody, who tells in it an exciting tale of the Yukon and of the Mounted Police of the North-West who kept some rough order there.

A Great Nature Writer

The vast area of Canada means that different districts have a life quite distinct from each other, and while, as we have seen, the crude life of the diggers and settlers in the goldfields of the Yukon gave rise to one kind of literature, and the trapping in the cold North to another, there was also the more settled ways of the cities, with their echoes of European society, and the—again close to Nature—pattern of living of the Maritime Provinces on the Atlantic side. The outstanding recorder of this last has been Theodore Goodridge Roberts, who was born in 1877. His many books deal with New Brunswick in partic-

ular. Their story-telling is often made a little jerky (as that of Dickens was) by the fact that he wrote largely for serial publication in newspapers; but apart from this he can tell a tale well. " The Wasp," which was published in 1918, is probably the best of these, and one other, a story for young people called " The Red Feathers," should be mentioned.

In recent years Canada has produced a host of able writers as the country has drawn up alongside the older civilisations in matters of culture. Two women novelists stand to the fore: Marjorie Pickthall, a sensitive, subtle writer who comes nearest to the older European tradition, and that now world-famous one of whom we have already spoken, Mazo de la Roche. Most young folk will certainly add to these the woman who created for their delight that lovely character " Anne of the Green Gables." This is Lucy M. Montgomery, and her Anne books ran into a whole series after she launched Anne in 1908.

Before we leave prose we must say a word for that purveyor of humour, Stephen Leacock (1869–1944). He was born in England but was taken to Canada when he was only six years old, and there eventually become a professor of economics and political science at the great McGill University. Perhaps in revolt from that over-serious subject, he began in 1910 those books like " Literary Lapses " and " Nonsense Novels." " I would rather have written ' Alice in Wonderland ' than the whole *Encyclopædia Britannica*," he said, and continued to keep us laughing with his sketches and stories of absurdities.

Canadian Poets

When we look back over Canadian literature it is surprising how many even of the best of the prose writers are also poets. Probably, like Australia, the Press has encouraged poetry by publishing it (we wish the British Press would copy this idea as they used to in the days before the First World War). Canadian poetry has tended to be fairly simple ballad and easy lyric. It may have lacked profound ideas or avoided being too clever in its use of difficult images and metres, but it is clear and certainly popular. Robert Service and William Bliss Carman (1861–1929) are the two best known of Canadian poets, Service, as we have seen, in swinging narrative poetry, and Carman with a sweet lyrical touch. His " Low Tide on Grand Pré " (1893) was his first book of lyrics. He sings of Nature and of the sea which he loves. In a group of books under the wide title of " The Pipes of Pan " he expressed that philosophy of mankind's unity with wild nature and the earth which has been a recurring note in all Canadian literature.

Capital Press, Ottawa.

A document unique in modern history, of which the first English and French copies are seen above, was presented in 1951 to Mr. Louis St. Laurent, Prime Minister of Canada, by the Rt. Hon. Vincent Massey. The document is the Royal Commission Report on National Development in the Arts, Letters and Sciences, an inventory of cultural development in Canada which took two years to prepare.

Charles Roberts, already mentioned as a writer of animal lore, was also one of the pioneer poets; his " Ode to the Canadian Confederacy," written when he was in his 'teens and published in 1880, brought him immediate fame. Its publication was the signal for a host of new writers of poetry to appear.

Archibald Lampman, a nature poet who beautifully describes Canadian scenery; Pauline Johnson, whose native name of " Tekahionawake " reveals her kinship with the Canadian Indians, and who sang the songs of her people; the line which began with the " poets of the 'sixties " has never slackened, though it is too soon to decide which of the more recent poets can be called great above their fellows. One of the quite early men who struck a distinctive note by creating characters and making them the mouthpiece or the subject of his narrative poems was William Henry Drummond (1854–1907). He has humour and a certain whimsical way with him as he writes of " Little Bateese " or " Johnny Courteau." Some of these poems are written in the dialect of the habitants and the voyageur; and their homely pictures of life and characters on the farm and the trail preserve for us the simple people who retain the pioneering tradition in a Canada fast becoming internationalised and sophisticated, and creating its new literature which is internationalised and sophisticated also.

AUSTRALIAN WRITERS

The early colonisers were too deeply engaged in strenuous, exciting and dangerous living to find time for the writing of books, even if they had had the ability to do so. Later, when they had gained a reasonable amount of security, they began to develop a literature of their own.

IN these new lands, with their demand for a busy, strenuous life from all the pioneers, there was little likelihood in the early days of getting good literature. It is rather easier, let us admit, to use a little leisure between digging and building, hunting and cattle tending and all the other hard physical activities of an early coloniser to write something than to use it for painting; but the kind of man or woman who chooses this busy, active life is not often the type who wishes to write at all. A rare letter home, interesting for its description of new life in a new land, is all we can expect. That is how it was for many years in both Australia and in Canada. So, as in the art of painting, we really have to wait until about the middle of the nineteenth century for anything worth while in literature.

Another trouble is that the writing kind of person so often found that the lack of an audience in the new land, and therefore the lack of publishers, booksellers, libraries and all the things which help to bring writings to the readers, made him yearn to be back in Europe even if he had been born in Australia. To-day, of course, with the swiftly growing cultural life of the great Dominions, this no longer applies as it did in the years of last century. Yet it may well account for the fact that Australia's two greatest writers—the woman novelist who wrote under the name of Henry Handel Richardson and the Greek scholar and translator, Gilbert Murray, both Australian born—became virtually English writers, because they came to England when they were still young and settled here.

On the other hand, that exciting, adventurous life and its " tough " people were splendid material for anybody who did choose to turn them into novels, short stories or poems. This was sometimes done by an English writer using his imagination and building upon the facts he could gather from the Australian newspapers and such sources. The first to write from his own experience of life in Australia was Henry Kingsley, the brother of Charles, who for a few years went out to Australia, joined the mounted police in the struggle against the bushrangers, was a gold digger, and often stayed with the squatters. This was the real thing; and when in 1859 he published his novel, " Geoffry Hamlyn," it was an excellent if slightly romantic picture of Australian life. There were other stories published about the middle of the nineteenth century which give us further pictures of that thrilling open-air life: William Howitt's " A Boy's Adventures in the Wilds of Australia," and Charles Rowcroft's " Tales of the Colonies " and " The Bushranger of Van Dieman's Land." These were the beginning, and soon two novelists of greater literary power arose: Marcus Clarke and T. A. Browne, who wrote under the name of " Rolf Boldrewood."

Two Great Names

Marcus Clarke (1846–81) wrote one magnificent novel describing the terrible life in the penal settlements, " For the Term of his Natural Life," and also numbers of short stories. The short story has always flourished in Australia along with the poem, because the best newspapers have always believed that it was their duty to publish good imaginative writing

and have found room in their columns for these shorter forms, and later for serialised novels. So it is natural that a man like Clarke should write sketches and short stories which would bring him immediate money, of which, indeed, he had little enough. He was only thirty-five when he died, worn out by the hardness of his life and by worry, leaving us at least that one great book.

Rolf Boldrewood (1826–1915) was

Specially drawn for this work.

FOR THE TERM OF HIS NATURAL LIFE

Born in England in 1846, Marcus Clarke emigrated to Australia at the age of 17 and, after working as a clerk and a farmer, engaged in journalism. He became a leader in Melbourne literary circles and founded the Yorick Club. His best-known novel " For the Term of his Natural Life," an incident from which is depicted above, is a story of convict times in Tasmania, but his greatest contribution to Australian literature was the fellowship among writers which his friendship encouraged.

equally an adventurous liver. He was himself a squatter and became a police magistrate and—toughest of jobs—a warden of the goldfields. His most famous story was the bushranger one, "Robbery under Arms," a story of Captain Starlight, the notorious bushranger. "The Squatter's Dream" was another realistic picture of this pioneering life in the hard days.

The Australian novelist with an international fame is the woman writer who published her novels under a man's name, "Henry Handel Richardson." She eventually married a professor at London University and settled permanently in London. The trilogy of novels written around "Richard Mahony," published in 1917, 1925 and 1929, give a full picture of life in the Australia of her youth. Her use of the name Handel in her pseudonym reminds us of another thing about this writer: how able she is to tell the story of a musician, as we realise when we read "Maurice Guest" and "The Young Cosima." Her writing is strong and was for a long time taken to be that of a man, a kind of Australian John Galsworthy, with a wonderful instinct for using the right word and a power to build up a long story of many characters set against a background of their society. Her book "The Getting of Wisdom" is one of the most magnificent of school stories.

During our own century the number of Australian novelists and short-story writers has, of course, increased enormously. Now the Dominion has its own great publishing houses, libraries and bookstores, so there is no longer the difficulty of finding a way to reach the public. Richard Furphy, whose finest book is called "Such is Life" (some people claim that it is the most important of all Australian novels); Katharine Pritchard, who writes terrifyingly real stories of life on the remote stations "out back," of timber-getting and cattle-breeding on the lonely places; Norman Lindsay, a

By courtesy of Messrs. Angus & Robertson Ltd., Sydney.

Best known as a great artist, Norman Lindsay was also a writer of some renown. Here is an amusing picture from a book for children he both wrote and illustrated, "The Magic Pudding." The story is about the adventures of Bunyip Bluegum and his Uncle Wattlebury, two Koala bears, and many other fascinating animals.

A THRILLING RESCUE

Specially drawn for this work.

ROBBERY UNDER ARMS

An exciting incident from Rolf Boldrewood's classic novel of bushranging and gold-digging days in Australia. Boldrewood was born in England in 1826; four years later his father, with his family and goods, sailed for Australia, settling in Sydney. For a time Rolf Boldrewood was a squatter, but droughts broke him and he became a Police Magistrate and Warden of the Goldfields.

writer of the earlier generation, who writes of young boys in an alarmingly outspoken manner; Vance Palmer, another Galsworthian portrayer of family sagas; and Frank Davison, the creator of thrilling pictures of life on the cattle stations in the wilds of Queensland—these are outstanding among the new writers. A good deal of the recent writing has been devoted to realistic—perhaps too realistic —pictures of city life; and the poor quarters of Sydney have had more than a fair share of attention; but Australian slums and slum-dwellers are very like those of anywhere else, and there is a truer and richer Australian flavour in the novels of the wide open spaces and the epic stories of the cattlemen, the sheep farmers and their kind.

Australian Poets

Along with the novel and the short story stands Australian poetry. As we would expect, it begins with simple songs and ballads; and if in more recent years it has lined up with the clever-clever intellectualist poets of Europe and America, the early vigorous and direct stuff written by men of action may eventually prove to have the lasting quality.

Foremost of these action poets stands that exciting person Adam Lindsay Gordon, Australia's best-known poet and the only one who has a memorial in the Poet's Corner of Westminster Abbey. Gordon was born in the Azores and was taken to England and educated at Cheltenham and elsewhere. He was from boyhood a wild character, an intrepid rider, boxer, sportsman of many kinds. Extravagant and romantic, he got into and out of many scrapes before he went off to Australia in his late 'teens. His mind was always full of poetry, the rather heady poetry of Swinburne and the action poetry of Homer. He loved horses and his whole Australian life is linked with them, first as a mounted trooper, then as a famous horse-breaker, steeplechase rider, livery stable keeper. So when he writes his

poetry it is full of the swing and rush of the horseman, and that above all else gives it its quality. Along with that romantic daring, unfortunately, went his inherited melancholy and a tendency to drink that he might forget his worries and money troubles. So, when he was only thirty-seven and those troubles became too much for him, Gordon walked out into the bush and shot himself.

Sport, especially steeplechasing, was the most exciting thing in life to him, and he sang its praises notably. It was his horse-riding poems, published in his volume " Bush Ballads," which earned him fame in his adopted country. " The Sick Stockrider " is probably the best of them, or " The Ride from the Wreck ":

" And faster and faster across the wide heath
    We rode till we raced. Then I gave her
    her head,
And she—stretching out with the bit in her
    teeth—
    She caught him, outpaced him, and
    passed him, and led."

The poems made the blood beat with their riding rhythms. There was his homely sentiment, too, which appealed to the unsophisticated Australians of his time:

" Life is mostly froth and bubble,
    Two things stand like stone,
Kindness in another's trouble,
    Courage in your own."

We know now that he was not a great poet, that even in his bush balladry " Banjo " Paterson (1864–1941) was at least his equal in this kind of Kipling narrative poem. Gordon's friend and protégé, Henry Clarence Kendall, was a better poet, and his pictures of Australian scenery are excellent. Nor was he afraid of being a realist, as his " Death in the Bush " shows. He recorded the cruelty and terror of the harsher aspects of Nature, the " fiery drought and burning sameness of the forest," and could describe a bush-fire terrifyingly. In life and temperament he, too, was overburdened and melancholy, and his work found practically no response during his lifetime.

The other famous and important bush balladist was Henry Lawson (1867–1922), who was also a prose writer. "While the Billy Boils," the title of one of his books, might be the key title to all of them, for he was a writer on the lonely outposts and stations. He set out, he said, to be "aggressively Australian "—that is, to throw off the influence of European literature and life in an effort to convey the spirit of his own country. Happily he had a delightful sense of fun as well as a passion for his native land, and both in the prose (especially the short stories) and the poetry of Lawson there is evidence of this humorous side of Australian living.

Pictorial Press.

This statue of Australia's famous bush poet is in Spring Street, Melbourne. Adam Lindsay Gordon loved horses, and the saddle under the seat is symbolic of the poetic theme he exploited with such great success.

An Age of Experiment

Round about the end of the nineteenth century and through the first decade of our own this self-conscious Australianism held. But the world of the fast steamship, the motor car and eventually the aeroplane is an international one, and the poets and novelists, the short-story writers and the critics, the newspapers which published sketches, and the rising publishers who put out Australian books, were all caught up in wider world movements. It was everywhere an age of experiment, and the younger poets in particular, especially after the First World War, were out for new methods. There were a great number of them—owing to the encouragement by enlightened newspapers Australia has long been "a nest of singing birds "—and they grouped themselves together sometimes under fascinating titles: "The Jindyworobaks," "The Angry Penguins," "The Barjoi." The pro-Australian note was still heard in all this, and that of the real equalitarianism which is so marked a force in Australian life. Bernard O'Dowd (born 1866), who called himself "the poet of the new democracy"; Christopher Brennan (1870–1932), whom some consider Australia's finest poet; Mary Gilmore (born 1865), a fine woman poet—these stand out among the older generation. Kenneth Slessor (born 1901), the author of "One Hundred Poems," is an outstanding modernist writer, a kind of T. S. Eliot who has tended to work back from the frustration of his early elegy for a dead friend,

" Five Bells," and in his more recent " Five Visions of Captain Cook " strikes a happier note. R. D. Fitzgerald (born 1902), at first a disciple of Brennan, is now one of the most important poets, his book " Moonlight Acre " being an enchanting volume.

Happily there is in every form of Australian literature the stirring of a people young and vigorous enough to be moving forward rather than depending on the past, either their own or that of the Motherland, yet established enough now to have a tradition upon which to build. Australian literature already has a noteworthy past, and it certainly has the promise of a wonderful future.

New Zealand Literature

The literature of New Zealand is equally one with a tradition dating back to the nineteenth century, gradually establishing itself, and now full of promise for the future. Katherine Mansfield, one of the finest of all short story writers, was New Zealand's great contribution to modern British writing, for she came to England, settled here, and produced splendid work. Now New Zealand has her own spirited literary life, remarkable for a country with only two million people. John Mulgan, Guthrie Wilson, Ngaio Marsh, and Nelle Scanlan are novelists whose names are well-known in their homeland and in Britain. Sir Peter Buck (1880–1951) is a world-accepted writer on the native Maori culture; there is a wealth of books on the pioneering days; and the richness of the country in poets and poetry is witnessed by such anthologies as Allen Curlow's " Book of New Zealand Verse " and Louis Johnson's " Poetry Year Book."

Specially drawn for this work.

AUSTRALIA'S NATIONAL WRITER AND POET

Henry Lawson was born in a tent in the goldfields near Grenfell, New South Wales, in 1867. Throughout his youth the family were often on the move and Lawson experienced all the hardships of a losing fight to win a livelihood in the bush. Though he married and settled for short periods in Sydney, visited New Zealand, and in 1900–2 was welcomed by London literary circles, it was always to the bush that he returned for inspiration.

Specially drawn for this work.

THE GOLDEN KEY TO THE LAND OF ENCHANTMENT

Children's books existed even before the printing press had been invented, and for more than four centuries books have been printed for both the instruction and delight of younger readers. They are "the Golden Key that opens the Enchanted Door." In this section an attempt has been made to compile a list of a hundred or more books, some of which have delighted many generations and are read with as much pleasure to-day as other books also given here, which have appeared in recent years.

IN the previous chapters we have read about the famous books which have been written during the past three centuries as well as the work of authors of more recent days. Of most of these books it can be said that they make their appeal to readers of all ages and classes.

Here in this chapter we turn to a particular class: the books specially written for younger readers between, say, the ages of four and sixteen. There are many books, of course, which were not originally written with the idea of appealing specially to younger readers, but have since come to be regarded in that class. "Robinson Crusoe" is an example. On the other hand there are books such as Stevenson's "Treasure Island" and "Kidnapped" which first appeared as boys' serials but became famous when published in book form and were hailed by grown-up readers as masterpieces.

Then there is Lewis Carroll's "Alice in Wonderland" told to three young girls on river picnics and afterwards written only in manuscript, with amusing but amateurish drawings, to give as a present to one of the girls because she had asked for it. That manuscript was sold seventy years later for £15,000, and grown-ups have enjoyed "Alice" just as much as children. Yet of no book could it be more truly said that it was "specially written for children." When the book was eventually published, the famous artist, Sir John Tenniel, illustrated it.

Nursery Rhymes and Adventure

Since 1865, when it first appeared, many other artists have illustrated the large number of different editions which have been published. Both "Alice in Wonderland" and "Through the Looking Glass," another story of Alice, have been translated into French, German, Italian and Dutch.

There were books written for children

well before Caxton set up his first printing-press. Generally they were written and copied by the monks in their monastery cells and they combined the teaching of reading with religious instruction. The first children's book ever printed in this country was probably "The Primer in English Most Necessary for the Education of Children," published about 1537. After reading came writing, and the first copy-book in England was printed about the year 1571. Later there were "Writing Sheets" or "School Pieces" and it is really from these School Pieces of the late eighteenth century that our modern Christmas cards developed.

Story books and nursery rhymes appeared later. Probably "Old Mother Hubbard" was the first of the nursery rhymes, though the earliest printed edition still in existence was only published about 1804, but the rhyme was well-known long before this. "The House that Jack Built" was published about the same time. History books had been written also and some publishers were quite anxious to avoid boring their young readers: "Choice Scraps, Historical and Biographical, Consisting of Pleasing Stories and Diverting Anecdotes, Most of them Short to Prevent Their Being Tiresome, Comprehending Much Useful Information and Innocent Amusement for Young Minds" was published about 1790.

Ralph Tubbs.

" WHERE I MAY READ, ALL AT MY EASE "

A library may be a cold, repelling room, but if it is intended as something more than a mere storehouse for books, then the more pleasant it is, the better for the reader. More attention is being paid to-day to the choice of a suitable room for the library in the newer schools. Our photograph shows part of the library at the High School, Richmond, Yorkshire.

TOM BROWN'S GREAT FIGHT

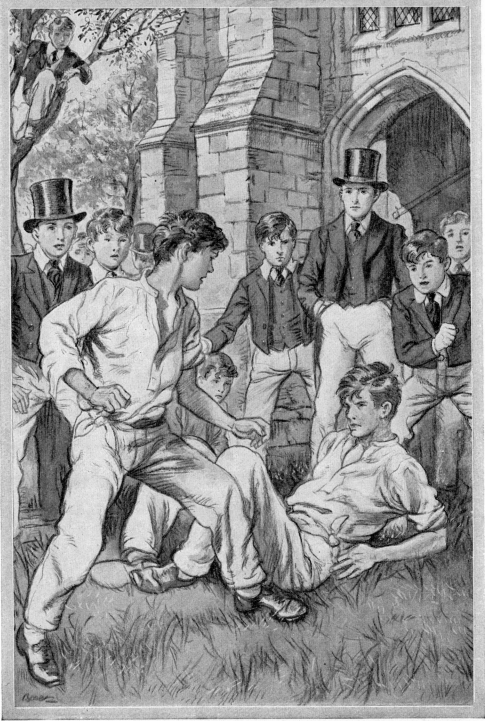

Specially drawn for this work.

Most famous of all school stories, " Tom Brown's Schooldays," by Thomas Hughes, was first published in 1856. It tells of the author's own life as a boy at Rugby under the great Dr. Arnold. Our illustration shows an incident in the desperate fight between Tom and Slogger Williams. Tom has just floored his opponent for the third time, but the issue is never decided as the Head himself appears on the scene and, in the author's words, " the ring melts away in a few seconds ! "

RIP VAN WINKLE RETURNS

Hero of a story in " The Sketch Book," by Washington Irving, published in 1819, Rip van Winkle fell asleep in the woods for twenty years. When he wakes and returns to the village he finds everything changed and himself practically forgotten. The story has been re-told in plays and comic operas and the name has become a household word.

More exciting books and adventure stories for young readers could also be bought. One of the earliest was " The Renowned History of Guy, Earl of Warwick, and containing his Noble Exploits and Victories," first published about 1700 and still being printed a century later. " The History of Robin Hood," which, with its many imitations, must be counted among the best-sellers of all time, appeared in different volumes before a collection of the stories was pub-lished in one volume in 1795.

Fairy Tales from France

The earliest fairy tales came from the French, written by an author's son, Pierre Perrault, and at least six of these stories are still popular: " The Sleeping Beauty," " Red Riding Hood," "Puss in Boots," " Hop o' my Thumb," " Cinderella " and "Blue Beard." These first appeared in France in 1697 and in due course English editions were published. " The Arabian Nights " also first saw the light of day in France and the stories of " Aladdin," " Sinbad the Sailor " and " Ali Baba and the Forty Thieves " were quite well-known to English children by the beginning of the nine-teenth century.

Suppose we were called upon to form a library of books which would be suitable for boys and girls ranging from four to sixteen. That would probably mean that some of the books would be suitable for reading aloud to children who were rather too young to read for themselves, while some of the books for the readers of fourteen to sixteen would suit readers of forty to sixty equally well. We shall, no doubt, overlook some that deserve to be in our library, but this is merely the beginning. Nor will we try to classify them too much by putting on labels for " Boys " or " Girls " though we may indicate such details at times. The truth is that many so-called boys' books are enjoyed by girls just as much as by their brothers.

Then there are books such as " The Wind in the Willows " by Kenneth Grahame which tells the story of Toad of Toad Hall, the humble-minded Mole and the practical Water Rat. This has often been described as a delightful book for a family of all ages. There are other books which come into the same category and it would need a very large volume to classify and comment on all the books that might deserve a place in our library.

Both New and Old

As a beginning, let us make a selection from books already mentioned in the previous chapters. Some of these have become classics in their own way and have been printed and reprinted for succeeding generations.

ANDERSEN'S FAIRY
   TALES. Grimms'
   FAIRY TALES.
ROBINSON CRUSOE.
   Defoe.
GULLIVER'S TRAVELS.
   J. Swift.
WESTWARD HO!
   Charles Kingsley.
LORNA DOONE. R. D.
   Blackmore.
THE CORAL ISLAND.
   R. M. Ballantyne.
MR. MIDSHIPMAN
               EASY.
   Captain Marryat.
LAST OF THE MOHI-
   CANS. Fenimore
   Cooper.
TOM SAWYER. Mark
   Twain.
UNCLE REMUS. J. C.
   Harris.
PETER PAN. J. M.
   Barrie.
FIRST MEN IN THE
   MOON. H. G. Wells.
ADVENTURES OF
   SHERLOCK HOLMES.
   A. Conan Doyle.

THE FOUR FEATHERS. A. E. W. Mason.
THE THIRTY-NINE STEPS. John Buchan.
GALLION'S REACH. H. M. Tomlinson.
TREASURE ISLAND. R. L. Stevenson.
KING SOLOMON'S MINES. Rider Haggard.
THE JUNGLE BOOKS. Rudyard Kipling.
BEVIS. Richard Jefferies.
TARKA THE OTTER. Henry Williamson.
FAR AWAY AND LONG AGO. W. H. Hudson.
DEAD MAN'S ROCK. "Q."
BRAZILIAN ADVENTURE. Peter Fleming.

To these we will add the two books already mentioned:

ALICE IN WONDERLAND. Lewis Carroll.
THE WIND IN THE WILLOWS. Kenneth Grahame.

Copyright.

IN THE ENCHANTED CASTLE

Among writers who created a new type of story for young readers was Edith Nesbit, and " The Enchanted Castle " is regarded as perhaps the best of all the many stories of magic, romance and adventure which came from her pen. Her characters, too, are altogether delightful and fascinating.

J. Hardman.

WHERE BEATRIX POTTER LIVED

The books of Beatrix Potter are among the smallest and shortest of all, but they became classics for younger children long before their author died in 1943. The illustrations by Beatrix Potter herself have special significance to Sawrey, the village in the Lake District where she lived for many years. She bequeathed to the nation Troutbeck Park Farm, seen in the photograph above and now in the care of the National Trust.

We have missed some that might have been included and only one from each author has been given in this first selection. Scott, Dickens and others have been left out because we should find them on the grown-up shelves when we reach that stage.

School stories are not, perhaps, as popular as they once were, largely because there is a wider variety to choose from these days, but some of them still have a charm of their own:

TOM BROWN'S SCHOOLDAYS. *T. Hughes.*
THE HILL. *Horace Annesley Vachell.*
A DOMINIE'S LOG. *A. S. Neill.*
THE FIFTH FORM AT ST. DOMINIC'S. *Talbot Baines Reed.*
VICE VERSA. *F. Anstey.*
STALKY & CO. *Rudyard Kipling.*
THE BENDING OF A TWIG. *Desmond Coke.*

JEREMY AT CRALE. *Hugh Walpole.*
GOOD-BYE, MR. CHIPS. *James Hilton.*

There are two writers whose books for girls have qualified them as classics in their particular sphere since they have been read by successive genera-tions and are still counted among the favourites by Royal Princesses and ordinary schoolgirls:

LITTLE WOMEN (and GOOD WIVES). *Louisa M. Alcott.*
WHAT KATY DID (and WHAT KATY DID AT SCHOOL). *Susan Coolidge.*

On the Children's Shelf

Now we might turn to the shelf which could be labelled " For the Very Young ": books that can be read to children or read by them as they grow older. Some of our famous authors have turned from novels to fairy stories or, like Lewis Carroll, have written tales to interest their own or other children. The author of "Vanity Fair" is rarely thought of as a writer for young readers yet one book of his deserves a place in our list:

THE ROSE AND THE RING. *W. M. Thackeray.*
THE KING OF THE GOLDEN RIVER. *John Ruskin.*
THE PRINCESS AND THE GOBLIN; and AT THE BACK OF THE NORTH WIND. *George Macdonald.*
THE STORY OF DR. DOLITTLE. *Hugh Lofting.*
WINNIE-THE-POOH (and THE HOUSE AT POOH CORNER). *A. A. Milne.*
MARTIN PIPPIN IN THE DAISY FIELD. *Eleanor Farjeon.*
THE GOLD OF FAIRNILEE. *Andrew Lang.*
JUST SO STORIES. *Rudyard Kipling.*
LITTLE BOY LOST. *W. H. Hudson.*
LEGENDS OF KING ARTHUR AND HIS KNIGHTS. *James Knowles.*

We might add two writers who attained popularity on both sides of the Atlantic and were among America's best-known writers in the nineteenth century. Washington Irving's "Sketch Book" contained two stories which have become classics and have been published in various forms since they first appeared over a century ago. Nathaniel Hawthorne though famous for his more serious work also wrote stories of ancient Greece which have been re-published many times since:

RIP VAN WINKLE & THE LEGEND OF SLEEPY HOLLOW. *Washington Irving.*
TANGLEWOOD TALES & A WONDER BOOK. *Nathaniel Hawthorne.*

There are two other authors whose books should go on this shelf and although in our list we will mention only two books from each, it is fairly

Specially drawn for this work.

A SCENE FROM "THE WHITE COMPANY"

Although Conan Doyle's great popularity was achieved mainly by his many stories of the adventures of the famous detective, Sherlock Holmes, yet he himself was inclined to place some of his historical novels on a higher plane than any other of his work. Few readers will disagree on reading those outstanding stories "Sir Nigel" and its entrancing successor "The White Company."

safe to say that some of the vacant space will soon be filled by more. Beatrix Potter's delightful little stories are for the very young and the children who have just learned to read, but older people enjoy reading them aloud, especially to the right audience. Edith Nesbit's books are much longer, but they are fairy tales that will fascinate young readers and continue to do so until they are quite grown up. Like the stories of Conan Doyle and W. W. Jacobs, they first appeared in the pages of the *Strand* magazine.

> THE ENCHANTED CASTLE. THE PHŒNIX AND THE CARPET. *Edith Nesbit.*
> PETER RABBIT. THE TAILOR OF GLOUCESTER. *Beatrix Potter.*

We should have a few pleasant books of poetry on this same shelf. Some famous peoms which one would like to have are not easy to obtain except in anthologies or grown-up collections. William Blake's " Songs of Innocence and Experience " are an example, and to these we will add:

> THE OXFORD BOOK OF ENGLISH VERSE.
> THE CAMBRIDGE BOOK OF POETRY FOR CHILDREN. *Edited by Kenneth Grahame.*
> POEMS FOR CHILDREN; THIS YEAR NEXT YEAR. *Walter De la Mare.*
> THE CHRISTOPHER ROBIN VERSES (WHEN WE WERE VERY YOUNG; NOW WE ARE SIX). *A. A. Milne.*
> A CHILD'S GARDEN OF VERSES. *Robert Louis Stevenson.*
> FAIRIES AND CHIMNEYS. *Rose Fyleman.*

To these add some amusing verses:

> THE BOOK OF NONSENSE AND MORE NONSENSE. *Edward Lear.*
> THE BAD CHILD'S BOOK OF BEASTS. MORE BEASTS FOR WORSE CHILDREN. *Hilaire Belloc.*

From Humour to History

While we are choosing humorous and light-hearted books, we could add another of the Dolittle books and some of the stories of that ingenious *enfant terrible*, William Brown, who has many volumes to his credit as well as having appeared on the stage and the screen:

> JUST WILLIAM. *Richmal Crompton.*
> DR. DOLITTLE'S CIRCUS. *Hugh Lofting*

At this stage, too, we might add one or two humorous books for the older boys and girls. W. W. Jacobs and J. K. Jerome are bound to appear in any list of humorous writers for young or old:

> DIALSTONE LANE. *W. W. Jacobs.*
> THREE MEN IN A BOAT. *Jerome K. Jerome.*
> SPANISH GOLD. *Geo. A. Birmingham.*

To speak of historical stories is apt to act as a warning to some young readers, and older ones too, who imagine that all historical yarns are heavy and old-fashioned. Some of them may be, but most of those given below are worth the hours spent in reading them, since they are stories that live in the memory long after others are forgotten:

> BEN HUR. *Lew Wallace.*
> THE BLACK DOUGLAS. *S. R. Crockett.*
> THE LAST DAYS OF POMPEII. *Bulwer Lytton.*
> THE WHITE COMPANY. *Conan Doyle.*
> CLOISTER AND THE HEARTH. *Charles Reade.*
> THE TOWER OF LONDON. *Harrison Ainsworth.*
> THE COUNT OF MONTE CRISTO. *A. Dumas.*

One or two others which we might add to our list, including one that has the air of recording history, though it is entirely imaginative, are " The Prisoner of Zenda " and one of Baroness Orczy's delightful stories about the French Revolution. This may not tell us much about the Revolution, but introduces us to Sir Percy Blakeney and may probably lead us to read the real history of these strange times:

> THE SCARLET PIMPERNEL. *Baroness Orczy.*
> THE PRIZONER OF ZENDA. RUPERT OF HENTZAU. *Anthony Hope.*
> THE SWORD IN THE STONE. *T. H. White.* (Fifteenth century boyhood).
> THE FIFTH OF NOVEMBER. *L. A. G. Strong.*

Animals and Schooldays

By way of a change, we might select a few books to appeal to those who love horses, including the famous " Black Beauty," first published in 1877, but still appearing in several publishers' lists; also one not specially written for children (" National Velvet "), but appealing strongly to many boys and girls.

> BLACK BEAUTY. *Anna Sewell.*
> SMOKY. *Will James.* (Told by a cowboy.)

Possibly we are filling our shelves in rather a haphazard way, but we can always go back. On the shelves for the younger readers, for instance, there must be room for some of Enid Blyton's delightful stories for children, and there are a few others for which we should find a place:

And for the girls' section, Angela Brazil's school stories of which there are many; in this school story section, too, we can select others from the books by Christine Chaundler and Agnes M. Miall, and the more adventurous stories of Bessie Marchant and Violet Methley. There are the modern school stories for boys, too, and here again the best plan is to choose from among those authors whose names are established, such as Gunby Hadath, Hylton Cleaver, Richard Bird and Jeffrey Havilton.

Mystery, detective and adventure stories by modern writers would need many shelves and we can only choose

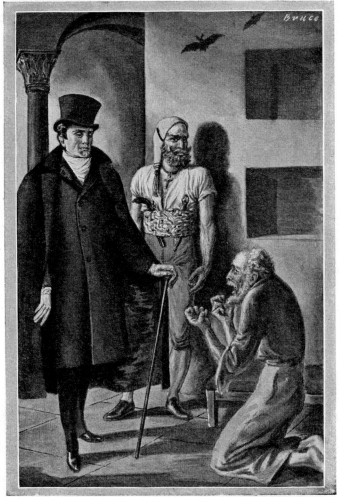

Specially drawn for this work.

THE COUNT OF MONTE CRISTO'S PARDON

Alexandre Dumas wrote many novels, but none has attained such world-wide fame as " The Count of Monte Cristo," written in 1845. It is a very long book, but its amazing plot, thrilling adventures, and atmosphere of romance set it in a class of its own. Our picture shows one of the final scenes in the story when Edmond Dantès' third and last enemy is forgiven and freed.

a rough selection, beginning with an author who is better known as the Poet Laureate but has written some wonderfully fine adventure stories as well:

To these we will add a mixed collection

of sea, air and adventure at home and abroad, spiced with one or two mystery stories:

GREAT NORTHERN (and all the "Swallows and Amazons" series). *Arthur Ransome.*
MYSTERY AT WITCHEND (and others in the "Lone Pine" series). *Malcolm Saville.*
BLACK IVORY. *Norman Collins.*
THE BOY CASTAWAYS. *Capt. Taprell Dorling.*

BIGGLES FLIES NORTH. *Capt. W. E. Johns.*
IN DANGEROUS WATERS. *Percy F. Westerman.*
THE FOURTH ENGINEER. *Lawrence R. Bourne.*
MOONFLEET. *J. Meade Falkner.*
CAPTAIN PEG-LEG'S WAR. *Peter Dawlish.*
WARDEN OF THE WILDS. *L. C. Douthwaite.*
THE KON-TIKI EXPEDITION. *Thor Heyerdahl.*

Stories of Wild Nature

Nearly a hundred volumes we have chosen so far and we ought to find space for a few fairly recent Nature stories, beginning with one for younger readers and ending with one for older boys:

BAMBI, THE STORY OF A FOREST DEER. *Felix Salten.*
SAJO AND HER BEAVER PEOPLE. *Grey Owl.*
ROMANCES OF THE WILD. *Mortimer Batten.*
WILD NATURE'S DAY. *Frances Pitt.*
THE FEET OF THE FURTIVE. *Charles G. D. Roberts.*
THE WOLF KING. *J. W. Lippincott.*

We might go on with other lists of books of Travel, Exploration, Science and Invention; or a short list of those delightful books such as "The Charm of Birds" by Lord Grey and others dealing with Flowers and Trees and all the wonders of the world in which we live. Or there are holiday books, such as "In and Out of Doors" by Amabel Williams-Ellis, which deal with all sorts of hobbies and amusements. Most of us have our own particular hobby and the special shelf of our library containing the books on our own subject is essentially an individual concern. In this chapter we have been chiefly concerned with stories and our complete list will be a general one

JUST WILLIAM!   *Copyright.*

It was in 1922 that the first volume of stories recording the adventures and misadventures of William Brown first appeared. Since then nearly thirty volumes have been published and William has appeared on the stage and the screen besides delighting millions of listeners to the radio broadcasts of his efforts.

with few that would not come under the broad heading of fiction.

In recent years the National Book League has arranged Children's Book Weeks in different towns throughout the country and so given young readers an opportunity of seeing a wide selection of books written for their pleasure and entertainment—and sometimes for their information and study as well. Then, too, the librarians of the many public and other libraries throughout the country have chosen their list of books for children which they say " should never be out of print."

All these will be found on one shelf or another of the library we have chosen here, with the exception of a special list of ten books which has been kept for our last addition to those already chosen. These books would have found a place in one or other of our lists but for the fact that they deserve to come in a special class all by themselves.

For some years past the Library Association has awarded each year, with the exception of one or two war years, the Carnegie Medal for the outstanding book for children, written by

By permission of the publishers, Macmillan & Co. Ltd.

" MRS. TAPER KNOCKED THEIR HEADS TOGETHER "

The story of the extraordinary adventures of Dinah and Dorinda in the village of Midmeddlecum is told in Eric Linklater's children's book " The Wind on the Moon," a tale crowded with both magical and natural incidents, all happening in a riotous world of mixed sense and nonsense. This book is among those which have been awarded the Library Association Carnegie Medal, and the illustration shown above is one of the many drawn by Nicolas Bentley.

a British subject living in the United Kingdom, which has been published during the preceding year. Here is a list of those books:

PIGEON POST. *Arthur Ransome.*
THE FAMILY FROM ONE END STREET. *Eve Garnett.*
THE CIRCUS IS COMING. *Noel Streatfeild.*
RADIUM WOMAN. *Eleanor Doorly.*
VISITORS FROM LONDON. *Kitty Barne.*

These are the books which, like so many of the older ones in our list, will stand the test of succeeding generations of readers. That is an important fact about a good book: it does not become out-of-date but often takes on a certain mellowness with time. There are books which enthrall us in our youthful days, but then they are put on one side and almost forgotten for years. One day we take up one of these half-remembered volumes again and begin to read, doubtfully, until the charm and fascination comes back and we are transported to the land of enchantment once more.

With over a hundred volumes on our library shelves we have made a very fair beginning. Probably some books have been omitted which another selector would have strongly recommended and some have been put in which he would leave out. Yet there lies the advantage of having a list: it recalls other books, suggests new ideas, and acts as a guide in building up a small library of books to interest all the younger members of the family—and some of the older ones whose minds are still young as well. We can all share that gift of which Andrew Lang wrote when he sang:

By permission of the publishers, Faber & Faber Ltd.

" GIRLS AND BOYS COME OUT TO PLAY "

Some of the most delightful fairy stories written in our own times have come from the pen of Walter de la Mare and appear in his " Collected Stories for Children." This book was awarded the Library Association Carnegie Medal for the most outstanding children's book of the year in 1947. Our illustration, drawn by Irene Hawkins, is taken from this volume and shows one of the amazing incidents in the story " The Three Sleeping Boys."

One gift the Fairies gave me—
The love of Books, the Golden Key
That opens the Enchanted Door.

J. Dixon-Scott.

STONEHENGE AT SUNSET

In this impressive photograph we see Stonehenge as it is to-day, silhouetted darkly against the setting sun. Such a view is particularly appealing in the wide and somewhat desolate expanse of Salisbury Plain. Stonehenge is believed to have been erected as a Temple of the Sun, and to have witnessed the evening shadows through a period estimated at thirty-six centuries.

IN THE DISTANT PAST

WE call our ancestors cave men because the first home of mankind was a cave. A hole in the rocks gave those naked, hairy folk shelter from the rain and snow, but not from the huge and savage beasts, such as the cave bear and sabre-toothed tiger, of those early days.

To protect himself against these monsters, it must have occurred to man at a very early stage to pile rocks across the mouth of the cave, and that rude stone wall was the first attempt at building.

The First Builder

Then some tribe that went wandering in search of food found itself up on a bare moor where there were no caves, but plenty of stones, and what is more natural than that its members should build a wall of loose stones around their camp? This wall protected them from wild beasts, but not from the weather and up on the heights the wind blew bitter cold, so someone got the idea of making a small enclosure just big enough for one family, and of laying sticks across the top to form the roof.

A Prehistoric Village

If you visit Dartmoor, that great tableland of South Devonshire, you may see for yourself just how those old folk built. On a high saddle between two tors near the eastern side of the moor lies the prehistoric village called Grimspound. It is a good sized space surrounded by a *double* wall of gigantic stones, and in it are the remains of a number of stone huts, one of which has been restored by clever scientists so that it looks just as it used to look when first built, perhaps thirty centuries ago.

Men's First Arch

You will notice that it is not quite circular, but that the rude stone wall is spiralled so that one end overlaps the other. Since the men who built it knew nothing of doors, they adopted this device to keep the wind from blowing straight in. The top, made of pieces of wood and rushes, is shaped like a beehive and was no doubt fairly weather-proof. With a good bed of dried grass and plenty of skins to cover them, we may well believe that the inmates slept snugly, even when winter storms raged over these bleak heights.

These primitive folk belonged to the Stone Age and had, of course, no metal tools, so they could not shape stones except by beating with other and harder stones. Therefore they picked such stones as were suited by their natural shape for their purpose, and filled the chinks with clay or moss to keep out the wind. Then as time went on they discovered tin and copper, two easily melted metals, and fused them together to make bronze.

Good bronze is very hard, and with bronze tools they were able to shape stones, to square them so that they would fit together. Once they had done this, they got on more quickly, and soon discovered how to make an arch by setting up the upright stones and placing across them a third stone. At Mycenæ, in Greece, there still exists an immensely ancient arch called the Lion Gate which is made on this principle.

All About Stonehenge

The first effort of the primitive architect was for defence against enemies, both man and beast; the second was for the building of temples in which to worship the unseen powers, and for the construction of tombs for the mighty dead.

The oldest ruins in England which still stand are the remains of the great temple of Stonehenge, a temple which we believe to have been erected for the worship of the sun, a work so colossal that it has stood through some thirty-six centuries, and still fills the mind of the spectator with wonder and awe.

The Hanging Stones

"Stanhengist" is the Saxon word, from which we have Stonehenge, and its meaning is "the hanging stones." The name shows how greatly impressed our Saxon forefathers were by the size of the lintels, the cross-pieces laid across the tops of the "sarsens" or pillar stones. Some of these lintels

A STONE HUT IN OUTLINE

Primitive man, maybe thirty centuries ago, built and lived in a stone hut of this shape. Knowing nothing of doors, he fashioned his wall so that one end overlapped the other, thus preventing the wind from blowing straight in.

Based on " Everyday Life in the New Stone, Bronze and Early Ages," by M. and C. H. B. Quennell, published by B. T. Batsford, Ltd.

HOMES IN THE STONE AGE

This illustration gives us a clear idea of the stone hut when it was finished. The stones for the base were of course carefully selected and their chinks filled with clay or moss to keep out the weather. For the upper structure, which makes one think of a beehive, there was a framework of wood neatly thatched with rushes. The floor was probably covered with dried grass.

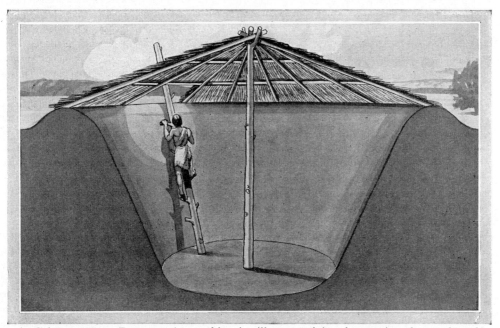

At Grimspound, on Dartmoor, is a prehistoric village containing the remains of a number of stone huts such as the one depicted in the upper drawing on this page. Another type of home was made in a pit, like the one here seen. Instead of rearing the walls of a house, as we do, primitive man dug holes in dry and suitable localities and roofed them with wood and thatch.

Drawings based on " Everyday Life in the New Stone, Bronze and Early Ages," by M. and C. H. B. Quennell, published by
B. T. Batsford, Ltd.

307   20—2

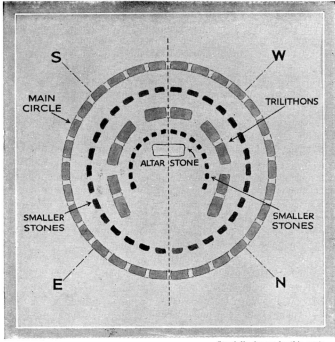

Specially drawn for this work.

STONEHENGE IN A SKETCH-PLAN

From this diagram we can easily imagine the shape and ground-plan of Stonehenge when first erected. You will notice that there were thirty huge stones in the outer circle. Each pair of these stones was capped with a lintel, or large horizontal stone. The inner trilithons also consisted of two uprights and one cross-piece, and the altar stone came in the centre.

savages. Not a bit of it, for they kept animals, such as sheep and cattle, they farmed the land and grew wheat, barley and other crops, and they lived in huts or houses. They knew how to spin and weave wool, they made good pottery out of clay, and they certainly understood a great deal about mining. They had undoubtedly some bronze implements with which they were able to cut wood and shape stones.

They also—their priests, at any rate —knew a lot about astronomy, for they " oriented " their stone avenues and stone temples correctly, so that the sun or some specially bright star shone upon them at some particular date.

are 15 feet long, 4 feet 6 inches wide and 3 feet 6 inches deep, and weigh nearly seven tons. Just think of lifting seven tons 20 feet off the ground! Nowadays, it is true, we could do it with a steam crane, but this task was accomplished about 1680 B.C., when our ancestors did not possess any sort of crane.

Who Built Stonehenge ?

The people who built Stonehenge were what we call Neolithic or New Stone people. They came from the shores of the Mediterranean, and their skeletons show that they were small folk. The men were not more than 5 feet 6 inches in height and the women about 5 feet. They were slenderly built, had rather dark complexions and long, narrow heads. Do not run away with the idea that they were

What Stonehenge Is

We have good reason to believe that Stonehenge was probably a temple of sun worship, for Professor Flinders Petrie has told us that it was plainly built so as to face the rising sun on midsummer day. The axis of the temple is a line drawn through the centre of the altar stone and the so-called slaughter stone to another stone beyond, named the Friar's Heel, and this line must have pointed exactly to sunrise when the temple was built. As we know, the place of sunrise varies slightly from year to year owing to the changes of the earth's course round the sun, and the great astronomer, Sir Norman Lockyer, has calculated that this line pointed exactly to sunrise in 1680 B.C. That is how we get the date of the erection of this strange and wonderful circle.

In Shape and Size

Stonehenge stands in the centre of Salisbury Plain on a circular earthwork 300 feet in diameter. There is an outside circle of " trilithons " (each a pair of the giant stone pillars with a crosspiece on top), and these were originally thirty in number. Inside this is a circle of smaller stones called " blue stones." In the centre is a horseshoe which was originally composed of five giant trilithons surrounding an inner horseshoe of blue stones. The pillars weigh from twenty tons up to fifty tons apiece.

Specially drawn for this work.

A BIRD'S-EYE VIEW OF THE TEMPLE

This pictorial diagram is a counterpart of the sketch-plan on the opposite page. Here you can see the outer circle, the ring of smaller inner stones, the horseshoe of trilithons and smaller stones and the altar. Some of the lintels are 15 feet in length, weighing many tons, yet they were lifted 20 feet above ground level.

How it was Built

The big stones or sarsens are of sandstone and have been roughly dressed. These stones are English, but not native to the district, which is all chalk. The blue stones forming the inner circle are not English at all, but were brought from across the sea, or possibly from Wales.

How did these primitive people bring them ? What ships did they use, and when the stones were landed, how did they carry them across many miles of hill and dale ? We may take it for granted there were no roads in those days; we know that then, and for hundreds of years after, nearly the whole of Southern England was swamp and forest. How did these little folk haul their huge boulders across such country, and how did they transport them across the wide rivers and over the soft boggy ground ?

Frankly, we do not know. We cannot even guess. The whole undertaking is a complete and utter mystery.

What About the Pyramids ?

People say " Look at the Egyptians. See how they built the Pyramids. They used bigger stones and more of them."

There is no comparison at all. Egypt is a fairly flat country with a vast river running through its centre on which great stones can be rafted. It has always had a big population, and the richness of its soil provides, and always did provide, plenty of food for vast armies of labourers. The Egyptians, when they wanted to build a pyramid, were able to gather a huge host of slaves on the spot and keep them there till the job was finished.

Salisbury Plain, on the other hand, is

TALES TOLD IN STONE

We should carefully preserve the fragments that have come down to us from the Stone Age, because they are almost all we have to tell us the story of primitive man. Here, for example, are some monolithic ruins to be seen at West Park, Jersey, in the Channel Islands. A monolith is a column or obelisk consisting of a single stone.

Photos: J. Dixon-Scott.

This picture also comes from Jersey, and the photograph was taken at Gorey. It shows us an ancient dolmen, the meaning of which is one large stone resting upon others to form a kind of inner chamber. In this instance there seems to have been a rampart of stone to protect the dolmen, and such a chamber may have been the centre of a grave-mound, known as a barrow.

A HUT CIRCLE ON DARTMOOR

Here is another example of a dolmen with the corridor or tunnel beneath the capstone plainly seen. This one is in Guernsey, and was undoubtedly a burial place. Picturesquely, it is said by the natives to be haunted by fairies. The dolmens of the Channel Islands are quite different from those found in England. Some thousands of such monuments survive in France.

Photos: J. Dixon-Scott.,

In this print we see the famous hut circle of Merrivale, on the windswept heights of Dartmoor. Each of these circles probably represents a hut with a stone base covered with a thatched timber roof, as illustrated earlier in this section. The men who arranged these stones may have lived a thousand years before the time of Christ.

Specially drawn for this work.

The Seven Wonders of the Ancient World were all connected with the two arts of architecture and sculpture, and the list of them was made about 2,000 years ago. The first four were: (1) The Colossus of Rhodes; (2) The Great Pyramid of Egypt; (3) The Mausoleum erected by Artemisia for Mausolus, King of Caria; and (4) The Statue of Zeus at Olympia (Greece).

Specially drawn for this work.

Continuing the list and pictures of the Seven Wonders of the Ancient World, we have: (5) The Temple of Diana at Ephesus, a Greek city in Asia Minor; (6) The Hanging Gardens of Babylon, associated with the great Queen Semiramis; and (7) The Pharos or lighthouse of Alexandria, an enormous tower of white marble built on an island at the mouth of the Nile to guide mariners.

313

an infertile stretch of country where crops were never grown, so even when the stones did reach their destination we are puzzled to know how the building was done. A large force must have been needed; for, if the giant stones were moved by man power, hundreds of men must have been required for the work. How, we ask, were all these men housed and fed on this barren upland? Yet it remains a question to which there is no answer. We do not know how the stones were brought to their present position or how, when brought, they were built up into a shape which has lasted for more than thirty-six centuries.

More Miracles

Remember, too, that Stonehenge is only a part, and a very small part, of the work done by those prehistoric builders. The Stone Circles at Avebury, a few miles from Stonehenge, were originally very much larger and more important than Stonehenge itself. Tremendous efforts are now being made to reconstruct this once mighty temple.

"This stupendous fabric," writes Mr. Colt Hoare, "which for many hundreds of years has braved the assaults of weather, and which . . . if left to itself would have lasted as long as the globe, has fallen a sacrifice to the wretched ignorance and avarice of a little village unluckily placed within it."

Some of these magnificent stones, brought here at the cost of untold toil, have been broken up to build cottages and pigsties. The loss to the student of past history is simply heart-breaking, but it is too late for useful repentance. All that we can do is to be very sure that no more of our ancient monuments shall be destroyed in so brutal a fashion.

Something About Bricks

No one can say who made the first brick, but we find bricks in Egypt, Assyria and Babylonia, which are at least 4,000 years old. In a country where there is plenty of clay but no stone, it is easy enough to imagine some enterprising person shaping lumps of wet clay and drying them in the sun for building purposes. Bricks, we know, were used to build the Tower of Babel, and in all parts of the world where clay is common and stone scarce early man took to building with clay.

The "adobe" houses of Mexico and Central America have walls made of clay mixed with straw and built up bit by bit, and in the county of Devon you may still see cottages and garden walls built of what is called "cob," which is nothing but the clay of the country built up in wooden moulds, course by course. Cob walls, if well made and protected by thatch at the top, will last as long as bricks and mortar.

The Romans made excellent bricks, and there are still in existence fine walls built by the Romans of kiln-burned bricks. One reason why these walls have lasted so well is that the Romans used a wonderful mortar of which the secret has been lost. Bricks were forgotten in England after the Romans left, and none was seen until the twelfth century, when they were made by Flemish immigrants.

The Seven Wonders of the World

Architecture, like sculpture, painting and other arts, seems to rise and fall in waves. It reached a great height in the fifth century before Christ, when in Greece, and more particularly in Athens, some of the most beautiful buildings the world has ever seen were erected. The best period was between 470 B.C. and 409 B.C. During those sixty years nearly all the buildings and sculpture which have made Athens the wonder of the world were completed. The Parthenon was finished in 438 B.C., the Propylæa at about the same time, and the Temple of Zeus at Olympia in 436 B.C.

The historian Plutarch says that the great sculptor and architect Pheidias

GATEWAY TO THE STONE AGE VILLAGE

Grimspound, the wonderful village settlement of primitive man still to be seen on Dartmoor, occupied a considerable area of ground and was surrounded by a double wall of gigantic stones, of which many definite traces remain to our own day. Here, as an instance, we see one of the entrance gates to this village of the Stone Age.

This interesting view of a portion of Stonehenge shows the stone called the " Abbot's Nose," as seen from within the main circle. The large upright or pillar stones are known as " sarsens," and this great Temple of the Sun takes its name from a Saxon word " stanhengist," which means literally " the hanging stones." Stonehenge is about two miles from Amesbury.

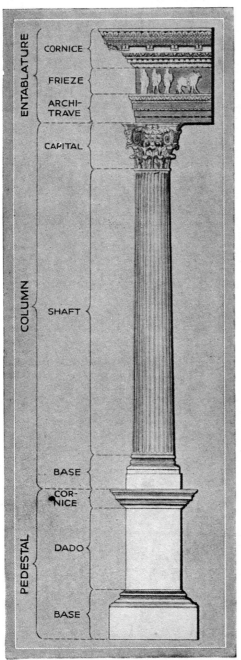

ENTABLATURE

CORNICE

FRIEZE

ARCHI-
TRAVE

COLUMN

CAPITAL

SHAFT

PEDESTAL

BASE

COR-
NICE

DADO

BASE

Specially drawn for this work.

TERMS IN ARCHITECTURE

The words printed on the left of this diagram come opposite the sections to which they refer, enabling us correctly to name the different parts which make up a pedestal, a column and an entablature. Very often in architecture the frieze is richly ornamented with figures in relief.

was in supreme control of all this wonderful work. The magnificent statues of Athena in the Parthenon and of Zeus at Olympia were the work of Pheidias' own hands. It is said that when the Zeus was finished the sculptor prayed that the gods would give him some sign that they were satisfied with his five years' labour, and in answer a thunderbolt fell at his feet.

The Olympian Zeus counted with the ancients as one of the Seven Wonders of the World, and, since these wonders were all connected with the two arts of architecture and sculpture, it will be well to give some short account of them before passing on to the story of architecture since the beginning of the Christian Era.

Why only Seven ?

Everyone has heard of the Seven Wonders of the Ancient World, and no doubt many have been puzzled as to why the number of wonders is only seven, when it might easily have been seventy. The reason is that seven was then, and always has been, a " mystic " number. There are seven days in the week, seven deadly sins, seven champions of Christendom, and all the ancient nations, Greeks, Romans, Hebrews and others, had the same belief in the sacred quality of the number seven.

Another question which may occur to you is who made the list of the Wonders ? The answer is that it was Antipater of Sidon, who lived about 2,000 years ago. But though he is the first to have written out the list, it was probably in existence a long time before he was born.

The Pyramids of Egypt

There are about seventy-five pyramids in Egypt, and all these were originally built as the tombs of kings. A few are of brick, but all the larger, including the Great Pyramid, are of huge blocks of stone, beautifully cut and fitted. The Great Pyramid is

THE COLUMNS OF THE GREEKS

Specially drawn for this work

DORIC · IONIC · CORINTHIAN

We refer to Doric, Ionic and Corinthian as " Orders of Architecture," and these three orders, illustrated above, belong to the Greek school of builders. The Doric is the oldest of the three orders, and the Ionic considerably more ornamental but not so massive. You can tell Ionic most easily by the scroll at its capital. The Corinthian order was greatly developed by the Romans, and is known by its acanthus leaves on the capital.

higher than St. Paul's Cathedral, and its base greater than the whole of Lincoln's Inn Fields. It is the oldest of existing buildings in the world, for it was erected some fifty-six centuries ago.

The more the Great Pyramid is studied the more marvellous it seems, for, besides the wonder of its making, its position and measurements go to prove that the men who designed it had a considerable store of knowledge. It seems clear that they fully understood the size and shape of our planet, all about its poles and equator, and were also deeply learned in the lore of the starry firmament. And so the Pyramids stand, eternal abodes of great kings, and to this day as impressive a sight as they were to the people of old time.

The Pharos of Alexandria

Another Egyptian Wonder was the Pharos or lighthouse of Alexandria, an enormous tower of white marble built on an island at the mouth of the Nile. Its purpose was to guide mariners into Egypt's principal port by day or night. Alas, there is nothing left of it! Not only the splendid tower, with its great spiral staircase, has vanished, but even the island on which it stood has sunk beneath the restless waves.

The Colossus of Rhodes

Rhodes, a large island lying close to the south-west coast of Asia Minor, was once a prosperous kingdom and immensely rich. Its capital was the best-planned city of the ancient world and had two ports. At the entrance to one of these ports stood the greatest statue of the ancient world, cast by Chares of Lindus about 280 B.C. It is said to have been 120 feet high, but there is no reason to suppose that it actually bestrode the harbour. Fifty-six years later it was overthrown by a mighty earthquake, but its remains lay where they had fallen for eight centuries till in A.D. 653 an Arab General sold them to a Hebrew as old metal.

Just like ourselves, the Ancients loved big things, and the statue of Zeus at Olympia, though seated, was 40 feet high. The father of the gods was represented on a throne made of ivory, and wore a mantle of gold. It was the work of the greatest of ancient sculptors, the Greek Pheidias, and with its ornaments of precious stones must have been a most glorious and beautiful sight.

Diana's Temple at Ephesus

Ephesus, in Asia Minor, was then a purely Greek city, and in St. Paul's time was the greatest trading town in that part of the world. The Temple of Diana stood a mile out of the city and was originally built by Chersiphron.

On the very night that Alexander the Great was born, a crazy fellow, called Herostratus, burned it down, but it was rebuilt more splendid than before with 127 magnificent columns, each 60 feet high. Its site was discovered in 1869, and diggings among its foundations have proved that Antipater was probably right in classing it as a wonder of the world.

Just as the Colossus of Rhodes has given us the word " colossal," so we now use " mausoleum " for a specially fine tomb. The original mausoleum was the tomb of Mausolus, King of Caria, built by his widow, Artemisia, in 353 B.C.

A wonderful lion-guarded stairway rose to a marvellous building of exquisite columns, with a pyramid-shaped roof crowned with statues of Mausolus and his wife in a chariot.

The Mausoleum lasted for some 1,500 years before it fell into ruin. Its site has been found and some of its remains are in the British Museum.

The Hanging Gardens of Babylon

Sixty miles round, Babylon in its prime was itself a Wonder of the world. The wall surrounding it was 200 cubits high, 50 cubits thick, and had 100 brazen gates. On the east side of the

SOME ORDERS OF ARCHITECTURE

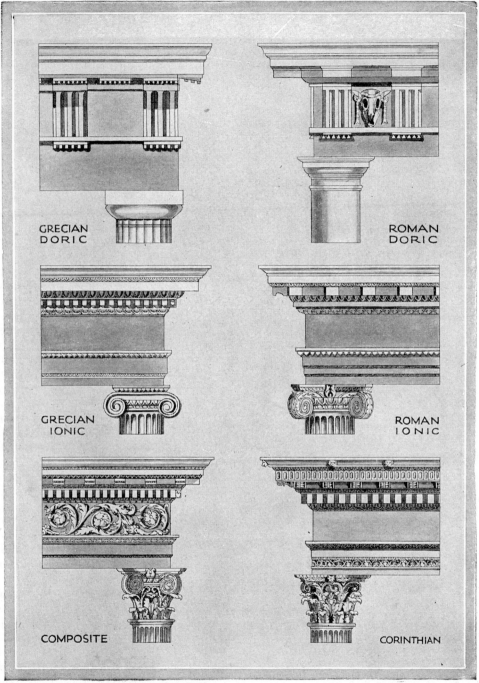

GRECIAN
DORIC

ROMAN
DORIC

GRECIAN
IONIC

ROMAN
IONIC

COMPOSITE

CORINTHIAN

Specially drawn for this work.

Though the Greeks were such accomplished builders and must have known about arches, they seldom used them, but made the openings in their structures square, the entablature or upper part being supported on columns which in turn rested on pedestals. We see here the great Doric and Ionic orders as they were fashioned both by Greeks and Romans; the Corinthian, as developed by Romans; and the Composite, a blend between Ionic and Corinthian.

river stood the newer part of the town, with the so-called hanging gardens of the great Queen Semiramis.

Babylon lay in the midst of flat desert land, and Semiramis, who came from the mountains of Media, pined for her native hills. So for her was built an artificial mountain of stone and brick, with vast terraces planted with trees and flowers of all sorts, and watered from the Euphrates which ran below. And there the Queen walked in the cool of the evening amid rich colours and scents. So huge was the pile that, although the city itself has totally disappeared, a mound remains to mark the site of this seventh Wonder of the world.

Ruin and Destruction

Athens in her prime must have been the loveliest city the world has ever seen. The Acropolis, rising high above the rest, was crowned with exquisite buildings of marble and cut stone, ornamented with the most wonderful sculpture.

Of all these beauties nothing now remains except the ruins of the Parthenon or Temple of Athena. When the Turks conquered Greece they stored gunpowder in this temple, which blew up and reduced it to a ruin; yet, broken as it is, its graceful columns are still a joy to the eye.

Discovery of the Arch

The Greeks, of course, understood the arch, for arches are found in some of the oldest buildings in the world. They are, for instance, common in old Egyptian tombs and temples. Yet the Greeks made no use of the arch in design and the first people to do so were the mysterious Etruscans, who, in days before Rome became a power, were the masters of Italy.

Alinari.

THE PARTHENON AT ATHENS

The Parthenon or Temple of Athena at Athens, even though in ruins, still shows us graceful columns. It was built in marble in the Doric order more than 400 years before the time of Christ, and richly decorated with sculpture by Pheidias. At the time of the Turkish conquest of Greece, gunpowder was stored in the Temple, and it was an explosion in the magazine in 1687 that brought ruin to the building.

"Words," says Sir Thomas Jackson, in his book, "Architecture," "can hardly express what this emancipation of the arch meant to architecture. It was the greatest revolution in the history of the Art. . . . Pillars and piers might be spaced widely apart without danger, the interval being safely spanned by an arch. . . . On this revolution by the Etruscans the whole system of subsequent architecture in Europe depended."

If you want proof of this, go into any great church or cathedral and you will see at once that the whole scheme of the building depends on its arches or upon the dome, which is, of course, merely a modification of the arch.

The Dark Ages

The world became Christian with the Edict of Milan, published A.D. 313, but the first churches built were simple enough. The walls were of plain brick, and the only costly part of such a church was the colonnade between the nave and the aisles, with pillars made of marble very often pillaged from some heathen temple. During the Dark Ages which followed the collapse of the Roman Empire, all the arts fell to a very low ebb. Civilisation seemed to go backwards, for the world was full of wars, and there was little peace or security anywhere.

E.N.A.

IN THE FORUM OF CÆSAR

Rome, like so many other great cities, grew up quite unsystematically. Julius Cæsar was the first to attempt some form of city planning, re-modelling old and adding new buildings, besides improving roads through the city. His successor, Augustus, completed Cæsar's plans, boasting with truth that he " found Rome of brick and left it of marble." In this photograph is seen the Forum of Cæsar, showing the Temple of Venus Genetrix.

Literature, painting and music almost vanished, but architecture still remained. Byzantium, which succeeded Rome as capital of the Roman Empire, suffered less from war and pillage than the western parts of Europe, and there the Byzantine style of architecture came into being. The principal feature of Byzantine architecture is the dome.

The City of Venice was the one part of Italy which remained faithful to the old Roman Empire, and the magnificent Church of St. Mark, consecrated in 1094, was modelled on the plan of the Emperor Justinian's Church of the Apostles at Constantinople. The plan was a Greek cross with equal arms and five domes, one in the centre, one over each arm of the cross. The great beauty of this church consists in the exquisitely carved capitals of the pillars. These capitals, it is believed, were imported from an island in the Sea of Marmora, where there was a school of sculptors who specialised in these wonderful carvings.

Poor England

Of all countries none suffered worse by the collapse of Rome than England. Romans had governed for nearly 400 years; the country was dotted with fine cities, splendid villas and great public buildings. Then all at once every Roman left the country, and wave after wave of barbarian invasion swept it for centuries. Civilised life simply disappeared, yet the Roman tradition died hard. With the Saxons, to build in stone was to build " more Romanorum " (in the manner of the Romans), but for at least 500 years there were very few buildings of anything better than timber, while poorer folk lived in mud hovels thatched with reeds.

Yet when the Normans came they found a good many churches soundly built of stone, some of which still exist. The best remaining example is at Bradford-on-Avon.

Anderson.

THE PANTHEON OF AGRIPPA

Referred to as the oldest building in the world in present-day use, the Pantheon at Rome was in ancient days a temple and is now a church. It was constructed by the Emperor Hadrian (who built Hadrian's Wall across the north of England) about the year A.D. 120. Features of this ancient building are a rotunda and dome, and a portico having Corinthian columns.

IN THE CRYPT AT DURHAM *W. F. Mansell.*

Durham cathedral contains a great deal of Norman architecture, for the present structure was begun in the eleventh century. The building was closely associated with a monastery, and in the above photograph we get a peep at the crypt beneath what was the monks' dormitory. This is a wonderful example of a vaulted roof. The majority of crypts are underground chambers used either for religious services or for burials.

NO sooner were the Normans settled in England than they set to work to build great churches and cathedrals. Before they had been a century in the country they had practically finished the great cathedrals of St. Paul's in London, Norwich, Gloucester, Winchester, St. Albans, Durham and Lincoln.

It was an achievement so marvellous that it almost reminds us of the creation of Stonehenge. Think what England was in those days. Her whole population was much less than two millions; roads, transport and building appliances were all of the most primitive kind. It is certain that the greater part of the people had to be employed in producing food, while a considerable number were kept under arms. The more one considers the matter, the more mysterious it seems that such immense and beautiful buildings could be created in so comparatively short a time.

The Growth of the Gothic Style

The Norman style of building is characterised by massive pillars and semicircular arches. Such arches put great pressure upon the side walls of the building. In the language of architecture, they "exercise a thrust," so the Romanesque and Norman builders dared not give a vaulted roof so broad a span as the nave of a cathedral. Beams were used instead, and cathedrals had wooden ceilings, the timber being usually oak.

The result was disastrous, for such churches were always getting burned. Nearly every great church in Normandy was burned between A.D. 900 and 1100. At Vézelay, in 1120, more than 1,000 of the congregation were burned to death in the cathedral. It became plain that the churches must have stone ceilings, so by degrees the Gothic arch was adopted, a pointed arch which could be raised to any height desired. It was a system of ribs and panels, the ribs forming a skeleton clothed by a ceiling of light masonry. In order to prevent too great a thrust upon the outer walls the flying buttress was invented, and on this outside prop the whole structure of a Gothic church depends.

Under a Taskmaster

Norman building was not only cum-brous, but very formal. The stones were all cut to one exact size, and we can imagine that the masons were forced to work entirely to the will of a taskmaster. But this taskmaster was often something of a jerry-builder, for we find that behind the even face-work rubble was used freely. Rubbish of all kinds, broken stone, or even mud, was employed to fill up the centres of massive-looking pillars.

With the coming of the pointed arch the workmanship improved, and we can see of what great things the English mason was capable when given a freer hand. The stones were no longer cut to one mould as though by machinery, and the workers' own taste and feeling shows plainly in the ex-quisitely varied details of the ornamen-tation. In the Transitional period, between the Norman and Gothic styles, the stone-mason seems to have played as great a part as the architect.

The chancel of Bam-borough Church, in the graveyard of which Grace Darling lies buried, is a fine ex-ample of this Transi-tional period, and nothing could be more perfect than the severe simplicity of this buil-ding. And everywhere in this church you can see how honestly the work was done.

French William

In Canterbury Cathedral you observe both the round and the pointed arches. The first Canterbury Cathedral was burned down only four years after the murder of Beckett. The people were so horrified at this destruction that

Specially drawn for this work.

THE NORMAN ARCH

When you see an arch semicircular in shape you may know it is in the Norman style. Such arches are very strong, but put a considerable thrust or pressure on the side walls. For this reason they are usually built on very substantial pillars. Norman arches have often a zigzag decoration.

they tore their hair and beat their heads against the blackened walls. A famous architect named William, who came from the town of Sens and was known as French William, was called in to see whether he could repair the ruin. After surveying the burned walls he realised that the only thing was to pull them down and begin again from the bottom, but it was a long time before he dared tell the monks "for fear the truth should kill them."

But he made a glorious piece of work of it. The capitals were wonderfully carven, and the new cathedral was far higher and finer than the old.

In the fourth year of the work a scaffolding broke and poor William fell and was "sorely bruised." For a time he managed to direct the work from his bed, but then he died and was succeeded by another William, "English by birth, small in body, but in workmanship of many kinds acute and honest."

Specially drawn for this work.

THE GOTHIC ARCH

A Norman arch is never pointed. When you see a pointed arch like the one above, you must think of the Gothic style. Gothic architecture figures in a great many of our most beautiful cathedrals, but in some (such as Canterbury) you will find both round and pointed arches.

Fine English Work

How splendidly those old craftsmen builded is proved by the way in which their churches have stood for so many centuries and are still good for centuries to come. The English were expert masons, and it must be remembered that in those days much more was left to the craftsman than is the case in more modern times.

Lincoln Cathedral is a very fine specimen of English work. It was begun in 1192 by Bishop Hugh of Lincoln, a man of most saintly character. Wild birds and squirrels came and fed from his hands, and even a wild swan followed him about.

Master Robert

While names of great painters and poets have always been preserved and have come down to us from the most ancient times, names of equally great artists—that is, the architects of many of our finest buildings—have been lost. Buildings, you see, are not "signed" like pictures or books—more's the pity. Even when we do know the name of the architect of one of these wonderful buildings we have nothing of his history.

Master Robert, for instance, the man to whom we owe that marvel of the builder's craft, Salisbury Cathedral— we know his name, but nothing about him.

The first Salisbury Cathedral was built in the hill fortress of Sarum in 1092 on a site that was " barren, dry and solitary." So in 1220 it was decided that a new cathedral should be built nearer the river; and as the site was quite open, the result is a church that is perfectly regular in shape and plan and the finest existing example of the architect's work of the thirteenth century. Some critics have said that it is too coldly severe, almost too perfect. It took 138 years to build, but the marvellous spire, 404 feet high, was not completed until several years later. It is the most perfect spire in the world, but its weight has greatly tried the foundations, which were not calculated to bear such an immense burden.

The Builders of Westminster Abbey

Dante describes Henry III. of England as " the king of simple life." But this Henry was a great patron of art, and it is to him that we owe the wonders of Westminster Abbey. The old Abbey had been built by Edward the Confessor, and was a heavy, ugly building. Henry began rebuilding in 1245, and put the work in charge of Odo, the goldsmith, with Master Henry of Westminster as architect.

Most of the great churches of that day were designed and built by monks, but in the case of Westminster Abbey the king's masons and architect were laymen. They had robes given them of squire's degree, and we hear of some of them rising to high positions and even becoming Members of Parliament. Westminster Abbey is the last Early English building in England, and is built in what is called the Middle pointed Style, in which the windows are decorated with delicate traceries cut in the stone.

Like many other new fashions, these

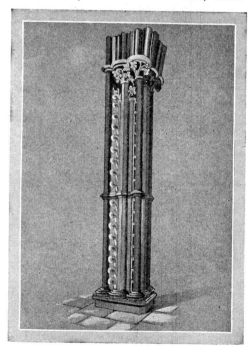

Specially drawn for this work.

PILLARS IN TWO STYLES

(1) The massive, barrel-like column is in the Norman style of architecture, and such pillars are to be seen in many of our churches, cathedrals and public buildings.

(2) This pillar is in the Gothic style, and the capital is decorated with foliage, or " foliated," to use the architectural term. In this case beauty conceals strength.

Painters mention is made of the amazing revival which occurred about this period in the art of painting—how the stiff Byzantine method had at last gone out of favour, to be replaced by the beautiful works of Cimabue and Giotto.

Exactly the same thing happened in the allied arts of sculpture and architecture. The revival in sculpture began with Niccola of Pisa, who was born in 1206. Niccola was an architect who broke away from the profession to follow sculpture ; and, basing his work on the marbles of the Greeks, turned entirely from the Byzantine style and founded a new school.

decorations became very popular, and were so overdone that early in the fourteenth century a reaction came, and architects went back to a severer style called the Perpendicular.

Architecture's Great Revival

While Westminster Abbey was being built great things were happening in Italy. In our stories of Great

Specially drawn for this work.

THE FLYING BUTTRESS

In this case the flying buttress connects the main building with a detached buttress, which may have been erected at a later date—perhaps if the main building " settled." The object of all flying buttresses is to support the main wall and help to carry the enormous weight of the roof, especially if this is stone-vaulted.

Norwich Cathedral, as seen from the south-east. The building exhibits several styles of architecture, and has fine flying buttresses, tower and spire.

Here you see the Choir of Norwich Cathedral, some of the arches being rounded and others pointed. The upper windows are of later date than the lower, and of different style.

This long corridor, which shows the Perpendicular style with a marvellous roof of fan-tracery, is in the cloisters at Gloucester Cathedral, considered the best in England.

In this print we see the beautiful Sedilia in Gloucester Cathedral. The sedilia in a church or cathedral are seats for the clergy, usually on the south side of the chancel.

HISTORIC PLACES OF WORSHIP

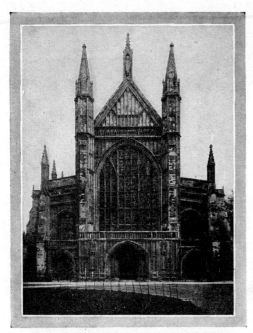

In this illustration we see the west front of Winchester Cathedral, in the Perpendicular style—you note the pointed arches. Only portions of the Norman fane remain.

The Choir of Winchester Cathedral, with its imposing roof and sculpture, is here seen from its western end. The building itself is 526 feet long.

W. F. Mansell.

The Cathedral of St. Albans, of which the Lady Chapel at the east end is illustrated, was started in Norman times and built largely from Roman materials.

St. Alban, the first English martyr, was put to death on the site long afterwards occupied by the Abbey Church. From the watching gallery above monks guarded his shrine.

W. F. Mansell.

The towering cathedral of Durham is the glory of the city, and a feature of its choir is the wonderful screen of stone here depicted. This cathedral held the shrine of St. Cuthbert, whose dust is said to rest beneath the high altar. Begun in Norman times, the building exhibits different types of architecture. Above the screen is a beautiful " rose window."

TOMB OF THE BLACK PRINCE

Among the royal tombs in Canterbury Cathedral is that of Edward the Black Prince, seen above, adjacent to Trinity Chapel. The Cathedral was rebuilt by the great French architect, William of Sens. The Black Prince visited the Cathedral after the Battle of Poitiers in 1356, and afterwards erected a chantry (in which priests chanted Mass for the souls of the departed). One can still see actual relics of the Black Prince near his tomb.

W. F. Mansell.

Here we have an interior view of the great Cathedral at Lincoln. It dominates the city, and was begun in Norman times. Some of its Norman architecture may still be seen, but as the building was the work of several centuries, we notice the styles of other days as well. In this photograph are the south aisle and nave. The roofs of both are of striking workmanship.

THE CHOIR OF PETERBOROUGH

W. F. Mansell.

This picture was chosen to present a contrast to the illustration on the opposite page. It shows us the Choir of Peterborough, looking towards the east, and you note the semicircular window arches of the Norman period, for the choir was completed about the year 1133. Norman architecture is heavier than Gothic. While Peterborough instances the first, Lincoln shows us the second.

GUARDED BY GARGOYLES

Photos: Donald McLeish.

This pelican gargoyle, on one of the towers of Notre Dame, is said to symbolise the virtue of Charity. He is in the company of other queer birds. Gargoyles nearly always stand at the corner of a roof gutter, and some of them are so designed that they carry the water out into space and allow it to fall to earth clear of the building.

THE SPIRES OF MILAN

Donald McLeish.

Milan is in importance the third Italian city, and contains one of the best-known cathedrals in the world, the building being faced with marble. Our picture shows a portion of the roof of Milan Cathedral, and it will be seen how the builders made use of marble spires. These spires were lavishly decorated with statues of most exquisite workmanship.

Then in the next century came Lorenzo Ghiberti, one of the greatest of all workers in bronze, who made the bronze doors for the Baptistery at Florence. He began them when he was twenty-five and finished them when he was seventy-four. He was the first sculptor to master perspective. Some of his panels contain as many as 100 figures modelled on different planes, so that those nearest to the eye appear larger and those further away smaller in proportion.

After Ghiberti came Donatello, born in 1386, one of the greatest sculptors who ever lived. His statue of General Gattamelata at Padua is one of the two finest equestrian statutes in the world, the second being the Colleoni at Venice, which was begun by Donatello's pupil, Verrocchio, and finished by Leopardi.

St. Peter's at Rome is the first great example of a Renaissance building, and our own St. Paul's is the finest English example.

St. Paul's is the work of Christopher Wren, who was not only the greatest of English architects, but one of the greatest of Englishmen.

The Crown of London

St. Paul's Cathedral has been called the " Crown of London," and well deserves its name. It is the third cathedral erected on the same site. The first was built in 610, the second was burned in the Great Fire, and the present building was begun in 1675 and finished in 1697 at a cost of about £750,000.

If you go into the Cathedral and up the stairs to the left you will be able to see the large model of Wren's first design, which is very different from the one he ended by adopting. On the south side is the library, with lovely carving by Grinling Gibbons ; and, in a case, the embroidered waistcoat and walking-stick which once belonged to the great Wren himself.

St. Paul's is 479 feet long, and the height of the cross on the dome is 365 feet. Though small when compared with St. Peter's at Rome, St. Paul's is a more beautiful building and

W. F. Mansell.

THE CORONATION CHAIR

Westminster Abbey was the last building to be erected in England in the Early English style. It is the burial-place of many notable people, and contains the British coronation chair and sword, here shown. The Coronation Stone itself is seen beneath the seat of the chair. It was used at Scottish coronations and brought to Westminster in 1296 by Edward I., and was stolen in 1950 but later returned.

MODERN ARCHITECTURE

Three Lions

New York City is famed for its skyscrapers. This type of building became necessary, as the city's business increased, for the simple reason that New York is built on an island and ground space is very limited. The foundations of these high buildings can, however, be based on solid rock. In this photograph is seen the tallest of all skyscrapers, the Empire State Building on the west side of Fifth Avenue. It is 1,248 feet in height and has 102 storeys above street level.

CENTRES OF LEARNING AND BROADCASTING

In this photograph is seen the comparatively new building of the London University in Malet Street, Bloomsbury. Dignified in appearance, and harmonizing with the Georgian buildings with which it is surrounded, the main feature and focal point of the building is the massive central tower. The whole design is of simple classical character.

Another great building that has arisen in the heart of London in fairly recent times is the home of the British Broadcasting Corporation in Portland Place, seen above. This is again an example of adopting a design to fit in with older surroundings. Broadcasting House follows the curve of the existing street, and its horizontal lines of windows follow those of less modern buildings on the left.

LONDON'S MODERN OFFICE BUILDINGS

Here is an excellent example of modern office buildings. There are really three great blocks, Thames House South, Thames House North, and I.C.I. House, fronting the River Thames at Millbank, London. The first two are connected by a bridge on the fifth floor, and the street runs between the buildings. A splendid view of the river is obtained from the office windows.

The Adelphi has earned a place in London's history since the famous terrace was first created by the Adam Brothers towards the end of the 18th century. In recent years rebuilding became necessary and here we see the large office building, Adelphi House, on the site of the old terrace facing the Thames. Built in brick with the front in stone, this new building is dignified and restrained in design.

DIGNITY COMBINED WITH PURPOSE

F. Jewell Harrison

As education progresses and improves, so do the school buildings embody new features in harmony with modern educational ideals. This photograph shows the exterior of the Bedford Girls' Modern School, an excellent instance of the simple dignity of well-designed building which has been carried out with special regard for the work done within its walls.

A. & H. Gibbs

In Australia the same outlook in regard to education is taken as in Britain. The Government of Victoria, for example, is spending some £4½ million annually on extensions to existing schools and in building new ones. An example of fine architecture is seen in this photograph of the Bairnsdale Technical School, one of several similar schools provided by the State.

CIVIC CENTRES OF TO-DAY

Stewart Bale Ltd.

Architecture is likely to be concerned to a considerable extent with buildings for public and social services for some years to come. The Swansea Civic Centre, seen in this photograph, is a very good exposition of modern design for public buildings. It is simple and dignified, but the beautiful lines of the main entrance, with the tower behind it, give scale to the whole group.

Southern Newspapers Ltd.

Here is another fine example of a Civic Centre, this photograph showing the one at Southampton. Contrast this with the Empire State Building on the first page. In the case of Southampton, plenty of ground was available, and the buildings, though covering a large area, have been well arranged to give easy communication between the long, low groups.

FOR LIGHT AND AIR

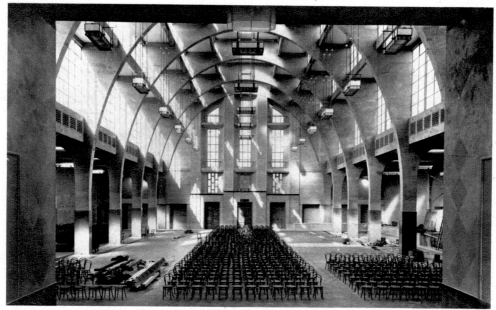

Sydney W. Newbery

This photograph shows the interior of the Royal Horticultural Society's Hall, Westminster. In the building of this Hall the use of reinforced concrete made considerable advance. Compare this interior with some of the old Gothic halls and note how thin are the concrete ribs of the roof in place of the stone-vaulted ceilings of bygone days. In spite of its great width the Hall is very light and airy.

Copyright

Here we have a block of flats in London, known as Highpoint Flats. The design is perfectly simple and achieves beauty by virtue of this simplicity. The arrangement of the windows and the balconies provides the maximum of light and sunshine in those rooms where it is most needed. The planning of the interior is considered in conjunction with a pleasing exterior.

IN CITIES OF THE DOMINIONS

Australian News & Information Bureau
For this typical modern building we go to Australia. These imposing and well-designed offices of a great insurance company are beautifully situated and overlook Hyde Park, Sydney.

Canadian National Railways
Canada vies with the U.S.A. in the skyscrapers to be seen in some of her big cities. This photograph shows the well-proportioned design of the Bank of Commerce Building in Toronto, Ontario.

Associated Press Ltd.
In this photograph we have the Royal Melbourne Hospital in the capital of Victoria, Australia. Notice how the design suits the purpose of the building in the wide sun balconies on each floor.

Commercial Photographic Co. Pty. Ltd.
Another excellent example of Australian architecture is seen in this picture of the Police Headquarters in Russell Street, Melbourne. The tall wireless mast adds to the dignity of the building.

THE HOME OF THE ARCHITECTS

It is natural that classical design should be given due regard in the home of architects. This photograph shows the exterior of the Royal Institute of British Architects in London.

Inside the Royal Institute of British Architects, the headquarters of the profession, is this modern staircase. The balustrade is of glass, with a beautiful design engraved upon it.

In this photograph we have an example of the modern architect's work when applied to the big department store, the main purpose of which is to display goods for sale. This picture shows the premises of Peter Jones Ltd., in Sloane Square, London. It is framed in light steel with a glass "skin," which provides ample light and is attractive to the customer.

W. F. Mansell.

Westminster Abbey, in several styles of architecture, is built in the form of a cross (" cruciform " is the word generally used). If you imagine the Abbey as a cross lying on the ground with its top to the east, the extreme easterly portion with the rounded end is Henry VII.'s Chapel, here illustrated, and regarded by many as the most magnificent part of the pile.

ST. PAUL'S, THE "CROWN OF LONDON"

In this print we are shown the Reredos (screen at the back of the altar) of St. Paul's Cathedral, London. The building is Britain's best example of Renaissance architecture.

Here is the famous Cross of St. Paul's, which was not completed until many years after the cathedral was finished. The ball will hold at least ten people.

Photos : W. F. Mansell.

In the crypt of St. Paul's Cathedral is the grave of Lord Nelson, as shown above. The site chosen is under the area of the dome. The remains of our great sailor were enclosed in a coffin made from the mainmast of a French battleship. We call the masonry structure in the centre over it a sarcophagus. This one is constructed in the Italian style.

HOW CHAINS EMBRACE THE DOME

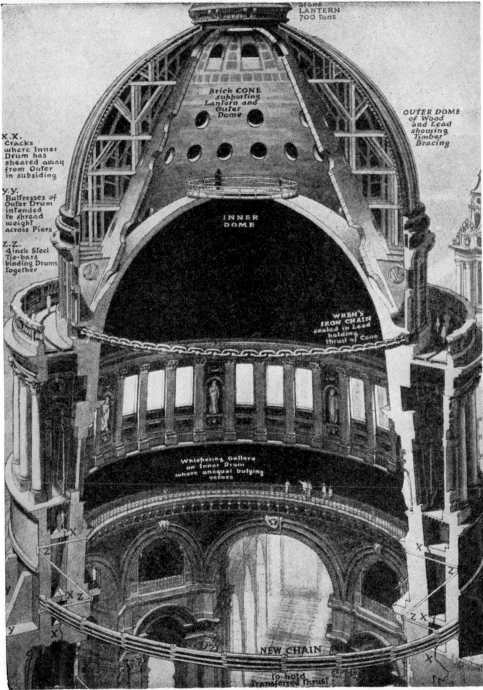

Stone LANTERN 700 tons

Brick CONE supporting Lantern and Outer Dome

OUTER DOME of Wood and Lead shewing Timber Bracing

X.X. Cracks where Inner Drum has sheared away from Outer in subsiding

Y.Y. Buttresses of Outer Drum intended to spread weight across Piers

Z.Z. 4 inch Steel Tie-bars binding Drums together

INNER DOME

WREN'S IRON CHAIN sealed in Lead holding thrust of Cone

Whispering Gallery on Inner Drum where unequal bulging occurs

NEW CHAIN

To hold transferred thrust

Not so many years ago a warning was issued by experts that, owing to the weakening of the foundations, the enormous structure of the dome of St. Paul's Cathedral, London, was becoming insecure. Cracks were appearing and ever-widening at the points marked X.X. in the above pictorial diagram. As a result work began on the strengthening of the eight great piers which support the dome, steel tie-bars being inserted at Z.Z. Further, a colossal new chain of chrome steel was made and built in position as shown to impart strength to the buttresses Y.Y.

better designed. The dome is particularly fine, and in order to hold it in position Wren fastened it with a great iron chain which runs all around it. So as to prevent the iron from rusting, he poured melted lead over and around it.

St. Paul's has stood up well to the wear of three centuries, but its mighty dome rests on a foundation of sand, and the great sewers and other underground works have drained away the water in this sand so that some years ago the warning went forth that the eight huge piers which support the dome were not as strong as they should be. In 1914 workmen began to strengthen these piers by " grouting " them—that is, squirting liquid cement into them, and now they are as solid again as man's skill can make them.

The reason why the grandeur of St. Paul's is not better understood is that the cathedral has been surrounded by warehouses and shops. Wren himself intended it to stand on the hill-top, quite alone, with broad streets running away like spokes in each direction. Many of the buildings around St. Paul's were destroyed or damaged during the last war and probably in the great plans for rebuilding London some of Wren's ideas may be put into practice.

Old St. Paul's was 586 feet long, while its spire rose to the great height of 489 feet. Some of its carved stones are preserved in the modern cathedral.

Inigo Jones

One of the most beautiful buildings of its type in London is the Banqueting

Donald McLeish.

HAMPTON COURT PALACE

The original part of Hampton Court Palace was built by Cardinal Wolsey in brick, and is one of the finest existing specimens of Tudor architecture. The Cardinal presented his magnificent home to King Henry VIII. It was in part rebuilt, and greatly added to, by Wren in William III.'s reign, and now contains over 1,000 separate apartments. It has not been occupied by a reigning monarch since the time of George II.

A GATEWAY TO THE PALACE

Donald McLeish.

The bricks of which Wolsey built Hampton Court Palace have now mellowed with age, and we can appreciate the size of the building when we realise that it housed the 500 people of which the Cardinal's household consisted. Here we are looking through Anne Boleyn's Gateway. On the left is the Great Hall.

House, Whitehall, now known as the Chapel Royal. Here is a specimen of pure Palladian (classic) style, which was planned and built at a time when this style was unknown in England.

The Banqueting House is a part of what was to have been a perfectly enormous royal palace, reaching from the Thames right back to the park and from Charing Cross to Westminster, and its architect was Inigo Jones.

A Builder of Churches

Inigo was the son of a cloth-worker who was sent by a rich patron to Italy to study landscape painting, but studied architecture instead, and came back full of the style of the great Palladio. He found himself employed in making scenery for Ben Jonson's plays which were being produced at the Court. Then he became surveyor-general of royal buildings and the first architect in England.

He lived into the troublous times of Charles I., and was shut up in Basing House during the famous siege. He was nearly eighty when he died in 1652.

St. Mary-le-Strand is a church well known to every Londoner, and, though grimed with London smoke, a very beautiful building. It is one of fifty new churches ordered by an Act of Queen Anne, and its architect was James Gibbs, son of an Aberdeen merchant and trained in Italy. He also built the Church of St. Martin's in Trafalgar Square, the Radcliffe Library at Oxford and the Senate House at Cambridge.

English Homes

Anything more hopelessly uncomfortable and inconvenient than the English home of the Middle Ages could hardly have been conceived. The rich man's house was a castle, built simply with the idea of being safe against the attack of enemies. The walls were tremendously thick—sometimes as much as 16 feet! There was a great central hall, in which everyone lived and ate, but the sleeping rooms were small, cold and inconvenient beyond words. There was, of course, no means of heating them, and since the windows were mere slits, they were very dark.

As for the poorer folk, they lived in the most miserable hovels, and the only people who had any comfort at all were the townsfolk. But the streets were so narrow that their homes were dark and ill ventilated, and, since there was no drainage or proper water supply, the towns were terribly unhealthy.

It was in the reign of the seventh Henry that matters began to improve and the first manor houses were erected. Tattershall Castle, built by Lord Cromwell in 1453, was the last of the old castles, and this noble was the first to build an unfortified manor house. That was South Wingfield, which set the fashion of a large open building with a courtyard in the centre.

Hampton Court

In 1515 the great Cardinal Wolsey took over the site of Hampton Court and began to build a stately home. He used brick for the walls and made mullioned windows and a great Gatehouse. Italian artists were employed for the decorations, both outside and inside, and presently there was built such a house as had never before been seen in England. Henry VIII. came to look at it, and rather curtly inquired of his cardinal why he was building such a palace. Wolsey was equal to the occasion.

"In order to show how noble a palace a subject may offer to his sovereign," he replied. That is how Hampton Court came to be a royal palace.

Huge Mansions

Wolsey had no fewer than 500 people in his household, and other great men of his date had retinues almost as large, so it is no wonder that some of those early houses were exceedingly large

CATHEDRALS OF OTHER LANDS

St. Peter's at Rome is the chief church of Roman Catholic Christendom, in which the Popes are crowned. The building, which is 450 feet wide and 615 feet long inside, is of several types of architecture.

This fine picture of St. Mark's at Venice shows the half-circle of mosaic work illustrating the Last Judgment, as well as the famous bronze horses overhead. The architecture is Byzantine.

Photos : Donald McLeish.

The Church of St. Anthony at Padua is a combination of Byzantine and Gothic architecture. To this church pilgrims come from all parts of Italy to be cured of ills.

Here we see the magnificent front or façade of Rouen Cathedral, dating from 1509. The upper part is adorned with statues of saints, prophets and martyrs.

OLD=WORLD ENGLISH BUILDINGS

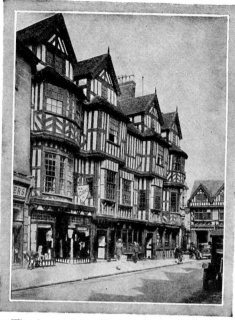

This entrance to the George Inn, Norton St. Philip, near Bath, is a splendid example of domestic architecture as followed in England about four centuries ago.

The houses here illustrated are known as Ireland's Mansions, and may be seen in High Street, Shrewsbury. This city is noted for its half-timbered buildings.

Photos: J. Dixon-Scott.

The Abbey of Glastonbury, in Somerset, was one of the most important in England, and thither went pilgrims from all parts. They stayed at the Pilgrim's Inn (now the " George "), the front of which we see in this print. The building was erected in 1475, and has a front of panelled stone with windows of singular charm and dignity.

THE HOUSE OF NINE WORTHIES

Not far from Yeovil, in Somerset, stands Montacute House, built in 1580 from designs prepared by John of Padua for Sir Edward Phelips. The east front, illustrated above, has remarkably beautiful Tudor windows. The statues, one in the centre gable and four on either side, are known as the " Nine Worthies."

Photos : J. Dixon-Scott.

Shall we in the future live in houses built on these lines? This very modern structure was designed by a New Zealand architect and erected on a hillside that overlooks the old-world village of Amersham, in Buckinghamshire. It certainly affords its inmates a great abundance of light and fresh air.

They had to be in order to provide sleeping rooms for such a number. Audley End is a tremendous house, yet is only about half its original size. Another immense mansion is Longleat, built for Sir John Thynne about 1567. Robert Smytheson, " fremason," was the builder, and it is interesting to learn that his wages were sixteen pence a day, together with " a nagge kept at your worshepe's charges."

At Knole the Earl of Dorset housed 200 people, and apparently all sat at meat in the great hall. There were eight at the high table, twenty-two at the parlour table, including the chap-lain, usher, secretary and pages; twenty-one at the clerks' table; and it is amusing to read that the carpenter sat at the nursery table. Besides these there were the long table, the laundry-maids' table, the kitchen and scullery table, at which sat six men, including John Morockoe, a negro.

Sir William Cecil had three houses— " one in London for necessity, one at Burghley of competency for the man-sion of his barony, and another at Waltham for his younger son." This last became the huge Theobalds, which James I. coveted and obtained. He gave Hatfield in exchange, where the Cecils still live.

Lovely English Ceilings

There is one amusing point about Burghley House. When the mansion was built Eng-lish architects were simply crazy on the Greek style of building, but of course the Greeks had no chimneys to their houses. So the architect made the chim-neys into Doric (Greek) columns.

Plaster work is a great fea-ture of the fine houses of the sixteenth cen-tury. The art may have come originally from Italy; but Eng-lish plasterers became famous,

Topical Press.

KNOLE HOUSE, SEVENOAKS

Our photograph, taken from an aeroplane, shows Knole House, for-merly the seat of the Sackville family, and owned in the fifteenth cen-tury by the Archbishops of Canterbury. It is regarded as one of the finest houses in all England. It has a great hall and there are said to be as many rooms as there are days in the year, *i.e.*, 365.

Photochrom.

ONCE OWNED BY CARDINAL WOLSEY

This picture shows the front of Knole House, Sevenoaks, one of several great English houses which, in recent years, have been handed to the National Trust to be preserved for the nation. Originally built before the fifteenth century, it became one of Cardinal Wolsey's homes and was taken from him by Henry VIII. Queen Elizabeth gave it to Thomas Sackville later. The massive gateway is probably the oldest portion of the structure which was rebuilt in the seventeenth century.

and even the names of the plasterers themselves have come down to us. One of the best-known was James Dungan, the King's plasterer, while another was Charles Williams, and a third was called Cobb, all true English names. There is a letter in existence from Sir William Cavendish, who wrote from Hardwick to ask for the services of " the cunning plasterer who had made divers pendants and flowered the Hall at Longleat." Hardwick Hall was built by the Countess of Shrewsbury, known as Bess of Hardwick, and though finished in 1597, remains very much as it was in the sixteenth century. It contains hunting scenes modelled very beautifully in plaster.

How a Style Committed Suicide

For centuries the art of building grew naturally. As we have seen, the Gothic arch succeeded the Norman because it gave greater scope to the builder. Each fresh step was based on the use of some new material or some new social demand (as, for instance, when chimneys followed a mere hole in the roof). It is an interesting point that these various changes came about almost at the same date in different countries.

Then came the Renaissance which was based on the revival of ancient learning. The literature of classic times was found to be so greatly superior to that of the day that a belief grew up that the ancient architecture must be equally superior to the Gothic art then practised, and everyone became enthusiastic about it. The classic orders were exalted as if they were divine, and it was supposed that nothing could be better.

You can easily see what the result

was. Natural growth stopped dead, and the great art of designing buildings was reduced to a state of utter stagnation. It was in Italy that people first tired of this utter sameness, and the Gothic style was revived in that country. Then the revival spread north of the Alps; and, by degrees, all over Western Europe. But the revivalists brought with them much of the Classic Style, and there are many famous buildings of the eighteenth century in which we can see this mingling of the two styles. At any rate, the old stagnation was ended, and to-day there is no art more experimental and progressive than that of architecture.

London's Best Buildings

Apart from St. Paul's, two other fine buildings in London are the Houses of Parliament and Greenwich Hospital.

A distinguished Frenchman visiting England once said: " You English are curious people. You put your poor into palaces and your princes into poor houses." The palace to which he referred was Greenwich Hospital, built as a home for old sailors, while the " poor house " was, of course, Buckingham Palace, which, though it has now been re-fronted, is certainly a very ugly building. Greenwich Hospital's west wing was built from the designs of the famous Inigo Jones, and the rest of the building had as architect Wren himself. Although the four separate blocks are of different heights, the general effect as seen from the river is very fine indeed.

The Houses of Parliament at Westminster were built to the design of Sir Charles Barry. In 1834 a workman having been ordered to destroy some

Campbell's Press.

DESIGNED BY INIGO JONES AND WREN

Greenwich Hospital, portions of which are here seen, stands on the banks of the Thames some five miles below London Bridge on a site once occupied by a royal palace. The present building was begun in the reign of Charles II., and some of the designs were by Inigo Jones, an English architect who travelled widely and introduced the Palladian style, so called after Andrea Palladio. Later portions of these buildings were designed by Sir Christopher Wren, who planned the present St. Paul's Cathedral and many of the City of London Churches.

WHERE CHARLES I. WAS TRIED

Walter Scott.

Westminster Hall, standing in close association with the Houses of Parliament, is one of the most notable buildings in England. It was started at the time of William Rufus, and enlarged by his successors. The wonderful oak roof, a marvel of capacity, was added by Richard II. in 1397. Much of the Norman workmanship remains, though largely re-lined. The roof is of stone slabs, supported by the huge beams, and there is no hall in the world so large whose ceiling is not carried by pillars, except of course steel buildings of our own day. King Charles I. was condemned in Westminster Hall.

old "tally sticks," burned them in a stove in the original House of Lords. The stove was not fitted for burning a lot of dry wood; it got red hot, and the result was a terrible fire which burned up almost all the old Parliament buildings. Only Westminster Hall, the Cloister of St. Stephen's Chapel and the Crypt were saved. Sir Charles Barry's idea was to make the new Houses of Parliament conform with the splendid old Hall, and very well he did the work, using what is called the revived Gothic style.

Fire again did its full share of destruction when the House of Commons was almost completely destroyed during the air attacks on London in the earlier years of the Second World War. Plans were approved for a new House to be rebuilt on the same site as soon as possible. The task was carried out and the new House of Commons was opened by King George VI. in October, 1950. Other parts of the Houses of Parliament have to be repaired owing to the damage done to the stonework by the smoke-laden air.

Campbell's Press.

IN THE TOWER OF LONDON

The above photograph shows us the entrance to St. John's Chapel in the Tower of London, which served as a place of private worship to our kings and queens who resided at the Tower. Norman architecture is here seen at its very best. You will note the massive pillars, and the arches with half-circle curves.

Stone and the Weather

The Houses of Parliament are by no means the only buildings in London to suffer in similar fashion, for the smoke which hangs so thickly over the great city, especially in foggy weather, rots most building stones. Some stones, however, are much more sensitive to smoke than others. Bath stone is particularly delicate. The best is that from Combe Down, where it is mined like coal, and must not be brought to the surface in winter, or it weathers hard. It has to be nursed and matured before it can be used, and unless it is set the right way of the grain it will not last.

The stone from Painswick in Gloucestershire, which will stand for centuries in a house built in the open country, powders rapidly away in smoke-laden air. This was the stone used about 120 years or so ago for repairing

Westminster Abbey, and in the present century every bit of it is found to be in a state of ruin and has had to be taken out and replaced by Portland stone.

The whole front of the imposing Carlton Club in Pall Mall, which was erected in the middle of the eighteenth century, crumbled considerably and called for repair a few years ago. This was of Caen stone, which cannot stand against London's foggy atmosphere. Even St. Paul's, about the stone of which Sir Christopher Wren took the greatest trouble, has suffered, and is covered with a crust-like stalagmite which consists largely of calcium sulphate.

The finest of all building stones is Aberdeen granite, which lasts practically for ever, but which is so difficult to "work" that it is not as much used as the cheaper granites from Norway, Sweden and Finland.

Campbell's Press.

ARCHITECTURE OF THE NORMANS

In this print we obtain a peep at the interior of St. John's Chapel, within the Tower of London, a very perfect example of Norman architecture. Each of the stones of which the great pillars are formed must have been cut to shape in advance by the masons. The pedestals and capitals are singularly massive.

London's Great Fortress

Someone has called the Tower of London a volume of England's history, a great quarto bound in grey stone, closed by massive clasps of iron. It was William the Conqueror who began this immense pile of grim buildings in the year 1078, and his architect was a Benedictine monk called Gundulf. "Gundulf the Weeper" he was called, but whether he wept or not he built the great Keep so well that he was made Bishop of Rochester, where he afterwards erected the famous Castle of Rochester. This Keep, now known as the White Tower, is 92 feet high with walls from 9 to 15 feet thick. It has a range of dungeons, a floor for the garrison, and, above that, a state floor, where the judges of the King's Bench sat. In the whole of the great building there are *only three fireplaces!*

Other kings slowly added to the Tower. The Inner Ward was enclosed by William Rufus, but Henry III. did most of the building and beautified his towers with sculpture and stained glass, none of which, however, remains to-day.

The Tower may not be anything wonderful from the point of view of the architect, but it is a very splendid and impressive pile of masonry, and its association with many of the great names in England's story since the days of the Normans gives it high place among our historic buildings.

Should Buildings be Signed ?

If you read a book which interests you, the first thing you do is to find out who wrote it, and if you see a picture which pleases, you at once ask who painted it. Now a fine building may be a greater work than a picture or a book, yet how many people ever think of inquiring the name of the architect ?

Take one of the finest examples of a modern English building, namely, Liverpool Cathedral, and the chances are that not one person in a hundred, either young or old, could tell you off-hand that the architects were Sir Giles Gilbert Scott, O.M., and Mr. G. F. Bodley. Sir Giles, whose design was chosen in open competition as being the best sent in, was only twenty-one years of age at the time. Liverpool Cathedral is said to be the finest example of a young man's genius, as applied to building, of which history has any record.

The Great Tower of Liverpool Cathedral, re-designed several years ago, will when completed be some 323 feet above St. James's Road. It is 104 feet square at the base. The inside height of the Cathedral is much greater than that of any other British Cathedral, and its perspective of lofty arches gives a most majestic effect to

Central Press.

GUILDFORD CATHEDRAL AS IT IS TO-DAY

Standing on Stag Hill, near the town, Guildford Cathedral is only the third entirely new Anglican cathedral to be built in England since the Reformation. The foundation stone, brought from Jarrow, the home of the Venerable Bede, was laid in July, 1936. Designed by Edward Maufe, the building will eventually be cruciform, 365 feet long, while the tower, only 85 feet high in this picture, will be 180 feet high. The chief building material is rose-coloured brick made from the clay of Stag Hill.

ST. GEORGE'S CHAPEL, WINDSOR

St. George's Chapel forms a part of Windsor Castle and is one of the most historic places of worship in the world. It is built in the Perpendicular Gothic style and has recently been extensively restored. In this picture we see the magnificent east window with the stalls of the Knights of the Garter to right and left and their banners overhead. Many of our Kings and Queens, including the late King George VI, have been buried in the Chapel, which has also been the scene of royal weddings. St. George's Chapel is situated in the Lower Ward of the Castle.

Specially painted for this work.

LIVERPOOL CATHEDRAL

This picture shows us the great Anglican Cathedral of Liverpool as it will be when finally completed. Standing on St. James's Mount, it dominates the city, and the magnificent building of red sandstone can be seen from the ships of all nations as they enter or leave the Mersey. The work of Sir Giles Gilbert Scott, this was the second cathedral to be erected in England since the Reformation and the foundation stone was laid in 1904. The design is Gothic and the vast tower is 104 feet square at the base. The mighty building rests on solid rock.

THE LADY CHAPEL AT LIVERPOOL

Stewart Bale.

When finally completed, Liverpool Cathedral, which belongs to the twentieth century, will be the largest and longest in England. In length it will exceed Winchester, at present our largest cathedral, by over 90 feet. Here we see the Lady Chapel, looking to the East. This was the first part to be opened for public worship, and it is as large as an ordinary parish church.

the interior. In the area of ground which it covers Liverpool Cathedral exceeds any other church in Britain.

Another modern cathedral which is being built to-day is at Guildford in Surrey. It was begun in 1936, but progress was delayed by the war and since its end the shortage of materials and funds has delayed the work still further.

Modern Movement in Architecture

In recent times there have been efforts to break away from old forms and traditions in architecture. New materials, new methods, and new purposes demand new forms of buildings. What is known as the Modern Movement or "live architecture" has become the vogue and created much controversy.

To some extent it is a rebellion against the ornament and decoration of Vic-

torian architecture. The modern architect has been anxious to show the functional purpose of his building. Civic halls, colleges, concert halls, power stations or railway stations shall indicate their functions by their design and not be imitations of Greek temples or Gothic churches.

The Festival of Britain in 1951 exhibited the new architecture in such buildings as the Royal Festival Hall, while the prize-winning design for the new Coventry Cathedral belonged essentially to the Modern Movement. One feature of the Festival of Britain was an Exhibition of Live Architecture in the Lansbury Neighbourhood Unit at Poplar, and this included not only houses and flats but a new Congregational Church, built on the site of the old church which was demolished by a bomb in 1944.

Central Press.

A MODERN CHURCH IN LONDON

In 1944 the Trinity Congregational Church at Poplar, in the East End of London, was destroyed during an air raid. A new church, designed on the austere strictly functional lines of modern architecture, was built on the old site and was dedicated at the end of September, 1951. The Church formed part of the Exhibition of Live Architecture at the Lansbury Estate in Poplar.

IN THE AGE OF STEEL

Sir Robert McAlpine & Sons.

PILLARS OF CONCRETE

The steel bars seen rising in groups in different parts of this illustration will presently be closed with moist concrete and so form pillars. Pillars of this type are referred to as being made of "reinforced concrete," the metal rods giving strength to the mixture of cement, sand and gravel. The photograph was taken when a big London hotel was in course of erection.

FOR thousands of years man built his houses of stone or clay, but when Bessemer found a way of making steel cheaply a new material for building came into being. To-day almost all great buildings in cities, especially offices, flats and hotels, are made of steel and brick or steel and concrete. Concrete, a mixture of Portland cement, sand and gravel, sets as solid as rock. Sometimes it is used plain, but the modern practice is to " reinforce " it with fine webs of steel, around which it is allowed to set.

" Skyscrapers "

When a steel building is to be constructed the metal frame is first erected, forming a huge bare skeleton of girders, strongly bolted and braced together. Then the walls are built in with brick or concrete, sometimes beginning at the *top* and continuing to the bottom.

The exceptionally tall buildings, called in America " skyscrapers," are invariably steel-framed. Indeed they could not be built in any other way. The cost of land in New York is so prohibitive that it is necessary for the owners to make the best possible use of it, and that is the reason why these very lofty buildings came into being.

A very famous example is the Woolworth Building in New York, which has no fewer than fifty-seven storeys and towers to the prodigious height of 792 feet above the pavement. It weighs 160,000 tons, and is based on solid rock far below the street level. It rests on sixty-six immense steel cylinders called " caissons," each of which is filled with cement. Thus the foundations are as firm as the solid rock on which they rest.

Although the space of ground on which the Woolworth Building stands measures only 200 feet by 155 feet, the building itself has no fewer than twenty-seven acres of floor space. Seventeen million bricks were used to make the walls, 7,500 tons of terra-cotta, and 2,500 square feet of cut stone. Seven million white hot rivets were required to bind together the 20,000 tons of steel which forms the skeleton of this giant erection. The building cost nearly two and a half millions, but was built in two years.

Higher and Higher

It is a town in itself, with its own restaurants, telegraph, telephone and post offices. It has in it doctors, lawyers, insurance agents, barbers, brokers and shops of all sorts.

Tall as is the Woolworth Building, it has been surpassed by two other New York giants, the Chrysler Building (1,046 feet high) and the Empire State Building. The last is the loftiest structure in the world. Including the 200-foot mooring mast for airships on its summit, it rises 1,248 feet above the pavement, and it has 102 storeys. As much steel (57,000 tons) was used in its construction as went into the Forth Bridge. Its walls have 6,500 windows in them, and its 71 lift shafts total seven miles in length. It is a curious experience to be at the top of one of these great skyscrapers in a gale of wind. The whole building seems to rock or sway, yet owing to its construction it is actually safer than a much lower building made of stone or brick.

Speaking to the National Association of Building Owners in Montreal some years ago, Mr. C. T. Coley, who is one of the chief authorities on steel building, said that the height of such buildings would be limited only by the efficiency limit of the lifts. He pictured offices soaring to immense heights and at the same time penetrating deeply below the ground. They would be served by double-decked high-speed motor streets.

By Light Rays

Lifts would have no operators, the opening and closing of doors being controlled by light rays, which would count the passengers and close the doors when the lift car was full. All offices, he said, would be equipped with wireless, so that business-men could listen in to the rise and fall

Sir Robert McAlpine & Sons.

BUILDING A HUGE LONDON HOTEL

This maze of metal rods formed the commencement of laying a floor at one of London's great new luxury hotels. These rods will have the openings round them filled with concrete to form a reinforced floor that will be actually three feet in thickness when finished. To-day almost all our very large buildings, more especially hotels and offices, are made of steel frames filled in with bricks or steel and concrete.

THE CHAINS FOR ST. PAUL'S

Topical Press.

When Sir Christopher Wren rebuilt St. Paul's Cathedral after the Great Fire of London, he bound the base of the dome with a chain of iron links encased in lead. In recent years, however, owing to a weakening of the foundations, the dome has been given fresh strength and support by a new chain of specially-hardened and non-rustable steel. Here some of the links in this wonderful chain are depicted, each, when standing on its end, at least twice the height of an ordinary man.

AN ADVENTURE IN ARCHITECTURE

The design and building of the new industrial town of Harlow, Essex, has been described as " one of the most exciting adventures in Britain to-day." New factories keep pace with the number of houses built and all the firms occupying the factories have come from London in accordance with the plan for decentralisation of industry and population. Above is a general view of the new town.

Topical Press.

This picture would scarcely be regarded as one showing a typical English country town, but it does show one of the experiments made by the architects in Harlow New Town. The skyscraper type of building, rising well above the roofs of the new houses, is a block of flats, all occupied by people working in the new industrial town. New industries have been started as houses became occupied.

UP ABOVE THE WORLD SO HIGH

Topical Press.

This photograph was taken during the construction of a great electrical power station in London. The crane is hoisting from street level two massive pieces that will be riveted into the parts of the girders which they were made to fit. The man may have travelled through space to save himself a long climb. It is more than likely, however, that the place to which the frames have to go can be reached only by this method.

HEADQUARTERS OF UNITED NATIONS

Unations.

Steel, concrete and glass are the chief materials which have been used in building the permanent headquarters in New York of the United Nations Organisation. Thirty-nine storeys high, it has nearly 6,000 windows. The Secretariat Building is the main structure, the Conference Building is in the foreground and the General Assembly Building just behind this on the right. Both the Empire State Building (left centre) and the Chrysler Building (extreme right), the two tallest skyscrapers, are seen in this picture.

Central Press.

A NEW GIANT IN WHITEHALL

This photograph was taken from Horse Guards Avenue and shows the new block of Government offices in Whitehall, London, when nearing the final stages in its construction. These great new offices, built in the modern way mainly of steel and concrete and costing over £5,000,000, are the new headquarters of the Board of Trade and the Air Ministry.

of stocks on the market and clerks could be called back to their offices when wanted.

Another great advantage of reinforced concrete as a building material is that it is, or can be made, fireproof. The new Sun Life Assurance Company's building in Trafalgar Square is said to be a perfect example of a building of this kind. The framework is of steel, the floors of steel, tile and concrete. Partitions are made of terra-cotta blocks and bricks, and even the doors and their frameworks are all of metal.

London is built mainly on clay, while New York has rock beneath it. That is the principal reason why there are no skyscrapers in London.

The highest block of flats in London is Queen Anne's Mansions in Westminster, which rises 180 feet above the pavement. The highest buildings in London are St. Paul's Cathedral, the Victoria Tower at Westminster (336 feet), and Westminster Cathedral, the tower of which rises 284 feet.

Since Queen Anne's Mansions was built the London County Council has put a limit on the height of buildings in all the area over which it rules.

Although London has no skyscrapers, the material—that is, concrete—which enables skyscrapers to be built is now being used in London and other English towns just as widely as in New York. Concrete was first used on a large scale

ARCHITECTURE IN THE DOMINIONS

Canadian National Railways.

Canada's largest city and commercial capital is Montreal, in the Province of Quebec. It stands on an island in the St. Lawrence and has direct railway communication with New York as well as Canadian cities. Our photograph shows the Montreal Terminal of the Canadian National Railways and gives an excellent idea of the modern architecture of this great Dominion city.

Australian News and Information Bureau.

Second largest city in Australia is Melbourne, capital of Victoria. In 1836 it consisted of 13 meagre buildings on the banks of the River Yarra. A century later it had a population of a million people. Our photograph shows a modern block of flats on the tree-lined St. Kilda Road, Melbourne. This block contains sixty 4- or 5-roomed flats, centrally-heated, with separate entrances and garages.

Associated Newspapers Ltd.

In the Old World it is the ancient cathedrals, abbeys and castles, mellowed by the centuries, that usually take pride of place as examples of a country's architecture. In the newer worlds of the West and South great cities have been developed within the past century or so, and their architecture is largely based on modern needs. Sydney, capital of New South Wales, and mother city of the island continent, has many notable buildings, and our photograph shows the offices of the *Sun*, one of the city's leading newspapers.

363

in London some forty years or so ago, when a huge concrete shop was built in Oxford Street with eight acres of concrete floors. The "Ritz," in Piccadilly, was the first large London hotel to be built on the modern principle with a framework of steel girders. The fine Science College at Kensington is another example of concrete work.

Not that there is anything new in concrete, for the Romans were using this material 500 years before the birth of Christ. The great dome of the Pantheon at Rome is made entirely of concrete, and a floor in the House of the Vestals consists of a slab of concrete 1 foot thick and 20 feet across.

Even in England concrete was used very long ago, for the foundations of Salisbury Cathedral are of this material, and so are the walls of Corfe Castle.

One great advantage of concrete is that such a building can easily be made with a perfectly flat roof. In old days the only covering for a flat roof was lead, which was heavy and extremely costly. Now concrete with a covering of asphalt is perfectly weather-proof and has made possible the formation of roof gardens, which are very popular in New York. Even in London, within a quarter of a mile of the Bank of England, grapes may be seen growing and fruiting on the concrete roof of a large building.

Luxury Flats

The greatest change in modern building is that from houses to flats. In London, Paris and Berlin, as in New York, people are flocking from the old-fashioned houses with their steep staircases, cold, draughty rooms and risks of frozen pipes, into flats.

The chief objection to the flat in the past has been the risk of being disturbed by noise made by neighbours above and below, but the architects of the new flats have made them almost soundproof.

Courtesy City Architect, Leeds.

A MODERN VILLAGE IN AN OLD CITY

In this photograph we have an example of how modern homes are built where slums once stood. The Quarry Hill Flats at Leeds comprise 938 dwellings to house over three thousand people. In addition there are shops, a restaurant, social centre, laundry and radio relaying station. Gardens, recreation grounds, with day nurseries and playgrounds for children, as well as other amenities, are all included in this self-contained community, with room for expansion in the future. Leeds existed in Anglo-Saxon times and was a great centre of the woollen industry even in the fourteenth century.

Rischgitz.

THE LAST DISCOURSE OF SOCRATES

It is from the written works of his pupil, Plato, that we know the teaching of one of the greatest of Greek thinkers, Socrates (470–399 B.C.) who was himself more concerned with meeting and debating with others than in writing. He was accused by his enemies on flimsy charges and sentenced to death by drinking the poison, hemlock. Our picture, by the famous French artist, David, shows Socrates with his friends as the end approaches, and this last discourse was duly recorded by Plato.

WISE MEN OF ANCIENT TIMES

MAN is an animal so far as his body is concerned, but he differs in one very important respect from all other animals. He is able to think and reason and does not rely upon instinct alone. Because of the fact that man possesses a thinking brain, great nations and civilisations have arisen and countless inventions and discoveries have been made about the Universe in which we live.

We all think for ourselves by means of our brains and though we are not all great thinkers we have the intelligence to recognise the truths and discoveries told to us by men whose mental powers are higher than our own or have special aptitudes which make them leaders in their own spheres.

We ourselves become wiser because of the knowledge they impart, or we benefit in one way or another because of the many inventions and discoveries made by others who have used their brains to good purpose.

Thales the Wise

One of the earliest thinkers of whom we have any record is Thales, who lived in Greece between the years 640 and 550 B.C. Thales was one of the Seven Wise Men of Greece and some of their sayings are still in common use to-day.

" Know thyself " and " Do nothing in excess " are among those credited to these wise men of Greece. Thales is regarded as the pioneer in the sciences of geometry and astronomy, and he was probably the first man to try to find out what we should now call a scientific reason for many things in the Universe instead of believing the ancient myths about the sun, moon and stars. He is generally believed to have been the first man to foretell an eclipse of the sun (585 B.C.).

It is rather curious that right through the ages the ordinary man has always been amused by stories of wise men making foolish mistakes or suffering some mishap which a less clever person would have managed to avoid. Right down through the centuries has come the story of Thales, the wise man, who, when out walking with his old maidservant, tripped and fell into the ditch. Whereon the servant, instead of sympathising with him, merely cried: " How can you, O Thales, expect to view the stars in heaven when you cannot see what is under your feet ? "

A Brotherhood of Scholars

Another famous wise man of Greece was Pythagoras who was born about 580 B.C. He was both a scholar and an athlete, and in the school which he founded discipline was strict. It is known that he was a wonderfully strong swimmer and gained prizes for running, jumping and wrestling, and it is probably due to Pythagoras that boxing became a sport.

It was, however, in the world of science to which Thales had first directed men's thoughts that Pythagoras really made his name. He is regarded as the real founder of geometry, and he believed in orderliness in everything : there must be the right proportions in architecture and concord in music. He is believed to have been the first man to discover the musical octave and to start men thinking in the right terms of music.

The multiplication table as we know it to-day is also due to him.

In his school he taught mathematics, gymnastics and music, and the pupils banded themselves together in what was known as the " Brotherhood of Pythagoras," and long after his death the principles he had set forth were taught by his pupils.

Euclid's Propositions

A third great thinker, or " philosopher " as such men were generally called, is one whose name is familiar to all of us. Euclid, who was born about 300 B.C., carried on the work of the mathematicians who had gone before him and wrote the famous " Elements of Geometry " on which all our modern geometry and methods of mathematical reasoning are based. Euclid thought in terms of lines, squares, triangles and circles, and put forward his famous " propositions " to prove the truth of what he taught.

At Alexandria he founded a famous school which was at that time the greatest seat of learning in the world. Of him, as of other early philosophers, little human stories are told which make these men more real to us. One of Euclid's students, having mastered the early stages of geometry, asked his teacher how much better off he was for knowing all that he had learned.

Euclid made no answer to the pupil but turned to his servant : " Give this gentleman a piece of silver since he cannot learn without making money."

Experiments of Archimedes

Archimedes, who lived between the years 287 and 212 B.C., went further than the philosophers and mathematicians who had taught before him. To a large extent they had been content with expounding theories, but Archimedes carried out experiments for himself. He had, too, that first qualification for the scientist, the enquiring mind that sought for an

WHAT A GLASS PRISM DOES TO WHITE LIGHT

A beam of the brilliant light from a "limelight," closely resembling that of the sun, is here being thrown through a triangular glass prism and magnifying glass on to a white screen. The effect of the prism is to break up the light into the series of colours, called the "spectrum," of which white light is composed. The colours are seven in number—violet, indigo, blue, green, yellow, orange, red. The artificial word VIBGYOR will help the reader to remember their order. The separation is due to rays of different colours being bent out of their original course in different degrees—violet most, red least. This particular spectrum, called the *solar* spectrum, is peculiar to sunlight of the same nature. Flames of various kinds produce distinctive spectra, so that the trained observer can tell what a substance is composed of by burning it in a gas flame and examining its spectrum by means of the spectroscope, an instrument containing a glass prism. The spectroscope even enables the astronomer to determine of what stars many millions of miles away are made.

A

B

C

D

E

HOW THE CAMERA HELPS IN REPRODUCING COLOURS

Printers make use of the fact that the three primary colours of the spectrum—yellow, red and blue—can be mixed to make any other colour. In C we have a three-colour reproduction of a famous painting. To reproduce this picture as shown in C three negatives of the picture are made with the camera, through colour " filters," which cut out respectively yellow, red and blue rays. Positive printing blocks are made from the negatives, and each is covered with ink of the primary colour which did *not* affect its negative. Printed separately, the " yellow," " red " and " blue " blocks would produce prints A, B and D respectively. In E red is printed on the top of yellow; and in C blue has been superimposed on E, giving a " three-colour " print in the actual colours of the original.

THE DISCOVERY OF SPECIFIC GRAVITY

Specially drawn for this work.

The great Greek inventor, engineer and scientist, Archimedes of Syracuse, is here explaining to his ruler, King Hiero, how he had detected the presence of base metal in a gold crown made for that monarch. The accidental overflowing of his bath had revealed to him the secret of specific gravity, which is the weight of a substance as compared with that of an equal bulk of some other substance taken as the standard; or, more briefly, the relation of weight to volume.

explanation of those apparently simple things that most people take for granted without asking " Why ? "

How this quality helped Archimedes and led to an important discovery has taken its place in history. The King of Syracuse had sent for Archimedes to ask his opinion on a crown of gold just made for him by his goldsmiths. For some reason or other the King was suspicious and had an idea that the goldsmiths, instead of using all the gold the king had sent them, had mixed a baser metal with the gold and in this way had been able to keep some of the gold for themselves.

In the Bath

Archimedes could merely say that he was unable to think of any test, but would consider the matter carefully. Some little time later Archimedes stepped into his bath which had been carelessly filled up to the brim. You can imagine just what happened : a great deal of the water overflowed from the bath and on to the floor.

The question at once came into Archimedes' enquiring mind: " Why ? " He made one or two very simple experiments and noticed that the lower his body went in the water the greater was the quantity of liquid which overflowed. It seems an obvious fact to us nowadays, but Archimedes was one of the first to realise that underlying these simple facts are important truths.

What Archimedes discovered as he pondered on the problem was that equal weights of different metals when weighed in water will no longer appear equal. The bulkier metal does not suffer the same diminution in weight.

The great scholar at once thought of the king's crown. If the crown were made of pure gold it would, when placed in a vessel full of water, displace the same amount as would a lump of pure gold the same weight as the crown. But if the crown contained some base metal it would not cause the same amount of water to overflow as would a lump of pure gold the same weight as the crown.

As soon as Archimedes realised the truth of his reasoning he leapt from his bath and ran through the streets crying out " *Eureka! Eureka!* " (I have found it).

Later Archimedes went to the king and made an actual experiment with the crown. When it was placed in a vessel filled to the brim with water it caused more water to flow over the sides than did a lump of gold of exactly the same weight. Therefore the crown contained some metal other than gold, probably silver as that is bulkier than gold.

Archimedes made many other discoveries and propounded theories about the lever and on hydrostatics. Some of these theories were not strictly accurate, but it was long centuries before other men discovered where they were at fault, and in doing so made further advances.

Among other inventions he discovered a means of raising water by the use of a screw and advanced the sciences of arithmetic and geometry very considerably. His method of making practical experiments to test his theories set a new fashion which has been followed ever since.

What is Truth ?

Another great man whose name is still honoured was Socrates, born about the year 470 B.C. According to all accounts he was thick-set and ugly in countenance, but possessed very great powers of physical endurance. It might be said that he began the " question and answer " method of arriving at the truth of any problem, and his great object was to convince others of the truth about themselves. He argued, especially with young people, about popular ideas and encouraged them to form their own views on politics and morals and to test these views by debate with others.

HOW ARCHIMEDES EMPTIED A SHIP

Specially drawn for this work.

The snake-like object occupying the centre of the picture is a device invented, so the story goes, by Archimedes for removing the water from a ship's hold. It consists of a coil of tubing, open at both ends, wound corkscrew-wise round a shaft. On the shaft being revolved, the water scooped up by the bottom end is raised through the coils, and delivered at the top.

Socrates himself did not put down his views and ideas in writing, but one of his pupils and admirers, Plato, took on this task, and acted towards Socrates much as Boswell, long centuries later, did to the famous Dr. Johnson. It is from the Dialogues of Plato that we know all that we do of what Socrates taught.

In 399 B.C. Socrates incurred the displeasure of the new government that came into power and was prosecuted on a charge of introducing new divinities in place of those recognised by the State. He was tried and sentenced to death, and despite the desire of many friends who could probably have contrived his escape, he drank the hemlock he had been condemned to drink and so died.

After Socrates' death Plato had only one mission in life and that was to carry on the work and teachings of the master he admired. Some of Plato's own ideas were, of course, brought into his writings and were not always on precisely the same lines as those of Socrates. Men have read the works of Plato ever since and they have had great influence on other thinkers who have drawn inspiration from his writings.

Others who studied under Plato carried on his work, and the most famous of these was Aristotle who is sometimes called the " Father of Learning." He was something more than a theorist, and carried his desire for scientific research to the study of animals, plants, rocks and minerals. Alexander the Great sent an expedition into Asia to capture and bring home strange animals in order that Aristotle might be able to study them.

Aristotle drew up a scheme of education which dealt with both practical affairs and the pursuit of culture. He wrote, too, on politics and different

ANOTHER FORM OF THE ARCHIMEDEAN SCREW   *J. F. Corrigan.*

This device acts in just the same way as the coiled tube of the preceding illustration. It is a moving metal spiral fitting tightly inside a fixed cylinder. The nearer half of the cylinder has been removed, to show how the water travels. Though the device is little used now for raising water, its principle is still employed in various kinds of conveyors.

Specially drawn for this work.

Our artist has here depicted Hero, a citizen of Alexandria, who lived in the first or second century B.C., making an experiment with steam. His servant is stoking a furnace below a boiler from which steam issues through a jet and strikes vanes on the rim of a wheel, causing the wheel to spin. Hero is credited with many inventions, including a fire-engine, a water-clock, and an organ worked by water power. He was also a great mathematician.

systems of government, but rejected all extremes of social or political programmes. Like Socrates and Plato, Aristotle taught men to think clearly and deeply.

One other great man of those ancient days is worthy of mention for a number of reasons. Hero of Alexandria lived about 130 years before the birth of Christ, and his name has come down to us for the discoveries he made in mathematics and science. It was Hero who discovered the formula to find the area of a triangle, and he was responsible for a number of mechanical inventions. One of these was the fountain, worked by means of air pressure.

The First Steam Engine

It was Hero, too, who is believed to have been the first man to realise the power of steam. He invented a small stationary steam engine and, although nothing very practical came of it until hundreds of years later, Hero was the first to make any use of steam at all.

To a very large extent these Greeks laid the foundations on which in due course others were to build. Some of their knowledge had come to them from the earlier civilisations of Babylon and Egypt. Astronomy was a subject on which the Egyptians had a rudimentary knowledge, but it was the Greeks who brought it to a stage where it became a science to be studied.

It was a Greek, Eudoxus of Cnidus (fourth century B.C.), who was the first to have an observatory, and to him is due the earliest systematic description of the heavens. Later came Hipparchus (160–127 B.C.) who invented several astronomical instruments and made accurate observations, dividing his circle into 360 degrees. In addition he made a catalogue of 1,080 stars and determined the length of the solar year with a fair amount of exactness.

Much of the work of Hipparchus was done at Alexandria where the Greeks had established the famous School of Alexandria. It had departments of literature, mathematics, astronomy and medicine and possessed the greatest library of ancient times, containing some 400,000 volumes or rolls. One part of this library was destroyed by the Christian Bishop Theophilus about A.D. 390, as he considered it a centre of pagan learning. The rest of this great library was destroyed by the Mohammedans in A.D. 640, whether purposely or purely by accident is not known, but its loss was certainly a great tragedy.

The Romans eventually succeeded the Greeks as the civilising power in the known world, but they scarcely advanced earlier knowledge to any great extent and were more concerned with the establishment of law and order and with the arts. In particular they were great builders as well as very able administrators. With their civil and military engineering they showed a genius for the practical side of life, but had little interest in knowledge for its own sake.

The result was that Science ceased to make any real advance during the Roman era. There were writers who touched on the subject, but they were content to record the knowledge of their time without attempting to add to it. The elder Pliny (A.D. 23–79) produced what might be called an encyclopedia of the knowledge of his time. In *Naturalis Historia* he dealt with man and his qualities, animals, plants and trees; geography, agriculture, fruit-growing, forestry, winemaking, metals, and with the fine arts, as well as magic and its usefulness. Plutarch (A.D. 50–125) wrote on the nature of the Moon and Roman mythology, and, with one or two other writers, passed on valuable information about Greek teaching and learning.

With the decline of the Romans, however, there came a long period when little or no advance in learning was made. The Dark Ages descended, and it was nearly a thousand years before scholarship and learning began to struggle towards further knowledge.

THE EARLY ASTRONOMERS

Rischgitz.

GALILEO BEFORE THE INQUISITION

For teaching that the Earth and other planets revolved round the sun the great astronomer Galileo was accused by the Church of heresy. In 1632, when nearly seventy years old, he was summoned to appear before the Inquisition at Rome, where he was made to kneel and affirm that his views were wrong. " I am at your mercy," said the aged astronomer, " and I must say whatever you wish me to say." But his beliefs remained unshaken.

LESS than 500 years ago men thought the world was flat and stood still while the sun and stars moved round it. Among the first of those who doubted this idea was Nicolas Copernicus, who was born in Prussia in 1473.

Copernicus was the son of well-to-do parents who sent him to the university of Cracow where he studied medicine, astronomy and mathematics. Telescopes were still unknown, and Copernicus spent many of his nights in a high tower watching the stars and studying their movements. He went to Italy for a time and then returned to his native land where after more years of study he told some of his friends his belief that the sun is the central body round which the earth and other planets revolve.

It was a long time before he could be persuaded to write a book in which his observations and theories were set forth. The first printed copy of this book, indeed, was brought to Copernicus shortly before he died in 1543. Other astronomers were able to read these theories, among them Tycho Brahe, though it was some years after Copernicus had died. Brahe was born in 1546, but it was in 1560 when an eclipse of the sun made him determined to study astronomy.

The King of Denmark built the largest observatory ever known up to that time in order that Tycho Brahe might pursue his studies, and for twenty years Brahe worked on the task of determining the positions of the moon, planets and stars.

His chief assistant was Johann Kepler, born in 1571, and after Tycho Brahe's death in 1601, Kepler succeeded him. There is no doubt that Kepler was one of the most brilliant men of his times and that his work in astronomy laid sound foundations on which other men worked after him.

It was an age when men were eager for new knowledge, and in Italy about the same time as Kepler was at work there was another brilliant scholar, Galileo, a professor of mathematics at Pisa and later at Padua. Hearing of an invention by Hans Lippershey in Flanders in 1609 of a glass which made distant objects seem much larger, Galileo carried out his own experiments and eventually constructed the first telescope.

Discovery of the Pendulum

He had already put forward several theories which made him unpopular, though some of his discoveries were destined to be of use for centuries afterwards. One such invention was due to his observation as he sat in church one day that the swinging of a lamp to and fro was perfectly regular. The idea of using a swinging weight as a means of measuring time came to his mind and as an outcome of this the first pendulum came into use.

It was by means of his telescope, however, that Galileo made his most remarkable discoveries. Copernicus had already put forth the idea that the earth and planets revolve round the sun; Galileo wrote a book setting forth the proofs of this theory. The Church at that time was strongly opposed to any such idea and Galileo was ordered to Rome. There, under the threat of torture and death, he was compelled to admit that his theories were wrong. Galileo was allowed to return to Florence where he spent his remaining years, not very happily, as he became blind, and he died in 1642.

It was not so many years after his death before the truth of his theories was confirmed by others, and to-day the name of Galileo is honoured by men of science throughout the world. He led the way which made the work of others who followed much easier

James's Press.

TYCHO BRAHE'S OBSERVATORY

This reproduction from an old print shows you the splendidly equipped observatory built for the great astronomer, Tycho Brahe (1546–1601), on the island of Hven, between Denmark and Sweden. It was erected at the expense of the Danish King, Frederick II., at a cost of over £20,000—a very large sum in those days. The name of Uraniborg, meaning "the castle of the heavens," was given to the observatory, in which Brahe worked for over twenty years.

IN ANCIENT GREECE—Plate 1

1

2

3

4   5

Not long after 2,000 B.C. Greek tribesmen came southwards from their Northern lands and settled in the country now known as Greece. Here they came into contact with the civilisation which had spread from Egypt along the Mediterranean coasts. The Greeks did not unite into a single nation but formed city states where through the centuries they gradually developed their own wonderful civilisation. Some idea of their wide interests is given in the Plate above: (1) Warrior in armour. (2) A Greek theatre. (3) Chariot race in the organised athletic contests for which they became famous. (4) Greek galley. (5) Musician playing the lyre.

6

7

8

9

10

Greek art reached its highest levels from about 500 B.C. onwards. Their sculpture and architecture, as well as the beauty of design in articles of common use, are still unsurpassed to-day. The Athenian vase-makers, for example, combined delicacy of drawing with great imagination. In the Plate above are shown: (6) The Parthenon, a famous temple dedicated to Athena, built 447–438 B.C. (7) A discus-thrower. (8) Sculpture, in which the Greeks excelled. (9) The Delphic Oracle, whose priestess delivered the utterances of the Oracle in the temple of Apollo. (10) Greek vases, which are still models of design and decoration to-day.

From the Eastern shores of the Mediterranean civilisation spread westward. It was from the Greeks that the Romans gained knowledge which they developed in time on their own lines. The " Meditations " of one of their Emperors are read to-day for their nobility of thought. This Emperor, Marcus Aurelius (A.D. 121–180) is seen in (1) pardoning his enemies. In (2) are the remains of one of Rome's most famous buildings, the Colosseum, built A.D. 72–80. It was here that the Early Christians were thrown to the wild beasts. Another great Roman city was Pompeii and in (3) is the amphitheatre in the city destroyed by the eruption of Vesuvius in A.D. 79.

Rome built her great Empire from about 264 B.C., when the struggle with Carthage began, until the triumph of the Goths and Vandals around A.D. 400 when Roman power had declined. Among her great Emperors was Trajan (A.D. 56–117), whose deeds were commemorated on the Trajan Pillar (4). The city itself was protected by mighty walls (5). Of the Roman temples that still survive the Pantheon (6), built by Hadrian, A.D. 120–130, is still used as a church. The Forum (7), reconstructed as it appeared in Rome's heyday, was the meeting-place of the assembly of the people, and here they were addressed by magistrates and others.

GALILEO AND THE PENDULUM

Specially drawn for this work.

While attending a service in the Cathedral of Pisa one day, Galileo—then a young man—noticed
that a lamp hanging from the roof was swinging slowly to and fro on its chain. Using his pulse
as a timekeeper, he found that, though the swings became smaller and smaller, the time taken
for a swing remained the same. As a result of his discovery pendulums came into use for clocks.

than it might have been. In the year that Galileo died Isaac Newton was born in Lincolnshire, and it was Newton who improved upon Galileo's telescope by his invention of the reflecting telescope.

Newton's Law of Gravity

The story of Newton and the falling apple is well known. Thousands of other people have doubtless seen an apple fall from the tree without puzzling their brains about it at all, but Newton asked the question—Why? It was from this that he gradually evolved his theory that some force in the earth must have pulled the apple towards it.

It was from this beginning that Newton elaborated his theories about the law of gravity. He proved that it was owing to this force of gravity that the moon was pulled round our world and that in turn the earth and other planets were themselves pulled round the sun. From this he went on to study the solar system and added greatly to men's knowledge of the sun and moon and the motion of the tides.

He found out that sunlight consists of seven differently coloured lights, and that these when combined together make ordinary white light. Shutting himself in a dark room on one side of which a small hole had been made to admit a ray of sunlight, Newton held a triangular bar of glass (a prism) in the ray of sunlight. A white sheet was fixed in front of this and the sunlight shining through the prism was broken into its seven different colours on the sheet.

In character Newton was modest, deeply religious and very just, but, particularly in his later years, he was apt to be absent-minded about the ordinary affairs of life. He was modest, too, about his own discoveries, and it was largely due to his friend, Edmund Halley, that his writings were published. A knighthood was conferred on Newton in 1705, and unlike some of our earlier scientists and

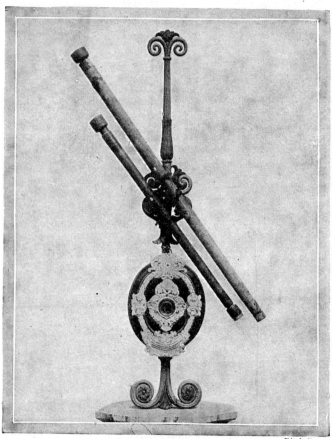

Rischgitz.

TWO OF GALILEO'S TELESCOPES

If ever you visit the Tribuna di Galileo at Florence, you will be able to see this pair of telescopes, made by the famous astronomer. Though not the actual inventor of the telescope —that honour belongs to Lippershey, a Dutchman—Galileo was the first person to produce a really serviceable instrument. His telescope had concave lenses as eyepieces, like those of a pair of field-glasses.

WHAT A FALLING APPLE DID

Specially drawn for this work.

In the year of Galileo's death (1642) there was born at Woolsthorpe, Lincolnshire, the greatest of natural philosophers, Sir Isaac Newton. This picture records the incident of the apple which fell from a tree and directed Newton's thought to the most important of scientific discoveries— the law that every atom in the universe attracts every other atom. This is known as the law of gravity, or gravitation.

astronomers, he was universally honoured and esteemed. He died in March, 1727, and was buried in Westminster Abbey.

The friend of Newton's, Edmund Halley, son of a London soap boiler, was born in 1656 and educated at St. Paul's School, where he showed great promise in mathematics. After studying at Oxford he went to St. Helena where he completed a map showing the positions of the fixed stars in the southern hemisphere. He became astronomer royal at Greenwich in 1720.

Halley's Comet

It was Halley who told us about the comet which bears his name. Halley's Comet takes approximately seventy-six years to travel round its orbit, and it has been possible to trace references to its appearance as far back as 240 B.C. Its appearance in 1910 was accurately calculated by the astronomers at Greenwich Observatory, and the forecasts

James's Press.

NEWTON'S REFLECTING TELESCOPE
This is the ancestor of most of the reflecting telescopes now used. The invention of Sir Isaac Newton, it is open at the top, and has a hollow-faced mirror at the bottom. The image is reflected forward on to a small flat, oblique mirror, which turns it into an eyepiece in the side of the tube.

and account given by Halley long years before have been fully borne out.

It is not always easy for us to discover how and why the knowledge of such men as astronomers and scientists affects the lives of ordinary people. It often happens that the man of science discovers some great principle, but it is left to another more practical man to make use of it for some everyday purpose. In the case of Christian Huyghens, who was born in 1629, we can see how the discoveries of science come to be applied to the things we use every day.

Huyghens made a number of improvements in telescope lenses, and in 1660 he visited England and helped Newton to develop his laws of motion. In 1678 he announced his wave theory of light by which he was able to explain reflection and refraction. He was also the first man to apply the pendulum to clocks, on Galileo's suggestion, while the first watch regulated by a spring balance was made under his direction and presented to Louis XIV.

It was Huyghens who discovered through his improved telescopes the ring around Saturn, though it was left to later astronomers to discover that this planet has several rings.

Somewhere about this time societies began to be formed so that the men of learning could exchange and discuss their theories and discoveries. One of the first was founded in Naples in 1560, and in 1651 another Academy was formed in Florence.

In England a society began to meet in 1659 at Gresham College in London, calling itself the Philosophical or Invisible College. Later this society was incorporated by Royal Charter as "The Royal Society of London for Promoting Natural Knowledge." Such societies did a very great amount of good in making known the work of scientists to others engaged in similar forms of research. To-day admission to the Royal Society (F.R.S.) is a high and jealously-guarded honour among all men of science.

Rischgitz.

WILLIAM HARVEY AND KING CHARLES I

The discovery by William Harvey of the circulation of the blood through the body was made known to the world in a book which he published in 1628. Ten years earlier he had been appointed special physician to James I. In this picture he is seen explaining his discovery to James's successor, to whom he was greatly attached. The boy watching Harvey so keenly afterwards ruled as Charles II.

IT is more than 700 years since Roger Bacon was born at Ilchester in Somerset. After studying at Oxford and Paris he became a friar of the Franciscan order and entered a monastery near Oxford.

During the years he spent here he invented the magnifying glass and an explosive compound of charcoal, sulphur and saltpetre, which was the first step towards our modern gunpowder. Bacon called it "Magical Fire." Among the prophecies he made were forecasts of ships that would sail the seas without sails, carriages that would move without horses, and of machines in which men would fly in the air.

Bacon's associates accused him of dealing in black magic, and he was ordered to Paris, where he was kept under restraint for eight years, and even forbidden the use of writing materials or instruments. A new pope, however, became interested in what Bacon had written earlier, and as a result Roger Bacon regained some of his freedom.

Then came another pope, and Bacon was imprisoned again. Bacon sent him a small book he had written, telling how to enjoy good health even in old age. The reward for this was his release, and he was allowed to return to Oxford.

Others followed in his footsteps, and though there were no outstanding men of science or scientific discoveries during the years that followed, men became more and more interested. In the reign of Queen Elizabeth a book was written by William Gilbert (1540–1603) in which the properties of Lodestone were explained and Magnets and Magnetism were dealt with. It was Gilbert, too, who found out that when substances such as amber, sealing-wax, and resin are rubbed they are able to attract other things to them.

Prophet of a New Era

The Greek word for amber is *elektron* and Gilbert called this curious power of attraction " electricity." It was long years before electricity as we now know it became the highly important factor it is to-day, but Gilbert led the way and lighted a path that others followed later.

Not much later than Gilbert came another man whose interest lay in other directions though he possessed that same enquiring mind as Gilbert. William Harvey (1578–1657) was educated at Cambridge, but took his doctor's degree in physic at Padua and then at Cambridge. He was physician to St. Bartholomew's Hospital and to King James I and later to King Charles I. It was Harvey who discovered the circulation of the blood and can justly be regarded as one of the pioneers in medical science.

A man of many parts, lawyer, statesman and philosopher, Francis Bacon (1561–1626) was the prophet of a new era and is regarded to-day by men of science as the originator of the school of experimental research.

He wrote " The Advancement of Learning," and in this and other books gave a summary of existing human knowledge and pointed the way to further advancement. He changed the ideas of men, induced them to experiment and asserted that Nature held many secrets still beyond men's imagination at that time, all of which could be discovered by patient research.

He even suggested lines on which science would develop and definitely anticipated the coming of the telephone.

In France about the same time, though a little later than Francis Bacon, a philosopher and mathematician, René Descartes, was also urging upon men the need for clear thinking. His three books on geometry opened a new era in that science. Descartes was not merely a clear thinker but was an excellent craftsman and could use his hands as well as his brains. Among the mechanical toys he constructed was a doll which even in these days would be considered a marvel of ingenuity.

This doll, capable of performing all sorts of movements, was sent by Descartes to a friend overseas. It was carefully packed in a box, but on board ship the rolling of the vessel had its effect on the doll's mechanism. According to the story, the captain of the ship became alarmed when he heard mysterious tapping sounds issuing from the box, and determined to open it.

Immediately the doll jumped out and began to dance about the ship. The captain was so scared that he seized the doll and flung it overboard into the sea—and that was the end of Descartes' " Wooden Daughter," as the doll had been called.

Boyle's Law

In 1627 there was born in Lismore in Ireland Robert Boyle, one of several sons of the first Earl of Cork. After leaving Eton young Boyle lived in France, Italy and Switzerland for five years and then returned to England. His interest in science made him one of the leaders in founding the Royal Society, but being a man of extraordinary shyness he spent most of his time in his study and laboratory, experimenting with minerals, liquids, and even foods to discover just what their constituents were.

He invented a compressed air pump and a new type of thermometer.

Rischgitz.

This is a very fine portrait of Francis Bacon, one of England's greatest thinkers. He held important public offices under James I, and was created a peer as Lord Verulam. His famous " Essays " are packed with pithy worldly wisdom; and his books on the science of reasoning are masterpieces. Certain people maintain that Bacon was the author of the plays that bear Shakespeare's name, and that their true authorship was concealed because play-writing was then looked upon as an unworthy pursuit for a man in Bacon's high position.

Boyle's Law relating to the volume of gases at fixed temperatures gave a new impetus to chemistry and began an era of chemical experiment on a vastly different plane from the methods of the old alchemists who worked in haphazard fashion and were chiefly concerned with discovering how to transform base metals into gold.

Other men worked on the same principles as Boyle, and by experiment and research steady progress was made. Among the great names that stand out during the century following Boyle's work was a Frenchman, Antoine Lavoisier (1743–1794). He first came into public notice by winning a prize offered for the best method of lighting Paris, and was later made director of powder works under the Government.

Lavoisier gave proofs that matter is indestructible and showed that any chemical action could be expressed by an equation. The system of naming chemicals in the way we do to-day was first begun by him. If Boyle sketched the plans it can be said that Lavoisier laid the solid foundations on which modern chemistry is based.

The French Revolution brought his career to an end. As the holder of a post under the government which had been swept from power, he was brought before the tribunal. To the plea that his work as a scientist justified his acquittal, the answer was " We need no more scientists in France! " and he suffered the fate of so many others during that period, and was beheaded.

Like Robert Boyle, Henry Cavendish was the son of a nobleman, Lord Charles Cavendish, brother of the Duke of Devonshire. Like Boyle, too, he was extremely shy and reserved and had no sort of desire to gain recognition of his work except among those who were carrying out experiments in the same way. Yet his discoveries about the nature of gases and his theories about electricity won him a reputation as a scientist throughout Europe.

His last important experiment is still referred to as the Cavendish Experiment, from which it became possible to calculate the mass of the earth. Others have worked on the same lines since those days, but with some degree of truth it can be said that Henry Cavendish was the first man to weigh the earth. Cavendish died in 1810 in his seventy-ninth year.

How Mineral Waters Came

A Nonconformist minister, Joseph Priestley (1733–1804) was much more interested in chemistry than his church work, though he held religious views far in advance of his time. In 1767 he published a History of Electricity and carried out many wonderful experiments, though it was another 100 years before the final proofs of his theories were forthcoming.

Turning his attention to chemistry, Priestley wrote a paper on " Different Kinds of Air," in which he told of his discovery of hydrochloric acid and nitric oxide. It was in this paper, too, that he suggested the saturation of water with carbonic acid, an idea for which many of us have reason to be grateful, since it was by acting on this idea that the manufacture of mineral waters began. Think of the good Dr. Priestley when you drink your next ginger-beer!

It was Priestley again who, in 1774, discovered oxygen, and this is really one of the landmarks in chemistry. Other gases were discovered by him, and by experiment he showed their different effects on plants and animals.

Now that men were beginning to understand the nature of gases they also learned how to make use of their knowledge. Young Humphry Davy, who had been born four years after Priestley discovered oxygen, developed an interest in chemistry very early in life. He was only twenty when he was made laboratory superintendent of an institute founded for the purpose of studying gases when inhaled. It was

DR. PRIESTLEY MAKES A DISCOVERY

Specially drawn for this work.

All his life Dr. Joseph Priestley held views, on both religion and science, which were in advance of his time. He became a Nonconformist minister, but it is as a distinguished chemist that he is now remembered. In 1772 he read his paper on Different Kinds of Air, in which several new discoveries were announced, including one dealing with the saturation of water with carbonic acid. This led to a new industry in the manufacture of mineral waters, which are as popular to-day as ever.

here that Davy discovered nitrous oxide, often called laughing gas, and afterwards largely used by dentists when extracting teeth.

Later Davy became director of the chemical laboratory at the Royal Institute in London, and during the period he was there he lectured on electricity and agricultural chemistry,

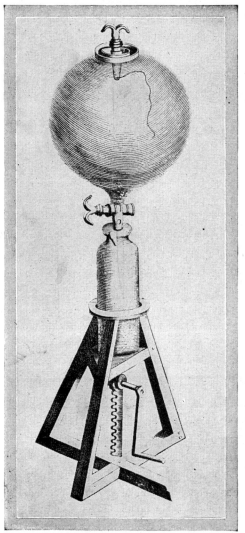

J. F. Corrigan.

BOYLE'S AIR-PUMP

This is one of the many pieces of apparatus made and used by Robert Boyle. The lower part of it is a cylinder with piston moved by a rack and handle; the upper, a spherical chamber connected with the pump through a stop-cock.

besides inventing the famous Davy lamp for miners. Davy was knighted in 1812, made a baronet in 1818, and died at the age of fifty in 1829. But in his comparatively short life he had advanced the cause of science and its usefulness to mankind very considerably.

The same may be said of Justus von Liebig, though his life was twenty years longer than Davy's. Liebig discovered a number of chemicals hitherto unknown and made many improvements in chemical apparatus. He was the first man to extract the nourishment from meat and store it in liquid form in bottles, and it was his studies on the chemistry of soils that had an enormous influence on the productiveness of farm lands by the use of the right fertilisers.

Between the years 1620 and 1800 different members of a Swiss family named Bernoulli became famous as mathematicians. In these days when water-power is being more and more used to create electric power the name of Daniel Bernoulli (1700–82) deserves mention. He wrote a remarkable book entitled " Hydrodynamica " in 1738, wrote, too, on the motion of tides, and laid the foundations of the science now known as Hydrodynamics. Switzerland to-day has cheap electric light in every tiny village, and many other nations have benefited by those early pioneer efforts of Bernoulli.

Chemistry was the main interest of John Dalton, a schoolmaster who became a professor of mathematics at New College, Manchester, in 1793. His writings on what became known as Dalton's " Atomic Theory " have fascinated investigators ever since, and some of the results were seen when the first atomic bomb played a great part in the final stage of the Second World War. If there are dreadful possibilities in this amazing power of the atom there are also high hopes that it may prove the greatest factor for universal peace ever devised.

Rischgitz.

A SCIENTIFIC ARISTOCRAT

The original of this portrait, Robert Boyle, a son of the Earl of Cork, has been called the " Father
of Chemistry," on account of the many chemical experiments that he made. He was even
more distinguished as an explorer of Nature's laws in other directions. We owe to him the
discovery of what is named after him " Boyle's Law," about the relation between pressure
and volume in gases. He invented the compressed-air pump, and made the first sealed-up
thermometer.

Weather was another of Dalton's
hobbies or interests, and he made
more than 200,000 observations over a
period of twenty-seven years. He also
discovered that he himself was colour-
blind and published the first scientific
paper ever written on this subject.

Another Manchester man, James
Prescott Joule (1818–1889) studied
under Dalton, and at nineteen pub-

25—2

lished his first paper " On an Electric-Magnetic Engine." During his experiments to measure electricity, Joule found out the mechanical equivalent of heat, and " joule " remains to-day the word used for the practical unit of electrical energy or work. A great deal of our knowledge on energy, that force which enables human beings to walk, an engine to draw loads, and a motor-car to move swiftly, is due to the pioneer work of Joule.

Nicolas Leonard Sadi Carnot (1796–1832) also was fascinated by this subject of energy, and it was through his writings that the modern science of thermodynamics was founded. He discovered the real nature of the connection between heat and mechanical work and put forward a theory of the reversible heat-engine.

It is due to these theories, evolved by men such as Joule and Sadi Carnot, that much of our progress with engines and machinery has come about.

Progress in Agriculture

Considerable though scarcely revolutionary improvements were made in Agriculture during the seventeenth and eighteenth centuries. It may appear curious, however, that in this oldest branch of knowledge, the production of food, there have been few tremendous changes or inventions comparable, for instance, with those made in transport.

Yet there were pioneers, and one name that is worthy of mention is Jethro Tull (1674–1741), a barrister who preferred farming to law and introduced new methods on his own land. Tull was probably one of the first farmers to study the soil scientifically and urged thorough cultivation or tillage. He also introduced the method of sowing in straight lines in drills.

Charles, second Viscount Townshend (1674–1738), a politician who was popularly known as Turnip Townshend, introduced turnips as a crop for bare arable land. Until then winter feeding of cattle had been impossible and salted meat formed the diet of most people during the cold months.

Rotation of crops was brought in during the reign of George III. Robert Bakewell (1725–95) was a pioneer in improving by selection the quality of cattle and sheep, while the brothers Colling established the famous shorthorn breed of cattle. Sir Humphry Davy gave lectures on agricultural chemistry around 1812.

Since then Science has taken an increasing interest in agriculture, and it may be that recent developments will bring forward far bigger changes in land cultivation and food production.

Gooch.

THE COAL MINER'S FRIEND

Sir Humphry Davy was the inventor of the miner's safety lamp, and as a scientist in chemistry, electricity and agriculture, stood in the forefront of all investigators at the beginning of the nineteenth century.

A PHILOSOPHER AND HIS PERSECUTORS

Baruch de Spinoza (1632–1677) the great philosopher, was a Jew by birth, but his studies made him give up the Jewish faith and dress, and even his Jewish name, which he changed to Benedictus. This drew down on him the hatred of other Jews in Amsterdam, where he lived. They insulted him, as our picture shows, and offered him violence. When at last he was attacked by a would-be assassin with a dagger he left his native city.

SO far in considering the work of the early astronomers and the pioneers in science we have read only about the great efforts of men to understand the forces of Nature. On the foundations which they laid wonderful strides have been made in the past century whereby these forces have been harnessed in the service of mankind. Of the men who carried on the work of these pioneers we shall read presently, but for a short time it is wise to pause and consider the work of other thinkers who have been chiefly concerned with man himself.

The Need for Wisdom

To-day many men are awakening to the truth that in some ways man has progressed almost too rapidly in his conquest of Nature, but too slowly, in proportion, in understanding and controlling himself. Scientists themselves have been warning us for some years past that we must learn wisdom in using the knowledge they give us; we must understand ourselves and other people so that we shall make wise use of the great machines and our amazing powers to use natural forces. Unless we do, the very machines man has made and the tremendous natural forces he has been able to harness will bring about his own downfall.

A famous modern scientist, Professor Soddy, put the question thirty years ago: " Physical force is the slave of science; Is it to be the master or servant of man ? The cold logic of science shows without possibility of an escape that this question, if not faced now, can have only one miserable end.''

More than a hundred years ago John Dalton gave his atomic theory, and for many years past scientists have told us of the tremendous forces existing in atomic energy. But it was merely a theory on which a great deal of knowledge had been accumulated when the war of 1939 broke upon us. Then under the stress of war the scientists of every nation sought desperately to discover the real secret of atomic energy.

British and American scientists discovered the secret as they worked together in America, and the atomic bomb was the result. It is the greatest destructive force ever known in the world. Its possibilities as a beneficial force for mankind, though not yet discovered, are immense. The question remains, however, much as Professor Soddy put it years ago: Is it to be the master or servant of man? Will man's mind be capable of using it wisely to bring greater happiness and understanding to the world, or will he use it only to destroy?

Problems of the Mind

That is why it is of the utmost importance that we should learn something about our own minds and the way we think; we must learn to think rightly and to be aware of that mysterious and little-understood something within us that we call our soul. Of course, many men have pondered and discussed such questions since the days when Christ taught on earth.

In one way it can be understood that the writings of those men who have been concerned with the things of the mind and the soul have rarely received the attention some great discovery in science has gained. Yet many of our great thinkers and philosophers have had the scientific mind also. Baruch de Spinoza, a Dutch philosopher who was born in 1632, was trained in the sciences of his day and approached the question of the working of men's minds in the same way that he would have tried to solve a difficult arithmetic problem.

Free or Slave?

Spinoza was not concerned with telling men what they ought to do. He simply tried to understand the reason for men's actions, and from this endeavoured to learn something about the souls of men. The human soul is only the idea of the human body, and according to whether these ideas are adequate or inadequate, man is either free or a slave. True freedom depends on the extent to which a man shakes off the yoke of his passions and identifies himself with God.

It was not easy teaching, but it is only by understanding one's own mind and trying to make it a better mind that we shall ever obtain a real knowledge of ourselves. John Locke, an Englishman born in the same year as Spinoza, was interested in much the

Rischgitz.

THE GREATEST OF MODERN PHILOSOPHERS

Immanuel Kant, a German who lived in the eighteenth century, had an almost dwarfishly small body, but the brain of a mental giant. His " Critique of Pure Reason " is one of the world's greatest books.

same line of thought as Spinoza. Locke, too, studied science, including medicine and meteorology, at Oxford, but some of his views differed very widely from those of Spinoza.

In 1690 his famous book, "Essay Concerning Human Understanding," was published, and one of his main contentions in this was that the source of all knowledge is experience. In other works he dealt with such subjects as "Toleration," in which he supported liberty of thought; "Education" (1693); and the "Reasonableness of Christianity," as well as "Civil Government."

No one would agree in these days with all that Locke said, but he made many men think about the subjects on which he wrote.

Gottfried Leibnitz, a philosopher and mathematician, also wrote about this time and put forth theories regarding the way in which the human mind works and the reason of it all. It was Leibnitz, too, who invented the differential and integral calculus about the same time as Sir Isaac Newton, and there was considerable argument as to which of the two had been first in the field.

A German of Scottish descent, Immanuel Kant (1724–1804) is among the great names in philosophy, and his books on "Pure Reason" and "Practical Reason" are still valuable. He asserted that certain truths such as the immortality of the soul, the freedom of the will and the existence of God, are established by the principles of practical reason. We cannot think of the wonderful things around us which are on the earth and in the skies without thinking of the One who created them all. That is God, and He alone is capable of understanding all things.

It was Kant, too, who first put forward the idea that the sun and stars were formed millions of years ago out of the great luminous clouds of gas which astronomers know as nebulæ. The famous French astronomer, Pierre Simon Laplace (1749–1827), who was

Rischgitz.

CHARLES DARWIN

This is a portrait of the author of a book "The Origin of Species," which has had more effect on human thought than any other yet printed, excepting, perhaps, the "Principia" of Sir Isaac Newton.

known as the French Newton, was able to prove this in due course by means of his powerful telescopes.

But Kant and men like him earned their places in history not because of their inventions or discoveries, but because they induced and taught men to think of their own minds and souls and the ultimate aim of mankind. Another man who helped men to use their own minds and to think for themselves, though chiefly in his case of material things, was Adam Smith, who was born in 1723. A university professor, first of logic and then of moral philosophy, Smith's claim to fame rests on his great book entitled "The Wealth of Nations."

This covers the whole field of economics; the product of labour and its distribution, the employment of stock, the progress of the different nations in wealth, and systems of political economy. It dealt with the work, trade and income of a nation as a science and not a haphazard sort of thing that just happened. Some of his ideas are no longer applicable as circumstances have changed, but even to-day this book forms the starting-point of the study of political economy.

The Theory of Evolution

Adam Smith died in 1790, and England had not then become a great industrial nation. It was in the nineteenth century, with the coming of the steam-engine, that the great industrial revolution began. Factories began to be built, and more and more coal was needed, the mills of Yorkshire and Lancashire caused towns to grow where before there had been merely villages.

It was during this period that two great thinkers wrote and lectured in Great Britain. Of Charles Darwin it has been said that his theories and views have had more effect on human thought than any other man, with the exception, perhaps, of Sir Isaac Newton. The story of Darwin's voyage in H.M.S. *Beagle* is told elsewhere in these volumes. As a naturalist he studied plants and animals, and in his book, " The Origin of Species," first put forward the idea that both plants and animals have " evolved "; they have become better and more adaptable during the course of the ages.

Awakening Men's Minds

He applied his theories to man himself and in another book, " The Descent of Man," endeavoured to show how at some remote period man himself had been closely related to the ape, but had slowly and gradually evolved into something far superior, and might of course attain something still greater as time went on.

His book aroused a good deal of argument, but Darwin was supported by another great thinker, Thomas Henry Huxley (1825-95) who had worked on much the same lines as Darwin. Huxley lectured not only to the scientists and learned societies, but toured the country speaking to the working classes and awakening in the minds of a far wider circle the desire to understand and reason about not merely the origin but also the ultimate aims of mankind.

He believed in freedom of thought and urged readers and listeners to rid their minds of prejudice and seek only the truth. Huxley was something more than a student, content to shut himself away from all distractions; he was anxious that others should learn, and became one of the first members of the London School Board when it was formed in 1870. He was a leader in political, social and moral reform as well as a scientist.

Mendel's Law of Breeding

Another man whose work was on similar lines to that of Darwin and Huxley was Gregor Mendel, an Austrian scientist who became a priest. Born in 1822 Mendel carried out many of his experiments in the garden of the monastery he joined when he was twenty-one. He discovered that it was possible to breed plants and animals which would not be attacked by the diseases to which their particular type had been subject.

It was Mendel who to a large extent discovered the laws in Nature which govern heredity, and it is by working in accordance with these laws that plants and animals have been improved by later workers. It was not until after his death in 1884 that the truth of many of Mendel's theories was accepted, but to-day the word " Mendelism " is used when speaking of the laws of breeding and descent first discovered by him.

The nineteenth century had many great thinkers, and the name of John Stuart Mill (1806-73) is remembered always for his famous essay, " On Liberty." Here again was a man who induced others to think for themselves. Happiness is the highest aim of human beings; not selfish happiness, but the happiness of all mankind. He was a great defender of the rights of the working classes and believed that women should have the right to vote at elections.

The name of John Ruskin (1819–1900) is not so much in the public mind to-day as it was fifty years ago, but he stands out as one of the great idealists of the Victorian era and as a man who led others to think more and more of art and beauty, not in a selfish way, but even as a guide in our moral lives. He himself inherited a large fortune, but lived on his earnings as a writer, devoting his fortune to educational and social reforms for the benefit of others.

To-day's Great Need

His best-known work is probably " Sesame and Lilies," a series of lectures he gave on reading and education, the crushing influence of industrial life on art and morality, and in general a plea for high ideals. In " Fors Clavigera " he addressed nearly a hundred letters to working-men on art, politics, trade, books, etc., written in his own vivid and sometimes magnificent prose.

All these men were concerned with teaching mankind to think, whether it was on the problem of how we came to be what we are to-day and of the process of slow change or evolution through the centuries, or whether it was about the fate and future of mankind. It was never

more necessary than it is to-day that men should think clearly and carefully. That great leader of the nation, Sir Winston Churchill, summed it up in an essay he wrote some years before the Second World War came upon us:—

" The busy hands of the scientist are already fumbling with the keys of all chambers hitherto forbidden to mankind. Without an equal growth of mercy, pity, peace and love, science herself may destroy all that makes human life majestic and tolerable."

Science has brought and will continue to bring many great gifts for the service of mankind. But it is essential that with this progress in scientific knowledge there should be equal progress in our capacity to use it wisely and for the good of humanity.

Rischgitz.

THOMAS HENRY HUXLEY

This English man of science, who lived from 1825 to 1895, was one of the greatest supporters of Darwin's theory of the evolution of plants and animals; that is, their gradual change in the course of ages to meet changing needs and conditions. Huxley's ruling passion was the search for absolute truth, whatever it might cost the seeker.

ELECTRICITY AND MODERN SCIENCE

Rischgitz.

MICHAEL FARADAY LECTURING AT THE ROYAL INSTITUTION

The Royal Institution, in Albemarle Street, London, has been the scene of lectures on scientific subjects for nearly 150 years, but none of the lectures delivered there has attracted more enthusiastic audiences than those of Michael Faraday, the English chemist and electrician. The picture seen above shows among Faraday's listeners the Prince Consort, who is facing the lecturer. The subject of Faraday's discourse on this particular occasion was evidently chemistry.

AS we have seen, most of the great inventions and discoveries made by scientists have been brought about by the work of several men, each succeeding experimenter carrying the work a stage further. In the reign of Queen Elizabeth, William Gilbert gave demonstrations of what he had christened " electricity." Gilbert might justly be called the father of electricity.

Other scientists of whom we have already read, Boyle and Newton, for example, helped to extend the knowledge of this subject. In America, Benjamin Franklin carried out a number of experiments, and his work led to the invention of the lightning conductor in 1749.

In Italy a professor of anatomy at Bologna University, Luigi Galvani (1737–98) made a curious discovery when dissecting a dead frog. He published a book on " The Force of Electricity in Muscular Movement." His theories were not by any means correct, but other experimenters had to discover this. Galvani's name is still commemorated in " galvanism " and other words derived from it.

Volt and Ampere

Another Italian professor, Count Alessandro Volta, made considerable progress in his experiments and was the first to construct a voltaic battery; in the word " volt " his contribution to discoveries in electricity is permanently commemorated. Others followed up Volta's discoveries, among them a Danish scientist, Hans Christian Oersted (1777–1851). During his experiments in 1819 he found out that a magnetic needle was deflected by a current in a wire passing below or over it. It was the beginning of electro-magnetism and the starting-point of the electric telegraph.

André Marie Ampère (1775–1836) added considerably to our knowledge of the connection between electricity and magnetism; he worked out the theory of electro-dynamics and laid down the laws which govern the science of electricity in motion. His

ELECTRICITY AND A FROG

Specially drawn for this work.

While dissecting a dead frog in his room one day, the Italian scientist, Luigi Aloisio Galvani (1737–1798), noticed that its muscles twitched when touched with his knives. Later on, he discovered the movements to be caused by electricity, though he thought that some kind of fluid passed through the muscles when they were electrified. This kind of twitching was called after him, " galvanism." We owe to his name also the words " galvanic " and " galvanise."

name, too, is perpetuated in the word " ampere." About this time G. S. Ohm published his work on the connection between current strength in a conducting wire and electromotive force. The word " ohm " has taken its place with " volt " and " ampere " among well-known electrical terms.

It was Michael Faraday, however, who made the greatest strides of all in our knowledge of electricity, and even to-day some of the pointers he gave are being followed up by investigators. Faraday was the son of a blacksmith and was born in 1791. He was apprenticed to a bookseller and was noticed by Sir Humphry Davy, a visitor to the shop, who was surprised to see the youth reading a scientific work.

How Wireless Began

As a result Davy took the youngster into his laboratory as an assistant. At first, Faraday's work was connected with chlorine, and he made certain valuable discoveries in this field. In addition he discovered new kinds of optical glass and this led to important investigations in electricity. His lectures attracted great attention, but never interfered with his work. There is no doubt that he was one of the most brilliant scientific investigators ever known, and to him must be given credit for the solid foundation on which our knowledge of electricity is based.

Another great British scientist, James Clerk-Maxwell (1831–79) carried on the work Faraday had begun, and. in 1873 he published his important work, " A Treatise on Electricity and Magnetism." He discovered the similarity between light rays and electrical vibrations, and it was his theories and discoveries in this connection which may be said to mark the beginning of wireless investigations.

William Thomson, better known as Lord Kelvin, was born in 1824 and was eighty-three when he died. He has deservedly been called the Grand Old Man of electrical science. Quite early in his career he published papers involving difficult mathematical research

" The Times."

AN HISTORIC MAGNET

Things that have been used by great men acquire a special interest. This very crude electro-magnet is treasured because it was made for Faraday, in 1845, for some of his famous experiments. The photograph proves clearly enough that in those days the construction of electro-magnets was in its early infancy.

THE FIRST ELECTRICAL BATTERY

Specially drawn for this work.

Count Alessandro Volta (1745–1827) was a fellow-countryman of Galvani's. To him belongs the honour of having first discovered how to produce a steady electric current by chemical means. Our picture shows him making sparks by touching together the ends of two wires connected with the poles of a contrivance of his own invention, named after him the Voltaic pile. This consisted of a pile of alternate copper and zinc discs, with a pad between each pair.

and was only twenty-two when he was appointed professor of natural philosophy at Glasgow, a position he held for fifty-three years.

Kelvin's Many Inventions

At first he was chiefly interested in thermodynamics, the science which deals with the relation between heat and work, in which, as we have read, James Joule did so much valuable work. But in 1854 Kelvin published a famous paper " On the Theory of the Electric Telegraph," and in 1857 took a leading part in laying the first Atlantic submarine cable.

It would take many pages to set forth a record of all that Lord Kelvin accomplished in his long life. He propounded the most difficult theories on such subjects as the Wave Theory of Light and on Vortex Atoms, but went beyond the mere theory and showed how they could be used in a practical manner. Over sixty inventions bear his name.

Another great name in the history of electricity is that of William Crookes, later Sir William, who was born in 1832, when the stage-coach was still the chief means of travel, and lived until 1919 when electric trains had long ceased to be a novelty and wireless was on the eve of becoming one of the recognised necessities of everyday life.

Electro-Magnetic Waves

Crookes discovered the rare metallic element Thallium and devoted a great deal of time to the investigation of radium. It was largely due to his work that X-rays were discovered by Röntgen, the story of which is told in another volume.

Crookes was a practical man as well as an investigator who put forward theories on which others could work. He wrote on the manufacture of beet sugar, a practical handbook on Dyeing and Calico-printing, and invented an eye-preserving glass for spectacles.

In the history of wireless or radio it would be impossible to omit the name of Heinrich Hertz (1857–94) who became keenly interested in the theories which James Clerk-Maxwell had written about electro-magnetic waves. The practical results he obtained were set forth in his writings, and the waves which he explained were known as Hertzian waves. Their importance cannot be exaggerated, since modern wireless communication is based upon them.

A young Italian, Guglielmo Marconi, born in 1874, became keenly interested, and when scarcely more than a boy made experiments in his father's garden in his attempts to send out wireless waves. In 1895–6 he carried his experiments still further, and in 1897 submitted his inventions to the British Government.

Turning the Knob

That was the real beginning of practical wireless as we know it to-day. The Marconi Wireless Telegraph Company was founded and in 1899 signals were transmitted across the English Channel. Improvements were made, and in 1901 communication was established between Cornwall and Newfoundland. One of Marconi's inventions in 1910 was a new valve receiver, and the next year wireless apparatus was installed in large ocean-going liners.

Meantime other men had been at work on these problems. Oliver Lodge, a professor of physics at Liverpool University, was making experiments on similar lines. One of his discoveries was a method whereby wireless messages could be sorted out so that one wireless station could signal to another without getting mixed up with a third station. He called this " tuning," and to-day we can " tune in " to different stations merely by turning a knob on our set.

Even so, wireless would not have become as it is to-day, an almost essential equipment in every home, if it had not been for the work of Sir

Specially drawn for this work.

This picture shows us Michael Faraday working as a young man in the laboratory of Sir Humphry Davy, the great chemist, who is seen standing behind him examining the contents of a test-tube. Like many another great man, Faraday had to begin right at the bottom of the ladder. Before his death he had reached the very top of it. More than a hundred years have passed since Faraday's greatest discovery—the true relation between electricity and magnetism.

J. F. Corrigan.

A MYSTERIOUS LITTLE MOTOR

This little device, which may sometimes be seen revolving in a
sunny shop window, is called a radiometer. It was invented
by Sir William Crookes. Four metal vanes, silvered on one side
and blackened on the other, are mounted on a spindle inside a
bulb from which air has been almost completely exhausted.
When exposed to light or heat the vanes revolve, bright sides
leading, showing motion caused by light.

Other scientists
improved the valves,
and broadcasting, as
distinct from wireless
communication, came
into existence as a
practical proposition
about 1920. The first
broadcast concert in
Great Britain was given
in July, 1922. Since
that date remarkable
developments have
taken place, and with
the coming of television
it is certain that wire-
less will have, and is
indeed already having,
a profound effect on
the lives of individuals
and of nations.

There have been
many other develop-
ments in the sphere of
electricity since the
days when those early
experimenters set forth
their theories. Tele-
vision and broadcasting
are described in another
volume; so, too, is the
development in another
branch of electricity, its
application to lighting.
It was not till 1880
that electric lighting
became a possibility
in the home, and even
to-day there are still
villages in our country
where the paraffin
lamp is the sole means
of artificial lighting.

Ambrose Fleming (1849–1945) who,
after being a University lecturer, became electrical engineer to one of the
big Edison companies. It was Ambrose
Fleming who invented the thermionic
valve which opened up a wider sphere
to wireless. No longer was it merely a
case of sending signals in the Morse
code; it became possible to transmit
the human voice.

There is little doubt that in the next
few years there will be no place in
Britain where it will be impossible to
connect up with the electric power
supply. In recent years we have made
greater use of water-power.

In offices and factories fluorescent
lighting has represented a big stride
forward in the science of illumination,

L.E.A.

This Grand Old Man of electrical science, Lord Kelvin, whose portrait you see above, began life as plain William Thomson. He was raised to the peerage in 1892, with the title of Baron Kelvin of Largs, in recognition of the great work that he had done in the field of electrical science. Among the scores of things invented by him may be mentioned especially the mirror galvanometer and siphon recorder, used for receiving messages sent through submarine cables, and his improved magnetic ship's compass (on which he is seen leaning).

and elsewhere in these volumes will be found a fuller description of this advance. Another type of lighting is due to the discovery by Sir William Ramsay (1852–1916) of a new element which he called Neon. By the use of this element neon lights possess a fog-penetrating quality which in these days of aeroplanes and fast-moving cars is of the greatest advantage.

The mention of fog is a reminder that despite our many inventions and our harnessing of the forces of Nature we are not yet able to control the weather. Science, however, has helped us very considerably in learning how to anticipate and forecast what the weather is likely to be. It is a long time since John Dalton made his regular observa-

tions concerning the weather, but most text-books on Meteorology quote Dalton's law as one of the bases on which the science has been built up.

Meteorology is of the utmost importance in aviation, and the " Met. Section " in the R.A.F. is one of the essential services on every airfield.

War's Aid to Peace

It is ironical in some ways that war, which is so largely concerned with the destruction of human life, should also be the means of bringing forth discoveries, inventions and improvements which are of immense value to mankind in peace. In medical science this has often been particularly true, and some

Post Office.

THE WIRELESS OPERATOR ON BOARD SHIP

Probably in no sphere of human activity has wireless been of greater value than on ships at sea. At the beginning of the present century there was no means of keeping in touch with a vessel once she was out of range of visual signals. To-day wireless is an essential part of the equipment of every ocean-going vessel. In this photograph is shown the wireless cabin on board ship.

PROFESSOR ANDRADE GIVES A DEMONSTRATION

Photo Press.

Perhaps the reader has been fortunate enough to attend lectures given at Christmas-time to young people at the Royal Institution by our leading scientists. However great may be their reputation, they put their knowledge willingly at the disposal of youthful listeners. Here you see Professor E. N. da C. Andrade talking to an audience which is as much interested in his explanations as he evidently is pleased to be giving them.

aspects of this are dealt with in a later chapter.

Wireless made great progress during the war of 1914–18, and even greater advances were made during the Second World War of 1939–45. Radar, for example, has proved of great value for the navigation of ships and of aircraft at night, or in foggy and cloudy weather.

It would be impossible to mention all the scientists who have contributed to the success of Radar, but men such as Sir Edward Appleton, Sir Henry Tizard, Professor E. V. Hill and Professor Patrick Blackett, working on ideas produced by Sir Robert Watson-Watt, were among the chief " Boffins " (as the Radar scientists were called) who, from the first experiment in 1924,

brought the invention to its present high state of perfection.

New Radio Layers

In the world of wireless as it affects us who sit by our receiving sets at home more remarkable progress has been made. Much work has been done in the investigation of " radio-layers " high above the earth. A new layer, 130 miles high, was discovered by Sir Edward Appleton. The Appleton layer has improved long-distance communications considerably.

A world survey has been made of the electrical strength of the Appleton and Heaviside layers in order to gain a better understanding of the reflecting powers of these layers. There was, too, an Eclipse Committee of scientists to study the 1945 eclipse of the sun from the point of view of its effect on wireless communication.

Engineering, too, has made great strides in many ways, and some of these are described in the chapter on Modern Inventions and Discoveries.

Team Work in Science

From the time when John Dalton propounded his theories of which we have read earlier, other men have studied his Atomic Theory and added greatly to the scientists' knowledge. Among them was Lord Rutherford (1871–1937) whose brilliant researches on the ultimate constitution of matter earned him a foremost place among the world's scientists. For his work on radio-activity Rutherford received many honours, and his discoveries concerning the atom have been the basis on which a large body of scientists worked during the war.

If the ordinary man as well as the scientist deplored the fact that the first use of the tremendous energy stored in the atom was made to destroy a city, there came, too, the knowledge that the end of the Second World War had come into sight more rapidly than we dared hope, and that great possibilities lay before mankind to abolish war for ever. Surely mankind has not progressed so far that he can solve the most tremendous secrets of Nature and yet still lack the intelligence to settle his petty disputes without destroying himself and the civilisation he has so painfully acquired?

Already the scientists are at work investigating and experimenting with this new power to find ways and means of converting it to useful and beneficial ends instead of purely destructive purposes. To-day our scientists no longer work as they did in days gone by, as lone seekers after new knowledge. In most cases they work as a team, exchanging knowledge with each other.

In this short review it is not possible to tell of all the great men who have contributed to human knowledge in the past fifty years or so. Sir William Bragg, who died in 1942, and his equally famous son, Sir Lawrence Bragg, have earned high place by their discoveries relating to X-rays, crystals and radio-activity. Lord Rayleigh (1842–1919) was responsible to some extent for Sir William Ramsay's discoveries of the gases argon, neon, krypton and xenon. Men such as Professor E. N. da C. Andrade have not only made valuable contributions to scientific knowledge by their own research work, but have also helped others to understand by their lectures, broadcast talks and writings.

Time and Space

Sir Arthur S. Eddington (1882–1944) was one of the most brilliant mathematicians and astronomers ever known, yet in the books he wrote he was able to impart his knowledge to the ordinary intelligent man as well as to his fellow-scientists. It has been said of Eddington that he was the only man capable of explaining to others the theories and discoveries of the famous Professor Albert Einstein on Time and Space.

Einstein was born in Germany in 1879, but for a number of years has lived in America where he is a permanent member of the Institute for Advanced Study at Princeton, N.J. There are many scientists who place Einstein on the same level as Newton as a discoverer of new truths which will profoundly affect the lives of all of us as we learn to understand them.

All these men have opened up new worlds of knowledge for the use of mankind. That is the purpose of the scientist. It is for others, the ordinary man of business as well as the statesman, and even more so for the boys and girls now acquiring knowledge as they approach maturity, to see that we make wise use of the great gifts the scientist brings to us.

THE FIGHT FOR GOOD HEALTH

Copyright, Wellcome Historical Medical Museum.

THE " FATHER OF MEDICINE " GIVES A LECTURE

Hippocrates (460–377 B.C.) was the first man to attack disease and illness in a commonsense way. Previously, medical treatment and religion had been linked together, to the great profit of the priests. Hippocrates, who is here seen lecturing his students under a plane-tree in his native island of Cos, taught that proper food and Nature's healing powers are two very good doctors, and that the treatment of a disease should be based on the nature of the disease itself.

IN that most important branch of Science which deals with the care and cure of our bodily ills, progress seems to have been slow and uncertain through the centuries until about a hundred years ago. There had been advances, it is true, but some of the root causes of disease and human suffering in a bodily sense had not become known.

Hippocrates, a Greek physician who lived between 460 and 377 B.C., is generally called the Father of Medicine. He was a member of a family of physicians, the Asclepiadæ, so called after the Greek and Roman god Æsculapius, the god of medicine. It is the symbol of this god, a staff with a serpent twined around it, which is to-day the badge of the Royal Army Medical Corps. Hippocrates treated disease with due regard to natural laws, giving simple remedies, and was probably the first to realise the value of diet as an aid to medicine.

Some of his writings can still be read to-day, and our modern doctors take the oath of Hippocrates when they become members of the profession.

The next medical man who wrote on the knowledge of his day was Galen, another Greek physician (A.D. 130–200), and he did much to help the limited development of medicine in his time. Some hundreds of years were to pass, however, before William Harvey, of whom we have already read, published his book on the circulation of the blood, in 1628.

Improvements in Surgery

It was just a century after that date when John Hunter was born, and it is on record that he acquired his wonderful manual dexterity while working as a cabinet-maker in his early years. Later he studied surgery, and became assistant to his brother William, also a surgeon. Hunter did a great deal to increase the doctor's knowledge of anatomy and by his skill as a surgeon brought about many improvements in the methods then in vogue.

One of Hunter's pupils in London was Edward Jenner (1749–1823), who later returned to the town in which he was born, Berkeley, Gloucestershire, where he practised as a doctor. Here he made his first studies into the problem of smallpox, a disease very prevalent in those days. As a result of this he made his first inoculation in May, 1796, and was able to show that the boy who had been vaccinated was immune from the disease.

There was at first a good deal of opposition, but Jenner's belief in vaccination gained steady support. In 1802 Parliament voted him £10,000 and four years later £20,000, practically all of which went towards furthering the cause in which he believed.

In some ways both surgery and

medicine made good progress during the first half of the nineteenth century, yet if one goes back to 1850 and compares conditions in that year with those of to-day there comes the feeling that it is in this past century that medical science (with other sciences) has leapt miles forward compared with the slow and painful inches gained during previous centuries.

It scarcely sounds like an epoch-making discovery to say that one of the greatest truths that became known in the latter half of the last century was that dirt was dangerous. Yet that is a simple way of stating a great fact. To-day all of us know quite a lot about germs and microbes, and if we cut a finger the first thing we are anxious to avoid is the risk of getting dirt into the wound. Acts of Parliament have been passed and all sorts of precautions are taken to ensure that

James's Press.

PASTEUR IN HIS SURGERY

Pasteur first defeated the ferments which cause trouble in the making of wine and beer. He then dealt with the terrible disease called anthrax, which had scourged cattle and sheep. Encouraged by his success, he next gave his attention to the dreadful malady named rabies, or hydrophobia, which affects animals and people bitten by animals already suffering from it. This picture shows us Pasteur in his surgery at Paris, to which patients flocked from all parts of the world to be " inoculated " by him.

JOHN HUNTER

Famous British surgeon and anatomist who began practice in 1763 and became a pioneer in improved methods of surgery. His collection of specimens is preserved by the Royal College of Surgeons.

EDWARD JENNER

An English doctor, and the discoverer of vaccination, Jenner studied under John Hunter in London, then returned to his native Gloucestershire where he made his first inoculation in 1796.

our food is kept free from dirt and that it shall not be sold if it has become tainted in any way.

But in 1845 there was no scientific justification for the idea that there was any connection between dirt and disease. Here and there a few doctors were beginning to suspect that the number of deaths after operations were due to uncleanliness. To-day every doctor is extremely careful to ensure that his instruments are absolutely clean, not merely from the dirt one can see with the naked eye but from all unseen germs as well.

There was one doctor in Vienna who had some ideas on this subject as far back as 1840, and he made his students at the hospital wash their hands with a solution of chloride of lime before going from one operation to another. The head of the hospital dismissed the fussy doctor even though he had been able to reduce the deaths after operations very considerably. The dismissed doctor, Semmelweiss, wrote a book about the subject of dirt, but nobody took much notice of it.

In America a famous author, Oliver Wendell Holmes, also wrote a book saying that dirt was dangerous. In England and the Crimea that great woman Florence Nightingale began a new era in nursing by her insistence on the need for cleanliness. She knew nothing at that time of the reasons why dirt was dangerous, and although people had ideas about catching certain diseases from other people there was no real belief in the danger of contagion.

Florence Nightingale was indeed very doubtful about contagion, but she certainly believed that dirt caused disease. There was no germ-theory about disease and therefore no ideas about killing the germs or preventing them from spreading. But in Paris a French chemist, Louis Pasteur, was carrying out experiments to find out why milk, wine and beer turned sour. It was through these experiments that Pasteur discovered that certain organisms called microbes found their way into the liquids from the air.

Pasteur made the further discovery that when a person is bitten by a mad dog certain microbes enter the blood of the person who has been bitten. The idea that the dreaded disease of hydrophobia was caused by these microbes was regarded by nearly everybody as too ridiculous to discuss. Pasteur, however, carried on with his theories and inoculated with other microbes a boy who had been bitten.

The experiment was successful and Pasteur carried on with his work. His theories about microbes, some good and some harmful, became known, and one man in England, who had already spent much time studying the subject of why the blood so often became poisoned after an operation, was quick to realise that here was one answer to his problem. That man was Joseph Lister (1827–1912) whose name is known throughout the world as Lord Lister, the father of antiseptic surgery, one of the greatest blessings ever given to mankind.

Lister took his medical degree in London in 1852 and became professor of surgery at Glasgow in 1860. Lister was appalled by the conditions under which surgeons had to do their work in those days when even the most trivial operation was liable to have a fatal ending.

Reading all about Pasteur's discovery, Lister realised that the big task of surgeons was to prevent these dangerous microbes from getting into wounds. The microbes must be killed before they had a chance of getting into the body. In the beginning he used carbolic and insisted on absolute cleanliness : instruments, dressings, hands that touched them, and even the operating theatre itself must be absolutely clean in the surgical sense. Everything was treated with carbolic.

His success with these new methods was dramatic. It was useless for critics to sneer when Lister could point to results, and a revolution had come about in surgery. The methods have been steadily improved since that day, and Lister himself, ever ready to consider any possible improvement on his methods, continued to experiment. He substituted for the antiseptic method, which killed the microbes, the aseptic method which aimed at keeping the microbes away altogether.

To-day the modern surgeon, in his mask, gown and gloves, follows in the direction Lister indicated ; in air-conditioned operating theatres with all dressings, instruments, gloves and gowns sterilised with heat before being brought into use there is no chance of any stray microbe entering the wound the skilled surgeon makes. Carbolic is no longer used because it had disadvantages, but in its day it helped a great deal.

First Use of Anæsthetics

There was another discovery of tremendous importance to doctors and sufferers, and we have to go back again to the middle of last century to realise the importance of what we now call anæsthetics, a word derived from a Greek work meaning insensible. When we go to the dentist to-day he may give us " gas " or may use a local anæsthetic. In any case he can take out a tooth without causing us any pain, thanks to the anæsthetic.

Until 1845 any operation, whether it was merely extracting a tooth or a major surgical operation, had to be carried out without any such aid to

Henri Manuel.

This photograph of the French chemist, Louis Pasteur (1822–1895), shows you a man to whom humanity owes a vast debt. As a result of long study he discovered that tiny living organisms, called ferments, bacteria and bacilli, are the causes of diseases in plants, animals and human beings. He also discovered ways of defeating these tiny enemies.

insensibility to pain as an anæsthetic. Humphry Davy had discovered laughing-gas, otherwise nitrous oxide, a long time before, and his pupil Faraday had found out forty years later that ether had a similar effect to that produced by laughing-gas. Like Davy, he suggested that pain might be abolished by its use.

Nobody took much notice of these suggestions at the time, but somewhere about 1840 two or three American doctors and dentists tried both gas and ether, though considerable improvements had to be made in the method of administering these before they could be regarded as reasonably safe.

In Edinburgh, James Young Simpson, professor of medicine at the University, also tried ether, but it was not too successful as it was slow and irritated the lungs. Simpson was a man of remarkable courage who dared to experiment on himself, and he inhaled the vapours of several different drugs to find out just how they acted. A chemist recommended him to try chloroform which had been discovered by Liebig some sixteen years before 1847, the year in which Professor Simpson tried it.

As a result of that experiment Simpson introduced chloroform into his own practice and to the medical profession. There was opposition, but the possibilities were too great for it to be pushed into the background again. Until then the surgeon had had to concentrate on speed when he carried out an operation; with an anæsthetic he had time to carry out his work with much more care.

Simpson was the founder of a new order in surgery and in 1866 his work was publicly recognised when he was made a baronet, four years before he died.

James's Press.

IN THE PASTEUR INSTITUTE, PARIS

In this laboratory microbes causing certain diseases are " cultivated " to produce liquids called vaccines.   A person suffering from, say, diphtheria is inoculated with diphtheria vaccine by having a small quantity of it injected into a vein.   This vaccine fights and overcomes the living microbes in the patient.   Pasteur Institutes are now to be found in many parts of the world.

There have been many improvements in anæsthetics since Simpson's day. In recent years a good deal of attention has been given to the application of certain drugs at the actual point to be operated upon. This method of giving a local anæsthetic has been entirely successful.

It will be seen that a very great revolution took place in medicine and surgery during the latter half of the nineteenth century : the discovery of anæsthetics and how to use them, combined with the further discovery of the germ-theory in relation to disease, followed by the introduction of antiseptic and aseptic methods.

Bacteria and Microbes

By the year 1880 it may be said that the germ-theory of infectious disease had become fully recognised. Pasteur with his treatment for the cure of hydrophobia by inoculating the person with other material containing the rabies germ in a weakened form, led the way for Lister to introduce his antiseptic and aseptic surgery. In a way, it might be said that Jenner had discovered much the same principles as Pasteur, but it was not thought that the idea of vaccination or inoculation could be applied to other diseases, and nobody had really established any theory about microbes or germs. Here again, however, it would not be strictly correct to say that earlier scientists had done nothing in this direction. A man named Kircher (1601–80), using a primitive magnifying apparatus, had discovered " minute living worms," as he called them, in decomposing meat and milk.

Then a Dutchman, Leeuwenhoek, in 1683 wrote to the Royal Society in London about certain observations he had made, and a Viennese physician in 1762 had the idea that infectious diseases were caused by a living microbe. But it remained for Pasteur to bring these odd notions to a practical shape, and he may be regarded as the

LORD LISTER   *Rischgitz.*

Joseph Lister (1827–1912) carried out investigations on the theories put forward by Pasteur. As a result Lister introduced the use of antiseptics and brought about one of the greatest advances in modern surgery.

founder of the modern science of Bacteriology.

Once the theories of Pasteur and Lister were understood, bacteriology became an important subject, sometimes called Microbiology, the science which deals with the study of bacteria and microbes. Not only in the fields of preventive and curative medicine, but in many commercial processes also, the science has been of tremendous importance and is being more and more generally used in industry.

Its industrial developments, however, are a different story. Here we are concerned only with the progress the science has made in connection with the prevention and cure of our bodily ailments. The war against dirt in all its forms still goes on, but the scientist has gained the upper hand and made further great advances within the past few years.

Henri Manuel.

THE FIRST GREAT WOMAN SCIENTIST

Madame Curie, the Polish wife of a Frenchman, Professor Curie, of Paris, shared with her husband the honour of discovering the marvellous element named by them radium. Their great discovery was made in 1898. This photograph shows us Madame Curie in her laboratory at the Sorbonne, Paris, where she succeeded her husband as Professor of Chemistry. She died in 1934.

CERTAIN discoveries were made towards the close of the nineteenth century and at the beginning of this present century which scarcely came within the sphere of medical science and yet have proved of immense value to the surgeon and the doctor.

X-rays were discovered by Röntgen in 1895 while making experiments in passing high-voltage electric currents through Crookes' tubes. Gradually, as the apparatus for making use of these rays was evolved, the possibility of their use as an aid in medical science was thoroughly explored. Photographs and the story of X-rays appear elsewhere in these volumes, but it is necessary to mention them here in order to have a complete picture of what the medical man has at his service to-day.

X-rays are of incalculable value in medical diagnosis, particularly in locating foreign bodies and detecting fractures and dislocations. With their aid the doctor can discover just what happens in the digestive organs, or identify the signs of disease in the lungs and other parts of the body.

Another great discovery came as the result of experiments carried out by Professor Curie and his wife between 1898 and 1902. They found a new metal called radium which had certain electric properties. To obtain even the smallest quantity of radium many tons of pitchblende are required. Professor Curie was accidentally killed in Paris in 1906, but his wife was appointed to his professorship and continued the experiments. She was awarded the Nobel prize in 1911, and by that date many other scientists had made further discoveries concerning radium. Madame Curie died in 1934.

To-day radium is extensively used by the medical profession. The substance itself is still exceedingly rare, and in both Great Britain and the U.S.A. there are Radium Institutes for dealing with the supply of the element, for research, and medical treatment. It is another weapon in the doctor's armoury with which he fights disease.

Importance of Vitamins

Science, as we have seen, is continually seeking fresh worlds to conquer, yet it still pursues its investigations into some of the very earliest problems that confronted mankind. Hippocrates, as we have noted, paid attention to the diet of his patients, and without much aid of a scientific nature there is no doubt that through the ages doctors have observed that certain foods produced beneficial effects. Even sailors such as Lord Anson discovered that green vegetables were necessary in diet if diseases which

attacked the seamen of his day, such as scurvy, were to be avoided.

But it was not until about 1880 that anything in the nature of a scientific study of diet was made, and after 1900 the subject was studied extensively. In 1912 Sir Frederick Gowland Hopkins, by experiments on rats, discovered what he called " accessory food factors," nowadays referred to as Vitamins. Many chapters and indeed many books have been written on this subject of diet in recent years, but it is only necessary to mention it here as one of the important details in the modern doctor's methods of preventing and curing certain ills. Science has given us within the space of the past fifty years a sound knowledge of what food we require to keep us in good health and able to resist disease.

The doctors' interest, however, must

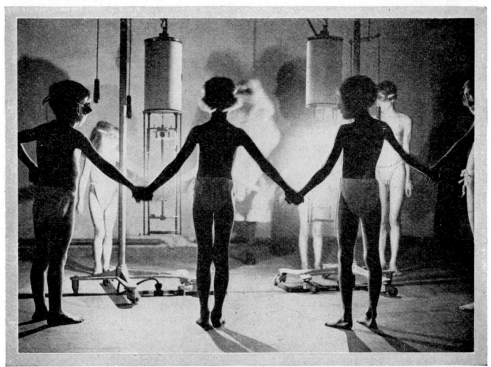

Fox Photos.

ARTIFICIAL SUNLIGHT AIDS THE DOCTOR

The beneficial effect of sunshine on the human body has been realised for centuries, but in the British Isles the sun's rays are all too frequently unseen and unfelt. Science can now produce rays of the same character as sunshine itself and our picture shows children in a modern clinic taking a sun ray bath to cure their ailments and restore them to good health.

still be in drugs that cure diseases, though it would be an unbalanced and unfair picture if nothing were mentioned about the work medical science has done in preventing disease. The war against dirt, in which is included personal cleanliness, proper sanitation, the prevention of contamination of our food by flies and other dirt-carrying insects, as well as germ-killing disinfectants, has gone on.

It is in the realm of bacteriology that medical science has made its greatest strides in recent years. Robert Koch (1843–1910) worked on much the same lines as Pasteur. In 1882 he was able to announce the discovery of the tubercle bacillus, and some years later he discovered tuberculin as an antidote. At the time it was believed that this was the certain cure for tuberculosis, but unfortunately it has scarcely fulfilled its first promise.

Drug versus Disease

Nevertheless Koch did much valuable work, and in 1905 was awarded the Nobel prize for medicine. If Koch failed to achieve all that he hoped, he showed the way to other men, especially in that branch of treatment which is known as chemotherapy. This aims at maintaining in the body for a considerable period a concentration of the right sort of drug to destroy any disease organisms.

Other investigators have followed different lines of investigation. Take the case of a young Canadian doctor, Frederick Grant Banting, born in 1890. He devoted his energies to medical research under the Canadian Federal Research Board.

Banting was the leader of a band of research workers who carried out long and patient experiments to find a cure for diabetes, and in 1922 it was announced that in co-operation with Professor Macleod and others he had discovered the cure. To the extract of the tissues of the pancreas of oxen, pigs or sheep they gave the name of Insulin. To-day thousands of sufferers from diabetes are alive and carrying on their work owing to the fact that they are receiving injections of insulin.

The Nobel prize for medicine was awarded to Banting and MacLeod in 1923, and Banting was knighted. The patent rights in insulin were presented to Toronto University which, in its turn, gave the British patents to the Medical Research Council. Sir Frederick Banting lost his life in an air accident in 1941.

Sometimes a great discovery is made almost by accident, though it would scarcely be fair in many cases to speak of the final result as accidental. Professor Alexander Fleming, working in his laboratory at St. Mary's Hospital, London, made one such discovery in that way and the outcome was penicillin, dealt with more fully in the section on Modern Inventions and Discoveries.

Medical science is making rapid progress, particularly in the field of dealing with infection and the diseases arising from all the different kinds of harmful microbes. There are still several serious infectious diseases against which there are as yet no effective weapons. It is highly probable that the branch of bacteriology which is known as chemotherapy will find the answers to the problems still remaining.

In surgery progress has been steady if not spectacular since Lister made his great discovery and improved surgical practice to an immeasurable degree. Instruments have been improved and new inventions have appeared.

A century ago the thermometer was scarcely ever used by doctors, though it had been known long years before. It was not until about 1866 that the doctor began to use it, and in 1868 the neat little clinical thermometer began to be made.

Electricity has come to the doctor's aid in many ways. The heart-motions can be accurately measured and so can the blood-pressure. Ultra-violet and infra-red rays are used for nerve and muscle complaints.

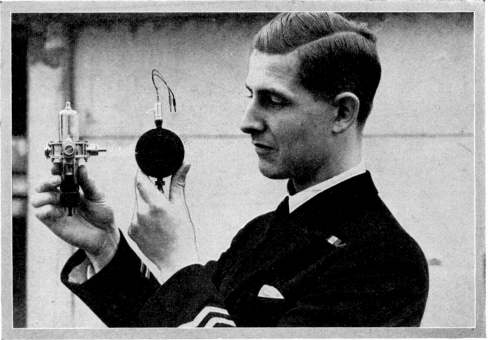

Fox Photos.

VALVES THAT WON A BATTLE

In the Royal Navy Radar played just as decisive a part as in the great victories of the R.A.F.
over the Luftwaffe. As we won air supremacy, so did the Royal Navy, largely with the aid of
these two tiny valves, the Sutton Tube on the left and the Magnetron transmitting valve on the
right, eventually win the long-drawn-out Battle of the Atlantic.

WAR is an evil. Yet it has its lessons just as it has its great stories of courage and sacrifice. If it destroys and brings ruin to lands and nations, it may also leave a legacy of beneficial inventions and discoveries for the days of peace. Wireless existed before the war of 1914–18, but its development was pushed forward very considerably owing to its usefulness in war, just as aircraft made big advances in design and speed during the same period.

Echo and the Magic Eye

In the war of 1939–45 both wireless and aircraft again made swift advances. The jet-propelled aeroplane came into being and was in actual use before the war ended. Wireless developed in several ways, and the story of radio-location or RADAR, meaning radio detection and range-finding, is a modern version of a fairy-tale, "The Magic Eye," and one that came true.

In 1933 the staff officers of the Royal Air Force were worried over the problem of detecting the approach of aircraft from a distance and of following the aircraft's course at night or in cloudy weather. The Air Ministry called on the scientists to help them and experiments began.

The first discovery they made was that by sending out high-powered radio signals they could detect objects on the sea or in the air by an "echo" which came back. The echo was converted by the scientists into a pattern of light on a cathode-ray tube.

Within six months or so after the experiments really began in 1934, the scientists were able to detect aircraft fifteen miles away. The big idea had

Fox Photos.

A RADAR AERIAL

The most powerful Radar transmitter in the world was used by the Royal Navy during the war, and our photograph shows the aerial of this Metre Band Long Range Warning set which was used both for transmitting and receiving.

been found, and after that it was a question of more and more experiments to improve on their early methods. New valves were invented which gave powers beyond anything attained before.

The men who carried out these experiments worked in absolute secrecy. Their first station in 1935 was at Orford, Suffolk, and by 1936 five radio-location stations had been set up on the East Coast. The scientists moved in that same year to Bawdsey Manor, and later Malvern College became the headquarters of the " Boffins," as the R.A.F. christened the scientists who were responsible for this amazing new device which was presently being fitted to some of their machines.

Radio-location was the name first used, and then for a time RDF, meaning radio detection and finding. By 1943, however, the word Radar, used in the U.S. Navy for radio detection and ranging, was officially adopted. The more accurate description of Radar would be " radio direction-finding and ranging."

By September, 1938, when the threat of war to this country had become acute, Radar could detect aircraft 150 miles away. More improvements and variations were perfected. By Good Friday, 1939, a twenty-four-hour Radar watch was begun around the British coast from Scapa Flow to Portsmouth. Sir Robert Watson-Watt, the first discoverer of radio-location, with a committee led by Sir Henry Tizard, and with more than ninety leading scientists, were at work in this year developing Radar.

When war came the men who manned the Radar stations sat in darkened buildings watching their luminous maps. The position of enemy aircraft coming from the Continent was indicated immediately they came within range and long before any faint murmur of engines could be heard. Our fighters were warned and could be told just where the enemy planes were and in

P.N.A.

AFTER THE FOG HAD VANISHED

FIDO was the name given to one of the many special tasks allotted to scientists during the war. Fog, Intensive, Dispersal Operations, led to devices by which the necessary heat was provided on airfields to bring about fog dispersal. The photograph above shows a Lancaster bomber taking off from an airfield cleared of fog by the continuous line of burners installed on each side of the main runway.

what direction they were flying. It was with this invaluable aid that our pilots won the Battle of Britain against the Luftwaffe.

Radar was adapted to serve other purposes. " GCI " was ground control interception, AI—air interception—was fitted to our night fighters; IFF—identification, friend or foe—was carried by all British and then American aircraft and automatically indicated whether the aircraft many miles away was enemy or friend.

H2S was the magic eye which enabled Allied night bombers to " see " their targets on the screen before them when visibility was bad, and with its help they were able to bomb their targets accurately. ASV—air to surface vessels—made it a simple task to locate the exact position of distant submarines and surface ships.

Signals from Rebecca

On the big 1,000-bomber raids the navigational aid named GEE, which came into use early in 1942, was able to tell the pilots exactly where they were when flying a thousand miles from their base. Another development was " Rebecca Eureka ": " Rebecca " is a radar beacon which is dropped in enemy countries to enable airborne troops coming later to know just where to land when " Eureka " on their planes picks up the signals sent out by " Rebecca."

Then Radar was adapted to the ships of the Royal Navy. The great handicap of fog had been banished and the guns of a battleship could be accurately sighted on an enemy ship that could not be seen or heard. It was Radar that helped to win the Battle of Matapan, assisted in the shadowing of the German battleship *Bismarck* as well as the attack on the *Scharnhorst*, and finally brought supremacy in the long Battle of the Atlantic.

In the Army the Radar equipment known as GL (gun-laying) was a great success. During the summer of 1944 eight out of every ten flying-bombs that came within range of our guns were destroyed.

Strictly speaking Radar was a war-time invention, and it was developed and brought to a high state of perfection owing to the needs of war. But its uses in peace time are just as valuable. It is now used in commercial and civil flying and helps to ensure the safe landing of aircraft. These are among other uses to which it has been adapted :—

Airports have greater control over machines in the air and are able to identify and locate aircraft before they appear in sight. It eliminates the danger of collision in fog, improves sea-rescue work, and helps ships to locate obstacles ahead in fog or darkness.

It is possible that Radar may prove more efficient than any other system for railway signalling, and its use in motor-cars is a distinct possibility. Time will be needed to develop and adapt Radar to the many purposes already foreseen, but the scientists who accomplished such wonders in war-time have been at work, improving and adapting their discoveries for the benefit of a world at peace. New ideas about valves and their manufacture were evolved during the peak period of the demand for Radar equipment. A single Lancaster plane required over 400 valves for its equipment. Nearly 40 million valves were made in the last year of the war.

Power in the Atom

Another tremendous discovery was made towards the end of the war, and one with a far greater threat to mankind than Radar ever possessed. Radar is in the main a magic eye which enables us to see dangers ahead though darkness or fog may be all around us. But the discovery of how to split the atom and release the energy it contains was an epoch-making event, possibly as important to the future of mankind as that great discovery long centuries ago when primitive man learned how to make Fire, and learned, too, how to control it.

An atom is the smallest particle of any element of matter. There are ninety-two elements known to scientists at present: hydrogen is the lightest and uranium the heaviest to be isolated. The size of an atom is about 1-20 millionth part of an inch, and it is, of course, impossible to see it with the naked eye.

A Continual Source of Energy

Yet this tiny speck of matter is a miniature solar system in itself. The scientist speaks of the nucleus, which is the core or centre of the atom, and this nucleus contains the energy, so amazingly powerful in proportion to its size.

Over a hundred years ago John Dalton gave his theory about atoms to the scientists of his day. For a good many years afterwards other scientists experimented with the atom and made further discoveries. Röntgen by his discovery of X-rays and the Curies by their further discovery of radium added more. Rutherford and Soddy found out that atoms were undergoing transformations all the time and gave out energy while doing so.

It was with the uranium atom that the Curies experimented. This is one of the most powerful radio-active elements and contains the greatest energy. When the bonds holding the atom together are broken down, terrific electrical energy is released. Rutherford was the first to split an atom. If a whole mass of atoms could be split at the same time—a sort of chain set up whereby the instant one released its energy all the other atoms in the mass would also release theirs—the result would be a terrific explosion. If this could be

P.N.A.

PLUTO PLAYS ITS PART

To keep the advancing Allied armies on the Continent fully supplied with all the petrol needed by their vast fleets of motor-vehicles of all kinds, Pipe Lines Under The Ocean (PLUTO) were laid. In our picture can be seen some 200 miles of the three-quarter mile sections of these Hamel pipes stored in readiness for winding on Gonun, the huge drum which was towed across the Channel to lay the pipe lines.

harnessed and controlled a great new source of power would be at man's service.

In various countries scientists were at work on the many problems connected with the atom long before war broke out. They were not trying to invent a new bomb; there were all sorts of possibilities and the production of immense power was certainly among them. New elements might be discovered owing to the changes that take place when the atom is broken down under a bombardment by neutrons.

When the war came it was known that German scientists had been experimenting with the idea of producing an atomic bomb. British and American scientists teamed up and set to work to beat the enemy. The story of the further development of atomic energy is told in a later chapter. It has even been suggested that by the use of this new power we may be able to control the weather, if we plan on a world scale.

The Allied team won, though it was a long and costly struggle to wrest these further secrets from Nature.

Practical Application of Knowledge

At present some of these forecasts sound like fantastic fairy-tales, but less than 200 years ago the prophecies of men who forecast carriages without horses, ships without sails, and machines that could be flown by men high above the earth were regarded as foolish imaginings. Scientists learned how to create and how to control the explosive energy contained in petrol and similar fuels. The result was the internal combustion engine, then the motor car and aeroplane. The great problem is not to foretell the wonders the scientists may achieve in the last half of the twentieth century, but to ensure that these new discoveries will be used for the benefit and not for the destruction of mankind.

Pure science had made many discoveries about atoms and radio-activity before the stress of war compelled them to seek a new agent of destruction. From some of the discoveries already made a new science has sprung. Electronics is the application of certain aspects of the knowledge gained by studying the electrons rotating about the positive nucleus of the atom, and the science of electronics is now being used in industry.

Electricity was known to the scientists years before their knowledge was applied in a practical way. In recent years artificial lighting has made great progress. In offices and factories Fluorescent Lighting has many advantages over any other kind of artificial illumination yet known. Another type of lighting is due to the discovery by Sir William Ramsay (1852–1916) of a new element which he called Neon. By the use of this element neon lights possess a fog-penetrating quality which in these days of aeroplanes and fast-moving cars is of great advantage.

Getting Rid of Fog

Radar overcomes fog and darkness, but it still has certain limitations. It can scarcely be expected to guide an aeroplane in such a way that it can make a perfect landing on an airfield blanketed in fog, though it is quite possible that future developments may enable it to do so. Meteorology helps the airman, and the " Met. Section " of the R.A.F. is one of the essential services. Even so, it is not always possible to forecast hours in advance all of the vagaries to which our British weather is liable. Fog is obviously one of the worst enemies with which an aircraft, returning to its base after a long flight, has still to contend, and during the war a special committee of scientists was set up to study it.

" Fog, Intensive, Dispersal Opera-

tions," was the wording of the task before them, and for purposes of secrecy the initial letters formed a code word FIDO when referring to the work being done. It was successful to a very considerable extent; bomber planes, returning after a long trip, were no longer faced with desperate risks if fog had suddenly clamped down on the airfield during the hours they had been away. FIDO had found remedies, and the fog in the vicinity of the airfield can now be dispersed to a very large extent so that incoming planes are able to land in safety. The great new London Airport (Heathrow, Middlesex) had this fog dispersal equipment installed, though its use is now limited.

What Mulberry Meant

Engineers have been called upon in recent years to tackle tremendous enterprises which in normal times would be rejected as utterly impossible. When the invasion of the Continent was planned it became obvious that an attempt to make use of the ports in enemy hands would mean a terrible sacrifice of life, and very probably if we succeeded in taking the port it would by then be utterly useless.

Yet without facilities for landing the tremendous quantities of supplies necessary for such a great undertaking the invasion would be a failure. That was the apparently insoluble problem. Engineers were called in and it was determined that the impossible should become the possible. Plans were drawn; experts dealt with every phase of the complex difficulties such an undertaking presented. Piers and landing quays were ordered to be constructed secretly in this country. Later they were towed across the Channel to be erected and made secure on the enemy coast-line while the troops made their initial landings to gain control of this strip of coast from patent landing-barges. It was a wonderful case of team-work and timing.

In constructing these harbours the

P.N.A.

A " MULBERRY " PORT ON THE NORMANDY COAST

For the Allied invasion of the Continent on June 6th, 1944, two prefabricated ports, each as big as Gibraltar, were made in sections in Britain, towed across the Channel, and set down off the coast of Normandy. These Mulberry harbours, as they were called, greatly simplified the Allied supplies problem. Our photograph shows the general view of the " Mulberry " in position at Arromanches.

need for secrecy made it necessary to have a code word. If the enemy had heard even the faintest whisper about artificial harbours he would immediately have altered his whole plan of defence. There would have been no need for him to concentrate on ports, leaving long stretches of what he regarded as impossible coast-line practically undefended. That was how it came about that thousands of workmen in different parts of the country were engaged on some queer task which went under the name of MULBERRY. The vast majority of those who worked on the job had very little idea of what Mulberry meant, but neither they nor those who did know gave any hint to the outside world. Not until D-Day in June, 1944, did the secret of the Mulberry harbours become known to the world.

The " Lily " Floating Island

One of the many new devices used in connection with Mulberry har-

bours was the " Swiss Roll "—a kind of floating pier or bridge that could be rolled up, carried on board ship, and then rolled out again across the sea from ship to shore. The original idea was the invention of Petty-Officer Hamilton of the Royal Navy. The Navy took it up, and complex mathematical calculations were carried out by Mr. Herbert, an Eton housemaster. Other developments of the idea followed.

One of these developments also rejoices in a nickname " Lily " from its resemblance to a carpet of lily leaves growing on a pond. It is a floating aerodrome, an island, or a landing-strip on the sea for aircraft, and is supported on a series of hexagonal buoyancy cans. The surface is flexible but can be controlled. The pier, bridge or landing-strip is considerably lighter than the Bailey bridge, another invention of incalculable value during wartime, and one that greatly eased the task of the Royal Engineers when faced with the construction of bridges across which whole divisions could pass with their equipment. The Bailey bridge was designed by Sir Donald Coleman Bailey, knighted in 1946 for his services with the Ministry of Supply. Both the Bailey bridge and the " Lily " strip have their place in peacetime developments.

Fuel for the Invading Armies

Another engineering feat carried out in wartime was the laying of an oil pipe-line from England to the Continent at the bottom of the English Channel. The project was known to those engaged upon it, who were of course under secret orders, as PLUTO, coined from the initial letters of " Pipe Lines Under The Ocean." Without PLUTO, and its capacity to feed fuel to the Allied armies in Europe

after the invasion had been successfully made, it would have been impossible to carry out the wide and rapid advances on all fronts which staggered and eventually overwhelmed the enemy.

Behind many of these inventions and discoveries are stories of personal adventure and experiment. The young sailor who wanted to test an idea of his own and borrowed a length of palings and some tarpaulin from a Surrey farmer was not likely to be thinking of D-Day and Mulberry harbours when he bridged a local ford with his weird paling and tarpaulin contraption. But he drove across his bridge on a motor-cycle and knew that his idea was sound. PLUTO might not have been constructed so efficiently if it had not been for two unknown Austrians who came to England after the Nazis had

A FLOATING FLEXIBLE ISLAND FOR AIRCRAFT

The " Lily " airstrip, or floating island, was the invention of Mr. P. M. Hamilton, and consists of hexagonal buoyancy drums, hinged together to form a flexible landing surface, 520 feet long by 60 feet wide, for aircraft at sea. Our picture shows " Lily " at Lamlash during tests, and a motor-launch, passing at speed, has caused the strip to undulate with the waves.

seized Austria. They brought with them the formula for processing synthetic rubber in a special way. It was that secret method which was eventually used to seal the joints of that long pipeline "Pluto" stretching from England, across the Channel, and then across Europe to give fuel to the advancing armies of liberation.

Parachutes and Insecticides

NYLON is the invention or discovery of the chemists. It can scarcely be classed as a war-time invention, but it certainly became a valuable aid in the years when everything was turned to use for the men and women of the Defence Forces. Nylon is a chemically-produced fibre, made by a complicated process from air, water and the by-products of coal.

In war-time it was used for parachutes and for the ropes required to tow gliders since it combined strength with lightness. In peace-

SIR ALEXANDER FLEMING

Penicillin is one of the most valuable discoveries made by medical science during the present century, and in the photograph above Professor Fleming, the discoverer of this powerful non-poisonous antiseptic, is seen at work in his laboratory at St. Mary's Hospital, London, where Penicillin was first used.

time it means silk-like stockings and beautiful fabrics. Nylon curtains and collars, suits and fishing-lines—there is no end, it seems, to the uses to which Nylon can be put. The fabric is mothproof, non-inflammable, and almost waterproof. Moreover it returns to its proper shape after being crushed, a definite advantage over almost all other fabrics.

Nylon is only one of several man-made fibres which have been developed recently. Orlon, a fibre made from car-

bon, nitrogen and hydrogen, is claimed to be better than nylon in some respects. It is said to be more resistant to soot and smoke and more able to withstand the effects of harsh sunlight. Dacron, another new fibre, is waterproof and will keep its creases even when wet or crumpled. Dynel is fireproof and has already been used to make curtains and bedspreads for modern liners. Two new fibres which have recently been introduced in Britain are Terylene, which draws its raw materials from the oil-cracking process, and Ardil, which has its origins in groundnuts. Both can be made into fabrics that will neither crease nor shrink.

But the chemists have yet to find a complete substitute for wool. The new man-made fibres have many advantages, but they·have disadvantages also. For example, most of them cannot be dyed easily. The artificial fibre that is most like wool is Vicara, but it lacks the strength of wool and cannot be used alone. It seems probable that fabrics containing both wool and man-made fibres will be the most satisfactory.

The Magic Mirror in Industry

Another recent invention which has made great progress is the "magic mirror"—television. The story of its development is told in another volume. Those of us who know television as a way of entertainment may not realise that it is also playing an important part in business, medicine and industry. Television is used by one of the big London banks to scan records that are kept many miles away in the country, by hospitals to show doctors and students how leading surgeons carry out new operating techniques, and by the fishing industry to study feeding and breeding grounds. The sunken submarine *Affray* was located on the bed of the English Channel by television, and the same means were used to track down the wreck of a Comet aircraft in the Mediterranean. The Comet, which had crashed between the islands of Elba and Monte Cristo, was located at a depth of 400 feet by a special underwater television camera. Special lights, which could be used "naked" in the water, lit the scene for the submerged "eye," which faithfully transmitted its pictures to a 14-inch television screen upon the salvage vessel. Such equipment can be used at depths of a thousand feet, but how much of the ocean bed or wreck can be seen by the camera naturally depends on the clearness of the water.

Killing Pests and Germs

In time of war when great numbers of men are compelled to live under conditions which breed disease, the fight against the germs which cause and spread these diseases is a desperate one. In this last war a new weapon was discovered, an insecticide and germ-killer, generally known as D.D.T., a very necessary abbreviation of its full and correct name of Dichloro-diphenyl-trichloroethane. Its discoverer, Dr. Paul Mueller, a Swiss scientist, was awarded a Nobel Prize in 1948.

During the war its effects were marvellous. The many varieties of flies and creeping insects that spread disease were annihilated wherever D.D.T. was used, and it certainly was used in such large quantities that not until the end of the war were any supplies made available to the general public. In peace-time it has been used to clear wide cattle-grazing areas of some of the most dreaded pests of the great American cattle ranches such as the horn-fly.

D.D.T. nowadays is supplied to the public carefully prepared at the right strength for the several different purposes in the home and garden or on the farm. Wherever D.D.T. is used the danger of contamination by flies and other insects is banished, while germs which breed diseases cease to exist.

Another insecticide has made its appearance since the war ended and has proved highly efficient against such pests as grain and blossom weevil, locusts, ants, mosquitoes, and similar pests. "Gammexane" is the name it has been given, but in these days when initials or nicknames have become the fashion it has also been christened simply "666" which, as in the case of D.D.T., is derived from its correct chemical name of Benzene hexachloride, the formula for which is $C_6H_6Cl_6$—hence the three sixes.

It is by attacking the disease in its first stage that the greatest success is obtained. Get rid of the pests that

Chas. E. Brown.

THE VAMPIRE IN FLIGHT

The first British jet-propelled aeroplane, designed by Air Commodore Whittle of the R.A.F., was successfully flown in 1941. Other types were developed later and our picture shows a de Havilland " Vampire " jet-driven aeroplane, fitted with de Havilland Goblin turbines, and having a top speed in the region of 600 miles per hour.

bring and spread disease and the disease ceases to exist. It is here that these new insecticides are proving their value.

The Fight Against Disease

There is a branch of medical treatment now known as chemotherapy. This aims at maintaining in the body for a considerable period a concentration of the right sort of drug to destroy any disease organisms. On these lines the scientists have spent a great deal of time in their efforts to find new weapons to overcome disease.

Among the recent discoveries is a drug generally known as M. & B. from the name of the manufacturing chemists May and Baker, whose research scientists first discovered it. Their experiments revealed that a drug usually referred to as sulphonamide had a wonderfully curative action in such diseases as pneumonia and similar infections.

Some thousands of related compounds of this type of drug were investigated. Sulphapyridine was even more effective in pneumonia cases, and " M. & B. 693 " has some wonderful cures to its credit. It has completely altered the mortality rates of several important diseases, while excellent results have been obtained by packing wounds and compound fractures with one of the sulpha drugs.

Sometimes a great discovery is made almost by accident, though the final result is anything but accidental. Professor Alexander Fleming, working in his laboratory in St. Mary's Hospital, London, noticed that on a dish upon which he had planted some of the microbes that cause boils and similar infections a greenish-blue fluffy mass had begun to grow. It was nothing more than what we call "mould," the sort of stuff that shows on a piece of bread that has been left lying about, or will start growing on a pair of shoes pushed away at the back of a cupboard for too long a time.

Result of an Accident

The dish might have been thrown away as useless because it had become contaminated. But there was something curious about it to the eyes of the bacteriologist. The little colony of microbes Fleming had planted there to develop had begun to dwindle. Apparently the mould was able to destroy the microbes!

It was an accident that mould appeared on his specimen dish, but the alert mind of the bacteriologist was needed to turn the accident to useful account. Nor did results come swiftly and easily. Professor Fleming identified the mould as a species of the large group known as *penicillia*, from a similar word meaning brush-like which describes the way the mould grows.

Fleming named the drug he was eventually able to produce " Penicillin." He wrote about it soon after he made the discovery in 1928, but the difficulty was that all efforts to concentrate it were useless and it was very unstable. It lost its power too quickly to be of any great use generally. The help of Professor Howard Florey was enlisted and some of the scientists working under him at Oxford began to study the problem. Professor (now Sir Howard) Florey, an Australian, had been Professor of Pathology at the University of Sheffield and was keenly interested in natural immunity—that is, the process whereby the body overcomes the harmful microbes with which it comes in contact.

There were many difficulties in the way before these scientists achieved success and were able to extract from the crude fluid on which the mould grew a powerful antiseptic to be used in curing microbic diseases. Many tests were made before they felt justified in speaking with absolute certainty. By 1944 Penicillin was being produced on a comparatively large scale, and to-day it is in universal use.

Honours for Scientists

Sir Alexander Fleming has been honoured for his great discovery both in this country and in others. In France the highest Order of the Legion of Honour was conferred upon him in 1945, and later he and his two chief collaborators, Sir Howard Florey and Dr. E. B. Chain, were jointly awarded the Nobel Prize for Medicine.

In no branch of science has more progress been made than in Aeronautics. It was generally agreed long before the last World War came upon us that air power would be a decisive factor. Germany's early successes against Poland, France, Belgium, Holland and Norway owed a great deal to the overwhelming superiority of her powerful Luftwaffe. It was only when in August and September, 1940, the British fighter aircraft, the Spitfires and Hurricanes, were able to take the air in sufficient numbers to have a semblance of a chance against the Luftwaffe that the German plans to gain air domination over the English Channel and our Southern airfields and ports were foiled. The Spitfires and Hurricanes, magnificently handled by well-trained British airmen, proved a match for the mighty Luftwaffe.

Planes without Propellers

One of the biggest developments was that made when the first British jet-propelled aeroplane made its successful trial flight in 1941. Its inventor, Air-Commodore Frank Whittle, had taken out his first patent for jet-propelled aircraft in 1930, but with the advent of war work was speeded up. Other nations had been at work on the same lines and the Germans eventually employed this jet system of propellerless propulsion in their pilotless V-1 planes, generally known as the Flying Bombs. The first of these fell in London in June, 1944, and for a time much damage and many casualties were caused by them in London and the southern counties until defensive measures lessened their effectiveness.

To-day the jet-propelled plane is

SECRETS OF THE SOUND BARRIER

The invisible wall of air resistance that we call the " Sound Barrier " creates special problems for aircraft designers. To help its designers to solve these problems, a large British aircraft firm has built this special trans-sonic wind tunnel in which models can be tested under exactly the same conditions as the real aircraft will encounter.

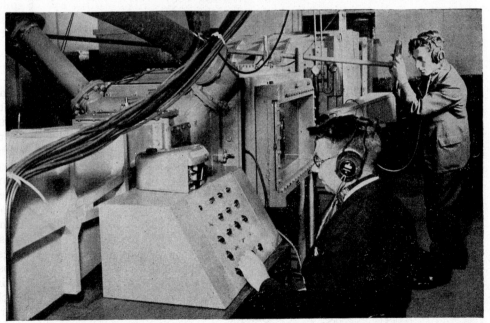

Photos: Sir W. G. Armstrong Whitworth Aircraft, Ltd.

The model has been fixed to the " sting " and is now inside the tunnel. The Chief Aerodynamicist is seated at the control panel, while his assistant turns the wheel to start the release of air. Thus, without risking a pilot's life or a valuable experimental aircraft, the designers will know exactly how the machine will behave during its passage through the " Sound Barrier."

being used for transport aircraft. A British Supermarine Swift F4 jet-plane set up a world record when it flew at 735·7 miles an hour in September 1953. This record has since been surpassed, but it was a milestone in the history of flying. In 40 years the speed of the aeroplane had increased from 10 miles an hour to over 10 miles a minute.

The great speeds at which aircraft can now fly have created many problems for the scientists and designers of the large companies engaged in making aeroplanes, and literally millions of pounds have already been spent on research work. When aircraft break through the invisible wall of air resistance which we know as the " Sound Barrier," disaster may result if the machines have not been properly designed for this high-speed flight. The aircraft may be subject to intense buffeting, go completely out of control, or even disintegrate.

To help their scientists to design aeroplanes that can pass through the sound barrier in safety, one large manufacturing company has built a special trans-sonic wind tunnel in which experimental models can be tested under actual flying conditions. Not many such tunnels exist in the world. But by positioning a model in the tunnel the specialists can study the behaviour of this type of aircraft under trans-sonic conditions without endangering the life of a test pilot or risking the loss of a valuable prototype aircraft.

The March of Progress

Progress leads to further progress. Development in one field frequently requires development in another. With every advance new standards are demanded. The metal component which must revolve at an incredible speed requires a far higher degree of smoothness than a similar component revolving at a quarter the speed. New machines for achieving this smoothness are evolved, and new methods of testing are devised to ensure that even the most infinitesimal deviation from the necessary standard has been removed.

Each new step forward opens up fresh vistas to our research workers and inventors, who thus find further opportunities for progress and endeavour.

Copyright.

MEASURING SMOOTHNESS

Some parts of modern machinery are required to have a very high finish on their surfaces. The photograph above shows an electrical instrument called the Tomlinson Surface Finish Recorder which measures and photographs the smallest deviation from smoothness. The slightest roughness on the surface can be shown on a screen 5,000 times enlarged.

ATOMIC ENERGY AND ITS MEANING

WATCHING THE GLEEP

The Gleep is the official name for the Graphite Low Energy Experimental Pile at Harwell Atomic Energy Station. Careful observations are made and records kept of all that takes place. Our picture shows the control room at Harwell, situated some distance from the pile so that the operators are not subject to stray radiations which might be harmful.

WHEN atomic bombs were dropped on Hiroshima and Nagasaki most people were made aware for the first time that scientists had discovered an entirely new source of energy.

The first bomb was dropped on August 6th, 1945, the second on August 9th, and Japan surrendered unconditionally on August 14th. This quick surrender undoubtedly saved the lives of many thousands of British and American soldiers who might have been killed if the war had had to be fought out using ordinary weapons and though the loss of life in the Japanese cities was very great, this may easily have represented a saving in human life as compared with the results of a long drawn-out war.

The atomic bomb provided the first practical demonstration that scientists had discovered this way of releasing immense sources of energy which man had never before been able to tap.

Many people, even to-day, still think that the most important application of this newly-discovered atomic energy is for the making of bombs to be used in warfare. This is very far from the truth. The fact that scientists have now discovered a method of releasing this locked-up energy in the atom has immensely greater possibilities than wholesale destruction.

How Heat is Produced

Many thousands of years ago some man discovered how to light a fire. It is possible that he may have used the discovery first for burning down the houses or villages of his enemies. The use of fire for purely destructive purposes is a very minor application of the wonderful discovery which was made so many thousands of years ago. For many hundreds of years fire has been the servant of mankind. The burning of coal in electric power stations makes electrical energy which is now available in nearly every home and workshop in the country. The burning of petrol in car engines supplies the energy, equal to many million horse power, which provides the motive power for cars, buses and commercial vehicles.

When the news of the atomic bomb was first broadcast to the world many people said it would have been far better if atomic energy had never been discovered. Many thousands of years ago, no doubt, many members of the human race who had only seen fire used for burning down their houses or crops may have given expression to the same feeling regarding the discovery of fire.

The heat which is obtained by burning things can best be described as molecular heat. That is to say, it is heat which is released when the molecules of a substance, such as coal or wood, begin to split up and form new combinations with the molecules of the air.

For a great many years chemists and scientists generally were of the opinion that though molecules could be split up to form other compounds it was quite impossible to split up atoms. They thought that a metal, such as copper or gold or lead, consisted of atoms of copper or gold or lead and that however much the material was sub-divided it would still be copper or gold or lead. The atom was, in fact, defined as the smallest possible quantity of a given

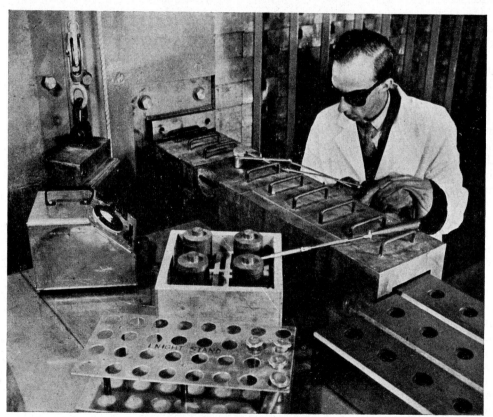

Crown Copyright.

MAKING ARTIFICIAL RADIUM

The valuable medicinal applications of radium have been greatly restricted in the past owing to its scarcity. Artificial radium or radio-active isotopes are now being produced at the Harwell atomic pile. Materials such as common salt are placed in small aluminium containers and inserted in holes in graphite blocks, as shown in the picture above. The radio-active properties persist for some time after the salt has been treated.

element, and it was considered to be indivisible.

It is now over thirty years since Sir Ernest Rutherford succeeded in splitting up the atom of nitrogen into two entirely different atoms, namely, oxygen and hydrogen. Before this time scientists were firmly convinced that oxygen, hydrogen and nitrogen were three entirely different substances which could not be changed one into the other.

Splitting the Atom

When Sir Ernest Rutherford split up a few nitrogen atoms in this way he found that a large amount of energy was liberated and that the oxygen and hydrogen resulting from the split-up nitrogen weighed rather less than the original nitrogen.

Crown Copyright.

A PISTOL WHICH PRESERVES HEALTH
The instrument shown above is known as a Pistol Monitor. It is used in connection with atomic research and provides a safeguard for the workers. By pointing the pistol at either persons or objects it is possible to tell whether they have been subjected to atomic radiations. If the pistol indicates that they have been affected the person can be treated at once and any harmful effects are prevented.

Some of the mass or weight of the nitrogen had been converted into heat. Rutherford succeeded in splitting the nitrogen atom by bombarding it with high-speed particles but he had to fire a great many shots with these particles before he was able to hit the centre or "nucleus" of the atom, which was the only way of causing it to split. Since then scientists have found ways of bombarding atoms so that they can be reasonably sure of splitting them up without having to fire too many shots.

This was the second stage in the discovery of atomic energy, but it was still not practicable to obtain useful energy, because the power used in splitting up the atoms was greater than the power which could be usefully obtained by splitting them up.

Scientists then began to experiment with the metal uranium. They found that some uranium atoms were continually splitting up by themselves and in doing so they released particles which bombarded the metal surrounding them and caused further splitting up, or "fissioning," to take place. The special kind of uranium which splits up or fissions by itself is called uranium 235.

If a piece of uranium 235 is less than a certain size most of the particles are thrown out as the atoms split up, and escape into the air, the metal continuing to fission at a comparatively slow rate. If, however, the piece of uranium 235 is made bigger than a certain size (the exact size is still a secret) each atom which splits up causes two or more other atoms to split up, and what is known as a chain reaction starts, causing the whole of the lump of uranium to explode, releasing a tremen-dous amount of energy in the form of heat, light and other radiations.

This in brief is the principle of the atomic bomb, but it is to be hoped that this particular aspect of atomic energy will in the future become less and less important, just as using fire for burning down houses is scarcely regarded as its most important use in these days!

Britain's Atomic Pile

Whilst the discovery of atomic energy is of vast importance, still more import-ant was the dis-covery of means by which this energy could be controlled and so brought into the service of man-kind. Although this problem of control has not yet been completely solved, scientists are already able to control atomic processes to a very large extent.

In Britain the chief research centre is at Harwell, in Berk-shire, where two experimental atomic piles were built. The larger of these is known as " Bepo " and is capable of developing about 8,000 horse-power or 6,000 kilowatts of energy. Inside each of these piles a small quantity of the mar-vellous metal uranium 235 is allowed to split up and in doing so it releases consider-able amounts of energy in the form of heat.

At present this energy is not used

Crown Copyright.

BRITAIN'S FIRST ATOMIC PILE

The first atomic energy station to be built in Britain is at Harwell, in Berkshire. Here scientists study the possibilities of this new source of power. The active material is surrounded by several feet of concrete which absorbs the radiations.

INSIDE A CYCLOTRON

This picture shows the interior of the Cyclotron constructed at the atomic research establishment at Harwell, Berkshire. One of the most important parts is a large electro-magnet, and the two poles are shown above. 700 tons of steel were used and the copper windings contain 70 tons of copper.

directly. A stream of air is blown through the piles to keep them cool. If the temperature of one of the piles rises too high for safety, rods of graphite or boron are automatically pushed into the pile and these have the effect of slowing down the action. At present these piles are being used chiefly for experimental work and for producing artificial radium, or, more strictly, radio-active isotopes of well-known chemicals.

If a small quantity of ordinary salt, for instance, is inserted into a cavity in the atomic pile and left there for a few hours it acquires properties very similar to those of radium. Many different chemicals can be treated in this way and these are being used in medical research and also in the treatment of cancer and other diseases which formerly required the use of rare and expensive radium compounds. These radio-active substances (radium, radon and radio-active isotopes produced in the atomic piles) are prepared for medical, scientific and industrial use at the radio-chemical centre at Amersham, in Buckinghamshire.

In February, 1954, the first zero energy fast reactor to be built in Britain was brought into operation at Harwell. This reactor, which has the name of "Zephyr," was designed for experimental purposes. With its help, our scientists hope to discover what use can be made of the process known as "breeding," *i.e.*, the creation of more fissile material than is actually consumed. The use of this process for the generating of electric power would mean that less fuel would be needed to operate the power station than is needed when other types of reactor are used.

A few weeks after the fast reactor had begun operating at Harwell, it was announced that a fast breeder reactor would be built at Dounreay, Caithness, where it would be housed in a large steel dome. It was said that this reactor might greatly reduce the amount of uranium needed for the atomic production of electricity and " would become a world-famous pioneer among the plants providing electricity in the next generation."

The time is now much nearer when it will be possible to use atomic piles instead of boilers for producing the steam necessary to drive the turbo-electric machinery in generating stations. In November, 1951, it was announced that atomic central heating had been tested successfully at Harwell, and in December of the same year electric power was produced from atomic energy at the National Reactor Testing Station at Arco, Idaho, in the United States. Near the Windscale works at Sellafield, Cumberland, where plutonium is produced, an experimental atomic power station is being built. The site is known as Calder Hall. Using uranium in its atomic pile, and producing plutonium as a by-product, this new station will eventually generate enough power to supply all Cumberland and Westmorland and certain parts of Lancashire. It will be the first atomic plant of its kind in the world and will probably generate, from every ton of uranium used, the same amount of power generated by burning 3 million tons of coal.

Meantime, other aspects of this amazing new power are likely to be revealed during the course of the work now being carried on at Harwell, where the secrets of atomic energy are being studied by British scientists, and at other research centres in the free world.

Inside a Uranium Factory

To find out how uranium ore is treated we must visit the Springfields factory at Salwick, near Preston, Lancashire. Crude ore comes to this factory in large lumps in sealed metal drums. The first job is

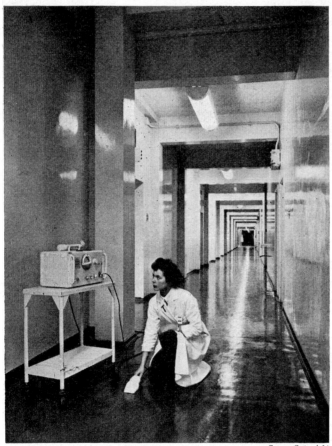

Crcwn Copyright.

PROTECTING THE WORKERS AT AN ATOM FACTORY
Great care is taken to safeguard the workers at British atomic energy factories from the effects of radio-activity. Special protective clothing and regular medical tests are provided, and the buildings themselves are regularly checked for signs of danger. This picture shows a girl making a routine check of the corridors of the Windscale laboratories.

IN A BRITISH ATOMIC FACTORY

British Official Photograph.

This picture shows us a part of the Springfields uranium factory at Salwick, near Preston, in Lancashire. At this factory, uranium is extracted from the crude ore. The ore is crushed into small pieces, then ground to a powder which is dissolved in acids in the crude oxide plant seen in this picture. The uranium oxide which results is then purified by a process called solvent extraction, which employs ether. A solution of uranyl nitrate is obtained, from which solid ammonium diuranate is produced. The latter is bright yellow, which reminds us that before atomic energy was discovered the only commercial use for uranium was to colour china.

to crush the ore into small pieces, care being taken during the process to prevent dangerous uranium dust from escaping into the air. The crushed ore is then ground into a powder. Water is poured into the mill and the resulting " slurry " (the water and its powder content) is then pumped into dissolvers employing a mixture of acids. Radium and other metals are extracted, and the uranium itself is precipitated as a crude uranium oxide which is removed by means of a filter-press.

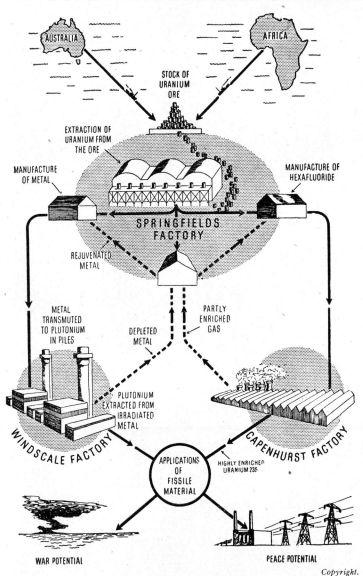

But impurities are still present, so the next stage is purification. By dissolving the oxide in nitric acid and evaporating the solution which results, uranyl nitrate is produced. This solution is then purified by the use of ether and the uranium is precipitated in solid form as ammonium diuranate. This solid compound is a vivid yellow colour and you have probably met it already without realising the fact. For it is to uranium that we owe many of the browns and yellows in our china. Until atomic energy was discovered, this was the only commercial use to which uranium was put.

The next stage is to make uranium metal from the ammonium diuranate. This is done by converting the diuranate to uranium tetrafluoride, which is then mixed with calcium and fired. This stage in the process is very spectacular. The mould containing the mixture of fluoride and calcium and its steel container are

AUSTRALIA

AFRICA

STOCK OF URANIUM ORE

EXTRACTION OF URANIUM FROM THE ORE

MANUFACTURE OF METAL

MANUFACTURE OF HEXAFLUORIDE

SPRINGFIELDS FACTORY

REJUVENATED METAL

METAL TRANSMUTED TO PLUTONIUM IN PILES

DEPLETED METAL

PARTLY ENRICHED GAS

PLUTONIUM EXTRACTED FROM IRRADIATED METAL

WINDSCALE FACTORY

CAPENHURST FACTORY

APPLICATIONS OF FISSILE MATERIAL

HIGHLY ENRICHED URANIUM 235

WAR POTENTIAL

PEACE POTENTIAL

Copyright.

HOW BRITAIN MAKES MATERIALS FOR ATOMIC ENERGY

In the past seven years, a new industry has been created in Britain. Its work is to produce materials which can be used to create atomic energy. The diagram shows how the industry is organised. Uranium ore from abroad is processed at the Springfields factory, which produces uranium metal for Windscale and hexafluoride for Capenhurst. At Windscale, plutonium is made from the uranium metal, while at Capenhurst uranium 235—the most suitable fissile material—is made.

enclosed in a steel compartment. Once the firing mechanism has been switched on, the heart of the mould glows red, the colour soon changing to a blinding white. Then, as the reaction is completed, the white-hot mass no longer spits out dazzling little stars into the darkness of its steel prison; the brightness fades and there, cooling, is the uranium metal itself. The rods later cast from the metal are enclosed in aluminium and are then ready for use in a nuclear reactor, or atomic pile. In Britain they are used at the Windscale factory for the production of plutonium, or in the experimental piles at Harwell.

If we did visit an atomic energy factory we should notice immediately how clean a place the factory was and how great were the precautions taken to protect the workpeople from harmful uranium or radium dust. Everyone wears white protective clothing, including rubber boots and gloves, there are special changing rooms, and clean-ing seems to be going on all the time. Special ventilation systems have been installed, there is a special medical service for the workpeople, and regular " radiation surveys " are made to ensure that no one is exposed to dangerous radio-activity. It all seems very different from conditions in many ordinary factories; and indeed it is, for these are the factories of a new age—the atomic age.

Yet, as we think of all the wonderful progress Science has made even within the past decade, it is as well to pause and ask the question: To what end will all these discoveries lead us ? It is of the highest importance that a right sense of proportion should be preserved.

That is why the work of the social scientists is just as important as that of the natural scientists : the sociologists, the psychologists who try to understand the working of the human mind, the psychiatrists who hope to remedy the ills of the mind or to test its varied

CAREFUL CHECKS ARE MADE AT EVERY STAGE OF PRODUCTION

In an atomic energy factory every process must be carefully checked. This operator at the Springfields factory, near Preston, Lancashire, is studying one of the many dials in the part of the factory where he works. Notice his protective clothing, which includes rubber boots and gloves.

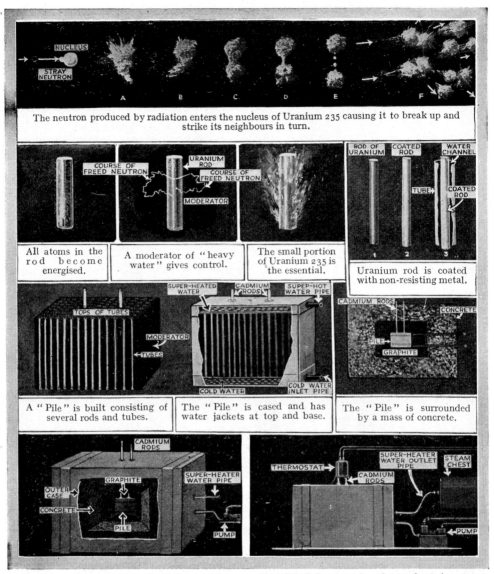

The neutron produced by radiation enters the nucleus of Uranium 235 causing it to break up and strike its neighbours in turn.

All atoms in the rod become energised.

A moderator of "heavy water" gives control.

The small portion of Uranium 235 is the essential.

Uranium rod is coated with non-resisting metal.

A "Pile" is built consisting of several rods and tubes.

The "Pile" is cased and has water jackets at top and base.

The "Pile" is surrounded by a mass of concrete.

Cadmium rods are used to control the working of the "Pile."

The "Pile" is encased and superheated water is converted to steam

HOW ATOMIC POWER MAY BE CHAINED

The drawings above explain very briefly how fission of the atom is produced, and show how the turbulence of colliding atoms produces heat. By means of water tubes surrounding the uranium rods, superheated water is produced under great pressure. When this pressure is lowered, superheated steam results, and this can be used for all industrial purposes in which steam-power is required.

capacities; the economists who study the production and distribution of wealth and include in their sphere the welfare of the worker. With these scientists there are, too, the preachers, the lec-

turers, writers and artists, who teach us to think and to admire beauty and the wonders of Nature. It is the broad well-balanced view that is necessary.

Atomic energy, as represented by the

WHEN ATOMIC ENERGY IS HARNESSED

The reality of atomic power is no longer a theory but a fact, though certain problems have to be solved before the possibilities shown in the picture above are fully achieved. The production of atomic heat creates an extraordinarily intense radiation which must be absorbed by protective shielding. This means new types of metal, and this question and others are being studied. Eventually the forecasts depicted above are likely to become realities.

atomic bomb, and that newer and even more terrible weapon, the hydrogen bomb, lead some people to say that there has been too much progress and that we are moving towards self-destruction. But already our scientists have shown how these new forces can be used for the good of all. So progress does not destroy Mankind—unless Mankind misuses it.

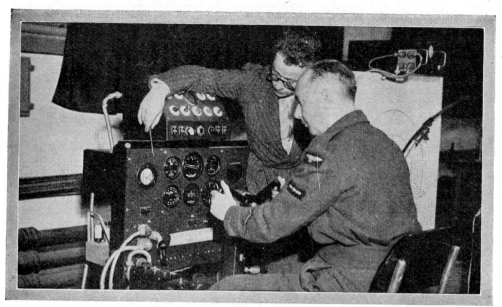

Keystone.

A PUPIL AT THE RADAR RESEARCH CENTRE

At the headquarters of Britain's Science Brains Trust research goes on continuously into the further possibilities of Radar. For that research work it is necessary to train men in the use of different instruments, and here we see an instructor explaining the working of an Air Interception Trainer Panel to a newcomer.

WE have read briefly in these pages of how the great thinkers through the course of many centuries have led man to acquire knowledge of the Earth on which he lives. Gradually man has begun to understand and to control to some extent the mighty forces of Nature, making them his servant instead of being his master.

It has scarcely been a steady progress and was indeed painfully slow in the beginning. Yet in the last hundred and fifty years this knowledge, and the capacity to use it, has gone forward by swift leaps and bounds. In 1800 the hand spinning-wheel, the hand loom, and the plough were very much the same as they had been for many centuries. The only means of travelling were by horse-drawn vehicles and by sailing-ship. A few inventions had been made and the spinning-jenny and mechanical weaving-loom were coming into use against much opposition.

Instead of hand-power the inventors made use of water-power, and a clumsy steam-pump was developed into a much more efficient steam-engine by James Watt.

Knowledge for Its Own Sake

This was the beginning of the great Industrial Revolution in Britain, and it spread throughout the world. It marked a new phase in the history of man's development which had begun with Greek culture. There had been other civilisations before Greece, but, as in the case of Egypt, wars came and the conquerors destroyed something they were unable to replace.

Yet some of the Egyptians' hard-won knowledge passed in due time by way of Crete to the mainland of Greece. With the Greeks, indeed, we enter the full light of history and know what their great teachers believed and taught from the written records they left. For a long time during which the Greeks were the leaders of the world, the great thinkers who investigated and made experiments were almost solely concerned with the pursuit of knowledge for its own sake, and that still remains the first aim of Science in our own day.

These early thinkers were not concerned with finding out new ways of lighting or heating their homes, or how to make bombs to destroy their enemies, nor even how to make a chariot or carriage travel more swiftly than horses could pull it. They were anxious to learn the truth about the Sun, Moon, Stars, and the Earth; how and why they existed at all, and how man should act and govern himself. Some of them were interested in numbers and the science of mathematics was evolved. They laid a foundation on which succeeding generations of thinkers were able to build. As an example, there was a school in Thrace about the fifth century B.C. which was known as the Atomists. They said that matter was formed of atoms "strong in solid singleness." Differences in the properties of bodies were due to differences in size, shape and movements of the atoms. Democritus (460–357 B.C.) put forward his atomic theory. Up to a point it was not much more than a lucky guess, but right through the centuries that followed this idea of the importance and power of the atom attracted men of science.

Powers of Radium

Dalton (1766–1844) formulated a much more advanced atomic theory; Lord Kelvin, Clerk-Maxwell, Sir William Crookes, Sir J. J. Thomson, all

British Council.

SCIENCE AIDS THE COTTON INDUSTRY

In the heart of Lancashire the Cotton Research Association has its laboratories where scientists test and carry out experiments with cotton to discover new and better methods of treatment and manufacturing processes. Our photograph shows girls at work preparing sorter diagrams to determine fibre length, fineness, etc., of the raw cotton.

added to the sum of knowledge. Lord Rutherford and Professor Soddy went still further, and in 1945 the power of the atom was dramatically and fearfully proved. But the atomic bomb is merely an offshoot of the knowledge scientists have now gained of the atom.

One aspect of atomic knowledge is seen in the work of the Curies and others. Radium is being increasingly used as experiments show its many powers. Radio-activity is one branch of Science which holds immense possibilities, especially in the treatment of disease. Substances can be made radio active—for a limited time. Radium itself remains potent for thousands of years, and if one were to inject radium into the human system it might cure the particular complaint quite quickly, but it would continue to act after that task was done and so start some trouble far worse. The remedy would be worse than the disease.

The scientists who are at work in the new atomic energy centres have made important discoveries in this connection as we have read in the chapter dealing with atomic progress.

When Wealth Increased

In Science we stand on the threshold of a new age and we need the wisdom to learn from the past. The Industrial Revolution that began about 1760 was wonderful, though it was from many points of view also tragic and depressing. It was nobody's business to control it. Production increased and wealth accumulated, but in the hands of a few. Masses of men were crowded together in mean, monotonous streets of ill-built houses ; they worked in badly-ventilated, insanitary, uninspected factories, and their children were born to a new slavery.

A new science came into existence to balance this state of affairs. Sociology, the scientific study of human life in organised communities, is as necessary to-day as biology. Some would say that Man has not changed in character

very much in the past two or three centuries. Yet old ideas that the weakest, whether in health, wealth, or influence, must go to the wall have little support to-day. Man has become conscious of himself as a member of a community and realises that he has duties towards others besides himself; he has a duty to humanity.

It is because we have these new ideas and this better outlook about our aims that we can look forward to the ever-increasing benefits Science can give us. There is a new hope that among the great nations of the world there is the wisdom, taught by the hard experiences of the past, to use the gifts the scientists bring for the good of humanity as a whole and not for its destruction.

Lines of Research

Even at the beginning of this present century the utilisation of the scientists' knowledge for manufacturing purposes so that the ordinary person could enjoy the result was often a matter of luck. The scientist or the inventor made a discovery and had to persuade some man or group of men that there was money in it before it became available to the public.

Some of the bigger manufacturers had their own laboratories and even their research departments, but it was not until the war of 1914–18 that the British Government founded a Department of Scientific and Industrial Research. This Department has an Advisory Council which includes the most distinguished scientists of the day. It provides funds, granted by Parliament, to the Research Associations formed by the industries themselves. There are some twenty-seven of these Research Associations.

There are three main lines of scientific research ; first and foremost, since everything else must depend on it ultimately, is the old ideal of " the pursuit of knowledge for its own sake." Then there is the research for the

Copyright.

MEASURING AND TESTING SCREW THREADS

In many scientific instruments screw threads and the teeth of gear wheels have to be very accurately formed. The instrument seen above has been designed to examine and test such threads. The component is placed in the beam of a powerful lamp and a suitable lens projects a greatly enlarged image on the screen. Any flaw can then be readily detected.

benefit of the people who consume and use the products of industry. Thirdly, there is research for the manufacturers on their own particular problems.

The Department has the National Physical Laboratory where, among other things, the testing and calibrating of scientific instruments and of chronometers is carried out. It also has research stations and special laboratories in different parts of the country. Food is a subject, for instance, with which the Government of the country is particularly concerned both in time of war and in peace. The Department of Scientific and Industrial Research has developed a method of gas storage for apples as well as new methods of storing fish in perfect condition for twelve months or even longer. This means that the fishing fleets can sail farther from our shores and the country will have fresher food. It means, too, that a glut of fish need not be wasted, as it used to be, but held for the lean period when there is a shortage.

New Comfort at Home

Bread has been studied by the scientists to discover just what nutritive value it has and how best it can be improved. Pests which attack the grain and lead to bad harvests have been the subject of other experiments and tests. Almost everything that enters into our everyday life has been or probably is at the present time undergoing scientific investigation. Most of us have had experience of woollen garments that shrink, but the Wool Industries Research Association has found a way to remedy this fault.

A long list could be made out of the everyday articles which are being studied by experts in chemistry and other branches of Science. Sometimes they seem to be a long way removed from the problems of pure science, or from the study of radio-activity or atomic energy. Boots and shoes for different occupations ; motor-horns that will give clear warning without being an annoyance to everyone in the neighbourhood ; building materials and printing inks ; domestic boilers and grates as well as the problems of heating and lighting in homes and factories: all these are under the microscope and are being tested and examined.

The Electron Microscope

The history of one of the most important of the scientist's instruments, the microscope, follows on much the same lines as those of so many other discoveries. Magnification by a curved transparent disc was known in ancient times, but the single lens gave a coloured and distorted image. It was not until the invention of the achromatic lens in 1729, followed by various improvements by Dollond in 1752, that any real use was made of the microscope.

During the next hundred years there was no great advance. It was only when Science realised the need for observing those tiny forms of life hidden from the naked eye that the microscope made big advances. In 1860 the first binocular microscope, giving stereoscopic vision, was designed. Improvements in the quality of lenses came with the discovery of how to make them from molten quartz, followed by a further advance when polarised light was used.

Now the electron microscope has been invented. This magnifies up to 50,000 times. Some idea of what this means

can be gathered from the fact that if a halfpenny were magnified to this extent it would cover three-quarters of the city of London. Germs and bacteria, so small that they have never previously been observed in detail, can now be properly studied.

It was after a good deal of experimenting by scientists in several countries that this type of microscope eventually became possible. The first electron microscope was produced in America in 1941 after big sums had been spent on research and experimental work. In our own country considerable progress had been made, but the final stages were suspended from the outbreak of war in 1939 until 1944 when it was found possible to resume the work. The first complete model was in use the following year.

The most recent model made in Britain is one hundred times as powerful as the best optical microscope ever devised. With the new electron microscope tiny organisms less than a millionth of an inch long can be examined on the greenish fluorescent screen of the type used in both radar and television. The cathode ray tube which made radar possible has also brought into being the electron microscope, a development which is wonderful in itself, but also opens up possibilities of new discoveries in many fields of research.

How Progress was Made

It is with instruments of this kind that the problems of one scientist may be solved by another working in a different field. One discovery links up with another ; the solution of one problem makes it possible to overcome a totally different difficulty. Atomic energy has been mentioned already, but because of its tremendous possibilities and because it has a bearing on so many other scientific and industrial problems it must inevitably crop up in many fields of research.

It is an epoch-making discovery ranking with the greatest of human discoveries. Fire was the first : man did not discover fire, or invent it, but long ages ago he learned how to produce it at will and to control it for his own purposes. We pass over many centuries before we come to anything comparable with this achievement. Steam was known to the Greeks and the first attempt to control it was made by Hero of Alexandria about 130 B.C. It was the seventeenth century before real progress was made. Then, in 1698, Thomas Savery invented an engine and used the term " horse-power." James Watt, Richard Trevithick, and finally George Stephenson gradually brought about the full revolution.

From Theory to Practical Use

Electricity, too, was known to the Greeks but without any knowledge of how to harness it. In England, Gilbert, the father of electricity as he has been called, published a book on the subject in 1600 and coined its name from the Greek *elektron*. Other scientists found out much more, but it was not until Edison invented an incandescent lamp and made an improved dynamo about 1880 that electricity became available for industrial purposes and for the home.

Due to the war immense strides were made by teams of scientists investigating the possibilities of atomic energy as a weapon of destruction. They knew how to split the atom ; they did not know how to split millions of atoms in a confined space all in the same instant and at the moment when the big explosion of energy was desired. They found the answer in Uranium 235, by which they were able to achieve " chain-reaction "—one atom exploding and causing the next atom to explode, as described in earlier pages.

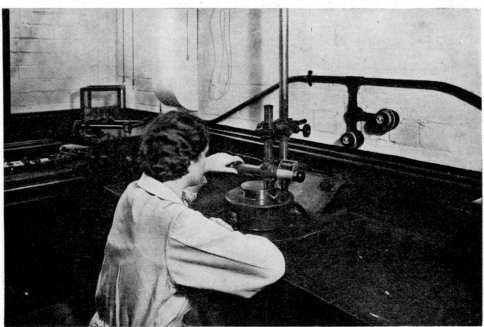

By courtesy of the B.T.-H. Co. Ltd.

MEASURING TO WITHIN A MILLIONTH PART OF AN INCH

On the top of the flat circular table can be seen two small rectangular bars: one of these is a highly accurate master gauge and the other is a duplicate which is being tested. When the operator brings the horizontal bar down so that the top rests across the two gauges, the tiniest difference in length is automatically registered on the indicator which is shown at the right-hand side of the bar.

New Worlds to Conquer

That is the beginning of the story of which the end is not yet known. Science has still to achieve much greater control. The theory is no longer in doubt ; the problem of putting it into practice depends on the solution to other problems. The right metals must be used to withstand the enormous pressures produced. Here the metallurgist comes in and his progress will be aided by the electron microscope. There are chemical problems for the chemist, and the engineer must be drawn in to design and improve the different parts of the pile. All these problems are being slowly but steadily tackled.

There are so many ways in which atomic energy may help other investigators. Wireless has progressed through the work of scientists in many different spheres. One of the most important aspects has been the discovery of " radio layers " high above the earth. The investigation of the stratosphere at new heights becomes possible by the use of rockets, propelled by atomic energy. These rockets would carry recording instruments which would supply important data for the scientists. Their construction would ensure their safe return to earth without damage to the instruments.

Rockets that travelled seventy miles above the earth, propelled by a series of explosions, were used by the enemy during the last war to act as long range bombs. They were launched in Holland and N. France and landed mainly in London and the Home Counties. With all their faults they were one of the most terrible of the new weapons employed in war. What of the use of rockets in peace ?

The Vastness of Space

Some system of atomic propulsion would have far greater possibilities than any previously-known method. On the strength of the knowledge gained from the first flights it would be possible to construct man-carrying rockets.

Man has conquered land, sea, and air, and has already penetrated the stratosphere. There is still the vastness of outer space to be explored.

H. G. Wells' imaginative forecast " The First Men in the Moon," is now well within the realm of probability. It is roughly 240,000 miles to the Moon. When atomic power is available for such a machine as the man-carrying rocket the journey might be accomplished in a matter of hours rather than days. The British Interplanetary Society is investigating the many problems to be solved before such a flight can be undertaken with confident hopes of complete success, both on the outward and return journeys. There are difficulties, but none that is beyond the power of modern science to overcome. It would not be a crazy trust-in-luck attempt. Every known risk and danger would be thoroughly considered by experts before the flight was begun.

Cosmic Rays

The scientific results of such a flight may be truly remarkable. There are many questions regarding space to which the scientists are seeking answers to-day. A study of cosmic radiation, for instance, gives information which is vital to the production of atomic energy. These cosmic rays are still one of the mysteries of science. They come from interstellar space and penetrate the earth's surface and are believed to be caused by disintegrating atoms in space.

Dr. Robert Millikan, an American scientist who was awarded the Nobel Prize in 1923, is regarded as the discoverer of the cosmic ray. His investigations showed that a certain type of cosmic ray is formed every time an atom of iron is formed. Among the deductions he made from the study of these rays was a belief that the world would never end.

Such investigations are not without a practical purpose. From these studies of the nature of the Universe comes knowledge that has its bearing on our own homes and on pleasures now regarded as essential. When you turn a knob and listen to a voice telling you just what is happening at that moment on a football field two hundred miles away, or on a sun-baked cricket-field six thousand miles away, it has all come about because scientists discovered the existence of electric waves in the ether similar to the waves of light and heat.

The astronomers who study the eclipses of the sun and the moon and those strange manifestations known as sunspots have given invaluable knowledge to the scientist experimenting with radio transmission. In the clinics and hospitals children and older people have sun-ray treatment by special lamps. The knowledge of these rays has been gained by scientists of several branches, and it is by this co-operation that progress is made.

From Stars to Ocean Bed

Other scientists are interested in the secrets that lie buried below the surface of the sea. Professor Piccard, who has ascended into the stratosphere in a special balloon he devised, has constructed a remarkable undersea balloon, known as a bathyscaphe. With this diving-bell new possibilities of scientific discoveries deep down in the ocean depths are probable. All such knowledge gives the scientist a fuller and more correct picture of the world in which we live.

Those early Greek thinkers who wanted to understand the sun and why it warmed the earth had no ideas about atomic energy or wireless transmissions.

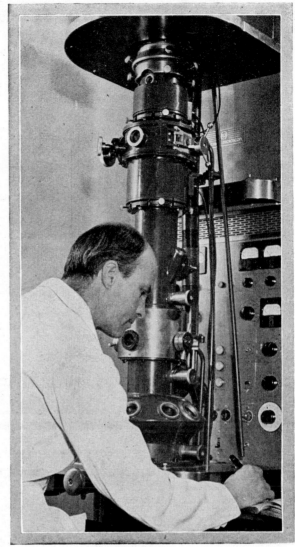

British Council.

THE ELECTRON MICROSCOPE

One of the most remarkable of modern inventions is the Electron Microscope. An electron stream passes through the transparency under examination and is focused on a photographic film. Magnification is approximately one hundred times greater than with the most powerful of visual microscopes.

They sought truth and understanding. To-day we are still far from knowing the full truth concerning the sun, but we are learning. We know, for instance, that growing plants collect energy from the sun and extract nutriment from the air and soil. The scientist has found that the green colouring matter known as chlorophyll enables the plant to collect this nutriment, which not only feeds the plant but will in due course feed man who lives on plants or on animals that eat the plants.

Good Health and Happiness

Science does not yet fully understand how the chlorophyll performs its work, but knows that it is chiefly carbon and that this particular carbon is radioactive. It is now possible to make ordinary carbon radio-active by that new and wonderful instrument known as the cyclotron. This mechanically bombards the carbon with neutrons and makes it radio-active. By studying radio-active carbon the scientist can observe what happens and so discover how the chlorophyll does its work.

This in turn may lead to discoveries of great importance to the health of mankind generally. Medical research and the fight for good health is obviously one of the highly important branches of Science. Like so many other sciences it has been until comparatively recent times almost entirely a matter of individual effort.

To-day it is largely team work and the research chemists of big industrial and commercial companies have made discoveries of great value. The largest chemical industry organisation in this country announced early in 1946 a new and revolutionary anti-malarial drug which they had named Paludrine. Its formula has been made public, so that all chemists will know how it is made.

At the end of 1948 this same company, I.C.I., announced the discovery of Antrycide, a cure and protection against all forms of cattle disease caused by the tsetse-fly. This new drug will be of incalculable value, particularly in Africa, which may well become a great cattle-breeding land.

In medicine, indeed, many advances have been made and in a number of cases these have been helped by the work of scientists in other fields. The electron microscope, for instance, has enabled investigators to discover new secrets of the body cells. A special award and the Garton Medal were awarded to Professor Dodds in 1948 for the discovery of Stilboestrol which has proved of great value in controlling certain forms of cancer.

Other drugs such as streptomycin have had highly beneficial results in the treatment of tuberculosis. Another remarkable weapon now used in the treatment of this particular disease is a vaccine known as B.C.G., first introduced by two Frenchmen, and the fight still goes on.

It has gone on for a long time, and it is by looking back over the history of the past that we realise how much progress has been made. A hundred years ago London was an unhealthy city, as it had been for a long time. Even in 1820 Jeremy Bentham, the philosopher who popularised the phrase " the greatest happiness of the greatest number," proposed that the country should have a Minister of Health. It was an impossible notion at the time, but in 1848 a Public Health Act was passed and in that same year London appointed its first Medical Officer of Health. A hundred years later a comprehensive National Health Service was inaugurated to ensure that everyone in the country had the full benefit of modern medical treatment when necessary.

Towards the Great Goal

Slowly but surely the advance in every branch of science goes on. It may take many years to develop all the new resources which are being placed at our service ; progress in one direction may not keep pace with the swift advances in others, or it may be held back or interrupted by the follies of man himself. But the great goal remains the same : the well-being and happiness of all mankind.